Cultural Hierarchy in Sixteenth-Century Europe
The Ottomans and Mexicans

This book argues that sixteenth-century European encounters with the newly discovered Mexicans (in the Aztec Empire) and the newly dominant Ottoman Empire can only be understood in relation to the cultural and intellectual changes wrought by the Reformation. Carina L. Johnson chronicles the resultant creation of cultural hierarchy. Starting at the beginning of the sixteenth century, when ideas of European superiority were not fixed, this book traces the formation of those ideas through proto-ethnographies, news pamphlets, Habsburg court culture, gifts of treasure, and the organization of collections.

Carina L. Johnson, a historian and former archaeologist, is currently an Associate Professor at Pitzer College and Extended Faculty at Claremont Graduate University. She is the recipient of a John Carter Brown Library NEH Fellowship, the Barbara Thom Fellowship at the Huntington Library, a Fulbright Award to Austria, and the Woodrow Wilson Postdoctoral Fellowship in the Humanities. She has been published in the *Journal of the History of Ideas*. This is her first book.

Cultural Hierarchy in Sixteenth-Century Europe

The Ottomans and Mexicans

CARINA L. JOHNSON

Pitzer College

CAMBRIDGE
UNIVERSITY PRESS

32 Avenue of the Americas, New York NY 10013-2473, USA

Cambridge University Press is part of the University of Cambridge.

It furthers the University's mission by disseminating knowledge in the pursuit of education, learning and research at the highest international levels of excellence.

www.cambridge.org
Information on this title: www.cambridge.org/9781107638983

First published 2011
Reprinted 2012
First paperback edition 2014

A catalogue record for this publication is available from the British Library

Library of Congress Cataloguing in Publication data

Johnson, Carina L., 1967–
Cultural hierarchy in sixteenth-century Europe : the Ottomans and Mexicans / Carina L. Johnson.
    p. cm.
Includes bibliographical references and index.
ISBN 978-0-521-76927-3
1. Europe – Intellectual life – 16th century.   2. Europe – Civilization – 16th century.
3. Reformation – Europe.   4. Ethnology – Europe – History – 16th century.
5. Mexico – History – Conquest, 1519–1540.   6. Turkey – History – 1453–1683.
I. Title.
D228.J64   2011
303.48´ 24009031 – dc22   2011015747

ISBN 978-0-521-76927-3 Hardback
ISBN 978-1-107-63898-3 Paperback

Contents

v

Figures

Acknowledgments

Finishing this book has reminded me that one of scholarship's great delights is that it is a collective enterprise. Over the years, as this project became a dissertation and then grew into a book, I met many people along the way who shared their ideas, advice, and scholarly enthusiasm with me. Finally, I can acknowledge them and the many institutions that welcomed and supported me. My first thanks are to the staff of the archives and libraries in Austria, Germany, Great Britain, Spain, and the United States who assisted me with my research, and my second to the many scholars who discussed sixteenth-century matters with me.

This project received institutional support, for which I am grateful, from multiple sources. The initial research and writing was funded by U.C. Berkeley, the Mabelle MacLeod Lewis Foundation, the Fulbright Foundation, the Program for Cultural Cooperation between Spain and U.S. Universities, the Social Science Research Council, and the Norddeutsche Landesbank's Warburg-Wolfenbüttel Fellowship. Rethinking, rewriting, and further research was supported by a Woodrow Wilson Postdoctoral Fellowship in the Humanities at Northwestern University's Alice Kaplan Institute for the Humanities and by Pitzer College. A National Endowment for the Humanities fellowship at the John Carter Brown Library and the Barbara Thom Fellowship at the Huntington Library deserve special thanks for making it possible to participate in the productive communities of the John Carter Brown and the Huntington Libraries.

Some material in this book appeared first in other formats: "Some Peculiarities of Empire in the Early Modern Era," in *Politics and Reformations: Communities, Polities, Nations, and Empires*, edited by

Christopher Ocker, Michael Printy, Peter Starenko, and Peter Wallace (Leiden: Brill, 2007); "Idolatrous Cultures and the Practice of Religion," *Journal of the History of Ideas* 67 (2006): 597–621; "Aztec Regalia and the Reformation of Display," in *Collecting Across Cultures: Material Exchanges in the Early Modern Atlantic World*, edited by Daniela Bleichmar and Peter Mancall (University of Pennsylvania Press, 2011); and "Stone Gods and Counter-Reformation Knowledges," in *Making Knowledge in Early Modern Europe: Practices, Objects, and Texts, 1400–1800*, edited by Pamela Smith and Benjamin Schmidt (The University of Chicago, 2007). All rights reserved. This material is used here with permission.

I would also like to thank my editor Eric Crahan, the production team, and the Cambridge University Press anonymous readers. The imaging staffs of the different museums and libraries who helped me acquire the visual materials for this book were wonderfully efficient. I am particularly grateful to Leslie Tobias-Olsen of the John Carter Brown Library Imaging Department, who gave me timely assistance during a snowstorm with Figure 3.

A debt of gratitude is owed to my dissertation advisor, Tom Brady, who encouraged me to follow the trail of my project wherever it led me and has always been available to give wise advice when I needed or wanted it. A parallel thanks must be offered to him and Kathy Brady for their warm and generous hospitality over the many years. I also thank those who helped steer this project to completion in its dissertation form – Randy Starn for his ongoing capacity to stretch my thinking, Elaine Tennant for sharing her rich understanding of things Habsburg, and Margaret Chowning for offering a Latin American counterpoint. Lee Wandel planted the seeds of this project by proposing, in a brainstorming session, that I look for traces of the Mexica in sixteenth-century Europe. I was fortunate to have the nurturing History Department at U.C. Berkeley as my base during the time that this project became a dissertation. Heidi Eberhardt Bate, Anne Keary, Amy Leonard, Ruth MacKay, Isaac Miller, Rachel Sturman, and Jonathan Zatlin all read portions of this work or helped me navigate its research and writing.

During the long process of turning the dissertation into a book, I received advice and encouragement from Antonio Barrera-Osorio, Peter Carroll, Duane Corpis, Dallas Denery, Doris Garraway, Anthony Grafton, David Luebke, Peter Mancall, Catherine Molineux, Ed Muir, James Muldoon, Allyson Poska, Jay Rubenstein, Jonathan Sheehan, Sam Truett, and Allan Tulchin. Many of them read parts or all of this work, and conversations with each have made it a better book. At the Claremont Colleges, I have benefited from the support and advice, in matters large and small, of Bill Anthes, Sumangala Bhattacharya, Ellen Finkelpearl, Alex Juhasz, Pamela Smith, Kathy Yep, and my colleagues in the history field group Stu McConnell, Dan Segal, and Andre Wakefield. Amanda James helped me with the bibliographic material, and Alexandra Margolin provided me, at multiple stages, with wonderfully careful proofreading and indexing assistance.

Judith Wolfsberger (formerly Huber) and Barbara Bartmann have, over many years, introduced me to Vienna's manifold charms and made it a welcoming home away from home. Diana Selig and Jay Fisher have been steadfast in helping me negotiate the logistics of writing this book. Sara Beam deserves special thanks, both as my trusted interlocutor since our first semester at Berkeley and for reading the manuscript at a crucial stage of the revision process.

Lastly but most importantly, I would like to acknowledge my family's support. Jian, Roy, Tim, and Maria have patiently tolerated my long preoccupation with this project. My grandmothers Lydia and Mung-Hsing offered me unstinting sympathy and generosity of spirit, and it is to their memories that I dedicate this book.

Abbreviations

ADB	*Allgemeine Deutsche Biographie*
AGI	Archivo General de Indias, Spain
AGS	Archivo General de Simancas, Spain
AKG	*Archiv für Kulturgeschichte*
AÖG	*Archiv für Österreichische Geschichte*
ARG	*Archiv für Reformationsgeschichte/ Archive for Reformation History*
AVA	Allgemeines Verwaltungsarchiv, Austria
BAE	Biblioteca de Autores Españoles
BSB	Bayerische Staatsbibliothek, Germany
BStA	Bayerisches Hauptstaatsarchiv, Germany
CDIA	*Colección de documentos inéditos, relativos al descubrimiento, conquista y organización de las antiguas posesiones españolas de América y Oceanía, sacados de los archivos del reino y muy especialmente del de Indias*
CDIE	*Colección de documentos inéditos para la historia de España*
CDIU	*Colección de documentos inéditos relativos al descubrimiento, conquista y organización de las antiguas posesiones españolas de ultramar*
CSSH	*Comparative Studies in Society and History*
FRA	*Fontes Rerum Austriacarum*
FSA	Frankfurt-am-Main Stadtarchiv, Germany
Heidelberg.	*Nicolai de Cusa opera omnia: iussu et auctoritate Academiae Litterarum Heidelbergensis ad codicum fidem edita*
HAHR	*Hispanic American Historical Review*

HHStA	Haus-, Hof- und Staatsarchiv, Austria
HKA	Hofkammerarchiv, Austria
JKSW	*Jahrbuch der Kunsthistorischen Sammlungen des Allerhöchsten Kaisershauses;* succeeded by *Jahrbuch der Kunsthistorischen Sammlungen in Wien*
JKMW	*Jahrbuch des Kunsthistorischen Museums Wien*
JHI	*Journal of the History of Ideas*
JWCI	*Journal of the Warburg and Courtauld Institutes*
MVGN	*Mitteilungen des Vereins für Geschichte der Stadt Nürnberg*
ÖNB	Österreichische Nationalbibliothek, Austria
RQ	*Renaissance Quarterly*
RTA	*Deutsche Reichstagsakten, jüngere Reihe*
StA	Stadtarchiv Augsburg, Germany
StAN	Staatsarchiv Nürnberg, Germany
SCJ	*Sixteenth Century Journal*
WA	*Luthers Werke. Kritische Gesamtausgabe*

A Note on Usage

Scholarship on the sixteenth century inevitably grapples with the historicity of terms. I have sought to use terms that retain important distinctions for, and would make sense to, the people who produced the texts, images, and some of the objects discussed in this book.

"Indian" and "Turk" were terms regularly used by sixteenth-century Europeans without intrinsically derogatory meanings. I have used them here when referencing European texts on peoples from the Americas or from the Ottoman Empire. For places in Meso-America, I have opted to use the term "Aztec Empire" to describe the polity that was replaced by the political unit of "New Spain" in the 1520s, the term "Mexico" to describe the roughly corresponding geographic area, "Mexican" when describing the peoples of that polity, and "Nahua" when referring to the Nahuatl-speaking peoples of that same polity. "Spain" and "Spaniard" in the sixteenth century referred to the geographic area of the Iberian Peninsula. To avoid potential confusion with the modern nation-state, I have used "Iberia" as the general geographic term unless "Spain" is called for by the original texts. I have capitalized "Empire" when referring to formal political units such as the Holy Roman, Aztec, and Ottoman Empires, but left it lowercase when discussing the Habsburg empire. The Ottoman Empire included territories on the continent of Europe, but the Ottomans were considered by Latin Christians to be based, by origin or formation, in the continent of Asia. They are thus included in my term "extra-European." Finally, I have used the term "reformers" to refer to those people calling for a religious reform of the Latin Christian church before the rise of the terms "Protestant," "Lutheran," or "Reformed."

For personal and place names, I have used anglicized forms when these anglicized names are commonplace and unconfusing, although there is inevitably some arbitrariness in my choices. In an effort to avoid anachronism, I have referred to rulers by the title they held at a given point of reference. So, for example, Ferdinand is first a Habsburg prince, then Archduke of Austria, then King of Hungary and Croatia, then King of the Romans, and finally Holy Roman Emperor. Western and central Europeans referred to the *Tlatoani* Moctezuma and the *Padishah* or Sultan Süleyman as kings or emperors; these rulers are occasionally titled as such in this book, reflecting usage in the Habsburg empire and much of the European continent.

Finally, because many sixteenth-century printed books mark leafs with roman numerals, I have used a superscript[v] (for example aiv[v]) to indicate the verso side and the lack of a superscript to indicate the recto side of a leaf.

Introduction

News of the World

This book examines the circulation of Mexican and Ottoman people and cultural goods through the Habsburg realms during the sixteenth century. In the early sixteenth century, the Aztec and Ottoman Empires were newly compelling to Europe: the Mexicans would be first encountered and then conquered, while the Ottomans began their expansion into Hungary and the Mediterranean. This situation, it has been argued, was met with modes of indifference in Europe, or with models of cultural superiority that had already been set in place in Latin Christendom by 1500. Such models are thought to have shaped the colonization of the Canary Islands and the early encounters in the Americas. Similarly, it has been proposed that once the shock of the 1453 fall of Constantinople had faded, Latin Christians who did not live in the Italian peninsula or Hungary ceased to pay much heed to the Ottoman Empire.[1]

J.H. Elliott's influential thesis argued that the New World had a "blunted impact" on the Old World that was Europe. Geography, botany, classical authority, and ideas about culture would eventually be reconceived, but these paradigmatic shifts in European thought only began

---

[1] John Tolan, *Saracens: Islam in the Medieval European Imagination* (New York: Columbia University Press, 2002); Benjamin Kedar, *Crusade and Mission* (Princeton: Princeton University Press, 1984); and Margarita Zamora, *Reading Columbus* (Berkeley: University of California Press, 1993). German disinterest in the Turkish advance as a direct concern before 1526 was argued by Stephen A. Fischer-Galati, *Ottoman Imperialism and German Protestantism, 1521–1555* (Cambridge: Harvard University Press, 1959), 1–25; for state policy, see Paula Sutter Fichtner, *Ferdinand I of Austria: The Politics of Dynasticism in the Age of the Reformation* (Boulder: Eastern European Monographs, 1982). For Iberia, scholars have proposed that attention was primarily focused on Andalusian and Valencian Muslims and *moriscos*.

some fifty years after 1492. This argument of initial European indifference, beyond fantastical or orientalist projections, drew on evidence of publication volume to gauge levels of interest.[2] More recent studies linking trading centers with the flow of news have traced significant and ready interest for early news about the New World, as well as some of the information networks that disseminated it. That work, along with earlier studies on the well-known Fugger information network, offers insights into the volume of news and interest in the Americas present during the early sixteenth century, and inspires further questions about the information order in the Habsburg empire.[3] By what means did information about the "Indians" or the "Turks" and their cultures flow? When was such information credible to the sixteenth-century recipient? What sorts of people probably received (read or heard) such news?

News about America and the encroaching Ottoman Empire flowed through the Habsburg empire in a variety of formats. Archival evidence demonstrates that news from far afield traveled in a variety of registers as court news, humanist and merchant epistolary exchanges, and printed newssheets, as well as by word of mouth. Courts and important trade cities (above all, Venice) were nodes for news gathering, and news

---

[2] J.H. Elliott described what he later termed "a blunted impact" of the New World on the Old in *The Old World and the New, 1492–1650* (1970, reprinted with a new preface, Cambridge: Cambridge University Press, 1992), 1–27. See also his "Final Reflections," in *America in European Consciousness, 1493–1750*, ed. Karen Ordahl Kupperman (Chapel Hill: University of North Carolina Press, 1995), 391–408. In Elliot's 1992 "Preface to the Canto Edition," in *The Old World and the New, 1492–1650*, he reiterated that "after the initial excitement of discovery, America tended to recede from the consciousness of many Europeans," and he continued to cite publication volume as a gauge of "the degree of interest in America shown by Europeans at any given moment, in so far as this can be measured by the books they were reading and writing," xii. Building on Elliott, Michael Ryan's influential essay "Assimilating New Worlds in the Sixteenth and Seventeenth Centuries," *CSSH* 23 (1981): 519–38 focused on paradigmatic shifts, arguing for a blunted impact, particularly in scientific thought, due to Europeans' assimilation of these cultures with historical pagan examples already available to them.

[3] Renate Pieper, *Die Vermittlung einer Neuen Welt: Amerika im Nachrichtennetz des Habsburgischen Imperiums, 1493–1598* (Mainz: Philipp von Zabern, 2000), "Die Berichterstattung aus der Neuen Welt im ausgehenden 16. Jahrhundert am Beispiel der Fuggerzeitungen," in *Die Neue Welt im Bewußtsein der Italiener und Deutschen des 16. Jahrhunderts*, ed. Adriano Prosperi and Wolfgang Reinhard (Berlin: Duncker und Humblot, 1993), 157–74, and "Informationszentren im Vergleich," in *Kommunikationsrevolutionen: die neuen Medien des 16. und 19. Jahrhunderts*, ed. Michael North (Köln: Böhlau, 1995), 45–60 was preceded by Viktor Klarwill, ed. *Fugger-Zeitungen* (Vienna: Rikola, 1923). C.A. Bayly's *Empire and Information* defines an "information order" as interpenetrated elements of state intelligence and social communication (Cambridge: Cambridge University Press, 1997), 1–9.

transmission followed well-established routes. News from the Indies (both east and west) came via the Portuguese and Castilian courts or official ports.[4] News on the Hungarian front or elsewhere in the Ottoman Empire circulated via Habsburg envoys or individuals living in Poland, Venice, Ragusa, and Vienna.[5]

These information networks grew out of fifteenth-century merchant and ambassadorial networks that had sought accurate information for trade and diplomacy. The practice of circulating letters and reports within these close and closed groups continued, even as the printing press began issuing copies, whether genuine or contrived, of informational letters. Merchants remained a crucial mechanism of news circulation, but in the broader information networks of the sixteenth century, connections between different social groups (particularly merchants, statesmen, and humanists) were crucial. To note a few networks: Philip Melanchthon was

---

[4] Martin de Salinas, *El Emperador Carlos V y su corte según las cartas de Don Martín de Salinas*, ed. Antonio Rodríguez Villa (Madrid: Real Academia de la Historia, 1903); HHStA Spanien Diplomatische Korrespondenz (Span. DK) 1/10, fols. 20–26ᵛ, 2/34; 2/37. *Ein missif oder sendbrieff newer zeytung/ betreffendt ein frydl zwysschen dem Allerdurchleuchtigisten großmechtigisten Fürsten vnnd herrn/ herrn Ferdinandus Röm. Kö. rc. vnnd dem Türckyschen Keyser / Außgangen zu Cracawl di 18. May. 1533 jar. gar schön vnd kurtzweylig zu lesen. Newe zeyttyng von einer wunderbarlichen Insel/ welche yetz durch des Königs von Portugals Schyffart ist gefunden worden. 1533. jar* [1533]. In one case, the news from Portugal then traveled to Toulouse. *Bottschafft des Groszmechtigsten Konigs David aus dem grossen und hohen Morenland/ den man gemeinlich nennet priester Johann an Babst Clemens den Siebenden/ zu Bononia vorhort in offnem Consistorio am xxix. tag Januarii Anno. 1533. Ein Sendbrieff des Königs von Portugal an Babst Clement den sibenden. Ein Sendbrieff des Morenkönigs an König Emanuel von Portugal. Ein Sendbrieff des Morenkönigs an König Johann von Portugal... Ein Sendbrieff des Bischoffs der grossen stadt Temixtitan in der Newen erfunden welt/ an die Väter parfusser Ordens... zu Tolosa in Franckreich vorsamlet. 1532* (Dresden: Wolfgang Stöckel, 1533). As evident in the title, this pamphlet includes fictive letters, letters from the kings of Portugal, and a letter from Bishop Zumarraga to a Franciscan. See Michael Giesecke, "Die typographische Konstruktion der, Neuen Welt'," in *Gutenberg und die Neue Welt*, ed. Horst Wenzel (Munich: Wilhelm Fink, 1994), 15–32 and Renate Pieper's "Informationszentren" for an analysis of the path of written news from the west Indies.

[5] For examples, HHStA Span. DK 3/57, fols. 370–6; 4/74, fol. 288; 10/10, fol. 33. Printed examples include *Newe zeyttung aus Polen/ von wunderlichen geschichten/ ynn Polen Vngern vnd Behemen/ auch von andern landen. Newe zeytung von Rom Venedig vnd Frantzosen* [1527]; *Ein missif oder sendbrieff...* [1533]; *Newe Zeyttung von Kayserlicher maiestat/ von dem Türcken/ und von dem grossen Sophi/ rc. Auß Venedig gen Augspurg geschriben.* (1535). One merchant chain extended from Adrianople to Constantinople to "Perso" [Bursa?] to Venice to the Holy Roman Empire. *Auszug aynes Brieffes: wie ainer so in der Türckey wonhafft/ seynem freünd in dise land geschriben/....* [1526]; *New zeytung auß Ungern des datum stehet zu Wienn am andern tag des Weynmonats M.D.xxvii* [1527].

at the center of a Wittenberg-based network among princes, other humanists, and merchants. Nuremberg humanist Christoph Scheurl got his news from merchants and the imperial court. In the 1520s, Augsburg merchant banker Jakob Fugger provided news to the Wettin princes of Saxony.[6] Central European merchants based in Iberia were closely involved in transmitting early information about the Indies to the German imperial cities. Baltasar Springer, author of the east Indies *Meerfahrt* (1509), was a printer and Welser factor. Valentin Fernandez Moravus, another Welser factor at the Portuguese court, provided Conrad Peutinger with early accounts of east India. In Seville, the first printer of Cortés's letters, Jacob Cromberger, was the father-in-law of Lazarus Nuremberger, a factor for the Hirschvogels in the east and west Indies and then for the Welsers in the west Indies. Although Lazarus Nuremberger traveled extensively, he maintained ties to his home town Nuremberg: one manuscript account of his voyage to the east Indies was sent to Nuremberg's leading humanist, Willibald Pirckheimer.[7]

News from the west Indies (soon reconceived as the New World) flowed through the conduit of the Castilian court. In Seville, the Casa de la Contratación had been established as the official crown depository of all information and treasure from the New World. Pilots' logs, treasure

---

[6] R. Grasshoff, *Die briefliche Zeitung des XVI Jahrhunderts* (Leipzig: C.W. Vollrath, 1877), esp. 15–57. Medieval merchant news, particularly letters prepared for public consumption, is explored in Margot Lindemann's *Nachrichtenübermittlung durch Kaufmannsbriefe. Brief-"Zeitungen" in der Korrespondenz Hildebrand Veckinchusens (1398–1428)* (Munich: Dokumentation, 1978). For merchant-bankers in the sixteenth century, Theodore Gustav Werner, "Das kaufmännische Nachrichtenwesen im späten Mittelalter und in der frühen Neuzeit und sein Einfluß auf die Entstehung der handschriftlichen Zeitung," *Scripta Mercaturae* 9/2 (1975): 3–51. Surveys include Lore Sporhan-Krempel, *Nürnberg als Nachrichtenzentrum zwischen 1400 und 1700* (Nuremberg: 1968); Karl Schottenloher, *Flugblatt und Zeitung* (Schmidt, 1922); Paul Roth, *Die Neuen Zeitungen in Deutschland im 15. und 16. Jahrhundert* (Leipzig: B.G. Teubner, 1914); Emil Weller, *Die ersten deutschen Zeitungen*, 2ed. (Hildesheim: Olms, 1962). For Saxony, see Götz Freiherr von Pölnitz, "Jakob Fuggers Zeitungen und Briefe an die Fürsten des Hauses Wettin in der Frühzeit Karls V, 1519–1525," *Nachrichten von der Akademie der Wissenschaften in Göttingen Phil.-Hist. Kl. 1941 N.F.* 3 (1941): 122–6.

[7] Heinrich Lutz, *Conrad Peutinger: Beiträge zu einer Politischen Biographie* (Augsburg: Die Brigg, 1958), 54–64; Enrique Otte, "Jacob und Hans Cromberger und Lazarus Nürnberger, die Begründer des Deutschen Amerikahandels," *MVGN* 52 (1963/4): 129–62; Clive Griffin, *The Crombergers of Seville* (Oxford: Clarendon Press, 1988), 56–70; Miloslav Krása, Josef Polišensky, and Peter Ratkoš, ed., *The Voyages of Discovery in the Bratislava Manuscript Lyc. 515/8 (Codex Bratislavensis)* (Prague: Charles University, 1986), 70. Christine R. Johnson analyzes particular uses to which German merchants and humanists put this information in *The German Discovery of the World* (Charlottesville: University of Virginia Press, 2008).

inventories, and conquistador reports were all to be housed and, it has been argued, guarded there from the prying eyes of rival states and all other undesirables.[8] Yet the court of Isabella of Castile and Ferdinand of Aragon also disseminated cultural information about the New World. When Charles succeeded his grandfather Ferdinand in 1516, his court became even more prominent as a nexus for such information.[9] Within the Habsburg family, much detailed information circulated: Charles's aunt Margaret, regent in the Low Countries, received descriptions both long (*relaciones*) and short (newsletters),[10] as did Charles's siblings Ferdinand and Maria. In the case of Ferdinand, he acquired much information from his own ambassadors to Charles's court. These ambassadors, well-trusted and lifelong servants of the family, received their news from Charles's councillors.[11] Early accounts of Hernan Cortés's and Pedro Alvarado's adventures, the Pizarros' early voyages and the discovery of Peru, and Marcos de Niza's travels to discover the Seven Cities of Cibola were all sent in manuscript form from Castile to other Habsburgs. Ferdinand's interest in receiving news about the New World extended beyond triumphal news: he also obtained reports on revolts against

---

[8] Bernhard Siegert, "Die Verortung Amerikas im Nachrichtendispositiv um 1500" in *Gutenberg und die Neue Welt*, ed. Horst Wenzel (Munich: Wilhelm Fink, 1994), 307–26; David Goodman, *Power and Penury* (Cambridge: Cambridge University Press, 1988), 53–65. Older studies mentioning these strategies are Jose Pulido Rubio, *El Piloto Mayor: Pilotos Mayores, Catedraticos de Cosmografía y Cosmografos de la Casa de la Contratación de Sevilla* (Seville: CSIC, 1950), 57–61 and Ernesto Schäfer, *El Consejo Real y Supremo de las Indias* (Seville: Carmona, 1935), 1:21–2, 19. For the debate on Portugal's efforts to control information, see Donald Lach's review in *Asia in the Making of Europe* I:1 (Chicago: University of Chicago Press, 1965), 151–62.

[9] Some Franciscan copybooks contain multiple excerpts from accounts of the east and west Indies and appear to be based on material from the Habsburg court. One, compiled at least partially in 1500 by a father Oliverius at a Franciscan monastery in Nuremberg, is in Krása, *Codex Bratislavensis*, 73. Another, compiled in the late 1520s, contains information from Nicolas of Herborn, who sent letters back from the Iberian Habsburg court to his home monastery in Cologne. Trier Stadtbibliothek, Codex 1374/140, fols. 220–9 and Ludwig Schmitt, *Der Kölner Theologe Nikolaus Stagefyr und der Franziskaner Nikolaus Herborn* (Freiburg im Briesgau: Herder'she Verlag, 1896).

[10] For published examples, see Karl Lanz, ed., *Correspondenz des Kaisers Karl V* (Frankfurt: Minerva, 1966) 1:286–91. The relevant archival material is in HHStA Span. DK and Span. HofKorrespondenz.

[11] Martin de Salinas, Ferdinand's representative in Charles's court from 1521–1539, and his office are described in Gerhard Rill, *Fürst und Hof in Österreich von den habsburgischen Teilungsverträgen bis zur Schlacht von Mohács (1521/22 bis 1526)* (Vienna: Böhlau, 1993), 118–25, 235. For Salinas's arrangement with Juan de Sámano, secretary in charge of the Casa de la Contratación, see Woodrow Borah, "The Cortés Codex of Vienna and the Emperor Ferdinand I," *The Americas* 19 (1962): 79–92.

Charles's authority in Peru, such as the rebellions of Gonzalo Pizarro and Lope de Aguirre.[12] From 1521, the date of Ferdinand's relocation to central Europe, through the 1550s, Ferdinand considered information on the New World a standard topic for his regular ambassadorial intelligence reports from Castile. Ferdinand's desire for all the news from the New World could, however, be thwarted by politics in Castile: when Cortés was in disfavor with Charles, the ambassador Martin de Salinas refused to forward Ferdinand's personal letters to the conquistador and claimed to be unable to obtain further information on Cortés's activities from court officials.[13]

News presented in printed broadsheets allowed for the possibility of broad social circulation beyond noble, merchant, humanist, and clerical circles. Printed news pamphlets, reporting on recent events, appeared in the late fifteenth century in the Holy Roman Empire and Italy (particularly Rome).[14] Breaking news of Ottoman military activities and of peoples encountered in the Indies were among the first types to appear in these printed pamphlets, and these two topics dominated the genre[15]

---

[12] Borah; ÖNB, Codex Vindobonensis S.N. 1600; Marcos de Nica, HHStA Hss. Blau 192 [1538]; HHStA Belgien PA 25 [1533], fol. 150–150ᵛ; HHStA Span. DK 2/37, fols. 122–54; 3/66, fols. 430–4; 6/118, fols. 166–182. Pedro de la Gasca lists the information sent in his letter of 1554, HHStA Span. HofKorrespondenz 1/4, fol. 104–104ᵛ.

[13] Salinas, 312, 318, 322, 632, 640. HHStA Span. DK 2/29; 2/31, fol. 28; Span. Varia 2/e, fol. 2. In the reports of Salinas's successor Guzman, "the Turk" and the Indies appear regularly in the weekly recapitulation of news at the Castilian court. For example, HHStA Span. DK 2/34, fols. 36–36ᵛ, 42ᵛ–43; 2/37, fols. 130, 163, 165–165ᵛ, 178; 4/74; 5/100, fol. 187. Ferdinand's interest could extend to patronage, as in the case of Gonzalo Fernández de Oviedo y Valdés. See Oviedo's letters in HHStA Span. DK 2/33, fols. 23–4ᵛ and HHStA, Staatskanzlei, WKL 5, fols. 75–6ᵛ; also ÖNB CVP 5542 and CVP 7195.

[14] Much news printed in the Habsburg Empire was produced in the Holy Roman Empire. For the role of Ottoman military aggression in promoting a market for printed news, see Margaret Meserve's discussion of the 1470 fall of Negroponte in "News from Negroponte: Politics, Popular Opinion, and Information Exchange in the First Decade of the Italian Press," *RQ* 59 (2006): 440–80, and for pamphlets in Italy more generally (verse histories dominated in Venice and prose news pamphlets in Rome), Raymond Wilhelm, *Italienische Flugschriften des Cinquecento (1500–1550)* (Tübingen: Max Niemeyer, 1996), 35–45, 90–92. Printers in the Iberian kingdoms produced few prose news bulletins (with the exception of lengthier accounts of voyages); see Griffin, 152–64, while in France, news pamphlets dealing with the west Indies and the Turks seem to have been sporadic in the late fifteenth and early sixteenth centuries. Clarence Dana Rouillard, *The Turk in French History, Thought, and Literature (1520–1660)* (Paris: Boivin, 1940), 646–55. The most comprehensive bibliographies of western and central European imprints are, for the New World, *European Americana*, ed. John Alden. vol. 1 (New York: Readex, 1980) and, for the Ottomans, Carl Göllner's *Turcica*, vol. I (Bucarest and Berlin: Academy, 1961).

[15] This generalization is based on surviving texts; see Göllner, *Turcica* I and Werner, 38.

during the first decades of the sixteenth century. In manuscript ambassadorial reports, newsworthy events were those with empire-wide significance. In printed news, the same guidelines prevailed; events of imperial scope were reproduced with various topics often bundled together
in a single pamphlet, just as in ambassadorial reports.[16] News from the
Ottoman court and of Turkish military activities appeared with some reg-
ularity along with other military matters and political news.[17] Sometimes
the Turkish news was printed alongside cataclysmic news, whether military events such as Charles V's capture of the king of France or the sack
of Rome, or agricultural catastrophes such as a horde of grasshoppers.[18]
Divine signs were announced in reports of many current events, and
important or significant events in the news pamphlets might reappear
in vernacular cosmographies of the 1530s and 1540s.[19] Links to ethnographic or cosmographic agendas were often made implicitly by printers, through their inclusion of descriptive news from the Turks and the
Indies. In 1522, 1533, and 1534, the years when information about new

---

[16] For example, one *Newe Zeytung* could contain information about the Netherlands,
Rome, Naples, Neustadt, and Austria. *Newe Zeytung Aus dem Niderlandt. Auss Rom.
Aus Neapolis. Auss der Newenstat Auß Oesterreych* (1523).

[17] Examples range from military matters such as conflict between the French and the Swiss
in 1515, the imperial conquest of Genoa in 1522, a 1510 truce between the king of France
and the pope, the 1525 siege of Pavia, the 1515 alliance between Austria, Poland, and
Hungary, and the 1525 siege of Pavia 1525 to news occurring around the Empire. See
VD 16 (Stuttgart: Hiersemann, 1989) 14: 464–506 and *Anzaygendt Newtzeyttung/ wie
es aigendtlich herren/ unnd mitt der schlacht vor Pavia* [Augsburg: Johann Schönsperger,
1525]; *Newe zeytung von Keyserlicher Mayestat/ vnd von Künig von Franckreych/ Auch
von vil andern Fürsten vnd Steten Welscher vnd Teütscher Nation/ geschehen im Jar.
M.D.XXviii. Von der Schatzung die Keyserliche Mayestat gefordert oder angeleget hat
alle seyner Geystligkeyt. Schatzung des Künigs von Franckreych aller Geystligkeyt. Newe
zeyttung von Graff Hans Weyda auß Hungern/ hat ein grosse legation durch.XXVI. die
er bey sich gehabt hat/ an den Türcken gesandt/ vnd des Türcken antwort darneben/
geschehen zü Betaw im Jar M.D.XXviii. Newe zeyttung vom Hertzog von Gellern/ vnnd
Bischoff von Uterich/ Geschehen am.xix. tag des monats May/ im Jar M.D.XXviii.*
([Nuremberg] Georg Wachter, 1528).

[18] *New zeytung. Die Schlacht des Turckischen Kesers mit Ludovico etwan König zu
Ungern geschehen am tag Johannis entheuptung. Item des Türcken feyndtsbrieff/ König
Ludouico zugesandt vor der schlacht. Item eyn kleglicher Sendbrieff so die Vngern
dem König im Polen zugeschickt/ nach der schlacht. Item etzlich naw getzeyten aus
Polen. New zeytung vom Babst zu Rome am xxvii. tag Septembris geschehen.* (1526);
*Warhafftige vnnd kurtze bericht Inn der Summa/ wie es ietzo/ im Tausent Funff hundert
vnd Siben vnd zayntzigsten jar Den vi. tag May/ durch Römischer Kayserlicher/ vnnd
Hispanischer Küniglicher Mayestet kriegs volck/ In eroberunng der Stat Rom ergangen
ist/ biß auff den xxi. tage Junii.* [1527]; *Newe zeyttung aus Polen/....* [1527].

[19] Examples include *Chronica/ Beschreibung und gemeyne anzeyte/ vonn aller Wellt
herkommen* (Frankfurt am Main: C. Egenolff, 1535) and Sebastian Franck, *Germaniae
Chronicon* (Augsburg: Weissenhorn and Steiner, 1538).

subject empires (the Aztec and Inca Empires) reached Europe, broadsheets bundled news from the Indies and the Ottomans.[20]

Printed pamphlets were cheap and quickly produced, often without printer's information. They included supporting information designed to reinforce their credibility. Not surprisingly, printed news pamphlets publicized their sources and their reliability. Unlike non-printed newsletters circulating in closed, familiar merchant and banking circles, printed pamphlets might emphasize and advertise their sources in the Habsburg court. News of imperial scope was delivered as published correspondence between Habsburg family members and courtiers, particularly letters to Archduchess Margaret, ranging from the discovery of Mexico to the marriages of her niece Mary and nephew Ferdinand.[21]

The pamphlet producer underscored the veracity of the news through several strategies. Most commonly, the text declared its origin as a letter from one known official or dignitary to another; alternatively, the letter might assert the authorship of an eyewitness who lived in a military hot spot. Reflecting the importance of the letter format,[22] acknowledged authors were located in a variety of social positions, ranging from the Habsburg family and other royalty,[23] nobles, councillors, named secretaries at the Spanish or Portuguese courts,[24] city secretaries, and

[20] *Translation uss hispanischer sprach zu Frantzösisch gemacht....* [Basel: Pamphilius, 1522]; *Newe zeittung von demlande. das die Sponier funden haben....* [Erfurt: Maler, 1522]; *Ein missif oder sendbrieff newer zeytung....* [1533]; *Newe Zeytung aus Hispanien vnd Italien. Mense Februario. 1534* [Nuremberg: Petreius, 1534].

[21] See *Translation uss hispanischer sprach....*; *Die abschrifft auß dem Original so der Turck sampt dem könig von Cathey vnd Persien allen Christlichen stenden des Römischen Reychs geschryben haben.* ([Nuremberg]: Friedrich Peypus, 1526); and *Die Stend des hailegen Römischen Reichs/ mit sampt aller Churfürsten vnd Fürsten....* (Augsburg: [Silvan Otmar] 1518), a letter from Johann Haselberg to Archduchess Margaret about the imperial diet of 1518.

[22] A preponderance of early pamphlets on the Turks appeared in letter form. See Göllner, *Turcica* I. The pamphlet in letter form, either as a "copy of a letter" or an "avviso," was popular in Italy as well as the Holy Roman Empire, appearing in the 1510s and peaking in the 1530s. Wilhelm, 205–73.

[23] *Bottschafft des Groszmechtigsten Konigs David....* (1533); *Copia de vna littera del Re de Portagallo mandata al Re de Castella del viaggio y successi de India* (Rome: Joanni de Besicken, 1505); Isabella Hunyadi, Queen of Hungary in *Vier warhafftige Missiven/ eine der frawen Isabella Königin vnd nachgelassene wittib in Ungern/ wie untrewlich der Türck vnd die iren mit ir vmbgangen. Die ander/ eines so in der belegerung bey der Konigin im Schloß gewest/ wie es mit Ofen/ vor und nach der belegerung ergangen. Die dritte/ eines Ungern von Gran/ wie es yetz zu Ofen zugehe. Die vierdte / des Türckischen Tyrannen an die Sibenbürter* [Nuremberg: Johann vom Berg and Ulrich Neüber, 1542].

[24] Peter Martyr of Anghiera's *De Orbe Novo* in *Opera* (Graz: Akademische Druck, 1966); Mayster Adolff in *Copey etlicher brieff so auß Hispania kummen seindt/ anzaygent die

merchants.²⁵ Accompanying woodcuts might illustrate the news being physically conveyed: for example, a text purporting to be a letter from the Ottoman ambassador to the Venetian Senate was illustrated with the image of an identifiably Turkish man bearing a letter with a pendant seal.²⁶ The earliest pamphlets about the New World often contained a woodcut of a ruler receiving his latest letters.²⁷ Each of these devices underscored the news' initial epistolary form.

News pamphlets often noted that their material had been translated from another vernacular language – one of the few times that vernacular-to-vernacular translating was touted in the early sixteenth century. News about the Turk might derive from sources closer to the front, "transferred out of a foreign tongue into high German" (in this example, via Belgrade),²⁸ or "printed in Venice and now word by word translated into German."²⁹ These translations were most commonly made from "Welsch" (Italian or another Romance language), Greek, or sometimes Latin.³⁰ The information that the news bulletin had been translated

---

eygenschafft des/ Newen Lands/ so newlich von Kay. May. Armadi auff dem newen Mör gefunden ist worden/ durch die Hispanier (1535); Jörg von Metha in *Ein missif oder sendbrieff* [1534]. Also *Copey eynes brieffes so miser Johann Baptista de Grimaldo/ seynem vettern Ansaaldo de Grimaldo/ vnnd andern Edlen gen Genua auß Hyspanien zu°geschribenn hat. M.D.XXiX* ([Nuremberg: Kunigunde Hergot], 1529) and a letter from Hungarian nobles to the king of Poland, *New Zeytung. Die Schlacht des Turkischen Kesers. . . . feyndtsbrieff* (1526).

²⁵ In 1517, a set of letters from a Christian merchant resident in Alexandria to the pope and from a city councilman in "Syo" described the war between Persian and Ottoman forces for Caspar Fry of Zürich in *Der krieg zwischen dem groszmechtigen propheten Sophi/ Turcken vnnd dem Soldan/ alle die ding die do geschehen seyndt in auffgang der sonnen rc. hat kundt gethan ein Christen Kauffman wonend zu Alexandria/ vnserm aller heiligsten vater dem Babst Im iar. 1517* [1518].

²⁶ *Ein Summari der Türckischen Botschafft werbung/ an die Herrschafft zu Venedig/ in Welscher sprach beschehen/ sampt des Venedischen Senats gegeben antwort* ([Nuremberg]: Johann Petreius] 1537).

²⁷ Amerigo Vespucci, *Mundus Novus* (Magdeburg: Winter, 1506); Cortés's second letter, *Carta de relacion* 2 ed. (Zaragoza: George Coci, 1523).

²⁸ "auß frembdersprach in Hoch tewtsch Tranßferirt." *Copey vnd lautter Abschrifft eins warhafftigen Sendbrieffs/ wie der Türckisch Kayser Solyman/ disen sein yetzt gegenwürtigen Anzug wider die Christenhait geordnet. . . .* [1532].

²⁹ "zu Venedig gedruckt/ vnd yetzt von wort zu wort verteutscht." *Ein Summari der Turckischen Botschafft werbung* (1537), 1.

³⁰ For example, *Ein Summari der Turckischen Botschafft werbung* (1537); *Die Ritterlich und lobwürdig reiß des gestrengen vnd über all ander weyt erfarnen Ritters vnd landtfarers/ herren Ludowico Vartomans von Bolonia. Sagend von den landen / Egypto/ Syria/ von beiden Arabia Persia/ India vnd Ethiopia/ von den gestalten / sitten/ vnd dero menschen leben vnd glauben. . . .* (Strasbourg: Joannes Knoblock, 1516); *Die beläagerung der Stat Wien Osterreich/ von dem aller grausamesten Tyrannen vnd verderber der*

seems to have added credibility. A related means to validate news was to emphasize its eyewitness origin.[31] All of these markers of credibility come together in an example from 1535: "[S]uch news has been translated out of Spanish into French, and then into Netherlandish and High German languages. A trustworthy man named Master Adolf, imperial secretary in Spain, has seen these two ships unloading."[32]

Although I have concentrated here on the circulation of information via links between courts and texts in the form of manuscript or printed pamphlets, word of mouth also played an important role in the transmission of information. Both written and verbal accounts of the New World exerted a persuasive pull during the late 1520s, serving as enticements to journey there.[33] The flow of verbal information from the Ottoman front is evident in municipal and court account books. The Vienna court as well as city councils got up-to-the-moment reports from returning soldiers and travelers.[34]

News and information were everywhere: lively interest in the west Indies and the Ottoman Empire formed the context for cultural descriptions of their inhabitants. In this first half-century of encounter, shifts

---

Christenhait dem Turckischen Kayser/ genandt Sultan Solimayn/ Nemlich beschehen/ im Monat Septembris des Newvndzwayntzigsten [1529]; *Copey unnd lautter Abschrifft ains warhafftigen Sandbrieffs/ wie der Türckisch Kayser Solyman/ disen seinen yetzt gegenwürtigen Anzug wider die Christenhait geordnet/ von Constantinopel außgezogen/ vnd gen Kriechischen Weissenburgk ankomen ist/ wie volgt* [1532]; *Duca de Albische Pardon... Auß Frantzösischer Sprach trewlich verdeutscht* (1570). In news from Hungary, translations from Latin into German occurred regularly. *Vier warhafftige Missiven/* [1542]; *Warhafftigen Neuwe Zeytung / aus dem Vngerlandt vnd Türckey ins Deutsch Landt geschrieben/ aus dem Latein inn Deutsche sprach verdolmetscht* (1546).

31 In a pamphlet detailing the siege of Vienna, *Ein kurtzer bericht vber die recht warhafftig Contrafactur/ Türckischer belegerung der Stat Wien/ wie dieselbig anzusehen vnd zuuersteen sey/ welche zu rhüm/ preyß/ lob vnd eer gantzem Römiscchem Reich/ Gemeyner Ritterschafft/ vnd in sonderheyt einem Erbern Rath der statt Nürmberg/ durch Niclaus Meldeman yetzt verfertigt/ getrückt vnd außgangen ist* [1529], ai[v] and Nicolas Federmann, *Indianische Historia* (Hagenau: Sigmund Bund, 1557). For the importance of the eyewitness, Michel deCerteau, "Ethno-Graphy: Speech, or the Space of the Other: Jean de Léry," in *The Writing of History*, trans. Tom Conley (New York: Columbia University Press, 1988).

32 "[s]olche zeyttung ist auß Hyspanischer sprach/ in die Frantzösische getransfertirt worden/ darnach in Nyderlendisch vnd hochteusch sprach. Dise zway schyff hat ein glaubwürdiger Mann mit nammen Mayster Adolff Kay. May. Secretari in Hyspania abladen sehen." *Copey etlicher brieff so auß Hispania kummen seindt....* (1535).

33 Jürgen Oohlau, "Neue Quellen zur Familiengeschichte der Spengler: Lazarus Spengler und seine Söhne," *MVGN* 52 (1963/64), 246–52 and Hans Staden, *Warhaftige historia und beschreibung...* (Marburg: 1557).

34 See Chapter 4.

in textual and visual representations of culture were strikingly evident, nowhere more so than in the comparatively visually rich German print culture. (Iberian and Italian printed works did not focus on visual images of New World cultures to the same degree.)[35] Some of the cultural flexibility of these descriptions lies in the visual representations and their references, as well as the texts. Print narratives of the Columbian encounters illustrate the flexibility of cultural associations accreting to descriptions.

In 1492, Columbus landed on an island in what would become the Caribbean. His descriptions of the peoples living there allowed them to be understood in Europe as a subset of the "wild man." The image of the wild man – a medieval motif of a hairy man living beyond the bounds of society or family – had by the fifteenth century become the symbol of a simple lifestyle, free from society's cares and woes. The inhabitants of the New World first appeared in print, in both text and image, within this framework. Simple barbarians on the very edge of the Indies, they were licentious cannibals without aesthetic cares, who wore feather headdresses and skirts, carried clubs or bows, and decorated themselves by attaching jewels to their skin. Finally, and most crucially, they held possessions in common and "had no government"[36] (See Figure 1). These points of cultural description had been drawn from Amerigo Vespucci's *Mundus Novus*. Beginning in 1503, Vespucci's text circulated broadly in first Latin and then vernacular texts: primarily in German (at least eight editions in 1505, the first year from which vernacular editions are extant), but also in Italian, Czech, and Low German.[37]

As interest in news of the world outside Europe ran high, printers hurried to produce pamphlets that met the demand. Even as the texts

---

[35] James Lyell, *Early Book Illustration in Spain* (London: Grafton & Co., 1926), 18. For formal precursors to the title pages of the first Castilian editions of Cortés's second and fourth *Cartas*, see the press of the Tres Compañeros Alemanes, 1498 in José L. Portillo Muñoz, *La ilustracion grafica de los incunables sevillanos (1470–1500)* (Seville: Diputación Provincial de Sevilla, 1980). The second *Carta* has even closer correlations with the production of (E)stanislao Polono (active in Seville, then Alcalá), particularly in the 1502 *Vita Christi*. The frontispiece arms in the Toledo 1525 first edition of the fourth *Carta* have a close approximation in Ruberto de Nola, *Libro de cozina* (Toledo: Ramon de Petras, 1525). See also Susi Colin, *Das Bild des Indianers in 16. Jahrhundert* (Idstein: Schulz-Kirchner Verlag, 1988).

[36] "Haben kein Regiment." *Dise figur anzaigt vns das volck und insel....* (Augsburg, 1505).

[37] See introduction to Jan van Doesborch *De Novo Mondo*, facsimile.... ed. M.E. Kronenberg (The Hague: Martinus Nijhoff, 1927) for some vernacular and Latin examples, 1–19. *European Americana* catalogs the numerous translations and abridgements: for 1503–1517, see 7–20.

FIGURE 1. *Dise figur anzaigt vns das volck vnd insel die gefunden ist.... Vnd haben kein regiment.* (Augsburg, 1505). Spencer Collection, The New York Public Library, Astor, Lenox and Tilden Foundations.

remained much the same, the images were often recycled and drawn from a variety of more or less evocative sources. The title page of a Low German translation of Amerigo Vespucci's *Mundus Novus* published in 1506 by Jacob Winter in Magdeburg contained one of these borrowed and spliced images. To create this image, Winter's press chose to copy two woodcuts that had appeared in fellow Magdeburger Moritz Brandis's 1492 *Legend of Belial*.[38] The press copied an image of Adam and Eve being expelled from Paradise after eating the forbidden fruit of the tree of knowledge. From the same moral work, they copied the figure of a king receiving a letter during a legal debate in which the devil Belial sought redress for the loss of souls harrowed by Christ from hell. Adam and Eve, as forebears of humanity, were suitable models to depict New World Indians. Such New World inhabitants were free from all cultural

[38] Colin, 188–9. Albert Schramm, *Der Bilderschmuck der Frühdrucke*, 12 (Leipzig: Hierse- mann, 1929), Table 62: no. 413 and Table 63: no. 422. The choice to reuse material from the Legend of Belial suggests a possible non-Christian identification for the peoples of the New World.

trappings and acquisitions, yet, like Adam and Eve, they bore the burden of original sin. Although the source of the borrowed image may not have been important to the pamphlet's producer, the reader would recognize Adam and Eve at humankind's simple beginnings. Elsewhere associations of New World peoples with wild men were strong and, by the time of Strasbourg preacher Johann Geiler von Kaysersberg's death in 1510, his sermons included a reclassification of the different types of wild men, with five subcategories – the *solitarii* (hermits such as St. Onofrius or Mary of Egypt), *sacchani* (wild men with horns such as satyrs), *hyspani* (people from the overseas islands), *piginin* (pygmies), and *diaboli* (devils).[39]

Perceived in practice as well as representation to be wild people without government and order, Caribbean peoples and their islands were quickly placed under Castilian dominance. Members of a 1512 junta of civil lawyers and clerics, convened at Burgos, applied the Aristotelian definition of natural slavery to inhabitants of the Indies. When the crown solicited a further opinion from one of the committee's members, the civil lawyer Juan López de Palacio Rubios, he emphasized the absence of civilized society. Palacio Rubios repeated the available evidence, that the Indians held all property in common, had no constituted families, were promiscuous, and had no technology or true religion.[40] Yet the vast kingdom of Prester John and the nations visited by the apostle St. Thomas might be encountered a few islands further away, regardless of whether you sailed east or west to India. Indeed, in 1517, Lazarus Nuremberger reported that an embassy from Prester John had met with a royal Portuguese envoy in subcontinental India.[41] The well-known Hans Burgkmair sketches of armed Brazilian Indians, as well as an image in Maximilian I's book of hours, reveal that there was some interest in ethnographic details at the Habsburg court. Similarly armed Indians also appeared in Maximilian's print "Triumphal Procession" (*Triumphzug*), but beyond the partial family of woman and child in this 1505 work,

[39] Geiler von Kaysersberg, *Die Emeis*, (Johann Grüninger: Strassburg, 1516), xl^v. His Lenten sermons were published posthumously. Wild men, along with the poor, burghers, and nobles, symbolized conditions of society. For an extended discussion of the wild man, see Richard Bernheimer, *Wild Men in the Middle Ages: A Study in Art, Sentiment, and Demonology* (Cambridge: Harvard University Press, 1952). The *Insula hyspani* is labeled in a 1493 Basel woodcut of Columbus's voyage.

[40] Pagden made this connection in his erudite *Fall of Natural Man* (Cambridge: Cambridge University Press, 1982). He, however, skimmed over the transition period (his text jumps from 1513 to 1537), noting in passing that a change reflecting the encounter with the Aztec and Inca societies occurred in the subsequent two decades, 50–3, 57–64.

[41] Krása, *Codex Bratislavensis*, 68.

Indians from the west Indies remained unassociated with other signs of social, political, or religious structures.[42]

Recent scholarship has often extended the predominance of this motif of the simple savage (either gentle or cruel, allegorical or real) in the New World through the entire sixteenth century. Too-heavy reliance on this idea elides the full range of perceptions about Indian culture and cultural hierarchy during the first half of the sixteenth century. As we will see, widely circulating news and images of Mexico and the Aztec Empire would mark significant changes in the evolving notions of Indian societies. Similarly, the fear of the Turk did not outweigh attempts to understand the Turks and their culture. The evidence for these changes is located in multiple media. Ideas in texts were not only instantiated but also developed in visual images and material objects: shifting cultural logics were expressed contrapuntally through recorded word and fashioned artifact.[43]

This book is divided into two parts. The first part, "Categories of Inclusion," examines the early circulation of Mexican and Turkish people, cultural goods, and representations in the Habsburg Empire. Pre-existing ideas of cultural similitude and natural religion allowed these societies to be understood, both conceptually and in practice, as relatively equivalent to those of Christian Europe. Habsburg and other elites quickly linked symbolic power to extra-European cultures. In a process of cultural appropriation and translation, they experimented with the status of Mexican and Ottoman people and the possession and display of Mexican and Ottoman cultural goods.

The first chapter argues that at the beginning of the sixteenth century, ideas of cultural similitude framed European understandings of the world's cultures. Fifteenth-century ethnographies and religious dialogues had conceptualized the world as a whole, where divergences in religious practice, trade, legal customs, or family organization revealed variation but not essential difference. The chapter then explores reports about

---

[42] Walter L. Strauss, ed. *The Book of Hours of Maximilian I* (New York: Abaris, 1974), 81. For a summary of the earlier literature on the two Burgkmair watercolors, see John Rowlands, *The Age of Dürer and Holbein: German Drawings 1400–1550* (London: British Museum, 1988), 187–8, nos. 158a, 158b; Max Geisberg, *The German Single-Leaf Woodcut, 1500–1550*, rev. and ed. Walter Strauss (New York: Hacker Books, 1974) II: 478–82; and for the relevant prints in the Triumphal Procession, Alfred Aspland, ed., *The Triumphs of Emperor Maximilian I* (Manchester: Holbein, 1873), II:123–4.

[43] Bourdieusian habitus and practice figure prominently in the conception of cultural change and expression employed here.

newly discovered Aztec culture (1518–1530) and pre-1532 representations of Turkish culture to explain Latin Christian understandings of religion and culture outside Europe and delineate emerging Reformation concerns in these cultural descriptions and cosmographies.

Chapter 2 examines the Habsburg court and its commitment to the ideal of world empire. It argues that initial responses to Mexican envoys in Castile occurred under this rubric; like Tunisian nobles, Aztec and Mexica elites were accepted as titled representatives of heterodox client states within a universal monarchy. The chapter closes with the mid-century development of segregationist ideas and policies. These policies set the stage for excluding all New World peoples from full participation in European secular and religious arenas.

Chapter 3 tracks the changing meanings of imperial symbolic display in the context of the early Reformation. After describing Habsburg treasure and gift giving, the Aztec treasure's initial incorporation into Habsburg treasuries as a conquered empire's regalia is detailed. The chapter then considers the treatment of both Christian and Aztec relics and treasures in the early Reformation's repudiation of spectacular display. Once desacralized and stripped of symbolic content, treasure could be melted down to finance Habsburg interests.

Part II of the book, "Experiments of Exclusion," examines the shift in categories of cultural comparison, from similitude to hierarchy. Reformation and Counter-Reformation thought and practices transformed conceptions of sovereign authority, repudiated "idolatrous" material culture, and redrew the boundaries of true religion. Ethnographers, diplomats, humanists, and other cultural actors contributed to the repositioning of Mexicans and Ottomans within these new frameworks. Mid-to-late-century Latin, German, and Spanish ethnographies and cosmographies depict the increasingly negative portrayals of extra-European cultures and their idolatrous religious practices.

Chapter 4 discusses the formation of cultural boundaries in sixteenth-century central and southeastern Europe, through practices and rhetoric involving Christian prisoners. Taking captives and hostages hardened the new political and religious border between a Christian Habsburg empire and a Muslim Ottoman Empire, even as it paradoxically regularized diplomatic relations to handle their captive redemptions. Negative attitudes of Christians toward Turks and Islam developed in this climate. During the mid-sixteenth century, the Latin Christian ex-prisoner emerged as the ideal and antagonistic transmitter of knowledge for a European audience.

Chapter 5 examines the secularization of Habsburg ceremonies of power during the later sixteenth century. Responding to solidifying confessions, the Habsburgs sought to represent their authority as non-confessional in print and in performative display. After exploring the range of efforts to shape perceptions of the Habsburgs, the chapter proposes the formation of the sybaritic Turk in the context of a new diplomatic relationship between the Habsburg and Ottoman courts.

The book concludes with the emergence of new definitions of culture in Europe at the end of the sixteenth century. Propelled by Protestant accusations of idolatry and the need to establish Catholic orthodoxy, sixteenth-century Counter-Reformation texts of cultural and religious description increasingly displaced idolatry to cultures beyond Europe or in the antique past. Catholic princely collections soon instantiated this move: Muslim and Indian treasures, once symbols of imperial authority, became conceptually conflated. Continuing this trend, New World and Turkish people and cultures were devalued from the category of "civilized" to a new cultural category of "idolatrous exotic." At the end of the century, then, Christian Europeans had elevated themselves above extra-European cultures through the exigencies of religious redefinition and confessionalism. Hierarchy had replaced similitude.

Throughout the sixteenth century, an information order, with interwoven elements of state intelligence and social communication,[44] spanned the Habsburg empire and most, if not all, of Latin Christendom. In the first half of the sixteenth century, the connectivity of the Habsburg empire was grounded in the ruler and policies of its dynasty. Habsburg courts were geographically separated from one another, with a Habsburg representative usually holding court in Castilian or Aragonese Iberia, in the Holy Roman Empire, and in the Low Countries. But while the Habsburg siblings Charles, Ferdinand, and Mary lived, their courts were deeply linked, sometimes to the consternation of local elites. Personnel were transferred from court to court to serve as diplomats, advisors, or attendants. Material objects passed from family member to family member, maintaining affective and symbolic bonds. Ceremonial practices and cultural ideas were shared between one court and another, to be shaped through sometimes regional cultural logics.[45]

---

[44] Bayly, *Empire*.

[45] Wolfram Krömer, ed., *Spanien und Österreich in der Renaissance* (Innsbruck: Institut für Sprachwissenschaft der Universität Innsbruck, 1989) and *1492–1992: Spanien, Österreich und Iberoamerika* (Innsbruck: Institut für Sprachwissenschaft der Universität

The connectivity was in part pragmatic: Charles's aunts, siblings, and children ruled portions of his vast empire on his behalf, and Charles's own unforeseen succession reminded the family that the Iberian succession often hung on one life. With Charles's abdication from all his titles in the 1550s, the balance of political power in the family shifted: the Central European Habsburgs were no longer subjects of the family's now-Iberian branch, "Casa Austria." Yet these cousins and siblings maintained multiple ties – educational, marital, and bureaucratic – that would continue to connect the two branches, their courts, and their cultural production throughout the sixteenth century. It is this broad Habsburg empire that served as the formative arena for the ongoing categorizations of extra-European peoples.

Innsbruck, 1993); volumes edited by Friedrich Edelmayer, including *Hispania-Austria II: Die Epoche Philipps II (1556–1598)* (Munich: Oldenburg, 1999); Christopher Laferl, *Die Kultur der Spanier in Österreich unter Ferdinand I. 1522–1564* (Vienna: Böhlau, 1997); and Bethany Aram, *Juana the Mad: Sovereignty and Dynasty in Renaissance Europe* (Baltimore: Johns Hopkins University Press, 2005).

PART ONE

CATEGORIES OF INCLUSION

I

Cultures and Religions

Reforming Description

In the fifteenth century, texts of cultural description proliferated in Latin Christendom. Such descriptions or ethnographies took several different forms and names, appearing as cosmographies or as works "on the customs, laws, and rites" of a people. Geographies such as Ptolemy's were gradually supplemented to provide cultural information along with their physical descriptions.[1] For models of cultural description, fifteenth- and early-sixteenth-century authors could and did draw on a range of classical and patristic sources, with Isidore of Seville's *Etymologiae* serving as a widely available reference. In the *Etymologiae*, Isidore sorted his information into categories: the earth, with its three continents (Asia, Europe, and Africa) and islands; cities; public buildings and sacred buildings; information on mineral deposits and agriculture; military matters,

---

[1] Relevant late-fifteenth-century ethnographic examples include Pius II's *Historia rerum ubique gestarum* (Venice: Colonia and Manthen, 1477), the ca. 1480 *Tractatus de moribus, condictionibus et nequicia turcorum*, ed. Reinhard Klockow (Vienna: Böhlau, 1993) by Georgius de Hungaria, and Bernhart von Breydenbach's *Peregrinatio in terram sanctam* (1486). The earliest Latin editions of Ptolemy's *Cosmographia* or *Geographia* (dating after 1406) contained few ethnographic or cultural notes, whereas the 1482 Ulm printed edition noted that several peoples in Africa (below Ethiopia) and in Asia (beyond the Ganges) were anthropophagi. Multiple editions were produced in the last quarter of the fifteenth century, with expanded cultural information added in 1486. See Margriet Hoogvliet, "The Medieval Texts of the 1486 Ptolemy Edition by Johann Reger of Ulm," *Imago Mundi* 54 (2002): 7–18 and J. Lennart Berggruen and Alexander Jones, *Ptolemy's Geography* (Princeton: Princeton University Press, 2000), 50–2.

ships, and smaller fabricated objects including instruments, tools, and clothing.[2]

By choosing to describe the world in its geographic expanse, Isidore had followed pre-established models in the Mediterranean world. Authors ranging from Herodotus, Diodorus Siculus, Strabo, and Pomponius Mela to Pliny, Solinus, and Martianus Capella had compiled expansive texts, styled cosmographies, chorographies, or histories that had organized material in geographical or chronological order. In Isidore's attention to cultural or material objects, he also drew from another tradition whose exemplar was Marcus Terentius Varro's *Antiquities*. Varro had attempted to describe "all the aspects of the life of a nation" in a systematic intensive fashion.[3] By the fifteenth century, Varro's categories had survived only through widely read third parties such as Isidore or Cicero. According to Cicero's report in *Academica*, Varro's text included the chronology and topography of Rome, its sacred laws, priests, domestic and military matters, and all other matters, whether human or divine.[4] The structure of Isidore's *Etymologiae*, incorporating geographic breadth and "antiquarian" depth of cultural description, seems to have provided the organizational categories utilized by subsequent authors.

Detailed cultural descriptions with Isidorean categories were employed in the thirteenth century to offer information about the unfamiliar Mongols (or Tartars). The Franciscan John of Plano Carpini's *Ystoria Mongalorum*, composed before his death circa 1252, included categories of marriage practices, social rank and its display through clothing and

---

[2] Isidore of Seville, *Isidori Episcopi Etymologiarum sive originum libri XX*, ed. W. M. Lindsay (1911; reprint Oxford: Clarendon Press, 1962). After Isidore's death in 636, his contemporary Braulio further organized the work. *Texts and Transmission*, ed. L.D. Reynolds (Oxford: Clarendon Press, 1983), 194–6, and Anthony Grafton, "The availability of ancient works," *The Cambridge History of Renaissance Philosophy*, ed. Schmitt et al. (Cambridge: Cambridge University Press, 1988), 784. Margaret Hodgen's survey of ethnographic texts in *Early Anthropology in the Sixteenth and Seventeenth Centuries* (Philadelphia: University of Pennsylvania Press, 1964) remains the introduction to the subject; she is primarily concerned with the categories of mid-twentieth-century anthropology.

[3] Arnaldo Momigliano's "Ancient History and the Antiquarian" distinguished between historians, who organized by chronology, and antiquarians such as Varro, who organized by system. *JWCI* 13 (1950): 286–9. For classical Greek ethnography, François Hartog, *The Mirror of Herodotus* (Berkeley: University of California Press, 1988), 204–6.

[4] Fritz Saxl noted Isidore's debt to Varro and his subdivisions of *qui agant, ubi, quando, quid* for human and divine in "Illustrated Medieval Encyclopaedias – 1. the Classical Heritage," *Lectures* ([1939]; The Warburg Institute, 1957), 228–41. Cicero, *Academica* I chap. 3 (I.9) (London: Heinemann, 1933), 418–19.

housing, possessions, religious practices, customs and laws both good and bad, food, history, and military organization and strategy.[5] Within a few years, this account was redacted in Vincent of Beauvais's *Speculum Historiale*, which would circulate widely in subsequent centuries.[6] Such descriptions of a people in terms of their history and customs, laws, and religious practices were repopularized in the fifteenth century, when contemporary eyewitnesses used the format to offer up information about a people, the "Turks," whose territorial gains drew the attention of their contemporaries.

By the fifteenth century, authors could not only draw from Isidore of Seville's or Vincent of Beauvais's categories of description and recently recovered classical ethnographies; they could also refer to the Aristotle's *Politics*, circulating in Latin Christendom since the 1260s.[7] The *Politics* defined a civilized state, in this case a city-state, as one that necessarily included households, family, property, government, arts, arms, religious practice, and adjudication.[8] Reliance on Aristotle also simplified the question of religion in the evaluation of virtue and good governance. For example, texts like the *Speculum Historiale* marked out doctrinal divergence as error,[9] yet such divergences were everywhere. In contrast, Aristotle expressed little concern about the details of doctrines and religious faith.

---

[5] Anastasius van den Wyngaert, ed. *Itinera et relationes Fratrum Minorum*, Sinica Franciscana I (Quaracchi, Florence: Collegium S. Bonaventura, 1929), 3–130. Franciscan William of Rubruck's account of the Mongols was written within the subsequent decade and included categories of housing, food, costume, customs and marriage, laws, and religious practices.

[6] Vincent of Beauvais, *Speculum historiale* (Strasbourg, 1473), Books 30 and 32.

[7] Jean Dunbabin, "The reception and interpretation of Aristotle's *Politics*," in *The Cambridge History of Later Medieval Philosophy*, ed. N. Kretzmann, A. Kenny, and J. Pinborg (Cambridge: Cambridge University Press, 1982), 723–37. For the availability of Cicero, Martianus Capella, Pliny the Elder, and Solinus, see *Texts and Transmission*, 124–31, 245–6, 307–16, 391–3. Diodorus Siculus's text was available in southern Italy ca. 1230, while Herodotus and Strabo circulated in the fifteenth century. Walter Berschin, *Greek Letters and the Latin Middle Ages: From Jerome to Nicholas of Cusa*, rev. and expanded ed., trans. Jerold C. Frakes (Washington, DC: Catholic University of America Press, 1988), 247, 396 and O.A.W. Dilke et al., "Cartography in the Byzantine Empire" in *A History of Cartography*, ed. J.B. Harley and David Woodward (Chicago: University of Chicago Press, 1987), 1:267–70.

[8] Aristotle, *Politics*, trans. Jonathan Barnes (Cambridge: Cambridge University Press, 1988), 1.1252a–1254b, 7.1328b. Joan-Pau Rubiés refers to a similar set of cultural attributes as constituting "civility" in his *Travel and Ethnology in the Renaissance: South India through European Eyes, 1250–1625* (Cambridge: Cambridge University Press, 2000).

[9] Vincent of Beauvais, Book 31, Chapters 96–8.

He argued instead that civilized states must contain a degree of organization in religious practice and institutionalized structure. Cicero, another classical influence on fifteenth-century humanist sensibilities about virtue, also emphasized the practice of worship rather than adherence to particular beliefs in *De natura deorum* and *De officiis*.[10]

Religious practice or worship, rather than religious beliefs, lay at the heart of Nicholas of Cusa's *De pace fidei* (1453). Composed during Cusanus's active engagement with his bishopric of Brixen, *De pace fidei* was a response to the news of Constantinople's fall to the Ottomans. Rather than a cultural description, *De pace fidei* consisted of a series of dialogues involving seventeen speakers, each representing a different people or *natio* and its religious "sect." Set within the framework of a vision sent by God to the narrator, the Greek, Italian, Arab, Indian, Chaldean, Jewish, Scythian, French, Persian, Syrian, Turk, Spanish, German, Tartar, Armenian, Bohemian, and English wise men each posed questions that were answered by the Word of God and the apostles Peter and Paul.[11] The men's questions focused on metaphysics and on rites, as the men sought the key to universal peace. The diversity of sects in the different peoples had been caused by the infinite Creator, who sent different prophets and teachers throughout world and thus generated the different sects. Would God the Creator continue to find the diversity of rites acceptable in the aftermath of the fall of Constantinople? Cusanus argued that the very unknowability and ineffability of the Creator made it likely that he would continue to be worshipped through a diversity of names and rites.[12]

Cusanus defined the necessary element of faith as belief in the Creator or "wisdom [which] is the one, simple, eternal God, the beginning of all

---

[10] See Cicero, *De natura deorum* (London: Heinemann, 1933) and *De officiis* (London: Heinemann, 1913). I thank James Muldoon for drawing my attention to Cicero's influence.

[11] The literature on Cusanus is extensive. Pauline Moffitt Watts, *Nicolaus Cusanus: a Fifteenth-Century Vision of Man* (Leiden: Brill, 1982) is an excellent starting point. For the metaphysics of Cusanus's phrase "religio una in rituum varietate," see Thomas McTighe's survey "Nicholas of Cusa's Unity–Metaphysics and the Formula Religio una in Rituum Varietate," 161–72, as well as James Biechler, "A New Face Toward Islam," 185–202; Pauline Moffitt Watts, "Talking to Spiritual Others," 203–18; and Thomas Izbicki, "The Possibility of Dialogue with Islam in the Fifteenth Century," 175–83, all in *Nicholas of Cusa in search of God and Wisdom*, ed. G. Christianson and T. Izbicki (Leiden: Brill, 1991).

[12] Nicholas of Cusa, *De pace fidei* [1453], ed. R. Klibansky and H. Bascour, O.S.B., *Heidelberg*. 7 (Hamburg: Felix Meiner, 1959), 6.

things."[13] Nonetheless, not all rites and doctrinal positions were equally desirable for Cusanus. Some doctrinal positions of the Latin Church were preferred and even necessary for the fullest possible understanding of God. Yet sects that disagreed with the Latin Church on doctrinal points, such as the Bohemians on the Eucharist and the Chaldeans on the Trinity, should still, according to Cusanus, be recognized and accepted as worshipping the Creator.[14] In *De pace fidei*'s final dialogue with the English speaker, Paul concluded the question of diversity by affirming its value. He argued that the diversity of rites might even increase devotion, as nations competed to make their own rites more splendid than all others. Cusanus ended his vision with a call for further concord: after carefully examining many authors who wrote about the diversity of religion, the foregathered wise men embraced the insight that, even as their nations worshipped through a diversity of rites, they all had faith in the Creator. They then adjourned in order to promote perpetual peace by sharing this insight among all peoples of the world.[15]

The dialogue between the Tartar and Paul revealed the extent to which religious practices or rites were extraneous to faith. The Tartar asked Paul about the bewildering array of practices found among other sects, particularly those involving marriage, sacrifice (including the Eucharist), and forms of visible and invisible physical marking: circumcision, branding, and baptism. In the preceding dialogue between the Bohemian and Paul, Paul had established that the sacramental practices of baptism and the sacrifice of the Eucharist were preferable but not necessary to faith. Cusanus, through the voice of Paul, noted that many men, including Christ and contemporary Ethiopian Jacobites, had experienced the practice of circumcision. Given that circumcision was a sign of respect for Abraham, Cusanus even suggested that it should be permitted or perhaps even adopted by all peoples, despite the Council of Florence's 1442 condemnation of the practice. Responding to the Tartar's questions, Paul reassured him that faith (*sola fides*) rather than rites justified salvation. Faith must be accompanied by obedience to God's only commandment, that people follow the law of love (*lex dilectionis*) toward God and humankind.[16]

---

[13] "Est igitur sapientia Deus unus, simplex, aeternus, principium omnium,... " *De pace fidei*, 14.

[14] *De pace fidei*, 21–6, 58–61.

[15] *De pace fidei*, 62–3.

[16] *De pace fidei*, 50–61.

Cusanus's discussion of idolatry moved beyond an examination of rites to an explication of the relationship between God and the sensible world. In the dialogue between the Indian and the Word of God, Cusanus began with the Latin Church's position on images: images were acceptable but should not be worshipped as though divinity inhabited the material objects themselves. Humans adored God as Creator and beginning of the universe. Because God was ineffable, human perception of him was always limited and partial. Elements of the natural, sensible world exemplified the separated parts of the beginning universe.[17] The elements that Cusanus chose to illustrate his argument were stars, humans, trees, and stones: all common objects of idolatry according to John of Damascus and the Book of Wisdom.[18] Implicitly, Cusanus validated the human tendency toward idolatry: it represented a genuine effort to worship God within the limits of human understanding. Because of human limitations, Indians would continue to venerate idols. This stance on idolatry drew on Cusanus's critique of affirmative theology in *De docta ignorantia* (1440). Organized religions' tendency to name and limit the divine, to worship the divine through rituals, often led to idolatry. Negative theology, Cusanus's "learned ignorance," provided the truer path to faith.[19]

Cusanus's 1456 sermon, "Ubi est qui natus est rex iudaeorum," extended his conception of diversity in religious rites to a broader consideration of human cultures and their diversity of customs and practices. Following *De pace fidei*, he asserted that although Jesus offered the most perfect *religio* to the "sect of the Christians," other peoples had received more distant versions of religion through their own wise men and prophets. The sermon also drew on his understanding of the human arts as a source of wisdom. In his 1450 *Idiota de sapientia* and *Idiota de mente*, he had already asserted that humans were best able to understand the true nature of wisdom through artisanal and commercial

---

[17] *De pace fidei*, 18–21. For Cusanus's development of these positions, see Watts, *Cusanus*, chapter 2.

[18] "Unde, quia Deum colentes ipsum adorare debent tamquam principium universi, in ipso autem uno universo reperitur partium multitudo, inequalitas et separatio–multitudo enim stellarum, arborum, hominum, lapidum sensui patet–omnis autem multitudinis unitas est principium, quare principium multitudinis est eterna unitas," in *De pace fidei*, 20–1. Cusanus does not emphasize another category, human-made idols, which appears in the Book of Wisdom 14 and in John of Damascus's translation of *Vita Barlaam et Joasaph*, ed. Michael Lequien, *Patrologia Graeca* 96 (Paris: Migne, 1891), 910.

[19] For a pre- and post-1440 periodization of Cusanus's thinking, Watts, *Cusanus*, 35, 55–61.

experience, as well as attendant numerical reasoning.[20] Within a culture, its ingenious men received divine revelation and, over time, were responsible for inventing the arts. In a vision of civilizational progress, Cusanus described humans separating themselves from animals, initially, through the invention of weaving, cooking, mechanical arts, agriculture, and trade. These arts might be followed by the creation of political and economic rules or customs that permitted virtuous living and peaceful governance. Finally, according to Cusanus, religion was achieved as a people's crowning development.[21] Cusanus's emphasis on the human arts reflected their importance as a source of wisdom in his thought. For Cusanus, diversity of custom and practice in both religious rites and other aspects of social organization was part of the process by which cultures became civilized.

Similar strands of thought appeared in other late-fifteenth-century authors. In common with Cusanus, Marsilio Ficino and Giovanni Pico Della Mirandola argued that some form of religious truth was possible outside of the Abrahamic tradition, articulating concepts often characterized as Neoplatonic religious universalism or natural religion. Unlike Cusanus, whose influence has been heavily debated,[22] Ficino and Pico are widely acknowledged as seminal influences for numerous Italian and German Platonists and humanists. Their search for a *prisca theologia*, predating Christ, was grounded in the belief that God had given wise men of all nations (most notably Plato) partial insight into his laws and mysteries. Careful study of these philosophers and the early Christian Platonists might allow the humanist scholar to learn their truth and wisdom.[23] Ficino believed that God had granted a form of religion to every region

---

[20] Nicholas of Cusa, *Idiota de sapientia, Idiota de mente*, ed. Renata Steiger, *Heidelberg.* 5 (Hamburg: Felix Meiner, 1983). For the Book of Wisdom's influence, Watts, *Nicolaus Cusanus*, 119–33.

[21] Nicholas of Cusa, "Sermon CCXVI: Ubi est qui natus est rex iudaeorum," *Sermones IV (1453–1463)*, ed. Klaus Reinhardt and Walter Andreas Euler, *Heidelberg.* 19, (Hamburg: Felix Meiner, 1996), 82–96.

[22] The debate can be entered through the work of Ernst Cassirer, a proponent of a direct link from Cusanus to Ficino and Pico in *The Individual and the Cosmos in Renaissance Philosophy* [1927], trans. Mario Domandi (Philadelphia: University of Pennsylvania Press, 1963), who moderated his position in "Giovanni Pico della Mirandola: A Study in the History of Renaissance Ideas," *JHI* 3 (1942): 123–44, 319–46.

[23] James Hankins, *Plato in the Italian Renaissance* (Leiden: Brill, 1990), 1:278–87; D.P. Walker, *The Ancient Theology* (Ithaca: Cornell University Press, 1972), esp. 1–21; Charles Trinkaus, *In Our Image and Likeness*, 2nd ed. (Notre Dame: University of

of the world, with different rites allowed to flourish in different places.[24] As outlined in *De christiana religione* (1474), Ficino's conception of non-Christian wisdom included the insights of Greek, Jewish, Persian, Indian, Egyptian, Ethiopian, Gallic, and Roman philosophers and priests; all of his examples were located in the ancient past.[25] Similarly, Pico worked to incorporate Jewish Kabbalists into studies of *prisca theologia*, but the scope of his work also focused on the learned men of past centuries rather than present-day cultures and religions.[26]

Members of the papal court, where Nicholas of Cusa's influence as cardinal and humanist was arguably greatest, grappled with the question of religious truth in the present world rather than the past. Several promoted the concept of harmony in the universe that reflected its creator. The Servite Agostino Filippi, preaching for Leo X at the beginning of the sixteenth century, invoked Cusanus's "learned ignorance" and, in language resonant with *De pace fidei*, affirmed that God was known in all the world's nations, which worshipped him through a diversity of ceremonies and rites. Augustinian Giles of Viterbo's concept of divine harmony explicitly encompassed non-Christians.[27] Giles's conception of cultural relativism and natural religion led him to consider that all languages other than Hebrew, the language of the Holy Spirit, should be redefined as "barbarian."[28] In "Sententiae ad mentem Platonis," he asserted that the Castilian and Portuguese voyages had revealed that people in every part of the world possessed a belief in God.[29] Giles also maintained active interest in ethnographic data. During Giles's service as papal legate to Castile in 1518, his ethnographic interest in the newly encountered lands of Yucatan prompted him to encourage fellow humanist Peter Martyr

Notre Dame Press, 1995), 722–34; Paul Oskar Kristeller, *Eight Philosophers of the Italian Renaissance* (Stanford: Stanford University Press, 1964), 37–71; and Charles Schmitt, "Perennial Philosophy: From Agostino Steuco to Leibniz," *JHI* 27 (1966): 505–32.

[24] Paul Oskar Kristeller, *The Philosophy of Marsilio Ficino*, trans. Virginia Conant (New York: Columbia University Press, 1943), 316–20.

[25] Marsilio Ficino, *Liber de cristiana religione* [Florence: Nicolaus Laurentius Alamus, 1476], Ai –Aiiᵛ.

[26] William G. Craven, *Giovanni Pico della Mirandolla: Symbol of His Age* (Geneva: Droz, 1981), 89–111.

[27] John W. O'Malley, *Praise and Blame in Renaissance Rome* (Durham: Duke University Press, 1979), 94–7, 129–32, 158–60 and, for a survey of papal court culture, Ingrid Rowland, *The Culture of the High Renaissance* (Cambridge: Cambridge University Press, 1998). Cusanus's sermon collection, as well as *De pace fidei*, could at that time be found in the Vatican library.

[28] John W. O'Malley, *Giles of Viterbo on Church and Reform* (Leiden: Brill, 1968), 77–83.

[29] O'Malley, *Giles of Viterbo*, 20–3.

of Anghiera (Pietro Martire d'Anghiera) to compose a fourth *Decade* of news from the Indies for Leo X's edification.[30]

Peter Martyr had served as Queen Isabella and King Ferdinand of Castile and Aragon's envoy to the Mamluk Sultanate before becoming Charles V's court historiographer. An active correspondent with other humanists in the papal court and with Charles's advisors Mercurino di Gattinara and Luigi Marliano, he embraced cultural evaluation as an inquiry into the divine. Cultural description was not mere entertainment for the curious. God, through his mediator *philosophia*, had caused the creation of city-states, human laws, militaries, architecture, agriculture, and medicine. Ethnography explored culture and *philosophia* to help humans better understand God.[31] At the beginning of the sixteenth century, then, platonic concepts of religion and wisdom were widely accessible as authors embarked on their proto-ethnographic projects of cultural description.

In late-fifteenth-century and early-sixteenth-century ethnographies, the very categories used to evaluate and describe culture supported a stance of religious relativism. Discussions of religion focused on practices, which were placed alongside other aspects of culture: trade, governance, family, and costumes. The practices of organized religion – places of worship, gods (whether singular or plural), priests, and rites and ceremonies – merited discussion, so that the reader would recognize different sects and the peoples defined by them. *Religio* was generally distinct from *fides* or *doctrina*: discussions of contemporary or historic *religio* centered on practice or *ritus*.[32] Latin Christian authors considered most forms of faith known to them, including Islam and other forms of Christianity, to be heretical,[33] yet cosmographers avoided judgment on these doctrinal points. Bernhard von Breydenbach's *Peregrinatio in terram sanctam* (1486), while containing elements of a pilgrimage text, exemplified this stance in his ethnographic description of Jerusalem's many peoples, their alphabets, religious and social practices, and brief mention of several Jewish and Orthodox doctrinal errors.[34] Cosmographers, then, focused

---

[30] Peter Martyr of Anghiera, *De novo orbe* (Alcala de Henares: Eguia, 1530), lvi[v].

[31] Peter Martyr of Anghiera, *Opus Epistolarum*, in *Opera* (1530, facsimile Graz: Akademische Drucke, 1966), lxxxviii[v], letter dated 1507.

[32] Ernst Feil sketches the shifting meaning and usage of *religio*, with component faith or doctrine and practice, in *Religio* (Göttingen: Vandenhoeck & Ruprecht, 1986–1997).

[33] Identifications of Islam as a sect date back at least to the late eighteenth century. John of Damascus, *De Haerisibus*, ed. M. Lequien, *Patrologia Graeca* (Paris: Migne, 1864).

[34] Pilgrimage texts differed somewhat in their treatment of religious faith, although Bernhard von Breydenbach's *Peregrinatio in terram sanctam* (1486) stands as a hybrid text: a

primarily on Aristotelian categories of description and religious practice. In the first decades of the sixteenth century, cosmographers increased the scope of their descriptions of "customs, laws, and rites" to include information spanning the globe so that readers might be able to make more concrete their visions of the world's peoples and realms.[35]

Johann Boemus's *Omnium gentium mores, leges et ritus* (1520) was arguably the most widely cited and reprinted cosmography of its day. Boemus described the peoples of the world through the categories made popular by Isidore of Seville and Aristotle: family, governance, and religious practices. While making it clear that he believed Latin Christianity was the true faith, he discussed a range of religious and cultural practices throughout the world. In his preface, Boemus commented negatively on beliefs that contradicted Latin Christian doctrine, but in the body of the book his discussion of practices was neutral. The book began with a discussion of creation. Boemus presented two explanations for the creation and early history of humankind, one based on scripture and the other a cultural-invention trajectory of humankind's developing civilization. He glossed one as true and the other as false, but nonetheless provided the reader with both.[36] From that springboard, Boemus turned to look at the peoples of Africa, Asia, and Europe in turn, devoting one book to each continent. On the subject of practices, Boemus acted as a relatively neutral cataloger. Although he noted that the Egyptians' worship of gods such as the sun, moon, famous men, and animals was idolatrous, he also gave the Egyptians credit for being the inventors of religious worship. As Boemus turned to discuss the different regions of the world, he cited the historic practice of idolatry by a variety of peoples, including the ancient Germans, who had replaced it with Christianity, and the Huns, who had not. He noted present-day idolatry among the Tartars, Muslims, and the peoples north of Livonia, and the Turks' charge of idolatry against Christians, while remaining silent on the prospect of idolatry in India

---

pilgrimage text and an ethnographic description of Egypt and Jerusalem's many peoples, their alphabets, religious and social practices, and a few doctrinal errors of the Jews and the Orthodox Christians.

35 Johann Boemus employed these organizational strategies in his widely influential cosmography *Omnium gentium mores, leges et ritus*, first appearing as *Repertorium librorum trium de omnium gentium ritibus* (Augsburg: Wirsung, 1520). Boemus was aware of the link with political empire: his dedicatory poem to the reader concludes with the question of governance throughout the world, aiii[v].

36 Boemus, Book 1 chapters 1–2. Also, Klaus Vogel, "Cultural Variety in a Renaissance Perspective," *Shifting Cultures*, ed. Henriette Bugge and Joan Pau Rubiés (Münster: Lit Verlag, 1995), 17–34.

proper (although he noted it in Cathay) and mentioning none among the Jews. Boemus's information is based on classical as well as contemporary sources: he cited Diodorus Siculus on Egyptian religious practice (including idolatry) and on the genealogy of circumcision, a practice adopted by the Jewish people during their time in Egypt. Boemus noted in passing that circumcision was still practiced among contemporary followers of Jewish law.[37] In his section on Christian people and faith at the end of Book II on Asia, Boemus was careful to discuss practices of baptism, marriage, and indeed all the sacraments in detail as well as the twelve articles of faith and the ten commandments. Nonetheless these articles lay folded within the book's attempt to delineate religious, governmental, and social practices around the world. Boemus's work was widely disseminated; from his death until the close of the sixteenth century, more than a dozen Latin and vernacular versions were printed.

Soon after Boemus's cosmography appeared, cultural descriptions began to reflect emerging concerns and debates of the early Reformation. Beginning in the 1520s, individual works were rewritten or reorganized to address these issues, redirecting attention to aspects of culture previously ignored. Translators and redactors were often responsible for these new versions,[38] but authors also responded directly to the era's debates. Polydore Vergil's *De inventoribus rerum* had first appeared in 1499, describing the origins and diversity of humankind's religious, marital, literary, and musical practices as well as the invention of music, mathematics, astrology, medicine, magic, law, governments, military, and other human arts. Like Boemus, he attributed the diversity of gods to demonic activity. Encouraged to religious error, people began worshiping celestial objects, particularly virtuous humans, and animals.[39] Polydore Vergil concluded his first chapter, "De prima deorum origine et que Veri Dei nullum est exordium," by praising Plato for his act of naming one god as the creator of the world.[40] In a major revision that appeared in 1521, Polydore Vergil added five additional books that described Christian religious

---

[37] Boemus, 10–26^v, 29^v, 33^v, 37–39, 48^v–57^v.

[38] See the discussion of Boemus translations in the Introduction to Part II: Experiments of Exclusion.

[39] Polydore Vergil, *De inventoribus rerum* (1499), b. See Margaret T. Hodgen, "Ethnology in 1500: Polydore Vergil's Collection of Customs," *Isis* 57 (1966): 315–24; for context, John Ferguson and Elizabeth H. Alexander, "Notes on the Work of Polydore Vergil 'De Inventoribus Rerum'," *Isis* 17 (1932): 71–93; and Denys Hay, *Polydore Vergil, Renaissance Historian and Man of Letters* (Oxford: Clarendon Press, 1952).

[40] "Et Plato quoque qui omnium sapientissimus iudicatur: unum deum nominavit: & ab eo hunc mundum esse factum confirmat." Polydore Vergil, *De inventoribus rerum*, biii.

practices and their historical development. His prefatory letters, written to introduce the five books and addressed to his brother Gian Matteo, underscored his heightened awareness of information on religion and its development. The first letter, dated 1517, explains that Polydore had decided to delve more thoroughly into the origins of Christian ceremonies ("ex ceremoniis ethnicorum") and local change or invention that led to "a river of many rites and many ceremonies"[41] in which all could bathe and be confident of their eternal salvation. This explanation for the five additional books was soon replaced by a more cautious preface, appearing in 1525. The second preface focused on a more genealogical interest in religious practices as evidence of Christianity's development beyond and improvement on the faith of the Old Testament. In this letter, Vergil called for the elimination of Jewish invented ceremonies that may have crept into worship of the divine, distinguishing between those introduced by Jewish people and those introduced by Christ, by apostles, and by later Church fathers.[42] Although still signaling his acceptance of Church authorities beyond scripture, Vergil had developed a reformed-era sensibility about "misguided" ceremony and the need to remove error. A growing ambivalence about religious error would also develop in descriptions of Mexican peoples.

The Yucatan and the Aztec Empire

By 1510, print descriptions of Christopher Columbus's and Amerigo Vespucci's voyages had introduced Caribbean island cultures to a wide reading audience in Europe. In those narratives, Caribbean peoples were licentious and either lived outside of or in a very rudimentary society, possessing few goods and limited regard for the ties of family and government. In 1517, after a few abortive and unremunerative excursions to the South American coast, Castilian conquistadors began exploring the Central American coast. Francisco Hernández de Córdoba and Juan de Grijalva led initial expeditions and, in 1519, a more substantive and unauthorized expedition led by Hernán Cortés founded a town, Vera Cruz, further west along the coast.[43]

---

[41] "tot ceremoniarum totve rituum flumen," Polydore Vergil, *On Discovery*, ed. Brian Copenhaver (Cambridge: Harvard University Press, 2002), 16.

[42] For both letters, Vergil, *On Discovery*, 12–23.

[43] References in Peter Martyr's *Opus Epistolarum*, *Opera*, suggest that news of these initial Yucatan explorations reached Iberia in 1518, cxl.

As news of these excursions reached Castile, Peter Martyr of Anghiera picked up his pen to compose a new *Decade* of his *De orbe novo*, about these recently encountered lands of Yucatan. *De orbe novo*'s first three *Decades*, published in 1516, had ended with a chapter that hinted of more civilized peoples found southwest of the Caribbean Islands. The people of Darien inhabited fortified towns and were "citizens" (*cives*) subject to laws. In the fourth *Decade*, first published in 1521, Peter Martyr confirmed reports that the people of Yucatan were even more civilized than those of Darien. They lived in well-constructed cities with paved streets, bustling marketplaces, and grand houses and temples built from stone. They possessed structured governments and judicial bodies, observed marriages, practiced religion under the supervision of priests, and produced books. Even the social elite in the Yucatan appeared in relatively familiar terms to the Latin Christian reader: they were sumptuously clothed and wore gold and jewels.[44]

Descriptions of religious practices were inseparable from political and economic matters, all part of Peter Martyr's cultural description. After detailing the use of stone and wood in architecture, Peter Martyr briefly described Yucatan ritual and economic practices: "They follow the cult of idols and are circumcised. They conduct business in the highest good faith, trading without money. They honor crosses."[45] For the city of Cozumel, he extended his discussion of religious practices to describe their ritual offering. It took place in "[r]ooms in the towers filled with marble statues and clay images of bears, which they invoke by singing in exalted unison. They burn sweet-smelling and fragrant offerings to these images, which they worship as Penates: a divine service is celebrated there, they are circumcised."[46] Throughout the fourth *Decade*, Peter Martyr repeatedly noted the presence of these two religious practices, idolatry and

---

[44] Peter Martyr of Anghiera, *De orbe novo decades* (Alcala: Arnaldus Guillelmus, 1516), i iᵛ. The *Decades* on the New World appeared in sets of ten books (decades). Peter Martyr of Anghiera's fourth *Decade*, *De nuper sub d. Carolo repertis insulis,...* (Basel, 1521) was addressed to the court of Archduchess Margaret, Charles's aunt and regent in the Low Countries, 3. He also sent letters describing the Yucatec peoples' laws and politics, *Opus Epistolarum, Opera*, cliᵛ (1520) and clxviii (1521).

[45] "Idolorum culturae indulgent, sunt Recutiti. summa fide negotiantur, permutando sine pecuniis. Cruces ornant." Peter Martyr, (1521), 5. In the second edition, *De rebus et insulis noviter repertisa sereniss. Carolo Imperatore* (Nuremberg: Friedrich Peypus, 1524), governance practices were clarified with the addition "legibus vivunt," aaiᵛ.

[46] "Cameras in turri reperere, statuis tum marmoreis, tum fictilibus ursorum simulacris instructas, quos unisono cantu elato invocant, suavibus adolent odoribus, uti Penates eos colunt: res ibi diuina celebrata est, sunt recutiti." Peter Martyr (1521), 9.

circumcision. Although neither practice was observed by Latin Christians, each had been accepted as sincere worship in Cusanus's *De pace fidei*. Each was popularly understood to be practiced by Jews and Muslims: both groups were believed to have committed idolatry in the past, and both were known to continue performing circumcisions in the present.[47] Idolatry and circumcision were initially interesting to the humanist ethnographer as religious practices, albeit erroneous ones, that demonstrated worship or a covenant with God.

Peter Martyr's initial books of the fourth *Decade* detailed Hernández de Córdoba's and Grijalva's expeditions. In these first books, the presence of human sacrifice was not discussed in the civilized city-states of Campeche, Cozumel, or Coluacan. Rather, Peter Martyr explained human body parts as the evidence of justice meted out through corporal punishment. Only in the fourth book of the *Decade*, describing an Island of Sacrifice located near an island inhabited exclusively by women, did he detail practices of sacrifice evoking Herodotus's description of Egyptian bull sacrifices. Hearts were removed from victims and burned, to create an offering of smoke, while blood was applied to the idol's carved lips and parts of the victims' arms and legs reserved for later eating.[48] The final books of the *Decade*, covering Hernán Cortés's expedition, were the first to suggest that human sacrifice was widespread in Yucatan. Even there, human sacrifice appeared as one of several religious practices: "[T]hey are idolaters and circumcised: they sacrifice boys and girls to zemes. The zemes are images of nighttime spirits which they worship."[49] Peter Martyr's brief description of religious rites in the fourth *Decade* of *De orbe novo* took on a new significance in the charged climate of the early Reformation. Deviation in worship and covenant would be increasingly read as signs of flawed religion mired in superstition. In subsequent accounts of the Yucatan city-states, idolatry became increasingly linked to human sacrifice and to Jewish error.

A year later, in 1522, Peter Martyr's Latin *De orbe novo* was supplemented by new information on the land of Yucatan (as it was then

---

[47] Michael Camille surveys late medieval assumptions about Jewish, Muslim, and pagan idolatry in *The Gothic Idol: Ideology and Image-Making in Medieval Art* (Cambridge: Cambridge University Press, 1989) and for thirteenth-century strategies, John V. Tolan, *Saracens* (New York: Columbia University Press, 2002).

[48] Peter Martyr (1521), 12 and Herodotus, *The Histories*, trans. Robin Waterfield (Oxford: Oxford University Press, 1998), 2.38–41.

[49] "[I]dololatras, & recutitos esse reperiunt: pueros puellasque Cemibus imolant. Sunt Cemes nocturnorum lemurum simulachra quae colunt..." Peter Martyr (1521), 21.

called). The Castilian-language text, usually identified as Cortés's second letter to Charles V, was dated October 30, 1520 but printed in Seville in November 1522 along with news from April 1522 that Tenochtitlán had been conquered. The pamphlet confirmed that Mexicans' manners, good order, and organization were comparable to "other peoples of reason" such as the Spaniards.[50] Cortés also declared the ceremonies and service at Moctezuma's court to be unrivaled by those of any sultans or other non-Christian lords. Given the Ottoman and Egyptian sultans' reputations for ceremonial display and wealth, this comparison may have been designed to emphasize the wealth and power of the Aztec court.[51]

Cortés admired the cities and peoples that he encountered. In his comparisons of specific Mexican and Iberian or European cities, the Mexican cities often outstripped the others in size and wealth. For example, in comparing Tlaxcala with the recently conquered city of Granada, Cortés explained that Tlaxcala had stronger walls, more beautiful buildings, and a larger population. Whereas Tlaxcala was comparable to the last Muslim kingdom in Iberia, other city-states that had allied with Cortés were depicted as republics, with governments similar to those of Venice, Genoa, or Pisa.[52] Tenochtitlán had an arcaded plaza like Salamanca's but was twice the size, while the tower on one of its temples was grander than the Giralda in Seville. The city itself was situated on a salty lake with straight roads and canals. Impressed by the very orderly mercantile buying and selling, Cortés emphasized that commerce encompassed a dazzling array of goods and services and that its participants numbered more than 60,000 daily. He provided a copious list of items for sale in the city. The streets were organized by crafts – here the street of apothecary shops, there the barbers. Saving best for last, Cortés explained the system of official regulation at the great market plaza. In the great square, ten or twelve judges kept trading people honest, adjudicated disputes, and

---

[50] This, despite their distance from those "other civilized peoples." "No quiero dezir mas: sino que en su servicio y trato de la gente della ay la manera casi de bevir que en España: y con tanto concierto y orden como alla. Y que considerando esta gente ser barvara y tan apartada del conocimiento de Dios y de la comunicacion de otras naciones de razon: es cosa admirable ver la que tienen en todas las cosas." Cortés, *Carta de la relacion enbiada a su S. majestad del emperador nuestro señor por el capitan general de la nueva spaña: llamado fernando cortez* (Seville: Cromberger, 1522), bviii.

[51] "porque ninguno delos soldanes ni otro ningun señor infiel delos que hasta agora se tiene noticia no creo que tantas ni tales cerimonias en su servicio tengan." Cortés, *Carta de la relacion* (1522), c.

[52] Cortés, *Carta de la relacion* (1522), av^v-avi, bii.

punished wrongdoers.[53] Overall, the city of Tenochtitlán reminded Cortés of Seville or Cordoba, both cities that had been taken from Muslim rulers centuries earlier.

In his discussion of religious practice and faith, Cortés focused on religious structures and institutions. The temples were impressively grand, the clerics were sons of lords and honored citizens serving during an abstinent youth. The idolatry of the Aztecs was mentioned and quickly addressed as an error of the "sect." After locating the most important idols, Cortés had them removed from the main temple and cast down the stairs below. The chapels were then cleaned of sacrificial blood and images of the Virgin Mary were installed in place of the discarded idols. He commanded that there be no further sacrifices of living creatures to the idols and called for the Aztecs to embrace the "one god, universal lord and immortal creator."[54]

While Cortés occasionally compared Mexican and Muslim costume, the pamphlet's April 1522 codicil also compared the fate of the Aztecs with that of the Jews, noting that more Mexicans died in the fall of Tenochtitlán than had Jews when Vespasian destroyed Jerusalem. Even in the face of this grim statement, Cortés's tendency toward triumphal comparison persisted: the pamphlet added that despite the greater number of fatalities, the population of inhabitants left living outnumbered that of Roman-conquered Jerusalem.[55]

Peter Martyr's and Cortés's cultural descriptions of a civilized state, with abundant foodstuffs, clothing, craft production, and agricultural or mineral wealth, could appeal not just to the humanist cosmographers, but also to the merchant burghers who formed a large portion of the audience for news. The 1522 pamphlet *Newe zeittung. von demlande. das die Sponier funden haben ym 1521. iare genant Iucantan* [New reports from the land that the Spaniard have found in 1521, named Yucatan][56] distilled

---

53 For the importance of trading in law, Cortés, *Carta de la relacion* (1522), bii-bvii; Francisco de Vitoria, *Relectio de Indis*, ed. L. Pereña and J.M. Perez Prendes (CSIC: Madrid, 1967), 77–80 and Anthony Pagden, "Dispossessing the barbarian," in *The Languages of Political Theory in Early-Modern Europe*, ed. A. Pagden (Cambridge: Cambridge University Press, 1987), 86.

54 "vn solo dios vniversal señor de todos..." also "...Ay enesta gran ciudad muchas mesquitas o casas de sus ydolos de muy hermosos edificios por las collaciones y barios della: y en las principales della ay personas religiosas de su seta que residen continuamente en ellas: para los quales de mas de las casas donde tienen los ydolos ay buenos aposentos." Cortés, *Carta de la relacion* (1522), bvi^v–vii^v.

55 "En la qual murieron mas indios que en Jerusalem judios enla destrucion que hizo Vespasiano." Cortés, *Carta de la relacion* (1522), div^v.

56 *Newe zeittung. von demlande. das die Sponier funden haben ym 1521. iare genant Iucantan....* [Erfurt: Michael Maler, 1522]. Although the secondary literature on images

the most exciting aspects of the news for the German-language reader. Like other early newssheets, it was printed along with other empire-wide news bulletins. The report from the Yucatan was bundled with a bulletin (dated March 1522) on the division of the Habsburg lands from Emperor Charles V's court in Brussels, and another from Hungary about the Turks besieging Belgrade. It began with familiar categories of cultural description, arguing that the Castilians had encountered a civilized city-state possessing good government and trade structures, stone houses and lofty churches, a city-council hall, marketplaces with monitored weights and measures, and books. The pamphlet described Tenochtitlán in concrete detail, emphasizing its qualities of urban order and government. Tenochtitlán, here dubbed "Great Venice" in recognition of its splendor, was the most magnificent city encountered in the New World. It was constructed on islands in a mile-wide lake, with gated towers guarding each of its five bridges. Much like the European city-state of Venice, it had three smaller dependent cities on the surrounding land. The aptness of Aztec Great Venice's comparison to one of the greatest cities in Europe continued. Canals of salty lake water ran through the city, but sweet drinking water was delivered via an impressively engineered aqueduct. Other aspects of architecture were impressive: each house had its own cistern, and the city's temples were constructed like castles. The possibilities for trade and commerce in Great Venice were also emphasized by the German translators. The numbers of people visiting its marketplace were provided (the given figure was lower than Cortés's by 10,000). Like other cities of Mexico, it had city council halls and a central market plaza where everything was bought and sold. Weights and measures were used to calculate sales. The pamphlet provided further promising details. Trade, it declared, seemed organized with the aid of merchant account books. Explicitly in contrast to other Mexican cities, which used cacao beans as currency, the pamphlet reported that Great Venice used metal currency in the form of copper coins. Although in reality this claim lacked foundation, the German reader would not have any reason to question this additional sign of civilization. This pamphlet also represented these civilized attributes through a new image of the capital city Tenochtitlán.

In the image, signs of cultural sophistication abound. The city is depicted as a European city (Figure 2). Five bridges are visible with their

of the New World attributes the pamphlet to an Augsburg printer, early-print scholars presently believe that it was produced by Michael Maler of Erfurt. I would like to thank Dr. Hans Jörg Künast for resolving this discrepancy in the secondary literature.

FIGURE 2. Tenochtitlán as Great Venice, *Newe zeittung. von demlande....*
Yucatan (Erfurt: Maler, 1522), Aiv. Courtesy of the John Carter Brown Library
at Brown University.

protective turrets, the surrounding lake is filled with ships, three outly-
ing towns edge the lake. Instead of the wooden and thatch huts shown
as dwellings in earlier images of the Indies, these towns are solidly-built
equivalents to European cities. Architecture as a marker of civilization
and culture was increasingly emphasized in European thinking,[57] and
this image reinforces the text's assertion of urban accomplishment. The
people of Tenochtitlán demonstrate that they are civilized rather than
wild through their clothing, as well. They are not naked or wearing gir-
dles of feathers. Rather, they are dressed as prosperous Europeans. In the
foreground, the peaceful action of the pamphlet is illustrated. To the right,
Cortés and Moctezuma meet. Moctezuma wears the robes of a wealthy,

---

[57] Stephanie Moser, *Ancestral Images: the Iconography of Human Origins* (Ithaca: Cornell
University Press, 1998), 52–9 discusses Vitruvius's *De architectura* and the structures
built during different ages of humankind.

high-ranking person: electors and urban patricians of the Holy Roman Empire often wore similar fur-collared clothing in portraits. To the center of the foreground, Moctezuma and Cortés walk together through the city. In 1522, not only the text, but also the accompanying woodcut has made the representational leap into a world somewhat familiar to the reader. Religion and faith aside, reports indicated that the Castilians had finally encountered a great polity with the attendant instruments and structures of good government and trade. In short, it was a land with burghers who had welcomed Latin Christians.

The mercantile and ordered city was significant news. A Latin translation of Cortés's letter, printed in March 1524 by Nuremberg printer Friedrich Peypus, made it accessible to readers in the commercial urban centers of Europe. The translation included a subtitle and summary that listed the civilizational attainments found in the Aztec Empire, and was issued with a second edition of Peter Martyr's fourth *Decade* and included a two-folio map of Tenochtitlán (Figure 3), in some examples colored blue, green, and brown.[58] The 1524 map of Tenochtitlán vividly impressed its plan and organization on the viewer. It displayed advanced city planning principles then in ascendancy. These aesthetic principles for Renaissance cities were grounded in the ideals laid out in Leon Battista Alberti's mid-fifteenth-century treatise on architecture. Above all, the city should be well planned: "The principal ornament to any city lies in the siting, layout, composition, and arrangement of its roads, squares, and individual works...."[59] Fifteenth-century humanist aesthetics had emphasized the importance of a city divided into sectors for different industries and functions.[60] Latin-educated, humanist-influenced readers would not be ignorant of these principles, and could not help but recognize them in the plan of Tenochtitlán, particularly in the main ceremonial plaza.

The public functions of Tenochtitlán's major plaza were familiar: the most important religious buildings and the palace of the secular authority were located there. Further, the main square was designed with arcades

---

[58] *Praeclara Ferdinandi. Cortesii de Nova Maris Oceani Hyspania Narratio Sacratissimo. ac Invictissimo Carolo Romanorum Imperatori* (Nuremberg: Peypus, 1524), ai, aiii–aiv, and foldout map. ÖNB 200,904-D is a colored vellum example, likely a presentation copy.

[59] Leon Battista Alberti, *On the Art of Building in Ten Books*, trans. Joseph Rykwert and Robert Tavernor (Cambridge: MIT Press, 1988), 191–2, 261–6.

[60] Christine Smith, *Architecture in the Culture of Early Humanism: Ethics, Aesthetic, and Eloquence 1400–1470* (Oxford: Oxford University Press, 1992), 179.

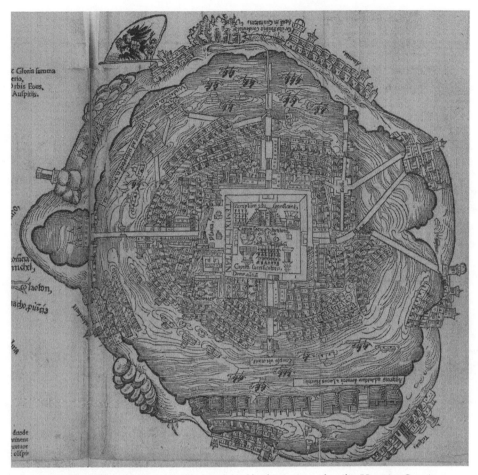

FIGURE 3. Map of Tenochtitlán and Gulf of Mexico (detail), Hernán Cortés, *Praeclara Ferdinandi. Cortesii de Nova Maris Oceani....* (Nuremberg: Peypus, 1524), foldout. Courtesy of the John Carter Brown Library at Brown University.

fronting the open center space. The significance of the ceremonial plaza was marked by the captions ("Temple where they sacrifice," "Stone idols," and "Heads of the sacrificed"). Although some religious functions of the square might alienate the literate Latin reader, other judicial functions were familiar in their physical brutality. The decapitated figure in the square echoed the display of public punishment apparatuses in European plazas. The ruler Moctezuma's palace quarters also fronted this main square, while a smaller but still grand plaza can be seen on the side. Demonstrating the close correspondence between this representation of

Tenochtitlán and city-planning ideals, Albrecht Dürer's plan for an ideal royal city, drawn three years after the Tenochtitlán map's publication, contained a center plaza and radiating street design that echoed the basic plan of Tenochtitlán.[61] In all these printed descriptions of Mexican cities as in contemporary European principles of city planning, good architecture was followed by good government: Tenochtitlán's magistrates and judges enforced civil law and commercial honest dealing.

The 1522 German pamphlet, the *Newe zeittung. von demlande...genant Iucantan* had also elaborated on Peter Martyr's and Cortés's cultural descriptions, not only by promoting an emphasis on urban order, government, and trade, but also by reworking the descriptions of religious practice. It provided an alternate detailed written and visual description of Mexican sacrificial ceremonies:

[T]hey make the children dance around the idols, in the temple, and there their priests take the children, one after another, and lay them on the abovementioned stone, on the round table, and cut off their hands and feet, which they save for eating. Then they pierce the body and take out the blood, coating the idol with it, and then they throw the bodies down the stairs.[62]

The pamphlet text embellished Cortés's printed account. Cortés had simply stated that the Aztecs made living sacrifices, in particular killing boys and girls by taking out their hearts and burning them before the idols. In the original Cortés's text, it was Cortés who had cleansed the temples by throwing the false idols down the temple steps, rather than Aztecs tossing

---

[61] Wolfgang Lotz, "Sixteenth-Century Italian Squares," *Studies in Italian Renaissance Architecture* (Cambridge: MIT Press, 1977), 74–116. See Setha Low, "Indigenous Architecture and the Spanish American Plaza in Mesoamerica and the Caribbean," *American Anthropologist* 97 (1995): 748–62 and Barbara Mundy's discussion of the Peypus map in "Mapping the Aztec Capital," *Imago Mundi* 50 (1998): 1–22 for derivations of the Aztec central plaza; for the European development of the central plaza, Marvin Trachtenberg's provocative *Dominion of the Eye: Urbanism, Art, and Power in Early Modern Florence* (Cambridge: Cambridge University Press, 1997), especially 12–25. David Friedman's *Florentine New Towns: Urban Design in the Late Middle Ages* (Cambridge, MA: MIT Press, 1988) provides examples of newly designed towns and their design principles, 77–119; also Paul Zucker, *Town and Square* (New York: Columbia University Press, 1959), 120–3.

[62] "[M]achen sie die kynder tantzen umb die apgotter/ so ym tempel seint/ darnach nehmen yre priester die kynder/ eyns nach dem andern/ unnd legen sie auff den obgemelten stain/ so auff dem runden tische leyth/ unnd schneyden ynen hende unnd fuess ab/ welche hende und fuess behalten sie/ fur sie zuessen/ darnach schneyden sie den korper auff/ und nehmen das gebluet herauß/ und bestreichen den apgot darmit/ dar nach werffen sie den Corper die stiegen hinab...." *Newe zeittung. von demlande*, [1522], Aii^v. Graphic details of sacrifice are also present in *Ein schöne Newe Zeytung so Kayserlich Mayestet auß India....* (Augsburg: Ramminger, 1522), Aiv^v–B.

children down the stairs. The pamphlet included sensationalized extra details from Peter Martyr, for example naming the demon a "zeme."[63] Yet Peter Martyr's description was also insufficient: added to this German text were details of forcing the children to dance and discarding their bodies.

The culturally favorable representation of the city, visually initiated with the "Great Venice" woodcut, contrasts with the negative implications of both the textual description of sacrifice and the pamphlet's other woodcut (Figure 4). Serving as a title page, this image is a composite representation of Aztec religious practices. Several richly associative images complement and dramatically expand on the contents of the text. The action in the middle ground is straightforward: the arrival of armed Spaniards under the Castilian flag follows the narrative events of the pamphlet. The top right-hand corner scene of the woodcut depicts the people described in the first paragraph of the 1522 pamphlet. When Cortés first landed, the pamphlet explains, he encountered two old women who belonged to a religious order. These women are consulted when the lords of the territories want to fight a war, to discover who will be victorious. The pamphlet clarifies that these women's powers are unholy: "[T]he women are great sorceresses, and make a pact with the devil, so that he comes and speaks personally to them."[64] The visual image reinforced this identification of their divinatory power, borrowing directly from late-fifteenth-century representations of witches consorting with the devil.[65]

In the background of the tower, we see the root of the Aztecs' religious deviance: they are idol worshippers. Idolatry is represented through the person genuflecting before a banner-bearing figure perched on a pillar, an image that would be very familiar to both the educated and the illiterate viewer. The iconic element of an idol on a pillar appeared in illustrations of the Old and New Testaments, particularly in representations of Nebuchadnezzar worshipping the golden calf or the Holy Family fleeing

---

[63] c.f. Cortés, *Carta de la relacion* (1522), bvii^v and Peter Martyr (1521), 21.

[64] "zway alte weyber/ welche weyber sie außgebenn fur geystlich/ unnd wen die hern von den Landen/ so do selbst in der selben gegenhayt liegen/ kriegen wollen/ einer mit dem andern/ so schicken sie zu den obgenanten zwayen weybern/ das sie ynen sagen soln ab sie victoriam haben soln/ ader nicht/ die selbigen weyber seint grosse zcauberin/ und beschwern den teuffel/ so kumbt ehr zu ynen / und redt personlich mit ynen/ in teuffellischer gestalt.... " *Newe zeittung. von demlande* [1522], A^v.

[65] Ulrich Molitor, *Tractat von den bosen weibern* (1490), see images in Albert Schramm, *Der Bilderschmuck der frühdrucke*, 5 (Leipzig: K.W. Hiersemann, 1923), table 77: no. 419.

FIGURE 4. Title page, *Newe zeittung. von demlande. . . . Yucatan* (Erfurt: Maler, 1522). Courtesy of the John Carter Brown Library at Brown University.

into Egypt to escape the Massacre of the Innocents (Figure 5). Similar figures on pillars, either clothed or not, can be found in depictions of Solomon and other Old Testament rulers, as well as in woodcuts of

FIGURE 5. Flight into Egypt, *Speculum humanae salvationis* (Augsburg: Zainer, 1473), gi^v. This item is reproduced by permission of The Huntington Library, San Marino, California.

various apostles, saints, and apocryphal heroes who vanquish idols either in the Holy Land, Europe, or the Indies.[66]

Bearing the woodcut's minor scenes in mind (the arrival of the Castilians, pacts with the devil, and idolatry), we can turn to the events depicted in the center and foreground of the woodcut. The central action of this interior tower scene is the sacrifice of children to an idol. As noted previously, the pamphlet text had embellished the source texts in this description, adding the round table and the staircase strewn with victims' bodies that appear in the image here. These additions gather a biblical weight in the accompanying visual image of sacrifice. The artist borrowed from

---

[66] Avril Henry, *Biblia Pauperum* (Ithaca: Cornell University Press, 1987), 56–9, 133–4; other examples in Camille, *Gothic Idol*, 1–9; Schramm 5, table 24: no. 134 and table 37: no. 241. The Indies were the location of the popular medieval romances Alexander (derived from Eusebius) and chivalric Duke Ernst, as well as the story of Barlaam and Josaphat. In *Barlaam and Josaphat*, Josaphat experiences a religious conversion from idolatry in India through the teachings of Barlaam, and eventually converts his father (the king of India) and the kingdom of India. The story of Barlaam and Josaphat provided a template for the conversion of an Indian kingdom, one that the first Franciscan missionaries to the Aztec people followed, however unintentionally, when they focused their conversion and educational efforts on noble sons. The story of Barlaam and Josaphat is thought to have originated as the Indian story of Siddhartha Buddha and translated from Greek to Latin by John of Damascus.

FIGURE 6. Massacre of the Innocents, Johannes Lichtenberger, *Prognosticatio* (Ulm, 1488), Bv^v. This item is reproduced by permission of The Huntington Library, San Marino, California.

contemporary depictions of the Massacre of the Innocents (Figure 6) to illustrate the dead children scattered down a staircase.[67] The visual reference here extends beyond this biblical story of Herod's perfidious actions. The child sacrifice at the round table itself is strikingly similar to images of the circumcision of Christ: figures gather around a child on a table, as a man reaches out to the child with a knife in his hand (Figure 7). Such scenes often could be found in late-fifteenth- and early-sixteenth-century woodcut series depicting Christ's life. Like many apocryphal legends of Christ's childhood, Christ's circumcision had gained popularity during

---

[67] Albrecht Altdorfer's 1511 print *Massacre of the Innocents* includes dead children cast down a threshold, Max Geisberg, *The German Single-Leaf Woodcut, 1500–1550*, rev. and ed. Walter L. Strauss, (New York: Hacker Art Books, 1974), I: 17; related are depictions of the Judgment of Solomon, in which a soldier with drawn blade threatens a child's life.

FIGURE 7. Circumcision of Christ, *Spiegel menschlicher behaltnis* (Speyer: Drach, 1495), xx. This item is reproduced by permission of The Huntington Library, San Marino, California.

the fifteenth century: Christ's circumcision was often understood as the first of his passions and thus the focus of much religious devotion. Circumcision itself was understood as the Abrahamic covenant, a practice left in the past by Christians whose covenant with God was symbolized by the more inclusive baptism.[68] Christ's generation should have been

---

[68] Bonaventura, *Das Leben unsers erledigers Jesu Christi* (Nuremberg: Johannes Stücks, 1514), viii–viiii[v]. Hans Schiltberger's fifteenth-century *Reisebuch* (Tübingen: Litterarischer Verein in Stuttgart, 1895) noted that Muslims followed Jews in circumcision, 86.

the last to suffer through the Old Testament ritual, and the continuation of circumcision was the sign of an imperfect understanding of religion.

Through the borrowings in this image, then, the woodcut artist implicitly invoked what Latin Christians believed were Jewish or Muslim practices drawn from the Old Testament: idolatry and circumcision. The woodcut echoed Peter Martyr's notice of idolatry and circumcision in the fourth *Decade*, even as it elaborated on Peter Martyr's description of Herodotean sacrifice with a focus on child sacrifice. In contemporary popular Christian perceptions, child sacrifice also was connected to Jewish religious practices developed when the Jews themselves began to err. In the Old Testament, Jews were described as occasionally falling into idolatry and worshipping Moloch by sacrificing their children.[69] Jews were not simply historic idolators, however, culturally equivalent to ancient Romans and Greeks, they were present-day perverters of religious ceremony: many Christians believed that they practiced ritual blood sacrifice.

Christian accusations of ritual blood sacrifice or ritual murder were leveled against Jewish communities in the late fifteenth and early sixteenth centuries. In the Holy Roman Empire, the best-known accusation and investigation occurred at Trent in 1475, sparked by the death of the young child Simon and popularized in Hartmann Schedel's *Liber chronicum*. Although higher levels of imperial justice discouraged these accusations and stopped them whenever possible, local communities suspected their Jewish residents when Christian children were found inexplicably dead. In several well-known cases, Jewish men were interrogated until they confessed to seizing children and bleeding them to mix their blood with dough for use in ritual perversions of the Eucharist (Figure 8).[70] The reader of the *Newe zeittung. von demlande*, while absorbing information on the peoples of Mexico, would recognize the allusions to biblical events and recent cases of alleged blood sacrifice, connecting these idolatrous human sacrifices with suspected Jewish rites. Religious descriptions of the Yucatan, then, resembled Jewish religious practices that were perceived to be either negative (sacrifice) or at the least irrelevant (circumcision). The text of the 1522 pamphlet itself was silent on

---

[69] Leviticus 18–20, 2 Kings 23, and Jeremiah 32.

[70] Hartmann Schedel, *Liber Chronicum* (Nuremberg: Koberger, 1493), cccliv^v; also Schramm 5, table 192: no. 501. See R. Po-Chia Hsia's *The Myth of Ritual Murder: Jews and Magic in Reformation Germany* (New Haven: Yale University Press, 1988) and *Trent 1475* (New Haven: Yale University Press, 1992), 4, 31.

FIGURE 8. Simon of Trent, Hartmann Schedel, *Liber chronicum* (Nuremberg: Koberger, 1493), ccliiii^v. This item is reproduced by permission of The Huntington Library, San Marino, California.

comparisons with Jewish people; the relationship was created primarily through the title page image. It evoked associations with the devilish inversions and practices like ritual blood sacrifice through its visual portrayals. Cortés's second letter (published in Castilian in 1522 and in Latin in 1524) made those connections explicit when he described Mexicans mixing victims' blood with maize in a parallel to the myth that Jewish ritual blood sacrifice sought children's blood to mix with dough for the making of unleavened bread.

The 1522 pamphlet's representations of urban idolaters rather than primitive ones arose as calls for religious reform began appearing. Other connections and tensions were implicit, remaining literally on the margins. An edition of Andreas Karlstadt's 1522 attack on idolatry in the unreformed Latin church, *Von abthieung der Bylder*, bore a title page with a recycled 1519 border, depicting people from the Indies (Figure 9).

FIGURE 9. Title page, Andreas Bodenstein von Karlstadt, *Von abthieung der Bylder,...* (Basel, 1522). Copyright: ÖNB Vienna, Picture Archive 79.W.87.

These figures are identified as Indian by their feather standards and head-dresses, and by the fact that they ride unfamiliar beasts (an elephant and a camel). An alternate edition of this pamphlet instead bore, as its title page, the Old Testament scene of Abraham and Isaac on their way to sacrifice Isaac according to God's command (Figure 10).[71] This image of the Abrahamic willingness to sacrifice, turned into the covenant of circumcision, had been selected to illustrate and introduce Karlstadt's warning against idolatry. In Latin Christendom, or at least in the minds of the printers who produced these Karlstadt texts, Reformation-era critiques of the veneration of images as idolatry could be illustrated, and thus associated, with both Jewish and Indian peoples and religious practices. An early example of these layered critiques can be seen in the 1515 printing of Lodovico de Varthema's (1510) travel to India (Figure 11). The 1515 version was careful to portray his reported encounter with an idol of the devil wearing a papal tiara.[72] The Augsburg printer, Hans Miller, sought to portray a culture mired in idolatry, but where was his critique directed? If papal critiques were beginning to be audible in 1515 when Miller printed his Varthema edition, Reformation debates were raging as the representations of Mexican culture were being produced. Michael Maler, who printed the 1522 German pamphlet, and Friedrich Peypus, printer of the 1524 Latin Cortés and Peter Martyr, were both open supporters of religious reform by the dates they printed those works.[73]

In March 1520, Friedrich Peypus had also printed an early, and perhaps the first, German-language pamphlet disseminating news of the Castilian excursions along the coast of Central America. Describing "a newly discovered island, the situation of the same, with native customs

---

[71] Joseph Koerner notes the substitution in *The Reformation of the Image* (Chicago: University of Chicago Press, 2004), 102. Schirlentz used the Old Testament image of Abraham and Isaac on the title page of other Karlstadt polemics against the unreformed church from December 1521 to February 1522, E. Freys and H. Barge, "Verzeichnis der gedruckten Schriften des Andreas Bodenstein von Karlstadt," *Zentralblatt für Bibliothekswesen* 21 (1904): 221–2, 227–9, while the feathered Indian border appeared in several pamphlets on the question of religious reform, published in Basel by Cratander in 1519–1520 (Girolamo Aleander, *Acta academiae Lovaniensis* [Basel: Cratander, 1520] and Ulrich Velenus, *In hoc libello gravissimis... probatur Apostolum Petrum non venisse... Romam* [Basel: Cratander, 1520]). For a visual parallel to the camel and elephant riders, see Geisberg, II: 512–3.

[72] "He has a crown... like a papal tiara...," Lodovico de Varthema, *Die ritterlich un[d] lobwirdig Rayss* (Augsburg: Hans Miller, 1515), facsimile ed. George Winius (New York: John Carter Brown Library, 1992), i iii^v.

[73] For Maler, *ADB* 20: 138; and Ulman Weiss, *Die frommen Bürger von Erfurt* (Weimar: Böhlau, 1988). For Peypus's early production of Protestant pamphlets, see Arnd Müller, "Zensurpolitik der Reichstadt Nürnberg," *MVGN* 49 (1959), 78 and Hans-Otto Keunecke, "Friedrich Peypus (1485–1535)," *MVGN* 72 (1985), esp. 52–61. The reformed educators Andreas Dieter and Sixt Birck translated the full text of Cortés's printed letters into German in 1550, after the letters had been banned in Castile.

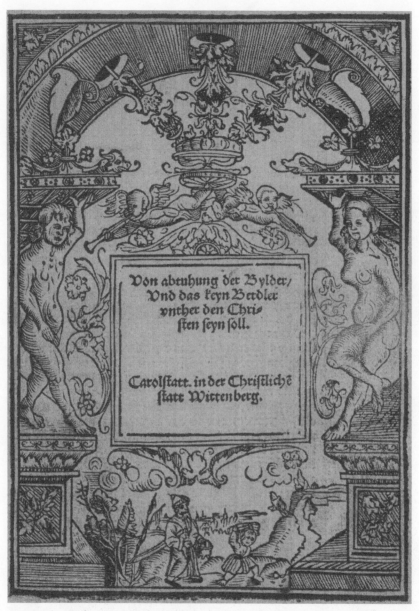

FIGURE 10. Title page, Andreas Bodenstein von Karlstadt, *Von abtuhung der Bylder...*(Nickell Schyrlentz, 1522). Copyright: ÖNB Vienna, Picture Archive *35.R.102.

FIGURE 11. Devil with a papal tiara, Lodovico de Varthema, *Die ritterlich un[d]
lobwirdig Rayss....* (Augsburg: Hans Miller, 1515), i iii. Courtesy of the John
Carter Brown Library at Brown University.

and habits contained within,"[74] the pamphlet focused on cultural attainments. The people of the Yucatan were a civilized people with fine cotton
or silk robes, social hierarchy and order, and skill in the mechanical arts
such as architecture. Religious practices revealed great devotion even as

---

[74] The pamphlet date reveals the speed at which news traveled. Peter Martyr first reported
on this news in December 1519, *Opus Epistolarium*, in *Opera*, cxlviii and the German-
language pamphlet is printed by March 1520. *Ein außzug ettlicher sendbrieff dem
durchleüchtigisten großmechtigisten Fürsten und Herren Carl römischen und Hyspanischen König... von wegen einer newgefunden Inseln/ derselben gelegenheit und inwonder
sitten und gewonheit inhatend vor kurtvershinen tagen zugesandt....* [Peypus: Nuremberg, 1520]. In the pamphlet's frontispiece, armed Spaniards in a ship approached a
coast where semi-naked peoples, in feather skirts and cotton drapes, wait to receive
them, led by a man with similarities to the pre-Christian kings and heroes in Maximilian
I's geneaology project. See Simon Laschitzer, "Die Heiligen aus der, Sipp-, Mag- und
Schwägerschaft; des Kaisers Maximilian I," *JKSW* 4 (1886), nos. 15–56. Along with this
sign of political and social order, the inhabitants are marked as idolaters through the
presence of their idol in the background.

they involved problematic sacrificial rites. On the final page of the pamphlet, it explains that the inhabitants

worship before their idols in whose service they dedicate themselves, and at times offer themselves... they pierce their tongues and ears, or let their blood run from cuts made with lancets and shears, which blood they offer to the idols, sprinkling the walls and strewing it on the altar. But they have another more cruel custom in their worship, that the Spaniards have seen. When they request something great from their idols, they take a young child or sometimes adults into the presence of the idol, cut out the heart and, while it is beating, offer it as a sacrifice... [75]

After this description of human sacrifice, the pamphlet emphasized the spiritual devotion of these people and concluded with confidence that, given their zeal, with a bit of correct instruction on "godly belief," these people would live in greater religiosity.[76] In 1520, Friedrich Peypus ends on an optimistic note of future reform rather than a dismissal of irredeemable error. By 1522, his fellow reformer Maler can only conclude his pamphlet by asserting that much of this idolatry was not simply devotion directed erroneously toward false images; it was directed toward the devil himself, held by these people as lord.[77]

The vernacular German interpretations of Peter Martyr's and Cortés's letters began producing cultural estrangement and religious alienation rather than an appreciation for the diversity of religious practice. The German versions, more than the originals, promoted the conflation of circumcision, human sacrifice, and the myth of Jewish ritual murder. The parallels of Yucatan religious practices with Abrahamic covenants were not celebrated but castigated as degenerate or unregenerate superstitious error. Protestant reformers[78] held circumcision in Europe and Asia to be

---

[75] "eeren sie vor ihre abgötter in welcher dienst sie weyrach/ und zutzeiten sich selbst opffern/... schneyden inen die zungen und oren ab/ lassen das blut auß inen selbst mit lentzlein/ und schermessern/ welches plut sie obffern den abgöttern/ salben die wend/ unnd werffens auff den altar. aber sie haben noch einen grausamern gebrauch in eererpietung dz etwa die Hispanier gesehen haben/ dan so sie etwas grosses von den abgöttern begeren/ ziehen sie herfür in angesicht des abgots die jungen kind/ und beweillen die gewachssen/ tödten das hertz/ und was lebendig ist bringen das zu einem opffer...," *Ein außzug ettlicher sendbrieff* [1520], Biii^v. For Cortés's version, see ÖNB Codex Vindo. S.N. 1600, 15^v-17^v and for Peter Martyr (1521), 12, 35–6.

[76] "So nun die Inselleut so geflissen sein/ des diensts der götter in denen sie etwas göttlichs sein vermeinen ist versehenlich/ wann sie in dem göttlichen glauben wurden underwysen/ das sie in grosser geistligkeit lebten." *Ein außzug ettlicher sendbrieff* [1520], Biii^v.

[77] *Newe zeittung.* von demlande [1522], Aiv^v.

[78] David Steinmetz, "Calvin and Abraham," *Church History* 57 (1988): 443–55.

an atavistic and unnecessary practice that reflected a neglect of the New Testament – an error, now, of Jews, Muslims, and some Eastern Christians. Those other errors that Jews and Indians might commit, sacrificing children and ingesting blood or body parts, were too problematic for use in explicit comparative critiques of the unreformed Church. In 1522, the year that news from Mexico reached Europe as well as the year of Karlstadt's attacks on idolatry, one pamphlet plays with this possibility. The visual image on the title page of Pamphlius Gengenbach's 1522 *Das ist ein iemerliche clag Totenfresser*,[79] a scene of the unreformed Eucharist, resonated with reports of Yucatan child sacrifice and subsequent cannibalism, freshly located in the Yucatan. The woodcut satirically critiques the clergy's greedy impieties, depicting clerics ranging from pope and bishop to nun gathered around a table to feast on a split-open corpse (Figure 12).

By 1522, the newly encountered Aztecs were not perceived as simple primitives. Such possibilities had been rejected as insufficient evaluations of an obviously complex society. Two new representational tropes circulated, instead, for the next several years. Yucatan and Mexican cultures included cities that functioned as important centers of craft production and commercial trade. Although this attainment was admirable, Aztec religious practices were increasingly perceived to be idolatrous and troubling. Implicitly, in the texts produced in the Holy Roman Empire, Mexicans were similar to the Jews. If, as was still believed in the 1520s, apostolic Christianity had reached everywhere in the world, the Mexicans fell into a cultural category with the Jews as peoples who had failed to embrace true faith and practice.

The second edition of the Peter Martyr's fourth *Decade* reveals the extent to which religious relativism could still be possible in 1524, the year Peypus produced it in conjunction with the Latin Cortés. The *Decade*'s Latin was edited and expanded slightly throughout, often improving its clarity. New margin notes were added to direct the reader. In a discussion of priests, the margin note compares the Yucatec priests to German clerics who had embraced the Reformation: the Yucatec priests were celibate and chaste, while the "heretics" argued that they ought to be allowed to marry.[80] Those margin commentary notes would be altered

---

[79] (Augsburg: Steiner, 1522).
[80] "Nota contra hereticos nostri temporis: qui volunt sacerdotes posse ducere uxores" and "Sacerdotes Celibes vivunt y incorrupti." Peter Martyr (1524), aaiv, bbiv.

FIGURE 12. Title page, Pamphilus Gengenbach, *Diß ist ein iemerliche clag vber die Todtenfresser* (Augsburg: Steiner, 1522). Copyright: ÖNB Vienna, Picture Archive 40.N.77.

in the next, posthumous 1530 edition. Sentences promoting perceptions of civilization and cultural comparability disappeared: printed margin notes no longer highlighted grand architecture or examples of governing or trade principles. The glosses contrasting Yucatan practices of clerical celibacy with reformers' demands for clerical marriage were removed. Instead, new glosses argued for the Yucatan peoples' uncivilized state, replacing the term "Indian" or "inhabitant" with "barbarian," particularly when discussing sacrifice.[81] These changes were, of course, subtle shifts in editorial comment, while the main content of Peter Martyr's and Cortés's ethnographic descriptions remained largely the same. Through 1530, these texts introduced the curious reader to customs and practices, both religious and non-religious, followed by the people of Mexico.

The Ottoman Empire

The last decades of the fifteenth through the first decades of the sixteenth century witnessed a proliferation of ethnographic texts about the Turks and commentaries about the Ottoman Empire's growing military presence along the Serbian, Hungarian, and Austrian borders. Both types of texts contained strands of Platonic or Cusan valuation. Open admiration of some aspects of Turkish culture, whether governance, social customs, or religion, can be seen in two fifteenth-century accounts that serve as starting points for this section. Konstantin Mihailović was an Orthodox Christian from Serbia, who was placed into servitude when the Ottomans formally conquered Novo Brdo in 1455. Mihailović's relationship with Ottoman authority was complicated. Elsewhere in his narrative, Mihailović claimed to have previously served in the labor levee sent by the Serbian despot for the conquest of Constantinople in 1453. Once a captive, the young Mihailović was sent to the Ottoman court, rising to a quartermaster position among the janissaries. Mihailović's servitude was relatively brief: after eight years, the fortress where he was stationed was recaptured by the King of Hungary. Mihailović returned to live in a Christian world, although now a Latin Christian one rather than the Orthodox Serbian one in which he was raised.[82]

Mihailović began his account with a description of Muslim practices. Muslims, in Mihailović's words, seemed to parallel or perhaps rival Christians in the piety of their practices: they were charitable without regard

---

[81] For example, "Qualia sunt simulacra quae Incolae illarum regionum colunt" and "Modum sacrificandi mortales in illis partibus," Peter Martyr (1524), aiii^v compared with"De crudeli immolatione quam Barbari Hiis suis exhibent" Peter Martyr, *De Orbe Novo* (1530), lviii. For a different interpretation of this paratextual material, Christine R. Johnson, *The German Discovery of the World* (Charlottesville: University of Virginia Press, 2008), 26–40.

[82] Konstantin Mihailović, *Memoirs of a Jannissary*, trans. Benjamin Stolz (University of Michigan, 1975). The text survived in Polish and Czech manuscripts, and was published in Czech in 1541 (a partial version) and again in the 1560s.

to the recipient's faith, they were abstemious and fasted, observed important holidays and the sabbath, and resolved disputes through councils
and a superior justice system. Mihailović understood Muhammad to be
a good and virtuous man, attributing the unidentified negatives of Islam
to his brother-in-law, Ali.[83] Mihailović's condemnation seemed primarily reserved for the Christian rulers whose conflicts and betrayals led to
Muslim victories. These rulers, whether Orthodox or Latin Christians,
showed few signs of virtue. They were murderers and even parricides,
vow-breakers, and opportunists. In contrast, with the exception of a military deception in deploying troops for the conquest of Constantinople,
the Ottoman sultan demonstrated judicious, although stern, judgment.
Mihailović's ethnography ended with a call for unity, arguing that Christians might stave off Ottoman expansion if they ceased their shortsighted
and self-interested actions. Despite this call to oppose Turkish expansion,
he did not devote particular attention to criticizing the Turk's customs or
religious practices and beliefs.

The distinction between practices or rites and doctrine also allowed
another former captive, Georgius de Hungaria (also known as Georgius
of Siebenburgen or of Hungary), to praise customs and practices of the
Turks, even as he critiqued the doctrines of Islam. In the *Tractatus de
moribus, condictionibus et nequicia turcorum*... (written before 1480),
Georgius depicted a world in which reasonable men explored differing
religious beliefs and cultures. For Georgius, this exploration was involuntary – captured in 1436, he remained a prisoner for more than twenty
years (until 1458). His imprisonment gave Georgius a special authority to
discuss Turkish culture and Islam. In his account, he emphasized his deep
immersion into Turkish culture, explaining that he had, for all practical
purposes, forgotten his mother tongue and had spoken only the bar-
baric Turkish during those twenty-plus years. Georgius offered an array
of information about religious faith and, beyond that thorny subject,
Turkish culture and people. The customs and practices of Turkish life
were carefully detailed. Social structure, the history of the land and its
ruler, gender relations (primarily the treatment of women), everyday practices, building construction, and costume were only some of the subjects
he covered.[84]

---

[83] Mihailović, chapters 1–8.
[84] Georgius de Hungaria, *Tractatus de moribus, condictionibus et nequicia turcorum*...,
ed. R. Klockow (Vienna: Böhlau, 1993), esp. 150–6 and, for "materna lingua," 408. For
a recent discussion in English, Albrecht Classen, "The World of the Turks Described by

Georgius included details of his life in captivity to explain the sources of his knowledge about the Turks. At first, his servitude as a prisoner increased his Christian faith. After his eighth escape attempt, however, Georgius entered a phase of religious crisis. He became increasingly attracted to Islam, which he saw as a sect of Christianity, and moved toward conversion. During six or seven months of studying Islam closely, Georgius gained a deeper understanding of Turkish culture and belief. But then, on the brink of conversion, God brought Georgius to his senses and he returned wholeheartedly to Christianity. For the next fifteen years, he had no doubts about his faith or that Islam's temptations were the devil's illusions, even as he continued to learn about Turkish customs and religious institutions. His understanding of Islam was so great that local people would seek out his pronouncements, and it led to his freedom: his master valued him more highly than his own son and eventually released him. While Georgius repudiated Islam, his understanding of virtue included his virtuous Muslim master.[85]

A Dominican monk by the time he wrote the *Tractatus*, Georgius presented Islam as a false branch of faith in God. It had structures, customs, and practices analogous to those of Latin Christendom and Judaism, chief among them churches, priests, fasting, baptism, holy days, and religious orders. Its falsity, however, was not immediately apparent: a thoughtful, inquiring man might easily be led astray in his exploration of Islam. Some aspects of it were particularly admirable: the Turks did not indulge in the sybaritic transgressions of Latin Christendom.

Captivity exposed Christians entirely too much to Islam, and Georgius warned that it was difficult to resist the pull of Islam in such circumstances. Some Christian prisoners were impervious to the allure of Islam and either died in captivity (Georgius called them martyrs) or were freed and returned home unscathed. The second group was in much greater peril than the first, who only faced bodily trials. Georgius fell into this group of people who studied Islam and the doings of the Turks, gaining close knowledge and, quite understandably in Georgius's mind, admiration of Islam's finer points. These people could only be spared the seduction of Islam through God's intervention. The third group could not escape this allure and embraced Islam as renegades from the Christian faith. Georgius pointed out that schism, invented laws, and a few perverse practices were instigated by the devil, but that this evident proof of the

---

an Eye-Witness." *Journal of Early Modern History* 7 (2003): 257–79. Georgius was also credited as the author of a mathematics text, *Arithmeticae summa tripartita* [1499].
[85] Georgius, *Tractatus*, 87, 298–304, 408–10.

demonic did not stop renegades from converting in ever greater numbers. Drawn in part to the reward of authority and power in the Ottoman Empire, even educated clerics could miss or willfully ignore the signs of the devil with those temptations. As examples, Georgius included stories of a Minorite and a Dominican who converted to Islam.[86]

In contrast to the easily beguiled Christian captives, Turks were increasingly impervious to Latin Christianity. According to Georgius this had not always been so: people in the past had converted sincerely and successfully, but now Islam had moved even further beyond orthodoxy. In Georgius's religious categories, offenders against God came in three different categories. Those who live outside of God's grace, as infidels and mortal sinners, could be converted through voluntary penitence. The second category, including heretics or those who "worshipped a false god," required an intercessor. The third category consisted of people who had given their souls to the devil. Although still convertible, these people were almost impossible to reach. Georgius believed that during the fifteenth century, the Turks had moved from the second to the third category of heterodoxy. Georgius bolstered his claim about the inconvertibility of Turks in the present day (1473) with a story of a group of "converted" Turks whose confessions and communions he had ministered. Their conversions proved false and the Turks soon fled. In sum, Georgius felt ["it had become impossible for Turks to accept Christian faith."][87]

With its mix of ethnographic social and material detail and discussion of religious inquiry, the *Tractatus* was very successful. The first known printed edition was produced in Rome in 1481, during the year that Ottomans held the southern Italian port city of Otranto.[88] By the following year, Jörg von Nürnberg had cribbed a portion for his own

---

[86] Georgius, *Tractatus*, 242–6, 346–50.

[87] "Deum ficte colentes" and "quod impossibile sit aliquem Turcum fidem Christi recipere." The increased power of the devil over the members of his "sect" had this effect. Georgius, *Tractatus*, 312–8, 370–3.

[88] The Ottomans captured Otranto on August 11, 1480 and were expelled on September 10, 1481 after the warring forces of Latin Christendom temporarily united under papal leadership. See the general survey by Robert Schwoebel, *Shadow of the Crescent: The Renaissance Image of the Turk (1453–1517)* (New York: St. Martin's Press, 1969), esp. 132–4 for Otranto. More recently, Margaret Meserve's *Empires of Islam in Renaissance Historical Thought* (Cambridge, MA: Harvard University Press, 2008) explores the complex cultural descriptions produced by fifteenth-century humanists, in particular those located on the Italian peninsula. Another important text was Theodore Spandones's *De la origine de principi turchi*, available in German as *Der Türcken heymligkeyt* (Bamberg: Erlinger, 1523) and in Castilian by 1520. See Jeremy Lawrance, "Europe and the Turks in Spanish Literature of the Renaissance and early modern period," in *Culture and Society in Habsburg Spain*, ed. Nigel Griffin et al. (London: Tamesis, 2001), 17.

German-language captive narrative *Ayn Tractat von den Türck.*[89] The
veracity of the *Tractatus*'s author seems to have been an important aspect
of the text's popularity. A 1487 annotation in Hartmann Schedel's copy
noted that the information within it had been verified by the exiled
Ottoman prince Calixtus during the prince's stay in Nürnberg.[90] The
Tractatus was linked, either through publishing history or textual borrowings, to most major sources and cultural evaluations of the Turks in
the Habsburg realms during the first half of the sixteenth century.[91] It was
reprinted in Latin, the majority of it first translated into German in early
1530, and an abbreviated German version bundled with Desiderius Erasmus's views on the Turks that same year. That January, Martin Luther's
forward introduced a Latin edition, both of which were quickly reprinted
by Friedrich Peypus in Latin as well as in a freely translated German
version by Sebastian Franck.[92] Erasmus's and Luther's evaluations of
Islam and Ottoman culture utilized cultural comparison to promote their
projects of religious reform.

Desiderius Erasmus's stance on the Turk evolved from his broader
irenic concerns. The question of evaluating Turkish culture first figured prominently in his Adage IV.i.7, *Dulce bellum inexpertis* [1514–
1515].[93] In it, Erasmus counseled against war and its social and economic

---

[89] (Memmingen: Albrecht Kunne, 1482).

[90] Klockow's introduction to Georgius's *Tractatus*, plate 3.

[91] For textual transmission and representations of the Turks in the sixteenth century, see
Clarence Dana Rouillard's authoritative *The Turk in French History, Thought, and Lit-
erature (1520–1660)* (Paris: Boivin, 1940) and the thoughtful response by Michael J.
Heath, *Crusading Commonplaces: La Noue, Lucinge and Rhetoric against the Turks*
(Geneva: Droz, 1986); for Venice, see Lucette Valensi's *The Birth of the Despot: Venice
and the Sublime Porte*, trans. Arthur Denner (Ithaca: Cornell University Press, 1993).
Representations of the Turk in Iberia have been examined in Albert Mas's two-volume
monograph, *Les turcs dans la litterature espanole du Siecle d'Or* (Paris: Centre de
recherches hispaniques, 1967) and Lawrance, "Europe and the Turks," 17–33. German works are discussed in Margret Spohn, *Alles getürkt: 500 Jahre (Vor) Urteile der
Deutschen über die Türken* (Oldenburg: bis Universität Oldenburg, 1993); Şenol Özyurt,
*Die Türkenlieder und Das Türkenbild in der Deutschen Volksüberlieferung vom 16. bis
zum 20. Jahrhundert*, Motive, vol. 4 (Munich: Wilhelm Fink, 1972); and Cornelia Kleinlogel, *Exotik-Erotik: Zur Geschichte des Türkenbildes in der deutschen Literatur der
frühen Neuzeit (1453–1800)* (Frankfurt am Main: Peter Lang, 1989).

[92] *Chronica unnd Beschreibung der Türckey mit eyner vorrhed d. Martini Lutheri*, introduction, xvii, WA 30:198–204.

[93] For the ambiguities in Erasmus's approach to the Turks, see Timothy Hampton's
"'Turkish Dogs': Rabelais, Erasmus, and the Rhetoric of Alterity," *Representations*
41(1993):58–82. Robert P. Adams, *The Better Part of Valor* (Seattle: University
of Washington Press, 1962), argues for the late composition date of *Dulce bellum
inexpertis*, 90.

devastation, calling instead for a peaceful united front of all Christians who should convert by example, not by the sword. War was, by its nature, "the kingdom of the devil," where Christians were led to commit terrible acts. If war was unavoidable, then motives for war determined a culture's virtuousness. Most motives for war, such as territorial aggrandizement or wealth, were demonic and inexcusable:[94] only defensive war was justifiable and truly Christian. The Christian kingdoms' failure to abstain from unjustified war provoked Erasmus's criticism: "We spit on the Turks and therefore see ourselves as good Christians, but perhaps we are more detestable to God than the Turks are."[95]

In the adage, Erasmus praised Turks, pagans, and Jews, as well as various peoples of Europe, Asia, and Africa, for their virtuous living. Actions beyond faith were important. In Erasmus's opinion, virtuous behavior was admirable because conduct worthy of Christ was the end and aim of faith in the Gospels, regardless of whether a person was Christian or not. Openly practicing Turks or Jews were less evil than Christian hypocrites, "Semi-christians" could be closer to "true Christianity" than most Christians. Such possibilities encompassed most peoples of Asia and Africa, who Erasmus believed were "Christians and half-Christians."[96] Throughout his text, Erasmus chose non-inflammatory language of cultural relativity. Eschewing the broad conflation of barbarian/wild-man/uncivilized with pagan/non-Christian,[97] Erasmus opted for more precise cultural terminology that distinguished between advanced society and enlightened (true) religious faith. He applied the term "barbarian" (along with the descriptor "barbarous") to those who waged war, regardless of faith[98]

---

[94] "vbinam diaboli regnum est," Desiderius Erasmus, *Dulce bellum inexpertis* [1515 ed.], ed. R. Hoven, *Opera Omnia* 2:7 (Amsterdam: Elsevier, 1999), p. 22 ll. 298–9. According to Erasmus, the brunt of war fell on farmers and peasants, as well as women and children: crops, herds, farms, villages, and churches were destroyed through pillage or excessive taxation.

[95] "In Turcas expuimus et ita nobis videmur pulchre Christiani, fortassis abominabiliores apud Deum quam ipsi Turcae," *Opera Omnia* 2:7 p. 39 ll. 807–8.

[96] *Dulce bellum inexpertis*, "Evangelicae fidei finis sunt mores Christo digni." p. 40 ll. 834–5; "Minus mali est palam esse Turcam aut Iudaeum quam hypocritam Christianum, " p. 40 ll. 855–6; "vel Christiani vel semichristiani" p. 39 l. 829; p. 40 ll. 841–2.

[97] See Anthony Pagden, *The Fall of Natural Man* (Cambridge: Cambridge University Press, 1982) for the conflation and negative judgments that could be attached to these terms. The rustic connotations of "barbarian" and "pagan" began in the classical era. 15, 18–21, 203.

[98] *Dulce bellum inexpertis*, p. 12 ll. 27–8: quam . . . barbarice geritur, non tantum ab ethnicis, verum etiam a Christianis;" p. 15 ll. 97–8 "barbaras cohortes;" p. 42 l. 913.

and preferred the term "ethnicus" to indicate people who were not followers of the Christian faith but instead were heathens. Good rulers,
whether pagan or Christian, fostered the "arts of civilization" throughout
their territories: where their subject people were primitive ("agrestes" l.
593), they instituted letters and laws; they built towns, bridges, and ports;
and they increased economic prosperity. The emphasis on practices and
custom[99] promoted the gathering of information about a culture's civilized attainments, because evaluations of virtue could depend, in part, on
levels of cultural attainment.

The battle of Mohács in 1526 and subsequent fragmentation of Hungary signaled the decisive (although not the first) Ottoman incursion into
Latin Christendom, but for most subjects of the Holy Roman Empire,
Ottoman forays into Austria in the 1520s and the siege of Vienna in
October 1529 proved perhaps more significant. The siege invigorated
print discussion about the nature of the Turkish people and threats they
posed. Erasmus returned to the question of how to regard Turkish people
and their religion in his *Vltissima consvltatio de bello tvrcis inferendo,
et obiter enarratvs Psalmvs XXVIII*, which first appeared in print just
months after the siege of Vienna, in 1530. His position on warfare did
not change substantively, although his rhetoric was more negative toward
the Turk[100] and equivalently more critical of Christians who failed his
standard of virtue. He took the opportunity to reject Martin Luther's
1518 proposition that the Turks, as a scourge of God, should not be
physically resisted, instead supporting the Paris theologians' countering
condemnation that secular authorities had the right to defend against the
threat.[101] Despite the increased threat of the Turks to the Holy Roman
Empire, Erasmus reiterated his argument that Christians should admit
and judge their own vices, the very ones they attributed to the Turks,
before using vice or doctrinal error as a justification to attack Turkish
people. Erasmus urged that religious concerns should not prompt military
conflicts, nor should religious authorities direct violence. Secular leaders
could, however, protect and defend the state from criminal aggressors,

---

[99] *Dulce bellum inexpertis*, pp. 31–2 ll. 590–6.

[100] Michael J. Heath, "Erasmus and War against the Turks," ed. Jean-Claude Margolin,
Acta Conventus Neo-Latini Turonensis (1980), 991–9. Timothy Hampton, "'Turkish
'Dogs'," 61–4.

[101] Desiderius Erasmus, *Vltissima consvltatio de bello tvrcis inferendo, et obiter enarratvs
Psalmvs XXVIII*, ed. A. G. Weiler, R. Stupperich, and C.S.M. Rademaker, *Opera
Omnia* 5:3 (Amsterdam: Elsevier, 1986), pp. 54–6 ll.428–444. By 1530, Luther had
also dropped this proposition.

be they Ottomans or any other peoples. Pursuing the distinction between secular and ecclesiastical authority, Erasmus emphasized that all subjects must obey their civil law and secular ruler but should not have their faith forcibly changed. To underscore this point, Erasmus cited the examples of Jews under Christian rule, Christians under the pagan Roman emperors, and Christians under Muslim Ottomans to remind the reader that peoples could be subject to rulers following a different religion.[102] Erasmus reemphasized that peaceful religious and cultural conversion were the Christian responses to the non-Christian.

Thirdly, if some cannot so quickly be persuaded, let them continue for a time to live under their own law, until gradually they come to agree with us. Long ago, Christian emperors used this method to abolish paganism by degrees. At first they allowed the pagans to live on equal terms with the Christians, in such a way that neither interfered with the other. Then they deprived the idolaters' temples of their privileges. Finally, after forbidding the sacrifice of victims in public, they abolished completely the worship of idols. In this way our religion grew gradually stronger, paganism was stamped out, and the signs of Christ's triumph filled the world.[103]

The rhetoric of the Reformation helped shape the categories in which religious practices would be evaluated: although Erasmus argued against compulsory conversion, he did employ idolatry as the standard of the false religious practice by which cultures and sects could be judged. Yet precisely which religious practices were idolatrous remained veiled in Erasmus's references. Islam was still understood as a sect formed from a mixture of Judaism, Christianity, paganism, and the Arian heresy.[104] Warning against any tyrant who called people to idolatry, Erasmus denied

---

[102] *De bello tvrcis*, pp. 58–9 ll. 512–9 here "ethnici principes."

[103] "Postremo si qui nondum possunt allici, sinantur aliquamdiu suis uiuere legibus, donec paulatim nobiscum coalescant. Sic olim imperatores christiani paulatim aboleuerunt paganismum. Initio patiebantur illos aequo cum nostratibus iure viuere, sic vt neutri alteris facesserent negocium. Deinde templis idololatrarum ademerunt sua priuilegia. Postremo victimas ab illis immolari palam veruerunt, mox omnem simulacrorum cultum submouerunt. Ita sensim inualescente nostra religione, paganismus extinctus est, et Christi trophaea mundum vniuersum occuparunt." *De bello tvrcis*, p. 82 ll. 142–50; English translation, *Collected Works of Erasmus* (Toronto: University of Toronto Press, 2005), 64:265.

[104] "Sectam habent ex iudaismo, christianismo, paganismo, et Arianorum haeresi commixtam." *De bello tvrcis*, p. 76 ll 984–5. The editor traces this interpretation of Islam back to Nicholas of Cusa's *Cribratio Alkorani*, (notes p. 77); in the *Cribratio Alkorani* Nestorianism rather than Arianism contributes to the development of Islam. Nicholas of Cusa, *Cribratio Alkorani*, ed. Ludwig Hagemann, *Heidelberg*. 8 (Hamburg: Meiner, 1986).

that Turks or other "barbarian nations" worshipped idols, arguing that they were halfway to being Christians.[105] In doing so, Erasmus hinted that the Turks were not necessarily the tyrants that he had in mind.

During the 1520s, the strategy of directing cultural comparison toward a veiled target was also evident in Martin Luther's discussions of Islam. He evaluated unreformed Christian and Muslim cultures and practices, noting positive and negative aspects in each. Just as Georgius had distinguished between Muslim practice and belief, Luther drew parallels between unreformed Christians and Muslims not only when they acted as bloodthirsty warring fiends, but also in everyday religious behavior. Luther's public statements on Islam and the "Turkish peril" were influenced by both the trajectory of the Reformation and the politics of the Holy Roman Empire. With Ottoman offensives safely directed away from Latin Christendom and toward Egypt during the first two decades of the sixteenth century, the Ottoman threat was largely abstract in the Holy Roman Empire. During this period, Luther rejected papal calls for armed aggression against the Ottomans, arguing in 1518 that the Turkish peril was a judgment visited upon sinful Latin Christendom by God. As such, non-resistance or at least defensive actions led by secular rulers were the only appropriate responses. Although Luther's views fell within the broad range of irenicist rhetoric promoted by influential writers like Erasmus, his position on the Turks was condemned by the papacy in 1520. Following the lead of Luther, many reformers argued that efforts should be devoted to correcting sinful behavior and erroneous religious belief rather than military offensives. In this context, what mattered to early reformers were self-examination and the recuperation of correct belief and doctrine, not the practices of a wayward sect like Islam. From Luther's condemnation in 1520 to 1526, he and his followers focused their attention on the papacy and its unreformed Christianity. Once Luther had been excommunicated, he quickly escalated his metaphors of papal godlessness. The papacy and its followers had devastated Christendom, "body and soul." The tyrannical pope held true Christians in a Babylonian captivity.[106]

---

[105] *De bello tvrcis*, p. 56 l. 437; "ad idolatriam vocanti tyranno," p. 59 l. 522; "de Turcis reliquisque barbaris nationibus, quarum, ut audio, nulla colit idola, sed demidiatum habent christianismum.," p. 62 ll. 634–6. The issue of the image appears also in Erasmus's discussion of the paintings of "Turkish cruelty" used to enflame popular sentiments against the Turks. p. 52 ll. 401–2.

[106] See Martin Luther's formal reply to the imperial diet on April 18, 1521, "Acta et Res Gestae D. Martini Lutheri . . . ", WA 7: 833.

By spring 1529, Luther agreed that changing circumstances required a new, more interventionist approach to thinking about the Ottomans.[107] In April, he published the *Vom Kriege wider die Türcken*, and after the conclusion of the siege of Vienna at the end of October, he composed the *Eine Heerpredigt wider den Türcken*. Both of Luther's pamphlets allowed for military defenses of Christianity but focused on the definition of a true Christian and how the true Christian should resist the temptations of false belief, be it Papist or Muslim. In *Vom Kriege wider die Türcken*, Luther was ready to give the Antichrist pope a "companion" and in a letter written the same year to Wenceslaus Linck, he paired the pope with the Turkish ruler as the "final Gog and Magog."[108] Comparisons between the papacy and the Turkish emperor and their tyrannies became favorites. This pairing allowed Luther to encourage readers' hostility toward the Ottomans (the tyrant outside Latin Christendom) to extend to the papacy (the tyrant within) again and again in his writing. Conflating the two also allowed Luther to advise true Christians in whichever captivity they found themselves. Luther implored every Christian to learn the basic articles of faith immediately, to avoid forgetting or abandoning Christ if they suddenly found themselves under the power of the antichrists. If the Turk, the devil, and the Pope were interchangeable, then his advice applied to situations in the Holy Roman Empire as well as in the borderlands of Hungary.

Although comparisons between the papacy and the Turkish emperor (as a synecdoche for Turkish culture) were among Luther's favorites, he employed cultural equivalencies to discuss or critique other incorrectly reformed groups. The Turks were more holy than the iconoclasts in the Holy Roman Empire because they tolerated absolutely no images, yet iconoclasts gladly accepted images on coins and jewelry.[109] In the

---

[107] Kenneth M. Setton's "Lutheranism and the Turkish Peril," *Balkan Studies* 3 (1962): 133–68 fleshes out the work done in George Forell "Luther and the War against the Turks," *Church History* XIV (1945): 256–71 and Harvey Buchanan, "Luther and the Turks 1519–1529," *ARG* 47 (1956): 145–60. For a broader context, see Stephen Fischer-Galati "Ottoman Imperialism and the Religious Peace of Nürnberg," *ARG* 47 (1956): 160–79.

[108] Martin Luther, 7. III. 1529, *WA Briefwechsel* 5: 28. As Luther shared the news of the siege's end, he remained focused on Christian reform but slightly moderated his position on the Turks: collaboration with the ungodly (those resistant to true reform within Latin Christendom) was permissible in common defense. *WA Briefwechsel* 5: 167–8. For the dates of the composition of the *Vom Kriege...* see *WA* 30 (2):96. For the *Heerpredigt*, see *WA* 30 (2): 149–50.

[109] *Vom Kriege...*, *WA* 30 (2): 128.

Heerpredigt, Luther distinguished between true Christians and those who followed the Bible yet lacked the articles of true Christian faith. Luther lumped together a broad array of people who all belonged in this second category of error: "the Jews don't have [true faith], nor the Turks and the Saracens, the Papists or false Christians, or any other unbelievers. Only the true Christians do."[110] Luther's negative rhetoric placed unreformed Christians on a religious level with other people whose faiths incorporated the biblical Old Testament. Throughout his discussions of the Turkish threat, Luther focused his energies on the question and problem of Christian reform.

In 1530, Luther also composed the forward to a new Latin edition of Georgius of Hungary's text, *Libellus de ritu et moribus Turcorum*. Here he acknowledged the appeal of Muslim religious ceremonies and practices, and of their clerics.[111] However, just as the true Christian must eschew the empty ceremonies of Roman Christianity through an understanding of correct practice and belief, he must also recognize the fallacies of Turkish Islam. Thus, study of Islam in the form of Georgius's ethnography was necessary. In the *Libellus* forward, Luther argued that the book's value lay in the neutral stance of the author toward Islam. Because Georgius was not filled with open hostility toward all aspects of Turkish culture and Islam, but rather love toward some, Georgius was able to describe this culture and religion more truthfully.[112] The value of non-negative cultural description might be overshadowed elsewhere by Luther's conflation of anti-Turkish and anti-papal rhetoric,[113] but in principle Luther favored a well-informed judgment of religious practice and faith.

In 1530, the same year that Luther's Latin introduction came out, Sebastian Franck produced a German-language version of the *Libellus* (the *Tractatus* with Luther's introduction) as a *Chronica unnd Beschreibung der Türckey mit eyner vorrhed D. Martini Lutheri*.[114] The *Chronica unnd Beschreibung der Türckey* appeared during Franck's early career as a writer, after he had left his post as a rural priest for a reformed,

---

[110] "Denn die Jüden haben des nicht, Die Türcken und Sarracener auch nicht, dazu kein Papist noch falscher Christ noch kein ander ungleubiger, sondern allein die rechten Christen." *Heerpredigt, WA* 30 (2): 186.

[111] "ex hoc libro videmus Turcorum seu Mahomethi religionem caeremoniis, pene dixerim et moribus, esse multo speciosiorem quam nostrorum, etiam religiosorum et omnium clericorum," "Martinus Lutherus Lectori pio" forward to the *Libellus de ritu et moribus Turcorum 1530, WA* 30 (2):206.

[112] "ex amore veritatis omnia narrantis," "Lectori pio," *WA* 30(2): 205.

[113] This rhetoric is furthered by Luther's close allies, for example Justus Jonas.

[114] (Nuremberg: Peypus, 1530), reprint (Augsburg: Heinrich Stainer, October 26, 1530).

married life in Nuremberg.[115] The last in his series of increasingly loose and interpretative "translations" to be printed by Friedrich Peypus, the *Chronica unnd Beschreibung der Türckey* arose from and depended on Georgius's and Luther's visions of cultural relativity yet extended beyond their positions. The Dominican-educated Franck created a redaction of the *Tractatus* that retained Georgius's descriptions of social and material culture, along with some of Georgius's experiences. Franck also liberally added his own material on religion and faith.

Many of Franck's points followed Georgius's and Luther's perceptions of the Turks. Like his preceding author and editor, he noted that the Turks had the appearance of godliness, more so than the Christians with their pomp. They reminded us that the Roman ceremonies, luxury and sin-loving clerics, and the acceptance of images and idolatry must all be reformed. The conversion of Turkish people was rare, but conversion could not come through the application of force. Expanding on Luther's conflation of Turks and papists into a single group, Franck explicitly defined a broader category of unbelievers "Turks, heathens, papists, false Christians and all unbelievers"[116] as those who fail to embrace Christ sufficiently.

Franck broke away from Luther in offering a more equanimous evaluation of religions. Embellishing the first paragraph of Luther's prefix to the *Tractatus*, Franck ascribed to Luther the desire to read the Koran because it was the Turkish scripture, analogous to the New Testament.[117] While repeating Georgius's assertions that the followers of Islam have splintered into four sects, Franck continued a step farther through a comparative chapter on Christian sects, a chapter not found in Georgius. Christianity had eleven nations or sects that he described in terms of their leaders, their geographical homes, their practices, and their beliefs. After sections on the Latin, Greek, Indian, Jacobite, Nestorian, Maronite, Armenian, Georgian, Syrian, Mozarab, and Muscovite sects, Franck concluded the main part of Chapter 30 by listing subsects within Latin Christendom itself, incorporating religious and lay orders into a long list. In his religious relativism, Franck developed a list of Christian sects that numbered sixteen by the second edition of December 1530. By 1532, this list was further

---

[115] For the details of Franck's life, including his education at the University of Ingolstadt and a Dominican college in Heidelberg, see Patrick Hayden-Roy's *The Inner Word and the Outer World. A Biography of Sebastian Franck* (New York: Peter Lang, 1994), here chapter 1.

[116] "Türcken/ Heiden/ Papistenn/ falsche Christenn/ vnnd alle vngleubigen," Franck, *Chronica unnd Beschreibung*, M.

[117] Franck, *Chronica unnd Beschreibung*, Ai^v.

expanded into twenty itemized sects and published independently.[118] In translating the *Libellus*, Franck hoped that the cultural description would inform the reader about the civilized nature of the Ottomans. The text would lay out their "qualities, knowledge, rules, orders, policy, religious forms, belief, and laws."[119] It was the beginning of a larger project, a cosmography of the world composed by an increasingly radical reformer.[120]

By the 1520s, Erasmian and platonic models of cultural evaluation could not stand alone. Other strictly negative accounts of the Turks, their military forces, and their bellicosity appeared alongside these models of cultural evaluation. The fall of Hungary in 1526 and the siege of Vienna in 1529 marked particular moments of embellishment on these negative themes. As with the evaluation of Aztec culture, these concepts were introduced in part through images. The Turks as the scourge of a punitive God, a theme employed by both Erasmus and Luther, were evoked by many writers. Such images, both visual and textual, were those that Erasmus criticized as inflammatory "paintings" of Turkish cruelty. One example from 1526, *Hernach volgt des Blüthundts/ der sych nennedt ein Türckischen Keiser/ gethaten/ so er vnd die seinen/ nach eroberung der schlacht/ auff den xxviii. tag Augusti nechstuergangen geschehen/ an vnsern mitbrüdern der Ungrischen lantschafften gantz vnmenschlich triben hat/ vnd noch teglichs tüt*,[121] demonstrates the associative dimensions of such representations of slaughter. Earlier, widely popular visual images included in pamphlets by Jörg von Nürnberg, Breydenbach, and the Steiner Augsburg edition of Franck's Georgius translation depicted strangely appareled men and women standing in towns, or a recognizable king, complete with crown and scepter.[122] In contrast, this 1526

---

[118] "Beham Pickarder/ Hußiten/ Barfusser Begeyner/ küttenn/ örden/ Luterisch/ Zwinglisch/ Teüfferisch/ vnd so vil hundert örden vnd secten," Franck, *Chronica unnd Beschreibung*, Kii^v. The December 1530 version published by Heinrich Steiner in Augsburg (*Chronica/ Abconterfayung vnd entwerffung der Türckey*). The stand-alone (reprinted in 1534) version was *(Z)weintzig Glauben oder Secten* (Frankfurt: Christian Egenolff, 1532).

[119] "Art vnd aygenschafft/ weyß/ pollicey/ regiment/ gestalten religionen/ glauben vnd gesatzen," Franck, *Chronica unnd Beschreibung*, 106.

[120] For another, Catholic-inflected cosmography of the world and its cultures, see Laurentius Fries, *Uslegung der mercarthen oder Cartha Marina Darin man sehen magl/ wo einer in der wellt sey/ vnd wo ein yetlich Landt/ Wasser vnd Stadt gelegen ist. Das alles in dem büchlin züfinden* (Strasbourg: Grüninger, 1527).

[121] Erasmus's painting metaphor is in *De bello tvrcis*, pp. 52–4, ll. 401–12. *Hernach volgt des Blüthundts/ der sych nennedt ein Türckischen Keiser/ gethaten / so er vnd die seinen/ nach eroberung der schlacht/ auff den xxviii. tag Augusti nechstuergangen geschehen/ an vnsern mitbrüdern der Ungrischen lantschafften gantz unmenschlich triben hat/ und noch teglichs tüt* (1526).

[122] Jörg von Nürnberg, *Ayn Tractat von den Türck [1480]*, facsimile in *Chronica unnd Beschreibung der Türckey* ed. Carl Göllner (Vienna: Böhlau, 1983), 109.

FIGURE 13. Title page, *Hernach volgt des Blüthundts/ der sych nennedt ein Türckischen Keiser...* (1526). Copyright: ÖNB Vienna, Picture Archive 20.Dd.937.

pamphlet drew on Old Testament images of persecution: the Massacre of the Innocents is strongly evoked in the two woodcuts. On the title page, turbaned men slaughter families in a town's main square (Figure 13). On the concluding page, three knights impaling infant boys, a common representation of the Massacre of the Innocents,[123] filled the entire page (Figure 14). Such comparisons between Old Testament persecution of the Jews and Turkish aggression against the people of the Hungarian and Balkan kingdoms became increasingly prominent.

---

[123] See Figure 6.

FIGURE 14. Massacre of the Innocents, *Hernach volgt des Blüthundts/ der sych nennedt ein Türckischen Keiser*... (1526), Aiv. Copyright: ÖNB Vienna, Picture Archive 20.Dd.937.

Despite the growing strength of negative representations, cultural description and comparison of Indian and Ottoman cultures in the early years of Charles V's reign were rich and complex. With that in mind, we can now turn to cultural practices toward Mexican and Ottoman in the subsequent decades of the sixteenth century.

2

Iberia after Convivencia?

As the Venetian ambassador Andrea Navagero traveled through the Iberian kingdoms during the 1520s, he wrote a series of letters describing his experiences. In Seville, he reported that "I saw some young men from the Indies, who have accompanied a [returning] friar... they were sons of important people in their land.... They have black hair, broad faces, blunt noses, almost like the Circassians, except that their complexion is more ruddy. They appear to possess cleverness and liveliness...."[1] These young men, casually seen in Seville, would soon be followed by others. During the 1520s, 1530s, and 1540s, a steady stream of well-born Nahuas traveled back and forth between New and old Spain. The practice of bringing inhabitants from the west Indies back to Castile had begun with Christopher Columbus. But unlike the illegally enslaved or servant Indians resident in Iberia,[2] indigenous nobles from Mexico received support and status through the attentions of Charles V's royal

[1] On May 12, 1526, "Vi también algunos jóvenes de aquellas tierras, que venían con un fraile... eran hijos de gentes principales en su tierra.... Son de cabellos negros, cara larga, nariz roma, casi como los circasianos, pero de color más rojizo; mostraban tener buen ingenio y viveza." Andrea Navagero, *Viaje a España de Magnifico Señor Andres Navagero (1524–1526). Embajador de la Republica de Venecia ante el Emperador Carlos V*, trans. Jose Maria Alonso Gamo (Valencia: Castalia, 1951), 57.

[2] Michael Palencia-Roth, "The Cannibal Laws of 1503," in *Early Images of the Americas: Transfer and Invention*, ed. Jerry M. Williams and Robert E. Lewis (Tucson: University of Arizona Press, 1993), 31–7. For the crown's interest in bringing Indians to Iberia, see AGI, Indiferente General (IG) 421 L. 11 fols. 305–311. The enslavement of West Indian peoples was rarely legal, but there were a large number of legal African slaves in Portugal and southern Castile and Aragon. See recent assessments in T.F. Earle and K.J.P. Lowe, ed., *Black Africans in Renaissance Europe* (Cambridge: Cambridge University Press, 2005).

court. Habsburg treatment of Nahua nobility illuminates the crown's perception of its territories in New Spain and its investment in a symbolism of Habsburg authority. During the first decades of Charles's reign, the crown worked to rehabilitate and reinvigorate the universal monarchy or world empire. Although the political ideal of the universal monarchy flourished only for a limited time, the idea framed Habsburg expansionism within and outside of Europe during those decades. For Charles's court officials and for his interested subjects in the Germanys and Iberia, this ideal gave shape and weight to projects and ambitions of empire.

The concept of universal empire had played an important role in late medieval struggles between papal and imperial authorities. Dante Alighieri's *De monarchia* (1313) had reshaped the concept of a universal monarchy to bolster Ghibbelline claims of imperial authority. Dante proclaimed that the monarch would renew the world empire (formerly the Roman Empire) and lead all peoples to a new era of peace and justice founded on Christian virtues. The ruler of the universal empire would be the pre-eminent authority in the world, independent of the papacy.[3] Debates over the balance of imperial and papal authority continued into the fifteenth century, during a period in which the papacy was first weakened by conciliarism and then regained its independence from church councils and secular authorities. In the second half of the century, prophetic and chiliastic texts continued to propose candidates for the position of last world emperor, and the Portuguese crown's imperial aspirations intensified with Manuel I's succession and its expanded activities in Africa and India.[4] At the beginning of the sixteenth century, the language of universal monarchy became associated with the papacy and, increasingly, the Holy Roman Emperor. Historians have described these reappearances as rhetorical flourishes variously inspired by the Neoplatonic conceits of the papal court, the overreaching dreams of Maximilian I and his propagandists, or the canny justifications of an avaricious

---

[3] Frances Yates's "Charles V and the Idea of Empire," *Astraea* (London: Routledge, Kegan and Paul, 1975), 1–28 is a seminal article whose ideas were expanded upon in Anthony Pagden, "Instruments of Empire," *Spanish Imperialism and the Political Imagination* (New Haven: Yale University Press, 1990), 37–63.

[4] Marjorie Reeves, *The Influence of Prophecy in the Later Middle Ages* (Oxford: Clarendon Press, 1969); Luis Felipe Thomaz, "L'idée impériale manuéline," in *Découverte, le Portugal et l'Europe*, ed. Jean Aubin (Paris: Touzot, 1990), 35–103; and Ivana Elbl, "Prestige Considerations and the Changing Interest of the Portuguese Crown in Sub-Saharan Atlantic Africa, 1444–1580," *Portuguese Studies Review* 10/2 (2002): 15–36.

Hernán Cortés.[5] Habsburg promoters of a universal empire aspired to make the ideal tangible, an empire greater than the Holy Roman or Portuguese Empires. In Charles V's court, the redefined ideal would be instantiated in multiple forms.

In the 1510s, even before Charles's election as Holy Roman Emperor, humanists at his Burgundian court heralded him as the universal monarch. In a 1516 speech honoring Charles's assumption of the role of master of the Order of the Golden Fleece, his court physician Luigi Marliano emphasized Charles's future world empire. Charles's inherited possessions were extensive: he was heir to his Iberian and Burgundian grandparents' territories, ranging from the kingdom of Castile and the duchy of Burgundy to outposts in northern Africa and in Caribbean Hispaniola, and he was expected to inherit his Habsburg grandfather's territories in central Europe. Charles's advisors celebrated the expanding empire whenever possible, as part of their propaganda campaign to promote Charles's candidacy for the position of next Holy Roman Emperor.[6] With Charles's election in 1519, the vision of a world empire gained new force. In his

---

[5] John W. O'Malley, *Giles of Viterbo on Church and Reform* (Leiden: Brill, 1968); Ingrid Rowland, *The Culture of the High Renaissance* (Cambridge: Cambridge University Press, 1998); Claudia Lazzaro, "Animals as Cultural Signs," in *Reframing the Renaissance*, ed. Claire Farago (New Haven: Yale University Press, 1995), 197–228; Hermann Wiesflecker, *Kaiser Maximilian I*, vol. 5 (Munich: Oldenbourg, 1986); Viktor Frankl, "Die Begriffe des mexikanischen Kaisertums und der Weltmonarchie in den *Cartas de Relación* des Hernán Cortés," *Saeculum* 13 (1962): 1–34. Yates emphasized the inspirational importance of the ideal, *Astraea*, 1–2.

[6] Earl Rosenthal, "The Invention of the Columnar Device of Emperor Charles V at the Court of Burgundy in Flanders in 1516," *JWCI* 36 (1973): 198–230. Mercurino di Gattinara is held to be the policy's main author. See John Headley's influential "The Habsburg World Empire and the Revival of Ghibellinism," *Medieval and Renaissance Studies* 7 (1978): 93–127 and his development of these arguments in "Germany, the Empire and *Monarchia* in the Thought and Policy of Gattinara," in *Das römisch-deutsche Reich im politischen System Karls V*, ed. Heinrich Lutz (Munich: Oldenburg, 1982), 15–33 and "Rhetoric and Reality: Messianic, Humanist, and Civilian Themes in the Imperial Ethos of Gattinara," in *Prophetic Rome in the High Renaissance Period*, ed. Marjorie Reeves (Oxford: Clarendon Press, 1992), 242–52. See also Reeves, *Influence*, 359–74; Franz Bosbach, *Monarchia Universalis: Ein Politischer Leitbegriff der Frühen Neuzeit* (Göttingen: Vandenhoeck & Ruprecht, 1988); Anthony Pagden, *Spanish Imperialism and Lords of all the World: Ideologies of Empire in Spain, Britain, and France c. 1500 – c. 1800* (New Haven: Yale University Press, 1995); and Karl Brandi, *Kaiser Karl V* (Munich: F. Bruckmann, 1937–8), chapters 2 and 3. For Iberian contributions to the ideal, Ramón Menéndez Pidal, *Idea Imperial de Carlos V* (Buenos Aires: Espasa-Calpe, 1941); José Antonio Maravall, *Carlos V y el Pensamiento Politico del Renacimiento* (Madrid: Instituto de Estudios Políticos, 1960); and J.A. Fernández-Santamaria, *The State, War and Peace: Spanish Political Thought in the Renaissance 1516–1559* (Cambridge: Cambridge University Press, 1977).

autobiographical reflections on the election news, Charles's advisor and chancellor Mercurino di Gattinara emphasized the Holy Roman Empire's important legitimizing role as a key step toward an ever greater empire and, in time, universal monarchy.[7] During the subsequent dozen years of Charles's reign, his advisors energetically promoted the identification of Charles and his territories with universal empire. Yet how did they intend their audiences to understand these proclamations of the coming world empire? What might the limits of that empire, whether ideal or real, be?

During those initial years of rule, Charles's advisors certainly drew on the late medieval prophetic vision of world empire that Dante had outlined. Recent scholarship has argued that early-sixteenth-century writers conceptualized the universal monarchy's territorial or geographic expanse as concurrent with Latin Christendom, or at most with the extent of Latin and Orthodox Christianity:[8] the envisioned state might more aptly be called the European rather than the universal monarchy. The concept of a Europe-wide empire, a Europe united under Charles V, was promoted for its strategic value: such a Europe would find the strength to stand against the Muslim Ottoman Empire. Yet the universal monarchy was not simply an answer to the question of temporal versus ecclesiastical authority in Latin Christendom, nor was it an empire restricted to Europe in antagonism to the Muslim world. Instead, the writings of Habsburg officials and supporters revealed a broader view of universal empire. The early-sixteenth-century Habsburg vision of the universal monarch and his world empire incorporated another strand of thought, one reflecting the ongoing exploration, territorial expansion, and cultural evaluation occurring beyond Europe and the Mediterranean. Charles's supporters drew on late medieval concepts of cultural evaluation and religious relativism to incorporate non-Christian peoples into their universal monarchy: they envisioned a global empire that could be religiously inclusive.

---

[7] Mercurino Arborio di Gattinara, "Historia vite et gestorum per dominum magnum cancellarium," ed. C. Bornate, *Miscellanea di storia italiana* 48, 3rd ser. 17(1915), 272–3. On the prophetic language of Charles's election, John Headley, "Germany" and Marie Tanner, *The Last Descendants of Aeneas: The Hapsburgs and the Mythic Image of the Emperor* (New Haven: Yale University Press, 1993), 109–13. Subjects also employed this language: Conrad Peutinger's 1520 address to Charles as "Caesarem Augustum et universi mundi dominum" on behalf of Augsburg was published in a 1521 oration. Heinrich Lutz, *Conrad Peutinger* (Augsburg: Die Brigg, 1958), 162, 378.

[8] Franz Bosbach's recent summary "The European Debate on Universal Monarchy," in *Theories of Empire, 1450–1850*, ed. David Armitage (Aldershot: Ashgate, 1998), 81–98, emphasized this point, surveyed in his earlier *Monarchia Universalis*. Yates and Rosenthal did not note geographic limits.

Charles's officials, both at his court and further down the ladder of imperial bureaucracy, explicitly extended the scope of universal monarchy beyond Christian Europe. In keeping with the continuing expansion of Charles's territories, his chancellor Gattinara framed the jurisdiction of universal empire as limitless. This scope was possible because Gattinara's understanding of imperial authority (*auctoritas*) included a rejection of imperial power as uniform or absolute, leaving space for multiple subordinate political entities and princes within the empire. This emphasis on *auctoritas* and an overarching, supra-political suzerainty rather than direct *dominium* had been developed in the Holy Roman Empire[9] and was well suited to the political realities of that incorporative empire. For Gattinara, this definition could be applied to all territories within a Habsburg Empire of whatever size, and he invoked the boundless empire regularly in addresses to estates and other formal bodies.

Although Gattinara focused on legal or political jurisdictions, other officials emphasized the geographical scope of empire beyond any given continent in their discussions of the universal monarchy. Examples of their promotional arguments appeared in print, as they sought broader audiences than assemblies of councils and estates. The imperial secretary Alfonso de Valdés, Gattinara's close ally and collaborator, marshaled the ideal of universal monarchy to explain the 1527 sack of Rome. Valdés produced several apologetics for a wide audience,[10] and in his efforts to justify the sack, Valdés promoted the notion of Charles as the destined emperor of the world. He began by directly addressing the question of imperial versus papal authority in the allegorical *Diálogo de las cosas ocurridas en Roma*. In this dialogue, Valdés affirmed that Charles's governing authority was independent of the papacy and argued that the sack of Rome was a consequence of the papacy's moral corruption.[11] The expansiveness of Valdés's concept became clearer in the *Diálogo de Mercurio y Carón*, where the characters of Mercury and Charon interviewed souls of the recently deceased. In that dialogue, Valdés proposed that people from foreign lands, "Moors and Turks as well as Christians," would flock to place themselves under a just universal monarch

---

[9] Headley, "Germany," especially 18–22 and, for the idea's geneaology, 29–30. Bosbach provides a partial catalogue of texts, *Monarchia Universalis*, 46–50.

[10] Yates, 12 and, for context, Marjorie Reeves, "A Note on Prophecy and the Sack of Rome (1527)," *Prophetic Rome in the High Renaissance Period*, ed. Marjorie Reeves (Oxford: Clarendon Press, 1992), 276–7.

[11] Alfonso de Valdés, *Diálogo de las cosas ocurridas en Roma* ([1528]; reprint Madrid, (1928), 77–105.

once they had heard of his good governance.[12] For Valdés, then, the empire's scope would not be bounded by the limits of Latin Christendom. Other Habsburg supporters saw the world empire not only as a future possibility, but also as a present jurisdiction. Jakob Köbel of Oppenheim, a mathematician and jurist, took this further step in his visionary text, *Glaubliche Offenbarung / wie vil fürtreffenlicher Reych vnd Kayserthumb auff erdtrich gewesen.* . . . Köbel had been contributing to the print debate on the balance between papal and imperial authority since the 1510s,[13] and in the *Glaubliche Offenbarung* he was unequivocal about the emperor's authority: there was no mediator between him and God, and thus he was not the pope's client. After describing the procedures of imperial elections and coronations, Köbel asserted that "heathens, Jews, and other foreign nations and people" were all subject to the Holy Roman Emperor as the emperor of the world.[14]

Charles's court and Habsburg supporters sought to reach audiences beyond assemblies of nobles or pamphlet readers: the idea of world empire was disseminated throughout Charles's realms not only in spoken and written rhetoric, but also in visual forms. Charles's world-imperial iconography was evident wherever Charles's coat of arms appeared.[15] Charles's personal arms – a coat of arms flanked by the pillars of Hercules (the straits of Gibraltar) and his expansionist motto "Plus Ultra" – often would be bordered by the many shields of his territories, overwhelming viewers with their numerical force. The imperial city of Nuremberg, by custom the site of a new emperor's first imperial diet, sought to make the imperial iconography accessible to all observers, whether literate or not.

---

[12] "Allende desto, muchas provincias, assí de moros y turcos como de cristianos, me embiaran a rogar que los tomasse por subditos, ofreciendo se de servirme y seguirme con toda fidel[i]dad" in Alfonso de Valdés, *Diálogo de Mercurio y Carón* (1528; reprint Madrid: Cátedra, 1999), 220. Valdés added that non-Christians would be inspired to convert.

[13] Köbel's *Dialogus libertatis ecclesiastice defensorius cum Imperatorum sanctionibus* (Oppenheim, 1516) responded to the concluded Lateran Council.

[14] Köbel explained the emperor is "on mitel von Got/ vnd keinen anhang von vnserm heiligen vatter dem Babst habe/. . . . " After the Roman King's election, he is " . . . ein Herre der welt genannt. Dann das Römisch reich ist das reich der welt / vnd beschleüßt in im / Heyden / Juden / vnd andere außlendische Nation vnd völcker" in *Glaubliche Offenbarung / wie vil fürtreffenlicher Reych vnd Kayserthumb auff erdtrich gewesen / wa das Römisch Reich herkomm /. . . . findestu inn disem büchlein zü eeren dem großmechtigsten Carolo dem fünfften Röm. Kay. angezaygt*, [Augsburg, Heinrich Steiner, 1532] Bv^v; also extant in a Mainz edition.

[15] Earl Rosenthal, "*Plus ultra, Non plus ultra*, and the Columnar Device of Emperor Charles V," *JWCI* 34 (1971): 204–28.

FIGURE 15. Carolus V, Hans Krafft, Nuremberg, 1521. © Victoria and Albert Museum, London.

The city councillors ensured that the iconography of Charles's expanding empire would appear in a multitude of places: they commissioned a new medal depicting twenty-seven of Charles's territories (Figure 15) and the pillars of Hercules on the reverse. They proposed to translate the motto for the non-Latinists from "Plus Ultra" to the German "Noch Weiter."[16] The city council also commissioned the redecoration of the imperial castle quarters. On the reception-room ceiling, the painter Hans Springinklee included the shields of Charles's territories, both real and claimed, over forty strong. The real included long-held Trastamara and Habsburg possessions as well as the new "Ocean Lands" and "Indian Islands"; the fictive and claimed territories included Jerusalem and Turcia, then held

---

[16] Rosenthal noted that the "Noch Weiter" translation appeared on several ca. 1518–1519 prints by Hans Weiditz, "*Plus ultra*," 224–5. Emperor Maximilian I had employed the symbolism of an extensive display of arms, for example in his *Ehrenpforte*, but under Charles, this collection of arms became broader. Hans Petz, "Urkunden und Regesten aus dem königlichen Kreisarchiv zu Nürnberg," *JKSW* 10 (1889), xliv–xlv, nr. 5829. For a similar 1532 design, see Max Bernhart, *Die Bildnismedaillen Karls des Fünften* (Munich: Otto Helbing, 1919).

by the Ottomans.[17] The second Latin edition of Hernán Cortés's conquest of Mexico (1532) reprised this visual strategy on its illustrated title page (Figure 16). There, Cortés's textual proclamation of Charles's expanding world empire was previewed by the plethora of shields that represented the empire semiotically.[18]

The efforts devoted to representing Charles's empire textually and visually reflected the awkward reality that Charles did not lack competition for the mantle of universal sovereignty. With the dissolution of the Byzantine Empire in the fifteenth century, most of his rivals could be found within Latin Christendom. Within the Holy Roman Empire itself, the Saxon Wettins had a long history of dynastic claims to world empire. Other candidates for world empire, such as the kings of France and Portugal or several Renaissance popes, were located outside the Germanys.[19] Charles's most threatening rival was the Ottoman sultan and emperor Süleyman I, the putative successor to the Byzantine Emperors. During the first two decades of Charles and Süleyman's imperial reigns, both courts claimed that their expansionist ambitions were legitimized by their sovereign's status as the destined world emperor. The more expansive vision of world empire proposed by officials like Valdés and Köbel was particularly useful in countering that challenge: Muslim territories and peoples could be governed by a Christian emperor. Advisors actively exploited the propagandistic value of this rivalry: in one example from 1527, Gattinara tried to extract more money from the Council of Castile by warning that, if Süleyman was left unchecked, he might achieve rule over the entire world.[20] Ferdinand tried to rally aid at the court by writing of Süleyman's "insatiable appetite to become monarch and universal lord."[21] The conflict between the two rulers has been depicted as one between the enemies of Islam and the enemies of Christendom, but the

---

[17] Hans Springinklee, Decke (ceiling), modern restoration, Emperor's reception room (Empfangszimmer des Kaisers), Nuremberg Burg; for the ceiling date, Josef Dettenthaler, "Hans Springinklee als Maler," MVGN 63 (1976): 146–7, 159–60. A listing of his 1521 overseas titles is in *Uff dem Rychstag....* (Speyer: Schmidt, 1521), ai[v].

[18] Hernán Cortés, *De Insulis nuper inventis Ferdinandi Cortesii...* (Cologne: Birckmann, 1532).

[19] Peter E. Starenko, "In Luther's Wake: Duke John Frederick II of Saxony, Angelic Prophecy, and the Gotha Rebellion of 1567" (Ph.D. dissertation, University of California at Berkeley, (2002). Gattinara, 273–6; Reeves, *Influence*, esp. 372–3, 354–8; Thomaz, *L'idée*; and Yates.

[20] "la monarchia de toda el mundo." Quoted in Headley, "Germany," 22, in a discussion of rivals, 18–22.

[21] Ferdinand to his ambassador at Charles's court in Brussels "insaçiable apetito de hazerse monarcha y señor vnibersal." HHSTA Belgien PA 6/2, fols. 22–23[v].

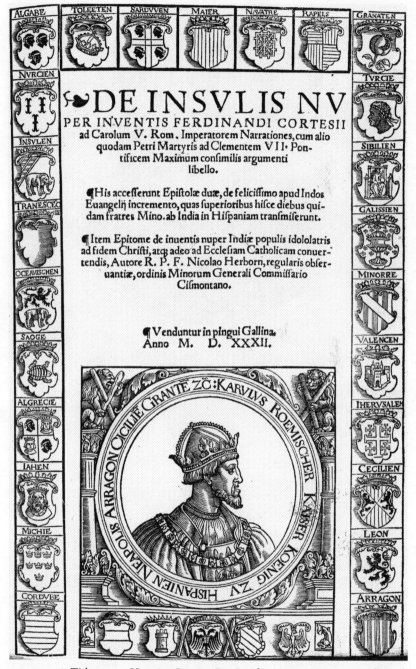

FIGURE 16. Title page, Hernán Cortés, *De Insvlis Nvper Inventis Ferdinandi Cortesii....* (Cologne, Birckman, 1532). This item is reproduced by permission of The Huntington Library, San Marino, California.

FIGURE 17. Charles V, Süleyman, and angel, 1532(?) Copyright © The Trustees of the British Museum.

two courts also saw it as a struggle to determine which ruler was the true heir to Rome and the prophesized world empire (Figure 17). In propaganda texts, Charles claimed sovereignty over Jerusalem; Süleyman countered by claiming sovereignty over Rome.[22]

Competition between the two rulers took material, tangible forms as well as rhetorical ones. In 1532, Süleyman wore a composite crown to receive ambassadors from territories in Latin Christendom. The crown, commissioned from Venetian jewelers along with European-style throne and scepter, combined secular and ecclesiastical symbolism with elements taken from the Holy Roman imperial crown, a military helmet, and the papal tiara. According to amused Venetian observers, the Habsburg envoys turned pale and speechless at the sight. The Habsburg envoys

[22] Cornell H. Fleischer, "Shadows of Shadows: Prophecy in Politics in 1530s Istanbul," *International Journal of Turkish Studies* 13 (2007): 51–62; Robert Finlay, "Prophecy and Politics in Istanbul," *Journal of Early Modern History* 2 (1998):1–31. The two rulers' rivalry was noted in the bronze medal (Figure 17), on which was inscribed "TE DECET O FELIX ULTRA PLUS PERGERE CESAR / CESAREO PRESENS DECIDET ENSE CAPUT" [It befits you, o fortunate Caesar, to proceed "plus ultra"/ the present head will fall by the imperial sword].

valued the "Imperial Crown" at 115,000 ducats, and the overall display at 1,200,000 ducats.[23] In 1535, Habsburg propagandists emphasized the symbolism of world empire when publicizing Charles's victory over Süleyman's North African vassal Hayreddin Barbarossa, particularly Charles's demonstration of mercy in sparing Tunis from sacking. Charles's court added new African titles to signal his expanding suzerainty and treated a gift of jewels from the king of Tunis as treasured regalia.[24]

Charles's subjects could observe the world empire triumphantly expanding beyond Europe and Latin Christendom. The Habsburg world empire had outstripped its immediate predecessor, the Holy Roman Empire, established by another Charles, Charlemagne. By incorporating lands outside Europe, the Habsburg empire evoked the precedent of the Roman Empire, which had geographically extended beyond Europe to the three continents of Europe, Asia, and Africa. The Roman Empire had also dated back to a time before Christianity and St. Peter, first bishop of Rome. By invoking the Roman Empire, imperial theorists could justify superceding the Christian "Holy" Roman and Empire and ignore the delimitations of present-day Latin Christianity and papal claims to supreme authority. Given that the world emperor's authority descended directly from God, however, the emperor's religious and moral virtue was crucial to Habsburg court conceptualization. The Habsburg world empire's promoters held their own religious practices and beliefs to be superior, and they certainly believed that the world emperor should be a Latin Christian rather than a Muslim. Yet in the religiously divisive 1520s, a theory of empire that could encompass even Jews, Muslims, and pagans allowed Charles V and his court officials to sidestep thorny questions of orthodoxy before a general council was convened to resolve doctrinal issues. Habsburg advisors could focus instead on Charles's moral virtue in good governance, whether that was signaled by the Habsburg reorganization of the imperial monarchy's bureaucracy or by Charles's treatment of conquered Tunis.

---

[23] Gülru Necipoğlu, "Süleyman the Magnificent and the Representation of Power in the Context of Ottoman-Habsburg-Papal Rivalry," *Art Bulletin* 71 (1989): 407–27 and *Wegrayß / Keyserlicher Maiestat Legation* (1532), Bii^v–Biii.

[24] *Keyserlicher Maiestat eroberung des Königreychs Thunisi/ ... den xii. Augusti hieher geschriben ist.* (Nuremberg, 1535), ii–iv and *Newe zeyttung Welcher massem römishe Kayserliche Mayestat/ im jüngstvershynen monatt Junio/ von Sardinia auß/ gehen Aphrican geschifft* (1535); AGS (Spain), Casa y Sitio Real Leg. 72, 1559 unfoliated inventory by Alonso de Baeça. Rudolf Beer published a 1555 version, "Acten, Regesten, und Inventare aus dem Archivo General zu Simancas," *JKSW* 12 (1891): cliii–clvii.

In Alfonso de Valdés's vision, the universal monarch's good governance followed Erasmian, humanist definitions. An Erasmian theory of governance for the universal monarch might sound oxymoronic, given that Erasmus was opposed to universal monarchy or *imperium*.[25] Yet despite any disagreement between imperial and non-imperial humanists over the possible extent of a ruler's dominion, Valdés's ideal of the universal monarch adhered to the Erasmian and Aristotelian principles of good rule laid out in Erasmus's *Dulce bellum inexpertis* [1514–1515]. Charles and his advisors could focus on fostering those arts of civilization (legal structures, trade and supporting infrastructure, literacy) laid out by Erasmus, regardless of their subjects' religious beliefs.[26] Erasmus's and Valdés's emphasis on virtue rather than religious faith could further help shape Charles's strategies. Erasmus's discussion of virtue extended the point further, arguing that peoples could be subject to rulers of different religions. Furthermore, just rulers should convert by example, not by force. The just ruler might gradually, over time, limit the public practice of peoples' religions, in the hopes that restricting certain acts would lead people into more preferred forms of worship.[27]

With questions about the evaluation of the Yucatec and Mexican peoples' religious practices and faith unresolved in 1521, Peter Martyr Anglerius had represented these cultures as civilized city-states that could be added to Charles's expanding world empire. The Habsburg court and readers throughout Charles's realm were enthusiastic about territorial expansion in the Americas as a sign that Charles was the true universal monarch. With the extension of his authority to Mexican lands, the prophecies of universal monarchy seemed to be triumphantly unfolding.[28] During most of the 1520s and 1530s, despite his brother

---

[25] For Erasmus's objections, see Yates, 19–20 and John Headley, "Gattinara, Erasmus, and the Imperial Configurations of Humanism," *ARG* 71 (1980): 64–98.

[26] Desiderius Erasmus, *Dulce bellum inexpertis* [1515], *Opera Omnia* 2:7 (Amsterdam: Elsevier, 1999), lines 590–6.

[27] Desiderius Erasmus, *Ultissima consultatio de bello turcis inferendo, et obiter enarratus Psalmus XXVIII*, *Opera Omnia* 5:3 (Amsterdam: Elsevier, 1986), lines 142–50.

[28] One such hopeful witness was the Franciscan Nicholas of Herborn, who rose to the rank of cismontane vicar-general and was at Charles's court during the 1520s and 1530s. His correspondence and manuscript of collected materials illustrates one understanding of the prophetic possibilities of this expanding empire, in *Epitome de convertendis Indianis* (Köln: Birckmann, 1532) and Trier Stadtbibliothek, Codex 1374/140 4° as well as letters reproduced in Ludwig Schmitt, S.J., *Der Kölner Theologe Nikolaus Stagefyr und der Franziskaner Nikolaus Herborn* (Freiburg im Breisgau: Herder'she Verlagshandlung, 1896).

Ferdinand's persistent pleas that he return to the Germanies more regularly, Charles remained whenever possible in Iberia, holding a court that embodied his world empire. The court's investment in universal empire went beyond textual and iconographic propositions and symbolism: it welcomed nobles from the Yucatan and central Mexico and incorporated them into its panoply.

A court's importance was represented symbolically through the magnificence of its spectacle.[29] In the 1520s, Charles's court was renowned for the array of people who were assembled there. Chroniclers took pains to broadcast that the court was particularly distinguished, beyond that of any other emperor or king, by the presence of ambassadors from distant lands. The range of non-subject notables attending the court in Iberia included at various times a papal legate; ambassadors from Latin Christian polities including France, Poland, England, Portugal, and the republic of Venice; and ambassadors from the rulers of Russia, Persia (Sophy), and kingdoms in Africa.[30] Subject ambassadors attending at Charles's court in Iberia represented territories throughout the empire; envoys from Austria, the Holy Roman imperial cities, and Italian states came to court, as did nobles from outside Europe's boundaries.

With the conquest of Mexico, Nahua and other Mexican elites began to travel across the Atlantic Ocean to attend their new sovereign's court. In the first passage back to Iberia from Mexico in 1519, the two Castilian delegates Puertocarrero and Francisco de Montejo brought rich gifts and news of the newly incorporated Spanish settlement Vera Cruz. They were

[29] Volker Press, "The Habsburg Court as Center of the Imperial Government," *Journal of Modern History* 58 (1986) suppl., 23–45; Ronald Asch, ed., *Princes, Patronage, and the Nobility: the Court at the Beginning of the Modern Age, c. 1450–1650* (London: Oxford University Press for the German Historical Institute, 1991), especially essays by Peter Moraw, "The Court of the German Kings and of the Emperor at the end of the Middle Ages, 1440–1519," 103–37; Volker Press, "The Imperial Court of the Habsburgs from Maximilian I to Ferdinand III, 1493–1657," 289–312; and M.J. Rodríguez-Salgado, "The Court of Philip II of Spain," 205–44. Recent work is represented in John Adamson, ed. *The Princely Courts of Europe* (London: Weidenfeld and Nicolson, 1999), especially Glyn Redworth and Fernando Checa, "The Courts of the Spanish Habsburgs 1500–1700, 43–65, 320–1 and Jeroen Duindam, "The Court of the Austrian Habsburgs c. 1500–1750," 165–85, 328–9; and Martin Gosman, Alasdair Macdonald, and Arjo Vanderjagt, ed., *Princes and Princely Culture 1450–1650* (Leiden: Brill, 2005), especially José Martínez Millán, "Charles V," 227–48.

[30] See *Uff dem Rychstag*, aii-aiiii[v]; Alonso de Santa Cruz, *Crónica del Emperador Carlos V*, 2 (Madrid: Patronato de Huérfanos de Intendencia é Intervención Militares, 1920), 164; Francisco López de Gómara, *Annales del Emperador Carlos Quinto*, ed. and trans. R.B. Merriman (Oxford: Clarendon Press, 1912), 72, 210; Prudencio de Sandoval, *Historia de la Vida y Hechos del Emperador Carlos V*, BAE 81 (Madrid: Atlas, 1955), 20.

accompanied by two high-ranking "Indians" (*indios*) and several other attendants. In Charles's request for this party's attendance at his court, he ordered them first to be outfitted in clothes of velvet, satin, and *grana*.[31] Once Moctezuma's empire was subjugated, other nobles of the former Aztec Empire came to Spain. In 1525, one of Moctezuma's sons and at least one other Nahua noble traveled to Castile to both demonstrate and confirm their vassalage.[32] (This group may have been that described by Navagero in 1526.) They were sent to a monastery in Talavera to learn Christian doctrine, given an annual income of 100 ducados, and within a year granted encomiendas by Charles. Don Rodrigo, a son of Moctezuma, apparently spent the next seven years in Iberia, reappearing in records in 1533 at the monastery of San Francisco, Madrid.[33]

The largest recorded group of Aztec (primarily Nahua) nobles in Spain accompanied Hernán Cortés on his first triumphal return in 1528. In an attempt to earn Charles V's favor, Cortés traveled to Spain with an elaborate following that included important fellow conquistadors, high-ranking Aztecs, Mexican entertainers, a menagerie of New World animals, and impressive gifts. These Aztec nobles included sons of Moctezuma and of the Tlaxcalan leader Maxixcatzin, as well as other prominent men described as *caballeros* and *señores*. Although Cortés's journey was only partially successful, with Cortés receiving only some of his requested titles and grants from Charles V, the conquistador and his entourage attracted great excitement and interest as they traveled to Charles's court. There, both artists and writers depicted the nobles. Although some chronicles were silent on the Aztec notables' presence in the entourage, both Gonzalo Fernández de Oviedo y Valdés and Francisco López de Gómara noted them. López de Gómara's account in particular placed them in the category of important dignitaries, along with the powerful conquistadors, whose presence bolstered Cortés's eminence, not in

---

[31] AGI, IG 420, L. 8, fols. 173ᵛ-175, 186. The papal nuncio described these nobles as ambassadors in *Prouinciae sive regiones in India occidentali* [1520]. For a 1509 example of early status-based restrictions on brocade and silk in the Indies, Richard Konetzke, *Colección de documentos para la historia de la formación social de Hispano-América 1493–1810* (Madrid: CSIC, 1953), 23–5.

[32] The nobles were Don Martin and Don Rodrigo. Vasco de Puga, *Provisiones, cedulas, instrucciones de su Magestad, ordenancas de difuntos y audiencia* [Mexico: Pedro Ocharte, 1563], 69; CDIA 41: 91–2, 142–4.

[33] CDIU 18:33, 46; Charles Gibson, *Tlaxcala in the Sixteenth Century* (New Haven: Yale University Press, 1952), 164.

the category of exotic entertainer.[34] The crown recognized its responsibilities for its subject noble visitors, supporting them financially and assigning crown officials to assist them personally during their Castilian travels. Records indicate that the crown took an intimate interest in these noblemen. In a decree from Charles overseeing their maintenance, thirty-six of the visiting Aztec are listed as individuals by name and rank. Although none of the Aztec notables appear to have gained new personal or corporate grants and concessions from the crown during this visit, the act and ceremony of acknowledging sovereignty was itself valued by both Nahuas and Castilians. In sixteenth-century Mexican historical memory, the journey's purpose was to offer fealty to and receive recognition from their new emperor and king.[35] Castilians also found the audience with Charles to be a significant marker. When the Audiencia of Mexico wrote to the crown about any one of these nobles, it clearly identified them as vassals who "had kissed the hands of your majesty."[36] Most of this large group of important Aztec traveled back to Seville in 1529, losing members to further journeys to Rome, and an alarming number to illness, before embarking for Mexico in 1530. Several of the principal nobles stayed behind in Castile – two at Charles's court, and two in Seville.

In its reception of the 1529 Nahua delegation and through its apportionment of favors among the visitors, the crown confirmed its support for a post-conquest social hierarchy within the indigenous nobility. During the early years of the conquest of Mexico, conquistadors had often maintained pre-existing social stratification, awarding the *tlatoque* (or pre-conquest rulers) the Iberian title of "don" upon baptism. Charles V legitimized this previously ad hoc practice. The Nahuas connected titles with individual position rather than a fully heritable familial condition,[37] and as colonial society evolved post-conquest, sons and nephews of

---

34 Francisco López de Gómara, *La istoria de la conquista de México* (Zaragoza, (1552), cxiii^v; Gonzalo Fernández de Oviedo y Valdés, *Historia general y natural de las Indias* 3 (Madrid: Real Academia de la Historia, 1853), 527–8; Christoph Weiditz, *Das Trachtenbuch des Christoph Weiditz von seinen Reisen nach Spanien (1529) und den Niederlanden (1531/32)* (Berlin: Walter de Gruyter, 1927), plate XXII.

35 "yendo a dar obediencia al Emperador Don Carlos, rey nuestro señor" in Diego Muñoz Camargo, *Descripción de la ciudad y provincia de Tlaxcala*, Relaciones Geográficas del Siglo XVI: Tlaxcala, 1, ed. René Acuña (Mexico: Universidad Nacion Autonoma de Mexico, 1982), 166–7.

36 "a besar las manos de Vuestra Magestad" in CDIA 41: 90–1, 110–11.

37 Charles Gibson, *The Aztecs under Spanish Rule* (Stanford: Stanford University Press, 1964), 154–6, 32–3; James Lockhart, *The Nahuas after the Conquest* (Stanford: Stanford

Moctezuma might hold the title of *don* or not, depending on their post-conquest fortunes. Once established, crown confirmation of title and rank remained a mark of recognition for heirs of indigenous nobles through the century, who were exempt from tribute and eligible for elected offices.

The crown made provisions for the care and maintenance of its visiting Nahua subjects that recognized gradations of rank, both by title and by appearance. Seven men were identified as "yndios principales," who either held the title of *don*, were the sons of the most important Aztec rulers, or possessed both attributes. Those identified as the most important nobles were the close allies of Cortés and had all played critical roles in determining the success of the Castilian conquest. One was the current ruler of Cempoala, a city known to Europeans as Cortés's first major ally. Another was the leader of Tlaxcala, the polity whose military force had enabled Iberian triumphs. A third noble was the son of a governor of Tenochtitlan who had risen from warrior ranks to become governor after Cortés executed Moctezuma's nephew and successor in 1525. Three more were the sons of the former emperor Moctezuma himself: Don Martin (identified in the Castilian as well as the Nahua records as the son of Moctezuma), Don Juan Coyanutle, and Pedro Gonzalez Aculan. In popular Iberian and European understanding, Moctezuma's role in the conquest had been perhaps the most generous and significant: Cortés claimed that Moctezuma had peacefully ceded his lands to Charles V in recognition of Charles's superior authority and sovereignty.

Along with other gifts intended to demonstrate Charles's favor to the group as a whole, these men were all dressed according to their status. As in 1519, these nobles were outfitted with velvet coats and caps, damask doublets, and capes and breeches of *grana*. The only Spanish-titled Nahua who was not included in this sumptuary class, Don Diego Yacamecaut, does not appear to fall into the category of close ally to the Habsburg crown. Other nobles, sons of ruling lords or members of Moctezuma's extended family, were not even acknowledged with Castilian titles. In keeping with their untitled status, each of them received less elaborate clothing.[38] By dressing these new subjects, the crown tacitly assigned them social distinction in terms meaningful to Spaniards. Contemporary

---

University Press, 1992), 126; S.L. Cline, *Colonial Culhuacan* (Albuquerque: University of New Mexico Press, 1986), 108–9.

[38] The news of Cempoala and Tlaxcala appeared in Cortés, *Carta* (1522), with Italian and Latin editions soon following. AGI Contratación 4675, fols. 172^v–175^v; Howard Cline, "Hernando Cortes and the Aztec Indians in Spain," *The Quarterly Journal of the Library of Congress* 26 (1969), 85–7.

descriptions of ceremonial court occasions suggest that the crown dressed the principal Indians similarly to lower-ranking courtiers, regidors (city councilmen), or corregidors.[39]

Traces of Nahua nobles who remained in Spain through 1533 can be detected in the archives. On January 25 of that year, five *indios* were sent by the crown to be housed at the Monastery of San Francisco in Madrid: Don Martin, Don Juan, Don Francisco, Hernando de Tapia, and Pedro. Their identification with the notables of 1528 is reinforced by a crown order describing three of the lodgers as "Moctezuma's son, his nephew, and a governor's son" who had previously paid homage to and petitioned the king. Although it is possible that these men were being trained for religious life at the monastery, the Council of the Indies' account books make it clear that the five men's previous movements had been closely connected to the royal court.[40] In July 1533, the Council of the Indies proposed that because expenses for the five notables were coming out of the crown's purse, they should serve at Charles's court: the son of Moctezuma in the household, two others in the honorary horse guard, and the final two in the honorary foot guard.[41] By January 1534,

---

[39] Regidors and the corregidor wore similar clothes in a procession greeting the queen in 1565, as did courtiers in another procession in 1566. HHStA, Spanien Varia 1, p and r. Heritage might restrict the use of luxury cloth: some types were prohibited for relapsed conversos reconciled with the church at the Time of Grace. Linda Martz, "Converso families in Fifteenth- and Sixteenth-century Toledo," *Sefarad* XLVIII (1988), 120. By 1572, the figure of the Indian cacique and his company were nobly clothed in an entrance-ceremony pageant (see *Relacion verdadera, del recebimiento, que la muy noble y muy mas leal ciudad de Burgos* ... 1572), xxx[v]iii along with the regidors (see *Relacion muy verdadera del alto recibimiento, que la ciudad de Burgos hizo....* [Valladolid: Bernardino de Santo Domingo, ca.1570]). See also Alonso de Santa Cruz, *Crónica del Emperador Carlos V* (Madrid: Patronato de Huérfanos de Intendencia é Intervención Militares, 1922) 3:258-9; P.E. Russell, "White Kings on Black Kings," in *Medieval and Renaissance Studies in Honour of Robert Brian Tate*, ed. Ian Michael and Richard A. Cardwell (Oxford: Dolphin, 1986), 151-63. Kate Lowe surveyed the comparable Portuguese engagement with African nobles in "'Representing' Africans: Ambassadors and Princes from Christian Africa to Renaissance Italy and Portugal, 1402-1608," *Transactions of the Royal Historical Society*, 6th ser., 17 (2007): 101-28.

[40] Vasco de Puga, *Provisiones, cedulas, instrucciones de su Magestad*, fol. 85ᵛ. These three men appear in the first Audiencia of Mexico's correspondence as nobles with inheritance difficulties stemming either from post-conquest social disarray or the noble's age. CDIA 41: 90-1, 110-11. Juan B. Olaechea Labayen proposes the thesis of religious training in *El Indigenismo Desdeñado* (Madrid: MAFRE, 1992); AGI, IG 422 L.15, fols. 213, 218-218v, L.16 fols. 48ᵛ-49.

[41] AGI IG 737, fol. 1. Charles's uncle, Prince Juan, kept horse and foot guards in his personal court before his death in 1497. Gonzalo Fernández de Oviedo y Valdés, *Libro de Camara Real del Principe Don Juan e Offiçios de su Casa e serviçio ordinario*,

the notables traveled to attend the court at Toledo. During the next few years, these five lived at court. Their costs were billed to Council of the Indies accounts, first on a crown bill and then subsidized by the sale of licenses for exporting slaves to the Indies. As was customary with court attendants at Habsburg courts, the crown occasionally refurbished their wardrobes and paid them annual salaries, in 1534 and 1535. When Don Juan fell ill and then died, the crown paid for the Confraternity of the Court to hold a proper funeral and reimbursed his companions for the expenses of his illness. After Don Juan's death, his fellow Nahua nobles announced that they wished to return home to New Spain and were granted leave to go. Hernando de Tapia, whose Nahua wife and son were with him, remained at court for another year, through the middle of 1537. Before his departure, the crown helped him recover valuable goldwork sent by his father.[42]

After the five resident Nahuas settled into life at court in 1534, they were joined for some months by envoys from Tlaxcala. The embassy was headed by the current governor, Don Diego Maxixcatzin, and included his *criados* Sebastian and Martin.[43] In the early 1530s, the Iberians perceived the Maxixcatzin family to be the hereditary rulers of Tlaxcala, and consequently Don Diego was an astute Tlaxcalan choice for envoy. Tlaxcala's reputation in Iberia at the time was very high. In court humanist circles, Tlaxcala was thought to be a republic, "somewhat democratic, somewhat aristocratic, as was the Roman government before it degenerated into a violent monarchy [i.e. despotic]."[44] The first bishopric in New Spain had been established there, and despite setbacks in 1527, the republic and particularly the nobility were believed to have embraced Christianity. Given this combination of corporate reputation and the high status of the ambassador, Charles readily recognized Tlaxcala's loyal service during the conquest of New Spain. Charles granted Tlaxcala a coat

Sociedad de Bibliófilos Españoles (Madrid: Sociedad de Bibliófilos Españoles, 1870). In 1542, Charles V had forty-two chamber attendants, seventeen foot guard, and twenty-four horse guard. Christina Hofmann, *Das Spanische Hofzeremoniell von 1500–1700* (Frankfurt a.M.: Peter Lang, 1985), 199.

[42] Don Martin, probably the son of Moctezuma, received a stipend double (40,000 maravedis) that of Don Francisco, Don Juan, and Hernando de Tapia (20,000 maravedis) in the allotments. AGI IG 422 L. 16 fols. 52–52ᵛ, 57, 107ᵛ–108, 201ᵛ–202, 231ᵛ, 267ᵛ–268, 276ᵛ–277ᵛ; IG 422 L. 17 fols. 17–17ᵛ, 103, 105–106; IG 1961 L.3 fols. 84ᵛ, 209; IG 1962 L.2 fol. 105, L.4 fols. 20–20ᵛ, 36ᵛ–37.

[43] AGI IG 422, L. 16 fols. 186–186ᵛ; IG 1961 L. 3 fol. 193.

[44] "Democraticae partim, partim vero Aristocraticae uti aliquando resp. Romana, priusque ad violentam monarchiam deveniret." Peter Martyr of Anghiera, *De Orbe Novo . . .* (1530) in *Opera* V:2, lxvi.

of arms and the title of "the Loyal City" (*La Leal Ciudad*), a title held by particularly loyal Castilian cities, and mandated that Tlaxcala become an inalienable province of the crown. As with other Nahua nobles, the crown paid for new silk clothes and the maintenance of the embassy while it remained in Iberia. They returned home in 1535, municipal privileges in hand, traveling with the first viceroy of Mexico, Antonio de Mendoza. This successful embassy was soon followed by another in 1539–1541 that petitioned the crown by reminding it that the Tlaxcalans were "loyal and good vassals." They asked the crown to confirm the city's status as an inalienable crown possession and to grant privileges for the preservation of the nobility and Tlaxcalan self-government, which the crown did. The crown also continued to provide the envoys with funds for their journey home.[45]

Even as the Tlaxcalans were successfully gaining corporate privileges, other Nahua nobles petitioned the crown successfully for individual awards. Nobles who were close allies of Cortés continued to receive the highest honors. Moctezuma's sons and other male heirs continued to travel to the Spanish court to confirm land grants and pensions. Because Charles V's sovereignty over Mexico was partially explained through Moctezuma's voluntary abdication of his regal or imperial throne, the crown continued to support many of his heirs' claims to nobility while it encouraged or demanded that they live in Castile during the first decades of Spanish rule in Mexico.[46] Some of Moctezuma's descendants were granted heritable titles, and some settled in Spain, including another Don Pedro de Moctezuma, who became *vecino* and regidor of Toledo. Following the Nahua example, Indian rulers such as Atahualpa's sons and lords of more recently conquered provinces of New Spain made their way to the Habsburg court to gain confirmation of their noble titles and properties.[47] Atahualpa, like Moctezuma, was accepted as the sovereign

---

[45] AGI, IG 422 L. 16 fol. 201, IG 1961 L.3 fols. 186–186ᵛ, 193, 269ᵛ–270; Gibson, *Tlaxcala* 164–5; AGI Patronato 275 r. 41, 1541.III.29; Bartolome de Las Casas, *Apologética Historia Sumaria*, Obras Completas (Madrid: Alianza Editorial, 1992), 8:1408–12. In recognition of their deeds during the conquest, AGI Patronato 74, n.1, r. 13.

[46] For Don Pedro de Moctezuma, Moctezuma's son, and his departure in 1541 after a 1540 audience, AGI IG 1963 L.7 fols. 217ᵛ–220. Carlos Álvarez Nogal, "El Conde de Moctezuma en el reino de Granada" in *El Reino de Granada y el Nuevo Mundo* (Diputación Provincial de Granada, (1994), 2:106. López de Gómara, *istoria*, xciiii. Other Moctezuma heirs appear in: AGI IG 425 L. 24 fol. 382ᵛ, IG 1085 L. 1575, L. 1576; Patronato 245, r. 10, 14, 25; Justicia 218 no. 2 r. 3, fol. 3; Pasajeros L. 8 E 1647.

[47] For example, AGI IG 425 L.23 fols. 71ᵛ, 111ᵛ, 311; Patronato 188 r.6; Contratación 5527 L.3. fols. 6, 16; M.P. – Escudos 77, 78.

of a kingdom or empire that had been conquered by the Castilians.[48] As in the Mexican examples, Atahualpa's descendants continued to receive recognitions of nobility longer than most other Inca or Andean noble families.[49]

This series of ceremonial acts – Nahua vassal envoys giving homage to and soliciting their sovereign, as well as Nahua nobles maintained as minor members of Charles's court – was accompanied by crown promotion of Nahua nobles' political authority during the same period. In 1530, Charles issued a writ urging the appointment of Indian regidors to town councils along with Spaniards. As colonial administration was increasingly regularized, the positions of Nahua nobles were as well. With the first viceroy's arrival in New Spain in 1535, the ruling *tlatoque* in many major Nahua polities were formally given the office of governor.[50] The Nahua nobles' presence at court was of course primarily symbolic; comparison with other members of the Habsburg court helps illuminate more fully the cultural position of these Nahua envoys and court attendants.

In the 1530s, their position was similar to that of other Habsburg subjects whose court attendance symbolized the dynasty's eminence. In keeping with the demands for magnificent spectacle in all its members, the crown financed the proper outfitting of not only Indian envoys, but also crown officials, returning explorers, and crown envoys on Indies business to other courts, all from the Indies accounts.[51] The court's concern with clothing was not exclusive to the matters concerning the Indies. Similar sums of money were spent on the dress of other envoys to the court, as clothing in general was both a major responsibility for a prince's household retainers and a major part of those court attendants' payment.[52] The crown also tapped into the Indies accounts to help support costs associated with nobles from another non-European and, in at least one case, non-Christian kingdom: Muslim princes who were members of the Tunisian Hafsid royal family.

---

[48] For Francisco Vitoria's acceptance of Inca vassalage, see his letter to Miguel de Arcos, *Relectio de Indis*, ed. L. Pereña and J.M. Perez Prendes (Madrid: CSIC, 1967), 137–9.

[49] AGI Pasajeros L.4 E3006 (1563.x.9), L. 4 E3100 (1564); Quito 211 L.2 fols. 197^v–198^v (1587), 207^v (1588).

[50] Gibson, *Aztecs*, 173; Lockhart, 31.

[51] AGI IG 422 L.16 fols. 123^v–124^v, 131^v–132; IG 425 L.23 fol. 141; IG 1961 L.1 fol. 63^v. For Indies including matters with Portugal, see AGI IG 425 L.23 fols.104–104^v.

[52] See Fernández de Oviedo's *Libro de Camara Real del Principe Don Juan*, 30, 36–7, as well as the Austrian Hofkammerarchiv account books (the *Hofzahlamtsbücher*) for Charles's brother King Ferdinand, extant from the 1540s onward.

With the Habsburg conquest of Tunis in 1535, the relationship between the Hafsids and Charles gained a new dimension. After being driven out of Tunis by the Ottoman vassal Hayreddin Barbarossa in 1534, the Tunisian king Muhammad b. al-Hasan (or Muley Hassan as he was known to the Castilians) accepted Charles V's offer of military assistance to recover his kingdom. Their combined forces retook Tunis in 1535. In consequence, Muhammad b. al-Hasan signed a treaty acknowledging Charles's suzerainty. The terms of the treaty made it clear that the rights of Christians in Tunis were to be protected and extended, but that there was no expectation of Muslim conversion to Christianity in the kingdom as a whole. Al-Hasan and Tunis could remain Muslim. The treaty did stipulate that Spanish *moriscos* would not be allowed to live in al-Hasan's territory.[53] The connections between Christian Spain and Muslim Tunis were even longer-standing than this well-known incident suggests. Hafsid princes had been subsidized at Charles's court since early in his reign: Charles had been subsidizing a Prince Juan of Tunis well before formal tribute status was established, and had paid for the king of Tunis's trip to Iberian territory in 1520.[54]

The king of Tunis was not the first Muslim ruler in North Africa to become a Habsburg subject: the king of Tlemcen had first offered tribute to the crown in 1512, and in 1535 became a client kingdom once again.[55] In a telling distinction, these charges were also paid out of Council of the Indies, rather than royal household or Council of Castile, accounts. As representatives of extra-European lands beyond the bounds of Charles's hereditary lands, the Mexican notables and North African kings were clearly in a different administrative category than, say, the Duke of Milan (although, in 1542, Bartolome de Las Casas argued that philosophically and legally, Mexico and Milan should be accorded the same treatment as conquered republics).[56] Yet the Habsburg court supported these nobles and, with the growing universal empire, saw nothing

---

[53] For the details of the campaign and the treaty itself, see Alonso de Santa Cruz, 3 (1922), 283–93, esp. 285.

[54] AGI IG 420 L.8 fols. 187–8; 1961 L.3, fols. 82^v–83; 1962 L.6. fol. 29–29^v.

[55] López de Gómara, *Annales*, 33; Jamil M. Abun-Nasr, *A History of the Maghrib in the Islamic Period* (Cambridge: Cambridge University Press, 1987), Chapter 4; also Mercedes García Arenal and Miguel Ángel de Bunes, *Los Españoles y el Norte de África, siglos XV-XVIII* (Madrid: MAPFRE, 1992), 83.

[56] In *De regia potestate* [1542], cited in Anthony Pagden, "Dispossessing the barbarian: the language of Spanish Thomism and the debate over the property rights of the American Indians" in *The Languages of Political Theory in Early-Modern Europe* (Cambridge: Cambridge University Press, 1987), 96.

contradictory in subject Indian aristocratic republics or Muslim North African kingdoms. These subject nobles embodied the rhetoric and theory of universal monarchy promoted by the Habsburg court, reinforcing the idea of Charles V as the true head of the prophesized world empire.

During the mid-sixteenth century, the importance of the universal monarchy began to wane in both material and rhetorical arenas. Envoys from the republic of Tlaxcala, seeking corporate privileges for their city-state, and noble descendants of close crown allies continued to travel to Iberia through the 1530s and 1540s. There, they offered fealty to their emperor Charles and in return had their grants and pensions confirmed. After a viceroyalty was established in Mexico in 1535, however, such grants could be confirmed in New Spain and the overseas journey was no longer necessary. In subsequent decades, Mexican nobles took advantage of their resident viceroy to obtain personal privileges from the crown – coats of arms or the right to carry a sword – without leaving home.[57] Increasingly, the Iberian court became isolated from its Mexican nobles. Intensifying this distance, the crown also began imposing protective limits on Indian travel to Iberia in the 1540s.

From the mid-1540s, decreasing numbers of Indians were present at court and in general society throughout Iberia. Citing the need for a protective segregation, the crown issued restrictions on all Indian travel as early as 1543.[58] In so doing, the crown rejected the applicability of the *ius perigrinandi* (the right of travel and access to all nations) to its Indian subjects only a few years after Francisco de Vitoria's argument in *Relectio de Indis* had unambiguously accepted this right as an argument for the Spanish conquest.[59] Initially, both Indian communities and the crown saw segregation as a positive policy. The Tlaxcalans themselves petitioned the crown and king in 1550 for permission to restrict Castilian access to their lands in New Spain, arguing that the Castilian presence had a deleterious effect on the common good of their republic.[60]

In the same decade, Charles and his court began to turn attention away from imperial expansionist projects and toward the resolution of internal

---

[57] See for example AGI Patronato 1748 leg. 55 no. 3 r. 4, 1536 referring to Don Juan Indio, señor natural de Cuyoacan, and Gibson, *Tlaxcala*, 163 for the Tlaxcalan Maxixcatzins.

[58] AGI IG 1963 L.8 fol. 278, L.9 fols. 8–9.

[59] For a description of Vitoria's use of ius peregrinandi (part of the *ius gentium*), see Pagden, *Spanish Imperialism*, 20–1. While it is tempting to read this action as denying Indians a natural right, it should be noted that in general, non-Castilians had not gained free access to New Spain by the 1540s despite Charles's 1517 proposal to allow his Flemish subjects to travel to his American lands.

[60] Gibson, *Tlaxcala*, 79–83.

religious divisions. Following a failed Algerian campaign in 1541, open military confrontations with Charles's rival Süleyman ceased by the mid-1540s. Large-scale hostilities in north Africa diminished and an uneasy peace established along a newly defined Hungarian border. A new generation of advisors replaced the Burgundian-based humanists with whom Charles had begun his rule in the 1510s. Religious divisions were hardening throughout his empire. In the Holy Roman Empire, Charles moved to wage war on his reformed princes and estates. In Iberia, Erasmians no longer sought to serve at Charles's court. Their theological positions were increasingly condemned as heretical, and humanists like Valdés often chose to flee to safe harbors outside Iberia.[61] The Cusan and Platonic idea, that diversity of practice was only human, was no longer tenable. Similarly, Erasmian ideals of good governance and conversion by peaceful example disappeared from print discussions, replaced by treatises calling for rulers to enforce adherence to true religion[62] during this phase of religious and political strife.

The resolution of the debate over Indians and natural slavery illustrated the changed intellectual climate. The cultural evaluation of non-Christians became tied to arguments of natural slavery and dominion rather than Gattinara's suprapolitical authority (*auctoritas*) of world emperors. Such arguments negated the earlier definition of a limitless world empire, instead delineating the legal boundaries of Charles's authority. In 1539, Francisco de Vitoria, a Dominican teaching at Salamanca and an important advisor to Charles on juridical and theological matters, argued that Indians could not be natural slaves. Because they were men with judgment who possessed dominion over themselves, they were by definition civilized. In line with previous Erasmian humanists and with Aristotle, Vitoria noted that the Indians "have order in their affairs: they have properly organized cities, proper marriages, magistrates and overlords, laws, industries, and commerce, all of which require the use of reason. They likewise have a form of religion.... "[63] Vitoria did not consider Indians in isolation: he compared Indians to Jews and Muslims

---

[61] Marcel Bataillon, *Erasmo y España*, trans. A. Alatorre (Mexico: Fondo de Cultura Económica, 1950).

[62] For treatises on good government, Ronald W. Truman, *Spanish Treatises on Government, Society and Religion in the Time of Philip II* (Leiden: Brill, 1999) and for ethnographies, see the Introduction to Part II.

[63] Francisco de Vitoria, *De Indis*, trans. Anthony Pagden and Jeremy Lawrence, *Political Writings* (Cambridge: Cambridge University Press, 1991), 250–1. "Patet, quia habent ordinem aliquem in suis rebus, postquam habent civitates quae ordine constant, et habent matrimonia distincta, magistratus, dominos, leges, opificia, commutationes, quae omnia requirunt usum rationis; item religionis speciem." *Relectio de Indis*, I.1.15, p. 29. For

as similarly civilized peoples who practiced religion and possessed the right to self-dominion. Yet Vitoria arrived at a very different conclusion on the question of religious inclusivity, a question he linked to dominion. Although Indians, Jews, and Muslims practiced religion, Vitoria asserted that sincere practice was not the decisive qualifier for inclusion in a Habsburg Empire. In their states of non-Christian or imperfectly Christian (in the case of converted Muslims, *moriscos*) religious faith and practice, such people lacked sufficient orthodoxy and its support of long-standing faith to be truly incorporated into a Christian polity.[64] Charles welcomed Vitoria's legal rejection of natural slavery, despite the consequent theoretical diminution of his imperial dominion. Over time, Vitoria's determination proved to have a lasting influence on both religious and political thought. His declaration that orthodox faith was necessary for full inclusion marked a lasting rejection of the previous decades' idealism.

The crown increasingly weakened Indians' abilities to act either symbolically or in practice as important or full members of an empire. Choosing to understand Indian polities as republics rather than fiefdoms, the Castilians had remodeled local governments by the end of the 1550s. The institutionalization of town government in a Castilian model (the *cabildo*) weakened the hereditary and unlimited authority of high nobles by defining these nobles as elected officials subject to the everyday authority of Castilian law. This diminution of noble authority was aggravated in non-Nahuatl-speaking regions, where a single hereditary lord had often held absolute power over his subjects in the Aztec era.[65] Las Casas, who had promoted the idea of the Indian republic so heavily, realized that hispanization had worked against his goals of inclusivity. In recognition of this, Las Casas spent his final years arguing for a restoration of Indian rulers as kings under a universal monarch.[66]

Vitoria's adherence to Aristotle's *Politics*, see Anthony Pagden, *The Fall of Natural Man* (Cambridge: Cambridge University Press, 1982), 71–3, 77–8.

[64] Vitoria, *de indis*, I.1.8, p. 20 and I. 2. especially pp. 55–72; also Appendix 8 "Parecer de Los Teologos de la Universidad de Salamanca sobre el Bautismo de los Indios," pp. 157–64.

[65] Judith Francis Zeitlin and Lillian Thomas, "Spanish Justice and the Indian Cacique: Disjunctive Political Systems in Sixteenth-Century Tehuantepec," *Ethnohistory* 39 (1992): 285–315.

[66] This shift radicalized Las Casas's position and motivations, well-known through the famous 1550–1551 Valladolid debate with Juan Ginés Sepúlveda. Juan Friede, "Las Casas and Indigenism," in *Bartolomé de Las Casas in History: Towards an Understanding of the Man and his Work*, eds. Juan Friede and Benjamin Keen (De Kalb: Northern Illinois University, 1971), 176–8.

Shifting attitudes in ecclesiastical matters closely paralleled changes in secular policies. Secular policies of segregation more clearly defined Indians as physically and innately different, and eventually ecclesiastical policies defined these people as intellectually or spiritually weak. Such a course was not self-evident in the first decades of evangelization in New Spain. Explicitly from at least 1532, the colonial Junta Apostólica supported Indians' full capacity for Christianity. Following the logical consequences of this idea and in keeping with papal pronouncements on the full Christianity of all, whether born gentile or not, the Junta decided to ordain educated Indians and mestizos in 1539. However, in the colonial uproar over the crown's proposed New Laws of 1542, the Junta reversed its position, claiming that Indians required secular and religious tutelage. In 1555, the First Mexican Provincial Council explicitly revoked the 1539 legislation and prohibited the ordination of Indians on the basis on their condition as perpetual neophytes who could never be full members of the Christian church. Placed in a category with moriscos, mestizos, mulattos, and direct descendants of people condemned by the Inquisition, Indians were persons whose "natural defects" prevented them from entering orders.[67]

This transitional mid-century devolution of the status of Mexican nobles and all Indians, as rule shifted from Charles to Philip, was accompanied by a change in the rhetoric of Habsburg monarchy. In 1549, Charles and the Habsburg crown once again revived the rhetoric of universal monarchy to support Philip's candidacy for election as King of the Romans. Philip toured the Burgundian cities in an effort to lobby for his election. By 1552, Charles recognized that the election was not possible, that his son Philip was politically unacceptable to the princes of the Holy Roman Empire.[68] The subsequent division of Charles's empire between his brother Ferdinand I (the Holy Roman Empire) and son Philip II

---

[67] When the Third Mexican Provincial Council in 1585 sent their decree, prohibiting the ordination of Indians and mestizos, to Rome for papal approval, the papacy altered the text. The Roman curia removed Indians from discussion, and instead of prohibition merely advised "great caution." See Stafford Poole's articles: "Church Law on the Ordination of Indians and *Castas* in New Spain" *HAHR* 61 (1981): 637–650 and "The Declining Image of the Indian among Churchmen in Sixteenth-Century New Spain" in *Indian-Religious Relations in Colonial Spanish America*, ed. Susan E. Ramírez (Syracuse: Syracuse University Press, 1989), 11–19.

[68] Bosbach, *Monarchia Universalis*, 47 and Juan Cristobal Calvete de Estrella, *El felicissimo viaje del muy alto y muy poderoso principe don Phelippe* (Antwerp: Martin Nucio, 1552), 13–18ᵛ, 117, 131–3, 152; *Beschreibung des Thourniers vnd kampfspeils, … zu Bintz gehalten des 24 tags Augusti An. 1549. …* [1550], aii-bvii.

(the Iberian possessions and the Low Countries) also shattered the geographic possibility of a universal monarchy. Philip occasionally tried to redeploy the rhetoric of universal empire in Iberia, with little enduring success. Indeed, when Tommaso Campanella proposed, around 1600, that Mexican elites be incorporated into priesthoods, monastic life, and imperial service, he did so as a heretic who had been shut away from the world.[69]

In 1549, the representations of Charles's sovereignty in his entries pronounced a redefined imperial authority. Fresh from the Battle of Mühlberg and his defeat of the Smalkaldic League of Protestant German princes, Charles was depicted as the victorious emperor who had defeated heretics of all kinds, including Turkish Muslims and German Protestants. Charles's decision to pursue religious uniformity in the Holy Roman Empire had necessitated the rejection of his inclusive supra-political world monarchy. His effort to impose religious orthodoxy on his German subjects had been conducted through military force. By choosing this path, Charles flouted the Erasmian definition of peaceful good governance in a polyreligious realm and repudiated a Cusan acceptance of religious diversity. And surely, if he tried to force religious uniformity on his German subjects, his potential subjects in other parts of the world would need to become doctrinally orthodox and faithful Catholics as well. A Christian or confessional empire could only be created by constricting the earlier, world-spanning imperial ideal and by abandoning its symbolic practices of religious and cultural incorporation.

[69] John M. Headley, *Tommaso Campanella and the Transformation of the World* (Princeton: Princeton University Press, 1997), 222–3.

3

Aztec Regalia and the Reformation of Treasure

The first news of Yucatan, with its civilized polities, arrived at Charles V's court in 1519. Along with reports, the Castilian conquistadors sent a cargo of treasure wrought from gold, silver, gemstones, and feathers by these newly-encountered people. Prominent humanists at the Castilian court produced admiring evaluations of these precious objects, and when Charles V went north the next year to be crowned as King of the Romans in confirmation of his election as Holy Roman Emperor, he exhibited his new treasures at his court in Brussels. Yet by May 11, 1535, a Habsburg court ambassador wrote to a fellow official: "[Charles] has ordered all the moneyers of his kingdom to come to this city [the port of Barcelona], so that they may melt down all the gold and silver of the Indies into coins..."[1] These gold and silver objects were melted down to finance Charles V's new offense against Tunis, which had been seized and held by an Ottoman client ruler, Hayreddin Barbarossa. Other objects from these early treasure shipments that could not be melted down seem to have disappeared from the written record for decades after the 1520s. What happened during the fifteen years between 1520 and 1535? One strand of scholarship has explained the sixteenth-century destruction or

---

[1] "Ha ordenado de venir en esta cibdad los monederos de todos sus reinos y hecho traer el oro y plata de las Indias para que aquí se labre por escudos, y desta moneda será proveido y servido. Aqui se han traido las tinajas del oro y plata para ser labrada la moneda." Martin de Salinas, *El emperador Carlos V y su corte segun las cartas de Don Martin de Salinas, embajador del infante Don Fernando (1522–1539)* (Madrid: Fortanet, 1903), 648. In 1535, Martin de Salinas was secretary and ambassador of Ferdinand, King of the Romans, Hungary, and Bohemia, at the court of Charles V.

disappearance of these objects as a European repudiation of, or oblivious-
ness to, a pagan aesthetic.[2] Such a narrative, however, neglects European
attitudes toward materiality, sacrality, and rulership. To explain both
the early reception of Aztec precious objects in Europe and their later
liquidation into specie, we must reconnect this history with that of treasure's changing cultural valence in the late fifteenth and early sixteenth
centuries, particularly during the Reformation's early years.

In the second half of the fifteenth century, treasure had become a necessary symbolic and material tool for rulers. Habsburgs Albert II, Frederick III, and Maximilian I, all elected Holy Roman Emperors during
the century, actively acquired treasure throughout their lives to promote
their wealth and splendor.[3] One of Maximilian I's monumental print
projects, the Triumphal Arch (*Ehrenpforte*), gathered together sources
and examples of Maximilian's fame and triumphs in many small prints
that together formed the spectacle of a paper arch. One woodcut, composed circa 1515, described the Maximilian's treasury (*Schatzkammer*)
through a caption and Albrecht Altdorfer's illustration of the space (Figure 18). In the secured room, treasure was displayed on separate platforms
and stored in chests. The illustration reveals a hierarchy of value, from
the viewer's left to right. The table on the left displayed plate, the center
ecclesiastical treasure of reliquaries, crucifixes and liturgical items. On
the table to the right, regalia and insignia, including a crown and the
collar of the Order of Golden Fleece, were arranged under a canopy. The
verse outlined both the materials valued as treasure and the treasury's
spectacular intention to outshine the possessions of other princes, both
through material value and attendant spiritual authority: "He alone has
the greatest treasure/ of silver, gold, and precious gems/ robes adorned

---

[2] Scholars have argued that such "barbarian handiwork" from the New World had no influence on sixteenth-century art and thus cultural production in sixteenth-century Europe.
See J.H. Elliott, *The Old World and the New, 1492–1650* (1970; reprint with a new preface, Cambridge: Cambridge University Press, 1992), 32. This argument forms the implicit
foundation of Anthony Pagden's influential *European Encounters with the New World*
(New Haven: Yale University Press, 1993), Chapter 1, and Michael T. Ryan, "Assimilating New Worlds in the Sixteenth and Seventeenth Centuries," *CSSH* 23 (1981): 519–38.

[3] Philip the Fair's marriage to Juana of Castile influenced the treatment of treasure at
the Castilian court, both through his own collection and through his son Charles V's
early education at the Burgundian court. José Miguel Morán and Fernando Checa, *El
Coleccionismo en España. De la cámara de maravillas a la galería de pinturas* (Madrid:
Cátedra, 1985), especially 41.

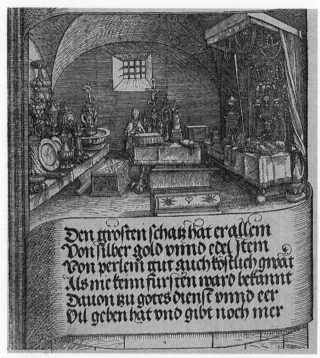

FIGURE 18. Albrecht Altdorfer, Schatzkammer, *Triumphal Arch of Maximilian I*, ca. 1515. *Photograph © 2011 Museum of Fine Arts, Boston.*

with valuable pearls/ as no other prince is renowned. He has given much to God's service and honor, and will give more."[4]

Not all treasure was inherited, so possessing treasure reflected first and foremost the abilities of an individual prince to obtain and retain treasure. Although Maximilian I's father Frederick left behind a treasure, he considered it his own personal trove and apparently felt no obligation to keep his son informed of where portions of it were secreted. Maximilian himself treated most of the Burgundian treasure of his deceased first

---

[4] "Den grosten schatz hat er allein/ Von silber gold vnnd edel stein/ von perlein gut auch köstlich gwant/ Als nie keim fursten ward bekannt/ Davon tzu gotes dienst vnnd eer/ Vil geben hat vnd gibt noch mer." Thomas Schauerte, *Die Ehrenpforte für Kaiser Maximilian I* (Munich: Deutscher Kunstverlag, 2001), 335–6, 395, 451–60; Franz Winzinger, *Albrecht Altdorfer, Graphik* (Munich: R. Piper, 1963), 70–4; also Hermann Fillitz, "Die Weltliche Schatzkammer – Wien," *Schatzkammern Europas: Weltliche Schatzkammern*, ed. Erich Steingräber (Munich: Hirmer, 1968), 37; Eduard Chmelarz, "Die Ehrenpforte des Kaisers Maximilian I," *JKSW* 4 (1886): 289–319 and the facsimile in the Supplement.

wife Mary as his own rather than as a dynastic possession. He utilized his treasure in two ways: both for its material value and for its ability to inscribe power relations in ceremonial display. Some treasure was more alienable than other, and Maximilian pawned and redeemed these types of treasure to ensure the flow of credit that funded his activities. Valuable tableware or plate, which traveled with the peripatetic court and later became a separate *Silberkammer*, could be easily pawned and redeemed. Maximilian also used some jewels as sureties for debts or treaties. The Burgundian jewels, possessing names and histories, were not closely linked to imperial authority, yet had value beyond the more material plate. In a reflection of this greater value or symbolic density, when the Fuggers acquired several lost Burgundian jewels, they did so with the intention of returning them to Maximilian in exchange for a large redemption fee. The recovery of renowned jewels could also become an important issue in peace treaties, as relations between dynasties and kingdoms were renegotiated.[5] A treasury contained these different types of secular treasure, as well as other treasure imbued with devotional or sacred value that made it even more culturally or symbolically dense, and thus less alienable.

Although a prince's possession of valuables was critical to his fame and reputation in the fifteenth century,[6] it was displayed primarily at ceremonial events. As depicted in Maximilian's triumphal arch, treasure was secured in storerooms and chests when not brought out for coronations, weddings, entrances, funerals, and other ceremonies that provided the appropriate public venues for such exhibitions. The distinctions between secular and devotional treasure, even when stored, were highlighted in another of Maximilian's commissioned triumphal print works, the Triumphal Procession (*Triumphzug*) series. Not all of the painted miniatures created for this propaganda piece were made into prints; among the draft scenes was one depicting wagons loaded with treasure. The wagons and treasure are separated into two categories as secular *Gebrauch* ("use")

5 Hermann Wiesflecker, *Kaiser Maximilian I. Das Reich, Österreich und Europa an der Wende zur Neuzeit* (Munich: Oldenbourg, 1986), 5:301–4. For a discussion of the symbolic density of objects, see Annette Weiner, "Cultural Difference and the Density of Objects," *American Ethnologist* 21 (1994): 391–403. The Fuggers purchased the jewels in 1504. Norbert Lieb, *Die Fugger und die Kunst* (Munich: Schnell & Steiner, 1952–1958), 2:137–41 and Joycelyne G. Russell, *Diplomats at Work: Three Renaissance Studies* (Wolfeboro Falls: Alan Sutton, 1992), 159.
6 Lisa Jardine, *Worldly Goods: A New History of the Renaissance* (New York: Doubleday, 1996); Thomas DaCosta Kaufmann, *The School of Prague* (Chicago: University of Chicago Press, 1988), chapter 1.

and sacral *Andacht* ("devotional"), labeled according to Maximilian's direction. This division delineates different spheres of a ruler's authority. Jewels and the hoard of gold were classified as more alienable or pawnable treasure, the secular *Gebrauch*, whose contents demonstrated a prince's grandeur primarily through sumptuous display. These treasures included ornate banquet vessels and platters, as well as works of art impressive for their expense and artistry.[7] Along with its alienability or convertibility, *Gebrauch* treasure possessed ceremonial significance. At coronations and weddings, the emperor was expected to dine off gold plate. At other times, it was the medium of ceremonial gift exchange between sovereign powers, or the offering of a prosperous imperial city to its ruler at his entrance, coronation, or wedding.

City councils typically incorporated a gift of silver or gold plate into entry ceremonies, held for a monarch's first official entry into a city. The entry reconfirmed the bonds between ruler and corporate body, with the citizenry assembling (often in armor, demonstrating their military readiness) to witness their ruler's ceremonial entry into the city. Upon entry, their ruler would be greeted by the most important people present, whether city councillors, ecclesiastical officials, or high-ranking nobles, and sometimes cities gave rulers tokens of sovereignty. Among the rituals of entry, city representatives would gather to present traditional gifts of hospitality to their king. Most practically, the city would gift their emperor or king with barrels of wine, oxen, and sheep (in Iberia, the Holy Roman Empire, and Italy). In the imperial city of Nuremberg, the city fathers regularly commissioned gold and silver plate to accompany the other perishable gifts of hospitality and fealty at the first entry of a Habsburg after he or she assumed a new title. The costs of these gifts were high, and often increased by filling the goblet or cup full of guldens in amounts of even thousands.[8] For example, for Charles's entry in 1541,

---

7 Franz Schestag, "Kaiser Maximilians I. Triumph," *JKSW* 1 (1883): 154–81; Franz Winzinger, *Die Miniaturen zum Triumphzug kaiser Maximilians I* (Graz: Akademische Druck, 1972), 1: 28–9, 2:50–1. For the alienability of Isabella of Castile's royal treasure after her death in 1504, Antonio de la Torre, ed. *Testamentaría de Isabel la Católica* (Valladolid: (1968).

8 StAN, Kronungsakten 1, fols. 105^v–106, 121^v, 132–5^v; StAN SIL 134 no. 19, fols. 1–34^v and no. 26; Vienna, Stadt- und Landesarchiv, OKAR 91 (1558), fol. 31^v. StAN, Stadtrechnungsbelege, 1515, 4; 1525, and throughout century. Jean Jacquot, *Fêtes de la Renaissance*, vol. 2 on Charles V (Paris: CNRS, 1956). Richard Trexler gives examples of entrance ceremonies for foreign princes, *Public Life in Renaissance Florence* (New York: Academic Press, 1980), 323–6. Valentin Groebner discusses gift culture in the Holy Roman Empire in *Liquid Assets, Dangerous Gifts: Presents and Politics at the End*

the drinking cup decorated skillfully with the seven planets cost over 460 gulden and was filled with 2,000 Nuremberger gulden. Gifts (mostly plate and calibrated according to rank) to members of his court ran to another 1,000 gulden.[9]

The second, sacral form of treasure (*Andacht*) also supported the authority of a ruler and particularly the Holy Roman Emperor as the possessor of sacred objects. A ruler's sacral treasures were not simply valued for the cost and artistry represented in the material objects; they were valued for their association with the divine. Sacral objects were understood to exert their beneficient power over all who came within sight of them.[10] Such items were almost never alienated from a ruler: a ruler might deposit a sacral object at a favored religious foundation or city, but his authority continued over either the object directly or the foundation. Alternatively, sacral treasure might travel with the peripatetic royal household. In Maximilian's Triumphal Procession, a host of these sacral objects were depicted for the viewer. One wagon carried gold vessels canopied under an eternal flame: reliquaries of body parts, crosses, monstrances, and liturgical apparati of tabernacles, censers, and chalices. Priceless silk garments were visible in a case on a second cart, and several other carts were closed and their contents hidden. Within the broad category of sacral treasure fell the imperial regalia and other insignia, archducal, and ducal regalia;[11] these were perhaps the most valuable and least alienable of a ruler's treasure, as they symbolized his authority to rule.[12]

---

of the Middle Ages (Philadelphia: University of Pennsylvania Press, 2000), 10–49. For the broader Habsburg empire, *La tryumphante Entree de Charles Prince des Espagnes en Bruges 1515*, ed. Sydney Anglo (1515, facs. New York: Johnson, 1973); Alonso de Santa Cruz's *Crónica del Emperador Carlos V*, 1–2 (Madrid: Huérfanos de Intendencia é Intervención Militares, 1520); Prudencio de Sandoval's *Historia de la Vida y Hechos del Emperador Carlos V*, BAE 81 (Madrid, 1955); Laurent Vital, "La relation du voyage de Charles-Quint en Espagne" in *Collection des Voyages des Souverains des Pays-Bas*, ed. Gachard and Piot, 3 (Brussels: Hayez, 1881).

9 StAN, Amts- und Standbücher Nr. 316: Geschenckbuch, fols. 9^v – 10.

10 For the medieval practices of relic gifts as well as their association with "articles of secular luxury" at courts, see Karl Leyser, "The Tenth Century in Byzantine-Western Relationships," 116–7 and "Frederick Barbarossa, Henry II and the Hand of St. James," in *Medieval Germany and its Neighbors 900–1250* (London: The Hambledon Press, 1982), 222.

11 Wiesflecker, 5:304.

12 Wiesflecker, 5:304.

FIGURE 19. Leonhard Beck, Karolus Magnus, *Saints connected with the House of Habsburg*, 1518. Copyright © The Trustees of the British Museum.

Three pieces of imperial regalia – the crown, the orb, and the scepter – were the symbols of imperial authority. As such, images of Maximilian and his ancestors often represented the emperor as the individual bearing these three treasures. In another Maximilian project illustrating the saints of the Habsburg house, the representation of Charlemagne highlights the regalia as his most important adornment (Figure 19). At his feet lie his treasure chests, filled with other sacral treasures made secondary by their placement in the image: fine cloths, a cross, reliquaries, and even two relics from Christ's passion.[13] Most crowns not only symbolized political authority, they also were holy relics: both a visible holy presence and an invisible symbol of kingship. Thus the crown of the Holy Roman Empire was considered not only to contain relics, but also as the relic of the emperor-saints Charlemagne and Henry II.[14] At the end of the fifteenth century, regalia, like a ruler's authority, spanned religious and temporal worlds, sacral and sumptuous meanings. Regalia also represented an individual ruler and the legitimacy of an ordered succession: at Maximilian's death, the regalia were displayed on a funeral bier in the Heilig-Geist-Spital chapel at Nuremberg, representing the dead emperor.[15] Regalia and other sacral treasure was displayed rarely, much less often than family jewels and gold plate. Part of the power of viewing it lay in its seclusion during times when it was not involved in rituals connecting the sacred and profane world. Even as the ritual viewings were rare, printed representations of these events began to circulate broadly in the age of print. In central Europe, among the very popular early pamphlets were the relic books (*Heiltumbücher*). Their profusion underscores the late-fifteenth-century emphasis on linked ritual culture and material treasure.

Relic books appeared in the German-speaking world in the second half of the fifteenth century. The first known relic book, printed in 1470, described relics in Maastrich and Aachen, but many subsequent pamphlets detailed relic collections and relic viewings in south-German provinces.[16] The relic books carefully ennumerated the relics held at a

---

[13] The whole project is reproduced in Simon Laschitzer, "Die Heiligen aus der, Sipp-, Mag- und Schwägerschaft' des Kaisers Maximilian I," *JKSW* 4 (1886): 70–288.

[14] Ernst Kantorowicz, *The King's Two Bodies: A Study in Medieval Political Theology* (Princeton: Princeton University Press, 1957), 339; Sergio Bertelli, *The King's Body*, trans. R. B. Litchfield (University Park: Pennsylvania State University Press, 2001); and for a recent discussion of the ambiguities of the Castilian case, Bethany Aram, *Juana the Mad* (Baltimore: Johns Hopkins University Press, 2005), 3–6.

[15] Karl Schlemmer, *Gottesdienst und Frommigkeit in der Reichsstadt Nürnberg am Vorabend der Reformation* (Würzburg: Echter, 1980), 327; also Max Geisberg, *The German Single-Leaf Woodcut* (New York: Hacker, 1974) IV: 111.

[16] Examples include *In disem puchlein stet vertzeichet das hochwirdig heiltum...zu Bamberg* (Nuremberg: Hans Mair, 1493); *Wie das hochwirdigist Auch kaiserlich heiligthum...Nüremberg* (Nuremberg: P. Vischer, 1487); *In disem puechlein ist verzaichent das hochwirdig heyligtum so man in der loblichen stat Wienn....* [Vienna: Joh. Winterburger, 1502]; *Diss Hernachgetrucktes wirdig Heyltum: ist funden worden / Im hohen altar im Thumbezu Trier* [1512]; *In dißem büchlin würt vil wirdigs*

particular sacred site. The relics and treasures were cataloged by sacral type, often in hierarchies of sacred value. Lists of relics functioned as a guide to the display order used on the day of the relic viewing, when the treasures would be carried to a special platform or balcony and displayed to the assembled viewers. The pamphlets often publicized the substantial number of days' indulgence that a viewer would receive for venerating the sacred treasure at such events. Annual ritual relic viewings (*Heiltumweisungen*) were tied to the medieval sacred calendar and, like many religious events by the end of the fifteenth century, were accompanied by a merchant fair. For institutions protecting a particular saint's relics, the viewing took place on the saint's day, and ritual viewings of the great sacral collections containing Christ's relics often occurred in Eastertide, linked to Christ's Passion.[17]

This rise in commemorated relic viewings, and the role of relics as material instruments of devotion, was linked to a late-fifteenth-century popular focus on the materiality of Christ's Passion. The individual instruments of Christ's Passion (*Arma Christi*) were depicted in altars and manuscripts to encourage empathic religious contemplation of his suffering. Each instrument – lance, rod with sponge, nails, hammer, scourge, bucket, crown of thorns, cloth of Veronica, and cross – helped the viewer contemplate a particular moment of the Passion. The appeal of these material objects lay precisely in their physicality; their tangibility allowed the viewer to access and comprehend the spiritual aspect of the sacred. What R.W. Scribner called the "sensual connection" between the viewer and the object functioned across a range of religious images and objects. A material like gold intensified the emotive magnificence of an object and would impress the viewer with its glory.[18] This focus of piety through a catalog of material objects informs the relic books' description of objects

---

heylthumbs so um sant Mathiis zü Trier [1513]. Josef Garber also cites Berg Andechs (1473), St. Georgenberg Tyrol (1480), Würzburg (1483), Augsburg (1483), Nuremberg (1493), Bamberg (1493), Vienna (1514), and reprints the *Hallnerischen Heiligthumb buch* [1520] in "Das Haller Heiltumbuch mit den Unika-Holzschnitten Hans Burgkmairs des Älteren," *JKSW* 32 (1915): i–clxxvii.

17 Examples of Easter-season viewings include Trier, Vienna on the Sunday after Easter, and Nuremberg on the second Friday after Good Friday.

18 R. W. Scribner explicates this point in "Cosmic Order and Daily Life," in *Popular Culture and Popular Movements in Reformation Germany* (London: Hambledon Press, 1987), 14. For the strength of the connection and reforming iconoclasts' eventual repudiation of images on these grounds, see Michael Baxandall, *The Limewood Sculptors of Renaissance Germany* (New Haven: Yale University Press, 1980), 70–93 and Lee Wandel, *Voracious Idols and Violent Hands: Iconoclasm in Reformation Zurich, Strasbourg, and Basel* (Cambridge: Cambridge University Press, 1995).

in text and image.[19] In Latin Christendom, emphasis on the material relics of Christ's Passion began to appear in representations of the miracle of the mass as confirmed by St. Gregory's vision of transubstantiation. In fifteenth-century paintings of this vision, tangible objects and the spiritual miracle are connected through Gregory's sight of a suffering Christ at the altar, with the Arma Christi arrayed around or on the cross behind him.[20] Instruments might also be lined up, sometimes on a crossbeam as in the 1487 Nuremberg relic book depiction of sacred garments and other regalia (Figure 20).[21]

The illustrations of the 1487 Nuremberg relic book reveal another critical aspect of the ceremonial relic display: the human presenter. Selected dignitaries (all clerics) hold the treasures aloft, facilitating the transmission of the sacred to the watchers below, arranged in two tiers and including a scepter-bearing man among the military rank (Figure 21).[22] The Habsburgs did not shy away from associating themselves with these ceremonies of sacred display, even crediting the existence of a relic viewing at Trier to Maximilian I's actions. In 1512, at an imperial diet held in Trier, "the front choir altar was opened, upon the serious command of his

[19] For example, *In disem puechlein.... Wienn*... [Vienna: Joh. Winterburger, 1502].

[20] Gertrud Schiller, *Iconography of Christian Art*, trans. Janet Seligman (Greenwich: New York Graphic Society, 1968), 2: 184–209, 226–7, especially plates 658, 806–71; for other examples from central Europe and Iberia, see Wallraf-Richartz-Museum, *Die Gemälde der Altdeutschen Meister* (Cologne: Gutenberg, 1939), inv. nos. 6, 59, 167; and Chandler Post, *A History of Spanish Painting* (Cambridge, MA: Harvard University Press, 1947), 9 (1–2): 13, 112, 299, 436, 445, 447, 482–5, 650. Miriam Chrisman notes that the graphic suffering of this "special devotion to the mysteries of the death of Jesus" appears in other popular types of printed manuals of piety in *Lay Culture, Learned Culture: Books and Social Change in Strasbourg, 1480–1599* (New Haven: Yale University Press, 1982), 117.

[21] *Wie das hochwirdigist... Nüremberg* (1487), Aiv^v.

[22] *Wie das hochwirdigist... Nüremberg* (1487), Aiv. Lists of religious and secular nobles allowed onto the display pavilions were kept, and included in Johannes Müllner's *Die Annalen der Reichstadt Nürnberg von 1623*, ed. Gerhard Hirschmann (Nuremberg: Stadtrats zu Nürnberg, 1984). For similar representations of acts of display, see *Ein warhafftiger tractat wie man das hochwirdig heiligthüm verkündt und geweist in der heiligen stadt Trier im thün... [1512]*, and *In disem puechlein... Wienn... [1502]*, aiii^v. See Schnelbögl's definitive "Die Reichskleinodien in Nürnberg, 1424–1523," *MVGN* 51(1962): 78–159, here 141–8. She also details how the relationship between emperor and city were negotiated through the imperial relics. I am grateful to Heidi Eberhardt Bate for introducing me to Schnelbögl's article and the subject of the imperial regalia while we were conducting archival research in Nuremberg. Bate's article "Portrait and Pageantry: New Idioms in the Interaction Between City and Empire in Sixteenth-Century Nuremberg," in *Politics and Reformations*, ed. Ocker et al., (Leiden: Brill, 2007), 121–41, which also explores the relationship between Nuremberg's civic display and the Holy Roman Emperor, offers a complementary analysis to the discussion here.

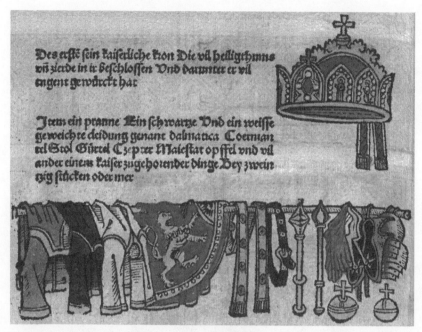

FIGURE 20. Imperial regalia, *Wie das hochwirdigist Auch kaiserlich heiligthum. Und die grossen Römischen gnad darzu gegeben....* (Nuremberg: P. Vischer, 1487), 240ᵛ. Bayerische Staatsbibliothek München.

Imperial Majesty (of which many have heard and read). After industrious search, the valuable treasure of the robe of Jesus Christ our savior was found along with many other relics."[23]

According to a pamphlet recounting these events, Maximilian witnessed the discovery in the cathedral choir, with the secular and religious nobles of the empire and selected ambassadors from the papacy and other kingdoms ranked behind him.[24] In a panel of his Triumphal Arch, designed a few years later, Maximilian took credit for the discovery.[25] The

[23] "Wart der obgemelt fron altar im Chor vffgethan/ und auß ernstlicher begerung Keiserli. M (welch vil dar von gelesen und gehort hat) Nach fleissigen suchen ist gefunden der köstlichschatz der ungeneiet rock vnsers erlößers Jesu christ mit vil anderem heilthum...," *Ein warhafftiger tractat... heiligthüm... Trier...*, Biiᵛ.

[24] *Diss Hernachgetrucktes wirdig Heyltum:... Trier* [1512], esp. Ai, Aiᵛ, Aiiᵛ.

[25] "Zu Trier in der beruembten stat/ Sein Kaiserliche Maiestat// Den Rock des Herren Jesu Crist/ Gefunden hat wie ir dann wist/" Schauerte, 329–30. Habsburg rulers in Iberia revived their association with important relic presentations in the second half of the sixteenth century. William A. Christian, Jr., *Local Religion in Sixteenth-Century Spain* (Princeton: Princeton University Press, 1981), 134–6.

FIGURE 21. Display of relics at Nuremberg's annual viewing, *Wie das hoch-wirdigist Auch kaiserlich heiligthum. Und die grossen Römischen gnad darzu gegeben....* (Nuremberg: P. Vischer, 1487), 240. Bayerische Staatsbibliothek München.

significance of the event is underscored by its position in the Triumphal Arch. As signs of divine favor manifested materially, the rediscovery of Christ's robe and the treasury panels formed the outside foundations of the arch, on the viewers' left and right, respectively.

The relics and regalia housed in Nuremberg and depicted in the relic books were intimately connected to imperial rulership. The instruments of the Passion and particularly the Holy Lance had been symbols of imperial authority long before 1424.[26] Emperor Charles IV first brought the imperial relics – both the instruments of the Passion and the imperial regalia – to Nuremberg. He promised to bring the imperial relics to Nuremberg or Frankfurt in 1352, at a time when he was also granting imperial cities various freedoms in exchange for election support. He then brought the imperial sacred treasure to the city in 1360 during the week after Easter, and again in 1361 to be used in the baptismal ceremony of his son Wenceslaus. The imperial relics were finally transferred to Nuremberg from Prague by Sigismund in 1424 to protect them from the threat of Hussite iconoclasm.[27] Annual public viewings were held on the second Friday after Good Friday. Printed copies of the Nuremberg relic book reviewed the appropriate order and hierarchy of the spectacle. It began with relics of Christ's life, family, and of other saints and martyrs, followed by the imperial regalia, and finally the instruments of Christ's Passion. First among the regalia was Charlemagne's imperial crown, "with many relics and precious decorations upon it," and next in prominence were an array of magnificent garments believed to be Charlemagne's – white, brown, and black dalmaticas, choirmantle, hat, gloves, shoes, and belts – followed by the ceremonial insignia of orb and scepter. The last objects listed before those of Christ's Passion were the swords of Charlemagne and St. Maurice.[28] In Nuremberg, the connection between imperial authority and regalia was strengthened by out-of-season private viewings, some authorized by the emperors for special guests as well as for themselves. At ceremonial entrances (most commonly a ruler's first official entrance), a prince, king, or emperor of the Holy Roman Empire typically visited the relics and heard a mass in connection with the viewing. Some went further: when Frederick III made his formal entrance into

---

[26] Schiller, 189–90.

[27] Müllner (1984), 4, 8–9, 24, 27, 35, 243–50.

[28] "Die vil heiligthums und zierde in ir beschlossen," *Wie das hocwirdigist... Nüremberg* 1487, aiii^v- bii^v; Schnelbögl, 102–3; and Müllner (1984), 244–6.

the city as King of the Romans, he viewed the sacral collection and also commanded an out-of-season ceremony of relic display for all others.[29]

By the end of the fifteenth century, no emperor or king of the Romans was crowned without being invested with and displaying the imperial regalia. Nuremberg patricians carried the imperial crown, robes, sword, orb, and scepter under armed guard to the coronations in Rome or Aachen. This guardianship of the regalia established the Nuremberg envoys' status when attending coronations and the subsequent feasts. The regalian robes were an important part of the coronation ceremony, which was considered ancient by 1520.[30] The emperor or king-elect walked to the cathedral in the robes of his own German lands (Charles appeared as an archduke of Austria, not a king of Castile), where he took a coronation oath. He then changed into the imperial ceremonial garments brought from Nuremberg and reappeared to receive the sword, scepter, orb, and lastly the crown. At his coronation at Aachen in 1520, Charles V required all of the imperial robes at the ceremony, although accounts varied as to whether only the silk choirmantle was laid on him, or if he was arrayed in all the imperial ceremonial robes.[31] The display of regalia at Charles's coronation, either way, reinforced sacral and temporal authority as it had for his grandfather Maximilian before him. The printed Nuremberg relic books also spread the description and images of the imperial sacral treasure throughout south Germany. The much-reprinted pamphlet inventoried the imperial sacral treasures, listing each jeweled gold or silver object or magnificent robe and its sacral worth, in terms of indulgences, for all to see. The symbols of imperial rule, sacred

---

[29] Müllner (1984), 268, 356–8. *Die Chroniken der deutschen Städte vom 14. bis ins 16. Jahrhundert* (Leipzig: S. Hirzel, 1864), reprint (Göttingen: Vandenhoeck and Ruprecht, 1961), 3: 365–7. By the end of the century, viewing the imperial relics became a common ceremonial activity for visiting, and entering, Habsburgs. Examples include *Die Chroniken der deutschen Städte vom 14. bis ins 16. Jahrhundert* (Leipzig: S. Hirzel, 1874), 11:516; Ferdinand's 1521 entrance, "Einritt Ferdinand I," *Anzeiger für Kunde der deutschen Vorzeit* 16(1869):161–2; and StAN, Krönungsakten 1, fol. 95–95[v].

[30] Nuremberg was one of only a few imperial cities with the right of attendance at this "prisca ceremonia," Hartmann Maur, *Coronatio Invictissimi Caroli Hispanarum Regis Catholici in Romanorum Regem* (Nuremberg: Friedrich Peypus, 1523), ci[v]–eii; Johannes Müllner, *Die Annalen der Reichstadt Nürnberg von 1623*, III (Nuremberg: Stadtarchivs Nürnberg, 2003), 457.

[31] See Schnelbögl, 103–5; RTA 2(1521), ed. Wrede (Gotha: Friedrich Andreas Perthes), 95–7; *Römischer Küniglicher Maiestat Krönung zu Ach geschehen* (Augsburg: Grimm und Wirsung, 1520), aiii–aiii[v]. Charles V commanded that a portion of the regalia be brought also to his first imperial diet, StAN SIL 134 no. 1.

authority, and release from purgatory all coalesced at a viewing of the imperial relics.

This was the cultural framework into which treasures from the New World arrived. A first shipment, accompanying the news that Hernán Cortés's expedition had founded the town Vera Cruz, arrived in Spain in November 1519 and was presented to the king at court in April 1520.[32] Initial reactions to the treasure were recorded by humanists at the Habsburg court. They praised the artistry of Aztec[33] treasure, emphasizing their firsthand encounters with these objects and supporting their judgments by citing the many attributes of civilization found in the Aztec Empire. Peter Martyr of Anghiera sent reports on the New World to members of the papal court and to other fellow humanists: he not only described the Yucatan and Mexico's cities, architecture, and government, he also lavished praise on these peoples' artistry. In a section of the fourth *Decade*, he praised them as having achieved genius, or come as close to it as humanly possible. "I wonder not at all the gold and gemstones, but at the skill and workmanship which far exceeds the value of the materials. I am amazed."[34] Charles, holding court in his Iberian kingdoms when the first treasure arrived there, was quick to display the objects.

In 1520, Charles returned to the Low Countries, holding an imperial court at Brussels before and after his coronation as King of the Romans in Aachen. Charles brought with him treasures from the Aztec Empire that Albrecht Dürer saw and described in an oft-quoted passage of his *Tagebuch*. Dürer had traveled to the coronation to reestablish his connections with the Habsburg court. His *Tagebuch* is filled with his impressions of the precious objects and artwork he saw in the Low Countries and the daily reckoning of his accounts, often settled with presentations of his own work. In Dürer's descriptions of the art and sights that he beheld, he signaled that Aztec treasure as distinct from more alienable and reducible treasure. He used the phrase *"köstlich"* (splendid), along with the occasional *hübsch* or *schön* to describe impressive artwork in

---

[32] Cortés's first *relacion* has never been located. What is now often called the first *relacion* for convenience's sake is a letter from the corporation of Vera Cruz detailing their actions. See the introduction to the *Codex Vindobonensis*, S.N. 1600, ÖNB, facsimile printed as *Cartas de Relación de la conquista de la Nueva España: Codex Vindobonensis S.N. 1600* (Graz: Akademische Druck, 1960).

[33] Cortés landed at a site now called Vera Cruz, which is thought to have been located within an Aztec/a sphere of influence that extended out from the Valley of Mexico.

[34] "Si quid unquam honoris humana ingenia in huiuscemodi artibus sunt adepta, principatum iure merito ista consequentur. Aurum, gemmasque non admiror quidem, qua industria, quove studio superet opus materiam, stupeo." Peter Martyr (1521) IV/9, 37.

the Netherlands. For a rare few spectacles, these words of praise were insufficient. For Dürer, Charles's coronation was defined as admirable as had not been seen before: "[T]here I have seen such lordly splendor. No-one, who lives among us, has seen more splendid things."[35] Dürer also employed this phrase to describe the treasure from the Aztec Empire:

> I have seen these things, which have been brought to the King (Charles) from the new golden land.... They are so splendid, that one would treasure them at a hundred-thousand guldens' worth. And I have in all my living days not seen anything, that delights my heart as these objects do. These are marvelously artistic things and I am amazed at the subtle craftsmanship of the people in the foreign land...[36]

Only the coronation, the Aztec treasure, and the sacred structure of St. Michael in Antwerp fell into Dürer's category of the never-before-seen or wondrous.

Both Dürer's and Peter Martyr's open appreciation for New World treasure depended on the recognition of its craftspeoples' artistry. Previous to the Yucatan encounters, Columbus and his successors had developed the practice of stripping local leaders, *caciques*, of their gold adornments and gold treasures in the Caribbean.[37] These ornaments had been perceived primarily in terms of their gold content and seem to have been melted down quickly. Peter Martyr, who saw the few worked Caribbean pieces presented to Isabel and Ferdinand, reserved comment on their

---

[35] "da hab ich gesehen alle herrlich köstlichkeit, deßgleichen keiner, der beÿ uns lebt, köstlicher ding gesehen hat,"Albrecht Dürer, *Schriftlicher Nachlass*, ed. Hans Rupprich (Berlin: Deutscher Verein für Kunstwissenschaft, 1956) I:159, 152.

[36] "Auch hab jch gesehen die dieng, die man dem könig auß dem neuen gulden land hat gebracht: ein gancz guldene sonnen, einer ganczen klaffter braith, deßgleichen ein gancz silbern mond, auch also groß, deßgleichen zwo kammern voll derselbigen rüstung, desgleichen von allerleÿ jhrer waffen, harnisch, geschucz, wunderbahrlich wahr, selczsamer klaidung, pettgewandt und allerleÿ wunderbahrlicher ding zu maniglichem brauch, das do viel schöner an zu sehen ist dan wunderding. Diese ding sind alle köstlich gewesen, das man sie beschäczt vmb hundert tausent gulden werth. Und ich hab aber all mein lebtag nichts gesehen, das mein hercz also erfreuet hat als diese ding. Dann ich hab darin gesehen wunderliche künstliche ding und hab mich verwundert der subtilen jngenia der menschen jn frembden landen. Und der ding weiß ich nit außzusprechen, die ich do gehabt hab." Dürer, I: 155. Jardine notes the connection between wonder, sensual delight, and the urge to acquire in *Worldly Goods*, 124. For further discussion of aesthetics and the marvelous, see Stephen Greenblatt, *Marvelous Possessions: The Wonder of the New World* (Chicago: University of Chicago Press, 1991), esp. 79–80 and Lorraine Daston and Katharine Park, *Wonders and the Order of Nature* (New York: Zone Books, 1998).

[37] Carl Sauer, *The Early Spanish Main* (Berkeley: University of California Press, 1969).

artistry, mentioning only that it was "gold cunningly worked."[38] More typically, he simply reported on the monetary value of the gold shipped back from Indies. In contrast, a significant portion of the Aztec Empire's treasure was not melted down before shipment to Spain. In describing what he had seen, Peter Martyr emphasized that the full value of the presented treasures could not be calculated materially. Hernán Cortés sent several further shipments of treasure: one sent in May 1522 but mostly lost to French pirates in the spring of 1523, and another in October 1524 to the king.[39] With the further presentations, Peter Martyr's appreciation of the Aztec treasure only increased. In his fifth *Decade*, he wrote: "They brought back many valuable collars, of great weight and value, beautifully wrought, in which the artisanal skill transcended the material. No doubt, they have the most cunning craftsmen in all arts, especially gold- and silver-smithing."[40]

Cortés's treasure cargo was accompanied by the public letters or reports (*relaciones*) written by Cortés for Charles's court. These reports were designed to support Cortés's petitions for political legitimacy[41] and to facilitate reception and desired understanding of his splendid gifts. Cortés's evaluations of Aztec culture reinforced the claim that he had subjugated a society that was civilized. In his letters, Cortés detailed Aztec economic organization, trading networks, urban development, skill in many crafts, agricultural ingenuity, and religious hierarchy and practice.[42] This strategy reinforced notions of Cortes's own military acumen in defeating such a powerful antagonist, as well as of his own

---

[38] "auri affabre laborati," Peter Martyr, (1516), fv.

[39] For the three inventory lists of the May shipment, AGI, Patronato 180 Ramos 84–5, 88, Indiferente General 420, L.9, fol. 91–1^v. The October shipment, carried by Diego de Soto, Cortés's servant, had to be escorted safely past pirates from the Azores to Seville, arriving in July 1525, according to Peter Martyr, *De Orbe Novo* in *Opera* (Graz: Akademische Druck, 1966), VIII:9: cxiii^v–cxiiii; AGI, Patronato 180, Ramo 86.

[40] "Praeter constandum aurum, monilia portarunt preciosa multa, magni etiam ponderis et valoris, perpulchre formata, in quibus ars materiam vincebat. Habent namque argutissimos omnium artium opifices, aurariae, argentariae que praecipue." Peter Martyr, *De Orbe Novo*, in *Opera*, V:3: lx^v.

[41] See Ross Frank, "The Codex Cortés: Inscribing the Conquest of Mexico," *Dispositio* 14 (1989): 187–212; Beatriz Pastor Bodmer, *The Armature of Conquest: Spanish Accounts of the Discovery of America 1492–1589* (Palo Alto: Stanford University Press, 1992), chapter two; "Hernán Cortés and the Creation of the Model Conqueror," 52–100; and Viktor Frankl, "Die Begriffe des mexikanischen Kaisertums," *Saeculum* 13 (1962): 1–34 for a discussion of Cortés's predicament and narrative strategy.

[42] Cortés's "Second Letter" was dated October 1520, and first printed in Spanish in November 1522 as *Carta de relacion enbiada a su majestad del emperador nuestro señor por el capitan general de la nueva spaña llamado Fernando Cortes* (Seville: Cromberger, 1522).

humility before the crown. Cortés was careful to represent Moctezuma as the ruler of a vast Aztec Empire in the language of magnificence intelligible to European readers.

Cortés's second letter emphasized the Aztecs' and Moctezuma's eagerness to submit to Charles V's authority. Moctezuma's authority to negotiate and cede sovereignty was crucial to Cortés's rhetoric of legitimation, particularly because the report admitted to a subsequent violent expulsion of the Castilians and their allies from Tenochtitlan. Wishing to impress and flatter Charles with the scope of his new lands, Cortés identified the Aztec territories as an empire. He also equated Moctezuma's status with that of emperor, describing Moctezuma's diplomatic and ceremonial acts as the gestures of European royalty. For example, after Cortés landed at Vera Cruz and met Moctezuma's "vassal" prince, an imperial Aztec messenger arrived to present gifts of welcome from Moctezuma to the powerful Castilian. In the arena of manners and spectacle, Aztec *servicio* and their ruler Moctezuma's magnificent wealth and treasury collections outstripped that of Castilian courts. Cortés was also careful to describe Moctezuma's material trappings as familiar symbols of rule: Moctezuma traveled in procession, he carried a scepter for public meetings, he had a throne, and he possessed a royal treasury.[43] These ceremonial identifications and settings helped identify and give meaning to the treasures sent back toIberia; Charles would be presented with the material artifacts of these symbolic acts.

Cortés's own dominance over Moctezuma was established for a European readership through his descriptions of symbolic interactions between the two men even before Cortés imprisoned the Aztec ruler.[44] The most familiar and compelling act was that of Cortés's entrance into Tenochtitlan and Moctezuma's reception of him. Once in the city, Cortés was met by Moctezuma's litter and procession. When the two greeted each other, Cortés tried to embrace Moctezuma but was prevented from touching him. (Peter Martyr added in his contemporary account that to touch the

---

43 Cortés, *Carta* (1522), bii–biiii. By mid-century, Cortés's secretary Francisco López de Gómara emphasized the regal symbolism of Moctezuma's procession and collections more heavily. See *La istoria de la conquista de Mexico* (Zaragoza, 1552), xl–xlv^v. The 1522 French translation of Cortés's second letter praises the treasure as more "exquisite" than any held by other princes in Europe or Africa, whether Christian, Saracen, Turk, or infidel. *Les coutrees des iles et des paysages, trouves et conquis par le capitaine* (Anvers, 1522), civ.

44 A decade later, this action would be paralleled by Pizarro's imprisonment of Atahualpa. See Patricia Seed, "'Failing to Marvel'," *Latin American Research Review* 26 (1991): 7–32.

ruler was sacrilege).[45] After a brief interlude in which Cortés was greeted by all others in the procession, Cortés went to Moctezuma and placed a necklace on him. Moctezuma then gave Cortés a much more valuable necklace, led him into his palace, and seated him on Moctezuma's own throne to receive a vast quantity of gold, silver, featherwork, and embroidered garments and then, finally, Moctezuma's speech of vassalage to Charles V.[46] Cortes's attempted desacralization of Moctezuma's person, and Cortés's symbolic assumption of authority through his enthronement and tribute,[47] were soon followed by Moctezuma's imprisonment. Certainly in Cortés's narrative, Moctezuma would never again be represented as an independent sovereign, and he died soon thereafter.[48] The rhetoric of Cortés's reports claimed legitimacy for Charles's domination of the Aztec Empire and familiar symbolic categories for the treasure itself.

Cortés had begun sending Aztec treasure along with his accounts back to Iberia as he maneuvered to gain Charles V's approval of his unauthorized conquest. Cortés hoped that the Habsburg court would value the goods, first as gifts from a potential client kingdom and then as tribute from a conquered one. The worked gold, silver, jewels, and featherwork, he wrote in 1522, had a value beyond their material worth: "they are so marvelous that, considering their newness and foreignness, they are without a price. Nor is it possible that any known prince of the world could possess any objects of such high quality."[49] The context of the treasures increased their value as gifts: they were both unique and presents of a

---

[45] Peter Martyr, *De Orbe Novo*, in *Opera*, V:3: lxviii[v].

[46] Cortés's account emphasized his willful interaction with Moctezuma's physical body in superseding what he understood to be Aztec ceremonial beliefs, as well as the celerity and legality with which Moctezuma then ceded his lands to Charles V. Cortés reports Moctezuma's speech as one of submission. J.H. Elliot pointed out that the speech echoed the New Testament by attesting to the ruler's corporeality in "The Mental World of Hernán Cortés," in *Spain and Its World: 1500–1700* (New Haven: Yale University Press, (1989), 36–7. Cortés recorded the phrase as "veys me aqui que so de carne y huesso como vos y como cada uno: y que soy mortal y palpable," *Carta de la relacion* (1522), bii[v].

[47] Accounts of this episode vary greatly. Bernardino de Sahagún's manuscripts, dating from ca. 1555 and 1585, make no mention of Cortés's gift, only of Moctezuma's. Bernal Díaz del Castillo's account dating from the end of the century rearranged the sequence of events and lacks any speech of vassalage during the ceremony.

[48] Pastor Bodmer analyses accounts of Moctezuma's death, *The Armature of Conquest*, 60–79.

[49] "las quales de mas de su valor eran tales y tan maravillosas que consideradas por su novedad y estrañeza no tenian precio ni es de creer que alguno todos los principes del mundo de quien se tiene noticia las pudiesse tener tales y de tal calidad," *Carta de la relacion* (1522), bvi.

newly subordinate wealthy empire and ruler, thus adding to Charles's real and symbolic worth. Although it is not known exactly how Cortés defined the gifts in the shipment of 1519, he did evidently include information about the sovereign Moctezuma and describe the treasure as presents from Moctezuma to Charles V.[50] Peter Martyr noted that the first gifts included a jeweled scepter, several gold collars, and two great discs, one of gold and one of silver, decorated with figures enthroned "like kings," who were actually divinities. Their reception at the Castilian court was just as Cortés wished: they were perceived as precious valuables and adornment from a newly encountered empire. After Charles finally saw the objects, he decreed that they belonged in the care of his Keeper of Jewels, Luis Veret.[51] Ambassadors to Charles's court also interpreted this first shipload of treasure through the symbols of court diplomacy. In a letter to the papal court in March 1520, the Archbishop of Cosenza identified the Indians accompanying Cortés's agents as ambassadors from a prince seeking a treaty with the Habsburg Empire. He categorized Moctezuma's major gifts as religious or regal symbols: the wheels of gold and silver were decorated with images of their gods, the scepter jeweled, a feather crown and other ornaments embellished with precious stones.[52]

The shipment sent in 1522 and seized by French pirates off the Azores had been more extensive. This treasure accompanied Cortés's third letter, in which he describes the violent conclusion to the military conquest of the Aztec Empire. With the changed political situation in Mexico, the symbolism of the treasure had shifted slightly while continuing to represent a subjected sovereignty. No longer gifts from a client empire, the precious objects became unique tribute from a newly conquered territory. Peter Martyr made the political distinction explicitly, describing the ornaments in the possession of Juan Ribera (whose ship made it safely to Seville) as Cortés's portion of the tribute from the conquest.[53] Two lists describe these gifts from Cortés to Charles V, now addressed as "most powerful Caesar." One list is a manifest of the royal fifth of gold and silver, describing each gold and precious stone ornament by weight and melted bullion by monetary value.[54] Cortés distinguished between these objects, with fairly calculable value derived from precious metals, and those in a

50 Moctezuma is "rex" here, Peter Martyr (1521), 30, 37–8.
51 CDIE I: 471–2.
52 *Prouinciae sive regiones in India occidentali* [1520], civ^v–dii.
53 Peter Martyr, *De Orbe Novo*, in *Opera*, V:10: lxxxiiii–lxxxiiii^v.
54 AGI Patronato 180, ramo 88, dated May 19, 1522.

second list. The ornaments of his second list were not evaluated in terms of weight, but rather described as artistically fashioned objects made from feather or precious stones and adorned with gold. A third list designated jeweled and feather ornaments intended for non-Habsburg recipients.[55] These categorizations of treasure by material – feather ornaments in one report and gold objects in another – would be continued in another shipment to Charles that accompanied Cortés's fourth letter.[56] Examining the planned distribution of objects allows us to piece together how types of Aztec treasure might have been understood.

In the shipment of 1522, Cortés distinguished between objects he had reserved for his king and those more modest feather crests and ornaments he had planned to present to religious foundations in the kingdom of Castile and to members of Charles V's court. The extant inventories provide a window into the strategems of gift giving and the transferability of this New World treasure to the Old. Only Charles was to receive items identified as regalia: miters, scepters, and the great wheels figured with divinities, as well as ornaments figured with eagles, in an evocation of the Habsburg eagle. Ceremonial items used in Aztec priestly sacrifices were reserved for Charles and for the shrine of the Extremaduran Virgin of Guadalupe, the king and other major Castilian religious sites were to receive plumed crowns.

Cortés's itemization of his gifts to religious foundations created a spiritual map of Castile. Along with the important shrine of the Virgin of Guadalupe, a favorite of conquistadors before him, Cortés gave a double quantity of ornaments to another religious foundation in Extremadura, the monastery San Francisco in his home town of Medellín. Next in quantity of gifts were some of the great shrines of Castile, Santiago de Compostela and the crucified Christ at Burgos, and two cathedral chapels of Marian devotion, the S. Ildefonso chapel at the Toledo Cathedral and the Virgen del Antigua chapel in the Seville Cathedral. He was careful to present treasure to the royal monastery S. Tomas in Avila and to Sta. Clara in Tordesillas, where Juana, Charles's mother and titular co-ruler of Castile, had retreated. Religious foundations in Oviedo, Toro, and Ciudad Real also were to receive treasure, along with the Hieronymites, named elsewhere by Cortés as acting governors of the Indies.[57]

---

[55] AGI Patronato 180, ramo 85 and 84.

[56] AGI Patronato 180, ramo 86 and 87, a shipment sent with Diego de Soto in 1524.

[57] AGI Patronato 180, ramo 84. Conquistadorial piety and particularly their Marian devotion were marked in the early conquest. For consequent syncretism, see Jacques Lafaye's

Cortés sent gifts to influential members of the Castilian court, both those nobles with hereditary positions and those *criados* who served on crown counsels or in the Casa de la Contratación.[58] As with the religious foundations, the gifts delineated the relative status of court officials. The Bishop of Burgos, Juan Rodriguez de Fonseca, who was responsible for all matters of the Indies until his death in 1524, received gifts similar in quantity and value to those given to important religious foundations: a robe, vestments, a bishop's staff. Other prelates, the Cardinal of Tortosa and the Bishop of Palencia, received the common-denominator gift of an ornamental shield or buckler (*rodela*). Every grantee received at least one of these ornamental shields. The practice of displaying trophy shields of conquered peoples in churches had long-standing antecedents in Castile,[59] and Cortés had described the military functions of the feathered shields in his second letter. The Aztec shield could represent the military triumph over the Aztec Empire. Cortés's hierarchization of treasure, with items reserved for sovereigns, helps explicate the symbolism of the gifts as they entered the Holy Roman Empire in the following few years.

Aztec treasure, while not the exclusive property of Charles V, was closely linked in these early years with him as the King of Castile and ruler of New Spain, the Aztec Empire's new name. Charles had returned to Iberia in 1522 to resolve the *Comuneros* revolt, and he remained there despite pleas that he travel to the Holy Roman Empire for the imperial diets held at Nuremberg in 1522, 1522–1523, and 1524. His aunt Margaret served as his regent in the Low Countries and Ferdinand as first his archducal representative in Austria and then as his representative

suggestive *Quetzalcóatl and Guadalupe* (Chicago: University of Chicago Press, 1976). William Christian discusses the increasing popularity of Marian devotion and identifications of the most important sixteenth-century shrines within Spain in *Local Religion*, 121–5. Cortés's interest in the two Sevillian Marian shrines might reflect his time in Seville before departing for the Indies. The connection between Marian miracles and St. Ildefonsus is described in Christian's, *Apparitions in Late Medieval and Renaissance Spain* (Princeton: Princeton University Press, 1981), 51–2. S. Tomas was a particular favorite of Isabella and Ferdinand until their son's death. For Cortés's perception of Hieronymite power in 1519, see *Cartas de relacion*, CV S.N. 1600, 3ᵛ–4.

58 In the sixteenth century, this office oversaw all traffic between Spain and the Americas. The Council of the Indies, created in 1524 when Juan Rodriguez de Fonseca died, supervised the Casa and other matters of the Indies.

59 "Las colecciones medievales que se instalaban en las iglesias, lo eran a menudo de *trofeos y objetos simbólicos* que expresaban ideas de victoria sobre pueblos y ciudades enemigas."[authors' italics] Morán and Checa, 17; Cortés, *Carta* (1522), aiiii. For other references to feather shields, *Ein schöne Newe zeytung so Kayerlich Mayestat auß India* (Augsburg: Ramminger, 1522), bii.

in the Holy Roman Empire. News of Moctezuma's "voluntary vassalage" and the fall of Tenochtitlan had reached Iberia via Cortés's third letter in spring 1523. Later that year, Charles sent new treasures from his new Aztec territory to his representatives, reminding all who saw them that the realms of the Habsburg emperor were expanding.

Margaret received Charles's gifts at her court in Mechelen in August 1523 and placed them within the public areas of her own suite of rooms, in the library.[60] Margaret's library served as her intimate receiving area, and displayed other princely ornaments and collected information about the world. Among the gifts were a silver wheel, most likely that displayed by Charles in 1519–1520, as well as a mirror and jeweled collars, all objects that Cortés had reserved for his sovereign. She also received weapons, shields, cloaks, and other clothing, decorated with precious stones and feathers. Margaret's own gift giving maintained this distinction between regalian treasure and the symbolically and materially less valuable objects. In 1528, while in the midst of complex treaty negotiations over Habsburg and Valois territorial claims, she presented a sword, helmet, shields, other arms and armor, a fan, and two animal heads to the duke of Lorraine's envoy. Another group of objects (*masse* of cournalines, shield, helmet, bannerette, fan, and a headpiece described as a *tocque*) was given to Archbishop Albrecht of Mainz.[61] Albrecht, who possessed one of the renowned treasuries whose relics were displayed at a relic viewing, had a crucial role in Holy Roman electoral politics. After Charles's election to the title of emperor, negotiations for the election of the next King of the Romans continued throughout the 1520s. Although Albrecht finally voted for the Habsburg candidate Ferdinand, he had promised his vote to a Wittelsbach prince as late as 1529.[62] Just as with feathered shields, Aztec weapons, armor, and feathered helmets could be understood as military trophies and sumptuary goods. Particularly on

[60] Dagmar Eichberger and Lisa Beaven, "Family Members and Political Allies," *Art Bulletin* 77 (1995): 238–44; Dagmar Eichberger, *Leben mit Kunst: Wirken Durch Kunst* (Brepols, 2002), 167–84; Deanna MacDonald, "Collecting a New World: The Ethnographic Collections of Margaret of Austria," *SCJ* 33 (2002): 649–63.

[61] Heinrich Zimerman, "Urkunden und Regesten aus dem K. u. K. Haus-, Hof- und Staatsarchiv in Wien," *JKSW* 3 (1885): cxix–cxx; M. Michelant, "Inventaire des vaisselles, joyaux, tapisseries, peintures, manuscrits, etc., de Marguerite d'Autriche … 9 juillet 1523," *Compte Rendu des Séances de la Commission Royale d'Histoire* 3rd series 12(1871): 61–5. Only the Vienna inventory lists items as gifts to the archbishop.

[62] Alfred Kohler, *Antihabsburgische Politik in der Epoche Karls V* (Göttingen: Vandenhoeck & Ruprecht, 1982): 98–159.

ceremonial occasions, European lords, soldiers and elite commoners wore helmets and hats decorated with elaborate feather plumes.[63]

Charles sent gifts from the Indies to Ferdinand on occasions when their display might expand public awareness of Charles's other new realms. In 1523, Ferdinand began acting as Charles's representative at several ceremonial events in Austria, where he had been sent when Charles took up rule in Castile and Aragon. Serving as Charles's regent in the Austrian Habsburg lands, he viewed the relics and regalia of Hall as part of the entrance ceremony confirming him as Count (*Landfürst*) of Tyrol.[64] During the imperial diet of 1523, Charles sent Ferdinand a letter with the latest information from the Indies, this time a map of Magellan's voyage, spice samples, and a bird said to be a battle talisman against death for kings in the Indies. The news spread quickly during the closing weeks of the diet.[65] For the imperial diet of 1524, Charles sent his brother more lavish gifts. The reception of these gifts, with their symbolism of imperial authority, subsequently became entangled with the onset of the early Reformation's attack against relics and empty ceremony.

The city of Nuremberg had hosted the imperial diets of 1522 and 1522–1523, which had addressed pressing issues of imperial legal and institutional reform, monopolies and taxation for the war against the Turks, and the religious reforms that continued despite the Edict of Worms (1521) ban on Martin Luther's teachings. The 1524 diet at Nuremberg was slow to convene, with the recess dragging on for months longer than planned. To exacerbate matters, the *Statthalter* (vicar) Count Palatine (*Pfalzgraf*) Frederick, whose appointment has served as a compromise between Habsburg and electoral interests, refused to continue serving. Ferdinand arrived in Nuremberg at the end of November 1523. After much negotiation, he was ultimately appointed *Statthalter*, a significant step up in his political authority. He and other representatives waited

---

[63] J.R. Hale, *Artists and Warfare in the Renaissance* (New Haven: Yale University Press, 1990), 42–77; and, for the prominence of feathered headgear, Alfred Asplund, ed., *The Triumphs of Emperor Maximilian I* (Manchester: Holbein, 1873); Pia Cuneo, *Art and Politics in Early Modern Germany* (Leiden: Brill, 1998), 162–76; and Gülru Necipoglu, "Süleyman the Magnificent and the Representation of Power in the Context of Ottoman-Habsburg-Papal Rivalry," *Art Bulletin* 71(1989): 401–27.

[64] Franz Schweyger, *Chronik der Stadt Hall 1303–1572*, ed. David Schönherr (Innsbruck: Wagner, 1867), 82–3.

[65] RTA 3, 896, 901; Jardine, 367–8. For other Christian European rulers' interest in parrots see H. Diener, "Die Kamera Papagalli im Palast del Papstes. Papagaeien als Hausgenossen der Päpste, Könige und Fürsten des Mittelalters und der Renaissance," *AKG* 49 (1967): 43–97.

through the end of the year for Charles's orator Jean Hannart and several princes (the electors of Köln and Trier and the duke of Bavaria in particular) to arrive. Ferdinand also was waiting for his own courier Hemricourt to return with personal instructions from Charles. The envoys from Charles V arrived in the first weeks of January. Hemricourt carried letters dating from August[66] and a set of gifts from the emperor. The gifts were treasure "that came from the said India newly encountered which is now called New Spain" and as such were entered into the inventory of Ferdinand's possessions on January 12, 1524.[67] On the same day, Ferdinand as vicar finally called the representatives together, and it was agreed that the diet would open without absent dignitaries on January 14, after a mass of the Holy Spirit at St. Sebald's.[68]

Ferdinand's new treasure – ten pieces from the vassal Aztec Empire – increased his personal collection of treasure significantly. In his pre-1526 ongoing archducal inventory, his holdings were modest. He had inherited some secular, alienable treasure from Maximilian's treasury: goblets and plate, along with some antique coins, and had subsequently acquired a few more pieces. His sumptuary goods, garments and tapestries, were fairly modest. They had only recently been increased by a gift of the habit of the English order of St. George, brought in December 1523 by an English embassy.[69] Ferdinand's chamberlain did not classify the Aztec treasure in that category of sumptuary goods, but rather as a more restricted category, under the heading *ornamentos* (adornments or ornament). Ornament as a category was implicitly tied to ceremonial adornment and regalia,[70] and Ferdinand's inventory entries support this sense.

---

[66] Wilhelm Bauer et al., *Die Korrespondenz Ferdinands I., Familienkorrespondenz bis 1526*, Veröffentlichungen der Kommission für neuere Geschichte Österreichs 11 (Vienna: Holzhausen, 1912), 93–4.

[67] "que vinieron de la dicha yndia nueva mente f[h]allada que se llama la nueva españa", ÖNB, CVP 7871, fols. 197ᵛ–199ᵛ.

[68] RTA 4:262, also 176–7, 54, 102.

[69] CVP 7871, fols. 1–59, 77–111; Carl Eduard Forstemann, *Neues Urkundenbuch zur Geschichte der evangelischen Kirchen-Reformation* (1841, reprint Hildesheim: Georg Olms, 1976), 121, 127; Zimerman, *JKSW* 3, xci.

[70] The word was used primarily to designate the emperor's ceremonial robes and other adornments. For example *Geschichts beschreybung/ Unsers aller gnedigist[.] Herrn/ des Roe. Kayser Carls des fünfften Belehnung umb das Hochloblich Ertzherzogthum Oster- reich/..durch Kai/ Mai. Brüder/ Künig Ferdinand* ... [1530] and later, *Habitus Prae- cipuorum Populorum, Tam Virorum Quam foeminarum Singulari arte depicti. Tracht- enbuch: Darin fast allerley und der fürnembsten Nationen/ die heutigs tag bekandt sein/ Kleidungen/ beyde wie es bey Manns und Weibspersonen gebreuchlich/ mit allem vleiß abgerissen sein/ sehre lustig und kurtzweilig zusehen.* (Nuremberg: Hans Weigel,

The other three sets of items to be cataloged as adornment were linked to Ferdinand's appearances at the imperial diets. The first lot, brocade robes embroidered with eagles and imperial crowns, had been prepared for the beginning of the 1522 diet. The second lot of ornaments (robes and jewels) were purchased during the 1522–1523 diet, and the third item, a square of black velvet,[71] was acquired before the start of the 1524 diet.[72] The detailed descriptions of ceremonial robes and regalia at coronations, diet openings, and other events in the early sixteenth century indicate that magnificence in dress was an important symbolic component of these events. The choice to place Ferdinand's Aztec treasure into the category of ornament, cataloged on the day that he resolved to open the 1524 diet, implies that these objects were understood or perhaps intended to be displayed in similar ceremonial contexts.

The inventory descriptions of the objects emphasized their provenience, drawing meaning from their distant and symbolically triumphant origins. They came from the Indies, and more specifically from a newly conquered kingdom of the Indies, "that was lord Montezuma's and now is named New Spain."[73] The treasure had been sent to Ferdinand by the territory's new overlord, the Emperor Charles, as Ferdinand was to preside over the imperial diet in his brother's place for the first time. Charles had sent Ferdinand objects drawn from those that Cortés had reserved for Charles or the most important religious foundations in Castile: feathered crowns and ceremonial religious robes of the Aztec Empire. The first four ornaments listed – a cape, two tunics, and a ritual instrument – were identified in the inventory as sacral items reserved for Aztec priests when making sacrifices to the gods and idols.[74] Forty years after Cortés landed in Vera Cruz, Bernardino de Sahagún's Nahua informants explained the significance of the gift of priests' robes in their accounts of Cortés's first encounter with an Aztec ambassador. The Nahua explained that on Moctezuma's orders, messengers had brought priestly ornaments and robes of Quetzalcoatl, Tezcatlipoca, and Tlalocatecutli to Cortés to

---

1577). "Ornamento" also designated ceremonial and clerical robes in *Testamentaría de la Isabel*, 264–336.

[71] His aunt Margaret had used similar textiles to display her Aztec treasure. Zimerman, *JKSW* 3: cxx.

[72] CVP 7871, fols. 196–197ᵛ.

[73] "la yndia nueva mente fallada *de que hera señor montezuma* que agora se llama la nueva españa", CVP 7871, fol. 197ᵛ.

[74] "se pone el sacerdote quando quere sacrificar a los dioses o ydoles" CVP 7871, fols. 198, and 197ᵛ–199ᵛ.

dress him and acknowledge him as their divine ruler.[75] Although it is not known whether the Nahua in 1519 interpreted Cortés as divine, or if any Europeans at the time understood the Aztec ambassador's gifts thusly, the descriptions of Ferdinand's ornaments indicate that the objects were understood to represent sacrality in the Mexican context, to be the regalia of Aztec priests. Five of Ferdinand's other Aztec ornaments were plumed crowns, acknowledged throughout the sixteenth-century Mediterranean world to be emblems of kingship in India. The final two gifts, a tunic and a feathered shield, supported the symbolism of military triumph.[76]

Before the beginning of the sixteenth century, the co-option of sacrality had been commonplace in Latin Christendom. In both the Holy Roman Empire and Castile, Latin Christians had appropriated Jewish and Muslim sacred spaces and objects and knew that the reverse, the conversion of Christian churches into mosques, also occurred in the Ottoman conquest of Constantinople. The sacred in one religion was convertible to another. In the Holy Roman Empire, Christians converted synagogues, recognized as sacred spaces, into Christian churches, often simply reconsecrating them. In part a symbol of the New Testament's triumph over the Old,[77] the practice was extended beyond the reuse of Jewish sacred sites. Reconsecration of a non-Latin Christian religious site was also more broadly a triumph of true Christianity over error. In New Castile and a reconquered Andalusia, Muslim shrines or mosques became churches often dedicated to the Virgin Mary or other Christian saints. As Castilian conquistadors traveled to the Indies, they anticipated the possibility of finding traces of the Apostle Thomas's passage and reviving lapsed religious practice. In the Aztec Empire, as the conquistadors first encountered indigenous temples, they chose to establish Christian churches within those religious

---

75 Sahagun's *Historia general de las cosas de Nueva España*, begun ca. 1555, is extant in the Nahuatl and Castilian Florentine Codex (1578–1579) and the 1585 Castilian revision. *We People Here: Nahuatl Accounts of the Conquest of Mexico*, Book Twelve of the Florentine Codex, trans. James Lockhart, Repertorium Columbianum 1 (Berkeley: University of California Press, 1993), 62–75 and Bernardino de Sahagun's *Relacion de la conquista de esta Nueva España, como la contaron los soldados indios que se hallaron presentes* [1585], ed. S.L. Cline (Salt Lake City: University of Utah Press, 1989), 156–64.

76 CVP 7871, fols. 198–9; Necipoglu, "Süleyman," 412–3.

77 J.M. Minty, "Judengasse to Christian Quarter: the Phenomenon of the Converted Synagogue in the Late Medieval and Early Modern Holy Roman Empire," in Bob Scribner and Trevor Johnson, ed. *Popular Religion in Germany and Central Europe, 1400–1800* (New York: St. Martin's Press, 1996), 75–6, 79. For an example from Iberia, Heather Ecker, "The Great Mosque of Córdoba in the Twelfth and Thirteenth Centuries," *Muqarnas* (2003): 113–41.

structures. They wrote triumphantly about replacing images of Aztec divinities with those of Mary and the saints and leaving the formerly idolatrous priests to tend the purified sacral sites.[78] Such recognitions of sacrality outside Latin Christendom could extend for Latin Christians, to non-Christian holy men: for example, Latin Christians noted in their ethnographic writing that the touch of the Shi'ite Safavid Shah Ismail was said to turn objects into relics.[79]

Moreover, in the case of imperial regalia, a shared interest in material magnificence and symbols of sovereignty crossed religious boundaries. Throughout Europe and Asia Minor, regalia's propagandistic appropriation by political rivals was popular. During the first fifteen years of Süleyman I's reign, which gained him the epithet "Magnificent," he commissioned regalia designed to be intelligible to Latin Christian viewers, as part of his claim to a world empire. In preparation for a serious westward campaign, Süleyman commissioned, along with a throne and a scepter, a "composite crown" from Venetian jewelers combining an imperial crown, a papal tiara, and a military helmet. In 1532, Süleyman received ambassadors from kingdoms in western and central Europe while wearing the crown and carrying other regalia.[80] Süleyman was also interested in pre-existing regalia of Christian monarchs. His agents approached the Fuggers about purchasing a Burgundian jewel in the 1520s, but their offer was refused when the Fuggers judged it ill-advised to sell a known Habsburg treasure to that dynasty's most prominent enemies.[81] The control of familiar regalia also had symbolic strength. To possess the crown or miter of a secular or ecclesiastical ruler was to retain power over them; Charles

---

[78] Amy G. Remensnyder, "The Colonization of Sacred Architecture: The Virgin Mary, Mosques, and Temples in Medieval Spain and Early Sixteenth-Century Mexico," in *Monks & Nuns, Saints & Outcasts*, ed. Sharon Farmer and Barbara Rosenwein (Ithaca: Cornell University Press, 2000), 189–219; Cortés, *Carta* (1522), bvii^v; Louis-André Vigneras, "Saint Thomas, Apostle of America," *HAHR* 57(1977): 82–90. Verónica Salles-Reese discusses the sixteenth-century debate about a possible apostolic sojourn in the New World, *From Viracocha to the Virgin of Copacabana*, (Austin: University of Texas Press, 1997), 136–56.

[79] Palmira Brummett, "The Myth of Shah Ismail Safavi: Political Rhetoric and 'Divine' Kingship," in *Medieval Christian Perceptions of Islam*, ed. John V. Tolan (New York: Garland, 1996), 351.

[80] See Chapter 2 for further discussion. Necipoglu, "Süleyman," 401–27. For the ambassadors' version, see *Wegrayß/ Keyserlicher Maiestat Legation/ im.32. jar/ zü dem Türcken geschickt...* (1532), bii^v–biii.

[81] Johann Jacob Fugger, *Das sibendt unnd letste Büech dises meines Oesterreichischen Ehrenwerkhs Welliches das ganntzherrlich leben mit allen löblichen und ritterlichen thaten des Allerkhünenisten Theürischen Khaisers Ertzhertzogen zue Oesterreich* [copy from 1598], ÖNB, CVP 8614, fols. 6–8; Lieb 2:137–8.

used and withheld the granting of regalia in his political maneuverings with both ecclesiastic and secular electors.[82]

Yet even as Ferdinand's chamberlain cataloged the new ornaments for sumptuous display and Ferdinand himself became Charles's vicar at the diet, hostility toward the connections between material lavishness and religious authority, as well as unreformed religion, was quickly mounting in Nuremberg. The first stages of city-sponsored evangelical reform would occur in this highly politicized context of the imperial diet. January 1524 began with traditional religious ceremonies, both masses for reopening the diet and a procession to purify the community. The storms and flooding in January were so terrible that Ferdinand requested a procession through Nuremberg to avert divine wrath, a request that the Nuremberg city council granted and that, in the eyes of observers, was fulfilled with appropriate piety by the city's people. When Charles's orator Hannart arrived in Nuremberg on January 25, his instructions confirmed Charles's continued opposition to Luther and his expectation that the Edict of Worms would be enforced in the Holy Roman Empire.[83] The followers of reform, and the Nuremberg city council, were not receptive to this demand. As the diet focused first on other issues, religious and political tensions continued to escalate in the diet and the city. Ferdinand reproached the city council for failing to suppress the adherents of the Wittenberg reform, particularly the farmer-turned-preacher Diepold Peringer who called for an end to the veneration of saints and the use of images in religious worship. Despite this pressure, the city council's public written response upheld their support of religious reform and for Peringer. As Ferdinand's stock diminished, a lampoon appeared on the wall of the Imperial castle mocking Ferdinand's reliance on his Castilian advisor Gabriel Salamanca and his Fugger bankers. The next day, Ferdinand that the city council attend him, but only four members of the council appeared.[84]

---

[82] R. W. Scribner, "Why was there no Reformation in Cologne?" in *Popular Culture and Popular Movements in Reformation Germany* (London: Hambledon Press, 1987), 220 for Maximilian's refusal to grant the archbishop of Cologne his regalia. For Charles's maneuvers with regalia, RTA 3:234 and *Warhafftig anzaygung wie Kaiser Carl der fünft ettlichen Fürsten auff dem Reychstag zü Augspurg im M.CCCCC.XXX jar gehalten/ Regalia und Lehen under dem fan gelihen . . .* [1530], Aiii–Aiii^v.

[83] StAN Ratsverlässe Nr. 699, fol. 5; RTA IV: 43, 290–5.

[84] Günter Vogler, *Nürnberg 1524/25. Studien zur Geschichte der reformatorischen und sozialen Bewegung in der Reichsstadt* (Berlin: Deutscher Verlag der Wissenschaften, 1982), 53–61, 135–45. For the events and the text of the Nuremberg city council's response, see Förstemann, *Neues Urkundenbuch*, 152–7; Kohler, *Antihabsburgische Politik*, 70–97; and RTA IV: 478–83.

Ten days later, at Ferdinand's request, the city council ordered a full procession for the formal entrance of the papal legate Lorenzo Campeggio on March 14. The event was marked by ill will. As the city recorded the event, all the imperial estates and clergy of the city gathered to honor Campeggio in a formal entry, but Campeggio failed to fully enact the entry ritual of making the sign of the cross and blessing the assembled people. Other sources suggest that Campeggio had responded to reformer sentiments by avoiding the ceremony. The following day, Andreas Osiander preached against the pope as Antichrist,[85] and public support for religious reform in Nuremberg continued to grow even as Ferdinand, Hannart, and Campeggio tried to muster support for the Edict of Worms. Osiander continued to preach for reform despite Ferdinand's explicit objections, and as Lent turned into Easter week, it was clear that the reform of religious ritual had begun. Traditional ritual practices were halted (including the procession of the *Palmesel* and laying a crucifix in the grave), and Nuremberg citizens and imperial nobles alike received communion in both kinds, asserting equal access to the sacred for both laity and clergy. On March 26, in the face of another denouncement of Luther, the city council declared that this year there would be no ritualized public display of the imperial relics, although the associated commercial fair would be held. Aware that this action cut against the sacral authority of the Habsburg emperor, the decision was recorded, unusually, as a majority vote without any councillor's name mentioned in the council minutes. On April 8, "lance and crown day" arrived,[86] conspicuously without any sight of lance, crown, or other imperial regalia.

The Nuremberg city council's decision to ban the annual viewing of the imperial relics cannot be separated from their determination to support a reformed Christianity and sever connections with late medieval ritual and veneration of material objects. While public safety and order

---

[85] "Welchs also geschechen und auch dieselb kirch eerlich zugericht und mit weppnern besetzt gewest. Aber der cardinal hat in seinem einreiten soliche procession lassen abschaffen, ist auch in die kirchen nicht kommen, darum soliche versamlung und gepreng vergebens gewest... sich keiner cruce zu machen wie von alter unterstanden." RTA 4:44. For Campeggio's failure to act according to tradition as cardinal, RTA 4:729; for the unceremonious entry, Förstemann, *Neues Urkundenbuch*, 158–60. Andreas Osiander, "Ain einfu(e)rung in den passion, in der karwochen durch den prediger zu(o) sant Lorentzen in Nu(e)rnberg gepredigt, 1524," *Gesamtausgabe*, ed. Gerhard Müller (Gütersloh: Gerd Mohn, 1975), I:133–6.

[86] "spere and kronetag," StAN Ratsbuch 12, fol. 229ᵛ and Ratsverlässe 701, fol. 13–13ᵛ; RTA 4: 738–744, 44, 242; Vogler, 60–1.

were always important concerns during the viewing, in previous years and during other imperial diets, the city council had increased its military protection to compensate for the numerous strangers present in the city and proceeded with the viewing.[87] In early 1524, the city council was not yet particularly concerned about unrest among the common folk. In imperial Habsburg eyes, the main source of unrest among the common people of Nuremberg had been the public preaching of Peringer, who had been protected despite Ferdinand's request for his silencing. The printed texts of Peringer's Lenten speeches allow us to discover which currents of evangelical reform were being heard and supported by the city council in Nuremberg. Much of Peringer's criticism focused on what he held to be the idolatrous reverence for saints.[88] Following the rhetoric laid out by Andreas Bodenstein von Karlstadt in 1522, Peringer assaulted the veneration of saints as diverting devotion away from Christ and the scriptures. Worship of the saints was mere idolatry, he argued, and the luxurious materialism of late-fifteenth-century sacrality promoted idolatrous thoughts even more. The resources of the pious would be better spent charitably, helping the poor and needy, than in creating new magnificent stagings for the sacred reliquaries or altarpieces.

In the general call for new forms of spirituality, late-fifteenth-century material forms of Christian culture, such as the veneration of images, the sale of indulgences, and other practices lacking a scriptural basis, were among the first attacked.[89] The church's avidity was condemned as contrary to the common good, and church decorations and reliquaries as symbols of the corruptness of the unreformed church. The city council's decision to not display the imperial relics was a criticism of the papacy's current policies of resistance to reform as well as the papacy's more historical proclamations: a 1452 papal bull had confirmed the imperial relics' presence in Nuremberg and established that now-canceled yearly public viewing.[90] The timing of the decision placed it in opposition to the papal nuncio, Campeggio, and the representatives of the emperor, Hannart and Ferdinand, as well: the city voted against the display on

---

[87] RTA 3:41–2; Schnelbögl, 106–116.

[88] *Eyn sermon gepredigt vom Pawren zu Werdt/ bey Nürmberg/ am Sonntag vor Faßnacht/ von dem freyen willen des mennschen/auch von anrüffung der hailigen* (1524) and *Ein Sermon von der Abgötterey/ durch den Pawern/ der weder schreyben noch lesen kan* (1524).

[89] Wandel, *Voracious Idols*.

[90] Müllner (1984), 244.

the same day that Charles's representatives issued another demand to the imperial cities and estates that they enforce the Edict of Worms absolutely.

The city council's decision to remove the imperial regalia from public veneration also transformed imperial ceremonial authority. By no longer participating in the production and reinforcement of an imperial sacral power, the Nuremberg city council moved to reframe sacrality away from material splendor. They rejected imperial religious spectacle as inappropriate, and in so doing divorced themselves from a previous source of city identity and reputation. The councillors' actions placed them within a broad south German attempt to separate sacrality from overlordship. While the more extreme manifestations of the communal reformation were soon suppressed, rejection of nonscriptural practice furthered the reform of religious ritual in Nuremberg. The annual viewing of relics would not be renewed even after the papal nuncio and Charles's agents Hannart and Ferdinand were gone from Nuremberg. The imperial regalia were stored away, the relics of Christ's passion mostly forgotten and the imperial ornamenta kept for the next coronation.[91] Correspondingly, Ferdinand's inventory reveals no more additions of ornament or splendid garments to his possessions in the next few years of further entries. Ferdinand's austerity, while perhaps a reflection of monetary concerns, also suggests a broader rejection of material "idolatry" in sumptuary display as well as art production and worship. By 1539, Johannes Faber, Bishop of Vienna, lauded Charles for eschewing the display of gold, silver, and ivory treasure, in contrast to his fellow emperor of the world, the biblical Solomon, who lacked restraint in all things and ended up an idolater.[92] In such a climate, the display of treasure was no longer possible.

The disjuncture between intended valuation and an emerging critique of material splendor appeared in the textual representation of the new Aztec Empire at Nuremberg in the spring of 1524. The first Latin translation of Cortés's second and third reports was printed in Nuremberg by Friedrich Peypus on the occasion of the imperial diet. The other books printed by Peypus in 1524, including Luther's vernacular Bible, all supported religious reform. The *Praeclara Ferdinandi Cortesii de Nova Maris Oceani Hyspania Narratio Sacratissimo. ac Invictissimo Carolo Romanorum Imperatori*[93] was translated by Pietro Savorgnano, secretary to the

---

91   For example, Maur, *Coronatio.*

92   Baxandall, 77; Johannes Faber, *Opera* (Cologne: Quentell, 1537–39), cxxxi.

93   (Nuremberg: Friedrich Peypus, 1524). For Peypus's early support of Luther, see Arnd Müller, "Zensurpolitik der Reichstadt Nürnberg," *MVGN* 49 (1959): 66–169.

then-bishop of Vienna, and printed with imperial privilege. Its Latin text spread word about the scope of Charles's territories. It promoted Moctezuma as a sovereign whose authority was manifest in his magnificent treasure and gestures of rulership, encouraging the interpretation of the Aztec treasure as regalian. The anonymous summary "Argument of the Book" listed Moctezuma's court ceremony and his political submission, but also reminded that the religious practices of idolatry and human sacrifice occurred there. The very symbolism of sumptuous treasure also contributed to Aztec culture's devaluation. The translation of the second letter was typeset by March 4, in time to be read during the escalating calls to abandon sumptuary religious display. Temples in the Aztec Empire, the "houses for idols," were described in charged language as more magnificently decorated than other buildings and filled with idols and images worshipped by the populace.[94] Cortés's second letter was not particularly concerned with human sacrifice; such acts were detailed primarily in the third letter as part of the horrifying flight from Tenochtitlan. But the letters and the map of Tenochtitlan had spelled out the very presence of idolatry. They proclaimed the expansion of Charles's empire to new worlds even as they depicted Tenochtitlan's main plaza decorated with a "stone idol" ("idol. lapideum") (see Figure 3). For readers in the imperial cities, descriptions of the splendor of Aztec treasure in temples would resonate with reformers' excoriations in Andreas Karlstadt's *Von abtuhung der bylder* (1522). By loving and ornamenting images, Christians like the Jews before them had created idols, turning churches into temples of idolatry. Karlstadt called individuals who gave gold and silver to images the "Devil's whores" and those images of saints "the Devil's heads." He dismissed images decorated with rich fabrics, gold, and jewels as idolatry and enjoined magistrates to lead the way in destroying all idolatrous objects.[95] Reformed tracts and sermons assaulted the idolatry of extravagant images and relics, papal luxury, and even symbolic or material cannibalism (see Figure 12).[96] In the next few years, rejection of relics became so widespread that imperial propandists like Alfonso de Valdés joined in ridiculing the profusion of relics through the example of

---

[94] Cortés, *Praeclara* 1524, aiii-aiv and "domus idolorum,"c^v.

[95] "Teuffelshuren," "Teuffels kopffer," Andreas Bodenstein von Karlstadt, *Von abtuhung der Bylder* (Schyrlentz, 1522), ciii^v, ciiii^v, di-di^v.

[96] In the following year, Zwinglian reformers attacked Luther and the Wittenberg circle as anthropophagi. Huldrych Zwingli, *De vera et false religione* [1525], *Sämtliche Werke* 3(1914); WA Briefwechsel 5: 170.

the three different foreskins of Christ. He concurred that relics served as a source of idolatry in his defense of the 1527 sack of Rome.[97]

The cultural valence of treasure shifted through the attack on sacral material display across Europe. Its sacral meanings, the source of its symbolic density, diminished even as the monetary value of treasure became more important in an era of increased warfare and threats to the Habsburg empire from the Ottomans. In 1526, while maneuvering to be elected king of Hungary, Ferdinand needed money to finance his election and military costs incurred by opposing the Ottomans and their client king, János Zápolyai. With the help of his widowed sister Queen Mary of Hungary, he gathered gold and silver objects from the former Hungarian treasury and had them converted to specie (despite their potential symbolic value in the face of a rival king) to fund his army. Luther noted that after the siege of Vienna, the papacy also authorized the Habsburgs to melt reliquaries in the Holy Roman Empire to fund the Ottoman wars.[98]

The break between the Habsburgs and their imperial city of Nuremberg, symbolized by the show of wills over the ongoing reform at the 1524 imperial diet, persisted. Despite the city's efforts to welcome their new sovereign Charles in 1520 after he was crowned King of the Romans, Charles had still not honored the city with a formal entry a decade later. Charles's failure to enter the city symbolized the fractured relationship between emperor and city; by custom, the new emperor entered Nuremberg soon after imperial election to hold the first imperial diet. In 1532, when Charles was once again in the Holy Roman Empire, the city learned that Charles chose not to visit them because the city was "Lutheran." Anxious to regain their emperor's goodwill and demonstrate their continued loyalty, Nuremberg sent an embassy to Charles in nearby Dinkelsbühl, bearing several non-sacral treasures as gifts: a valuable jewel and some pieces of gold. The city council began organizing festivities for the hoped-for visit, planning a procession (including banners with Charles's arms and the imperial eagle on either side) and a welcoming

---

[97] For mockery of foreskin relics, see Jacob Strauß, *Ein kurtz Christenlich vnterricht des grossen irrthumbs/ so im heiligthüm zü eren gehalten/ das dan nach gemainem gebrauch der abgötterey gantz gleich ist* (Erfurt: Michael Büchführer, 1523), Bii^v; Alfonso de Valdés, *Diálogo de las cosas ocurridas en Roma* (Madrid: Espasa-Calpe, 1928), 189–92 and David Goodman's discussion in *Power and Penury: Government, Technology and Science in Philip II's Spain* (Cambridge: Cambridge University Press, 1988), 16, 44.

[98] HHStA, Hofsachen, Karton 103, 123–38; Zimerman, *JKSW* 3 (1885): cxxv–cxxix, cxl–cxli; WA, Briefwechsel 5:216, 218. Arjun Appadurai discusses regimes of value in "Introduction: commodities and the politics of value," in *The Social Life of Things* (Cambridge: Cambridge University, 1986), 3–63.

mass at the church of St. Sebald. Yet even in these plans to demonstrate its continued loyalty to Charles, Nuremberg did not soften its stance on symbolic matters of religious reform: Charles would be greeted by the clerics of the city with the exception of monks, and St. Sebald's would be decorated with fine altarcloths and tapestries, but not with the display of sacred relics.[99] Negotiations at the imperial diet over military and financial support of troops for the Ottoman front were the pragmatic focus of concern, but the contentious issue of the appropriate symbolism or sacral components of imperial authority was not resolved or set aside. Charles would not make a first entry into Nuremberg as emperor until 1541. The city council did display the coronation regalia in 1540 for Ferdinand and Charles in 1541, but records note explicitly that the relics of Christ's passion were not included. Similarly, with debates raging over the form of mass, the traditional mass of thanksgiving celebrated upon rulers' entry was not possible. Rather than the sacral displays of pre-Reformation entry, Charles's entry in 1541 was marked by classical and battle themes presented in triumphal arches, pageants, tableaux, and performances for the newly arrived emperor.[100]

Nuremberg persisted in its repudiation of sacral treasure. Some statuary and other ecclesiastical art may have been saved by, or returned to, their original donors, and liturgical vestments continued to be used. With a few exceptions of religious orders' or brotherhoods' collections,[101] gold and silver reliquaries and other sacral treasures were never reassociated with their donors. Reliquaries, except for the shrine of St. Sebald and some of the instruments of Christ's passion, suffered another fate. They were gathered at the Frauenkirche, St. Sebald's, and St. Lorenz's, where they were inventoried, weighed, and eventually utilized by the city of Nuremberg to offset monetary burdens.[102] A few items had been sold in the late 1520s and 1530s, and as early as 1530, the city had compiled inventories of their ecclesiastical treasure holdings in preparation for this

[99] StAN, Krönungsakten 1, fols. 101–13, esp. 103ᵛ, 128; SIL 134, no. 19 fol. 9. This hostility toward Lutheran practice was echoed by Ferdinand upon his entry in 1540. Krönungsakten 1, fols. 120ᵛ–1.

[100] Albrecht Kircher, *Deutsche Kaiser in Nürnberg* ((Nuremberg: Verlag die Egge, 1955), 49–72 and more generally, Roy Strong, *Art and Power* (Berkeley: University of California Press, 1984), 75–97.

[101] Carl C. Christensen, "Iconoclasm and the Preservation of Ecclesiastical Art in Reformation Nuernberg," *ARG* 61 (1970): 205–21; Jörg Rosenfeld, "Reformatorischer Bildersturm – Export ins Nichts?" *ARG* 87 (1996): 89.

[102] StAN, SIL131, No. 22.

liquidation. City officials simply weighed the relics along with their containers to calculate the material value of the reliquaries. Artistry or sacral power were no longer considered in these evaluations. When the final reckoning of the gold and silver weights was made, the relics were listed along with iron, wood, glass, copper, bronze, and stones as dross weight. No recognition of their potential value as sacral objects is mentioned, and there is no record of what became of the relics themselves in the smelting process.[103] The majority of the reliquaries and liturgical objects were melted down in 1552 to yield a sum of about 16,000 florins, when the city needed money for a continued resistance to its former lord, the Margrave of Brandenburg-Ansbach.[104] The treatment of relics as desacralized treasure occurred in other imperial cities. For example, in Strasbourg, the bone relics of St. Aurelia were placed in the charnel house with other peoples' bones, and some of the ornaments and treasures were given to city charities.[105]

The imperial regalia survived to be used in future coronations, but they were now even further removed from public view, appearing only once a generation rather than once a year for the public to see, admire, and, if they were Catholic, gain indulgences.[106] The value of minor regalia had diminished or evaporated as their sacral nature was repudiated as idolatrous. In two decades when the Holy Roman Empire and the Habsburgs were concerned with mustering armies and funds to fight internal and external enemies, much treasure was needed as specie. Charles V's decision, then, to liquidate much, if not all, of his gold and silver treasure from his empire in the Americas thus becomes more comprehensible.

The example of the first treasure from Peru underscores this transition. That first Inca treasure arrived in Castile during the last weeks of 1533. News of this gold- and silver-rich Indian state, the Inca Empire, and its preliminary conquest circulated widely and quickly.[107] The Inca

---

[103] StAN, SIL 131, No. 22, fol. 27–8.

[104] Christensen, 220, Gerald Strauss, *Nuremberg in the Sixteenth Century* (Bloomington: Indiana University Press, 1976), 184–6.

[105] Wandel, 116, 124–7.

[106] By the 1620s, the city council's action was seen as saving the imperial regalia from misuse and idolatry. Uwe Müller, "Herzog Wilhelm V. und das Reichsheiltum." *MVGN* 72 (1985): 118–19.

[107] Within a few months, *La conquista del Peru, llamada la nueva Castilla* (Seville: 1534); Francisco de Xérez, *Verdadera relacion de la conquista del Peru* (Seville: B. Perez, 1534), and *Newe Zeytung aus Hispanien und Italien* [1534] appeared in Habsburg territories alone. In his visit to the court at Toledo in 1534, Hernando Pizarro presented

Empire was the second American empire to be conquered, and descriptive accounts of it presented the familiar triumphal ring. As they had in Mexico, the Castilian conquistadors reported that the inhabitants lived in an organized polity ruled by a sovereign and "natural lord," and that the religious practices included idolatrous ones. They also reported that, as in Mexico, subject peoples in the empire quickly became willing vassals of Emperor Charles V, and that their ruler Atahualpa was easily captured and ransomed. Not surprisingly, the conquistadors described their gold, silver, and feather treasures as dazzling.[108] News of this kingdom was shared within the Habsburg family as had been the news from Mexico. However, Charles V did not make an effort to send any of this treasure to Ferdinand and his new regent in the Low Countries, his sister Mary, the widowed queen of Hungary.[109] Magnificent display of treasure was no longer part of this universal emperor's representation of authority, at least in the territories where calls for religious reform had attracted significant followings.

Certainly, Inca treasure was received in Castile with less attention than Aztec treasure, although it similarly encouraged viewers to seek their fortunes in the Indies. Initially, the crown proposed leaving the treasure, which consisted of gold and silver plate and other objects, at the Casa de la Contratación in Seville. When Hernando Pizarro asked for permission to present Charles with some of the treasure directly, he employed the familiar rhetoric of the marvelous and unique. He promised that the treasure was worth seeing because its like had never been seen before. Pizarro believed that nothing similar had been possessed by another prince.[110] Charles granted Pizarro's request, allowing him to bring "some pieces which are most unusual and of little weight,"[111] but ordered the rest melted down. Charles then relented further, calling a halt to the melting. He further agreed to place no restrictions on the size or monetary value

a declaration of the conquest and the imprisonment of Atahualpa. AGI Patronato Real [2460] Leg. 93 n. 4 r. 4.

[108] For Atahualpa's sovereignty, Xérez, esp. Bii^v and Alonso de Santa Cruz, *Crónica del Emperador Carlos V*, 3 (1922) chap. XXXIV, 164–73. The rhetoric of Inca "tyranny" emerges later in the century.

[109] Mary did receive one set of greves from her aunt Margaret's collection. Michelant (1871), 61.

[110] "son de ver . . . porque cosa que fasta oy no se ha visto en *Indias* otro semejante ni creo que lo hay en poder de ningun Principe." *Libro Primero de Cabildos de Lima* (Lima: 1888), 3:127.

[111] "algunas piezas de las más estrañas e de poco peso," *Libro Primero de Cabildos de Lima*, 3:128.

of the treasure Pizarro was to bring to him, emphasizing that he still wished to see the pieces that were "estrañas," or unusual and foreign. Pizarro presented Charles with two gold and one silver vessels, a retable with two images, a cornstalk of gold, and a little gilded tambor.[112] The extant descriptions do not suggest that the victorious Castilians ascribed asymbolism of sovereignty to the objects. Instead, descriptions identified them as plate (vessels, platters, goblets) and, with the exception of the retable, convertible secular treasure. After viewing his new treasure, Charles sent it to his stronghold at Medina del Campo.[113] Charles's ambitions were focused not on the Americas but rather on his most dangerous rival to world empire, the Ottoman sultan. Planning to attack Ottoman power in North Africa symbolically, Charles mustered all the financial recourses available to fund the assault on Tunis in 1535. Within months, he renewed the orders to melt all the plate for his upcoming confrontation. With its symbolic value as the sacralized symbols of lordship absent, treasure was just so much more alienable metal, like the once-splendid Hungarian treasure in 1526, well-sacrificed to pay for the cost of empire.

---

[112] *Libro Primero de Cabildos de Lima*, 3:129–30. The exact description of Pizarro's gifts vary. For slightly different lists, see Xérez, f. [cvii^v]; Rafael Loredo, *Bocetos para la Nueva Historia del Peru: Los Repartos* (Lima: D. Miranda, 1958). 42–3; *Nouvelles certaines des Isles du Peru. Lyon, 1534*, trans. by Raul Porras Barrenechea, *Las Relaciones Primitivas de la Conquista del Peru* (Lima: 1967), 76–7.

[113] Salinas, 562.

PART TWO

EXPERIMENTS OF EXCLUSION

B etween 1535 and 1540, the artist Peter Flötner designed a distinctive pack of playing cards. Like most German playing cards, the deck had four suits (acorns, leaves, hearts, and bells) with three face cards (king, over-valet, under-valet). Doubtless, its popularity depended in part on the bawdy and scatological images of the individual number cards. Those images commented on daily life and its risible qualities. Yet the face cards, and particularly the kings, also offered a more sober commentary on government and authority (Figure 22). The four kings are all emperors carrying the symbols of rule: royal crowns and scepters. The acorn and leaf suit kings are identifiable as Maximilian I and Charles V.[1] Charles V, the leaf king, wears the insignia of the Order of the Golden Fleece and stands in a pose familiar from printed images of the new discoveries in the Indies: a messenger hands the king a letter in the foreground while a voyaging ship lies in the background. The two sovereigns in the heart and bell suits are equally recognizable. The king of hearts is the Ottoman emperor, wearing his distinctive turban-crown. His bellicose nature is symbolized by the slaughter of infants at his feet and a military camp of tents. Lastly, the king of bells is an Indian emperor whose crown is reminiscent of a papal tiara but lacks two tiers. He is accompanied

---

[1] Detlef Hoffmann identifies the king of acorns as Maximilian in *Altdeutsche Spielkarten, 1500–1650* (Nuremberg: Verlag des Germanischen Nationalmuseum, 1993), 96–103, 185–7. For roughly contemporaneous portraits of both Charles and Ferdinand, see the titlepage of Friedrich Nausea's 1532 *Friderici Nauseae Blancicampiani, . . . Evangelicae veritatis Homiliarum Centuriae tres, nuper excusae* (Cologne: P. Quentell, 1532). Laura Smoller's "Playing Cards and Popular Culture in Sixteenth-Century Nuremberg" discusses the broad social appeal of carnivalesque card images in *SCJ* 17 (1986): 183–214.

FIGURE 22. Peter Flötner, The kings in a deck of playing cards, Nuremberg, ca. 1535–1540. Beinecke Rare Book and Manuscript Library, Yale University.

by a bow-carrying, feather-wearing Indian attendant, while an elephant symbolizes India. Some of the face cards' more political associations and meanings are revealed in a specific version of the deck, one produced on the occasion of Charles V's long-awaited entry into Nuremberg for his ceremonial acknowledgment of the Protestant city's loyalty in 1541.[2] The deck, designed for a member of the Este family, had a song written on the reverse side of the deck: each card carried a commentary verse, and the kings' card verse reminded the card player of the importance of political legitimacy: "Where the common good is found, there is good government."[3]

In 1541, as ideas and information about extra-European cultures and societies proliferated, propositions about cultural similitude and political virtue in the world could be found everywhere, even on a pack of cards. Although each of the kings ruled a suit, they were not equal; suits could trump one another. If the deck of cards represented a hierarchy of kingdoms, it could also be read as a critique of Charles V and, perhaps, his vision of world sovereignty. Although Charles trumped the Turkish sultan or an Indian king, he ranks below his grandfather Maximilian, despite Charles's claims to be the triumphal universal monarch over a far larger expansive territory. The focus of cultural description, or knowledge about other cultures, was beginning to shift by the mid-century. In the following half-century, an expanding hierarchy among the different societies (Christian European, Ottoman, and Indian) can be traced not simply in suits, but instantiated in cultural practices. Christian Europe would, over time, become conceptually categorized above all other peoples and cultures. Such distinctions developed most visibly in ethnographies, and it is there that we turn first, to frame the second half of this book.

Cosmographies of Exclusion

Drawing on ideas of political organization, natural religion, and *prisca theologia*, cultural descriptions of Mexicans and Ottomans, or Indians and Turks, initially affirmed these peoples and their empires as civilized. During the 1520s, ethnographic explications of New World idolatry, circumcision, and child sacrifice resonated with popular beliefs about

---

[2] Ute and Wulf Schadendorf, "Anhang" to "Peter Flötner's Spielkarten für Francesco d'Este" by Wulf Schadendorf, *Anzeiger des Germanischen National-Museums 1954–1959*, 169.

[3] "Wo gemeiner nutz gefodertt wird, da ist gut Regimente, " Hoffmann, 96–103.

historic and contemporary Jewish and Muslim practices. Jews were documented, biblically, as committing all three acts, while Turks were believed to limit themselves to two. They refrained from sacrificing children, but as popular illustrations reminded the viewer, they did kill children during warfare. In the 1530s and 1540s, when confessional doctrine was increasingly defined, texts of cultural description drew on those earlier works while continuing to expand the breadth of their coverage and to sharpen their cultural valuations. Some of the large volumes produced in these decades advertised themselves as compendia of individual ethnographies. Thus, Simon Grynaeus's 1532 *Novus orbis regionum ac insularum veteribus incognitarum*[4] compiled sources about lands outside of Latin Christendom that he presumed were unfamiliar to his readers. Along with descriptions of the east Indies, Sarmatia, Prussia, Muscovy, Tartaria, the Holy Land, and the African coast, he included several sources on the west Indies: Columbus, Vespucci, and Peter Martyr of Anghiera's first four *Decades*. Grynaeus reprinted Peter Martyr's New World descriptions without alteration, although he chose not to include the already published fifth through eighth *Decades* detailing Cortés's conquest of Mexico. Grynaeus did not devote much coverage to the Ottoman lands, either, perhaps considering them not sufficiently "unknown." In reproducing Peter Martyr's fourth *Decade*, Grynaeus included a description of Yucatec religious practices for his readers. Even so, Grynaeus marshalled arguments against other non-Christian religious doctrine: while living in Basel, he blocked a proposed Latin print edition of the Qur'an in 1536 ostensibly on religious grounds.[5] Two years after Grynaeus's compilation appeared, Michael Herr produced a German version of Grynaeus's work as *Die Newe Welt* (1534). Herr rejected neutral description of the diversity of rites and announced that his cosmography would instruct the reader about the devil's activities in the world.[6]

A cultural description that continued to argue for religious relativism risked being criticized for heterodoxy. The series of cosmographies begun by Sebastian Franck in 1530 and concluded with his *Weltbüch* in 1534

---

[4] *Novus orbis regionum ac insularum veteribus incognitarum* (Paris: Jehan Petit, 1532). Grynaeus was a Protestant scholar based in Basel. For an introduction to the text and Grynaeus's interest in the physical world, see Jan. N. Pendergrass, "Simon Grynaeus and the Mariners of *Novus orbis* (1532)," *Medievalia et Humanistica*. n.s. 19 (1993): 27–45.

[5] Hartmut Bobzin, *Der Koran im Zeitalter der Reformation* (Stuttgart: Steiner, 1995), 185. For economic motivations, see Mathew McLean, *The Cosmographia of Sebastian Münster* (Aldershot: Ashgate, 2007), 42.

[6] *Die Newe Welt* (Strasbourg: Georg Ulrich von Andla, 1534), *iiii^v.

demonstrate the difficulties of such a project. Soon after the appearance of Franck's *Chronica und Beschreibung*, a 1530 German translation and reinterpretation of Georgius's *Tractatus* and Luther's forward, Franck left Nuremberg to avoid censure for his heterodoxy and settled in Strasbourg. There, his earlier text was soon superceded by the *Chronica, Zeytbuch vnd geschychtbibel* (1531) and the *Weltbüch* (1534), lengthier chronicles discussing the religion and histories of empires, peoples, and rulers of all the world. The *Weltbüch*, the culmination of his cosmographic efforts, discussed the world in four books: Africa, Europe, Asia, and finally America. Although Franck had begun his ethnographic writing relying on Georgius of Hungary, his sources in the *Weltbüch* ran the gamut of available classical and contemporary texts (including an open reliance on Boemus, Vespucci, and Cortés).[7] Franck's world-spanning compendia expressed his increasingly extreme position of religious relativism. In these texts, Franck continued the categories of cultural description utilized by earlier cosmographers: social customs, government organization, regulations, established religious practices, doctrine, and laws.[8] As he expanded his cosmographies, Franck laid out the basis for his position of relativity: errors could be found throughout the entire world and each sect contained only a portion of divine truth.[9] For Franck, only the spirit determined godliness.[10] This tenet allowed Franck to admire spiritual possibilities beyond works or faith, Muslim or Christian, Catholic or reformed, of "ein frech/ rauch/ wild leben" ("a bold, raw, wild life").[11]

---

[7] Franck's publication record is in Christoph Dejeung, "Sebastian Franck," *Bibliotheca Dissidentium* 7 (Baden-Baden: Valentin Koerner, 1986), 39–117. Franck also published a translation of the *Tractatus*, a portion of Erasmus's *Vlti. Consultatio* discussing Turkish origins, Sabellicus's report on Turkish military strength, and additional material on the sects of Christianity in *Auß Rathschlage Herren Erasmi von Roterdam/ die Türcken zubekriegen...* [Egenolff, 1531]. In *Weltbüch* (Tübingen: Ulrich Morhart, 1534), Boemus is referenced on vi^v–vii, Vespucci on ccxxv^v, and Cortés on ccxxix.

[8] Franck listed his topics in the self-consciously preliminary *Chronica unnd Beschreibung der Türckey* (Augsburg: Steiner, 1530) as "art vnd aygenschafft/weyß/ pollicey/ regiment/ gestalten religionen/ glauben vnd gesatzen," Oiii^v and in the Weltbüch as "leben/ wesen/ glauben und regimenten...manifaltig sect...dz schier sovil glauben und Gotsdienst seind," iii.

[9] "[I]ch glaub/ yrthum gee durch die gantze welt aus vnd kein sect hab es gar errathen," Sebastian Franck, *Chronica/Zeytbuch und geschychtbibel* (Strasbourg: Beck, 1531), kii.

[10] Patrick Hayden-Roy, *The Inner Word and the Outer World* (New York: Peter Lang, 1994), 27–30, 95–8 discusses Franck's charge of heresy against Erasmus for his disagreement on this point.

[11] Franck, *Chronica...der Türckey*, Oiii. This pair of adjectives *rauch/wild* was also applied to post-biblical Europe in *Ain über Schönlesen/ Von den Wilden rauhen menchen*

Such a life could be lived by a wild man, free from society's constraints in the forests of Europe or the New World. Franck's cosmographies sought to detail the range of cultures in the world, including ones perhaps closer to God than reformed Christianity. As a reformer who critiqued empty ceremonies and rites, all human art and human-invented wisdom (including superstitious practices like idolatry) was fruit from the poisoned tree of knowledge.[12] Thus, the Qur'an, Talmud, and papal decretals were all comparable.[13] Franck inverted the positive evaluation of civilization found in previous cultural descriptions, thereby rejecting humanist, Platonic praise of human invention and wisdom.

Franck closely associated idolatry with human sacrifice, reminding the reader of sacrifice's origin: it had originated with the Ammonites' worship of the idol Moloch, as they copied Abraham's willingness to sacrifice his son.[14] After listing historic examples of idolatry and human sacrifice, Franck turned to a severe critique of Latin Christendom for its idolatrous practices. Following Karlstadt and Zwingli, he argued that unreformed churches were worse than "heathen temples" because they were adorned with idolatrous objects. Unreformed Latin Christians were "vain heathens and idolaters" like the Jews and the Turks; they practiced "magic and idolatry" more than had the Egyptians.[15] Comparing Yucatec and Mexican religious practices with more familiar Jewish and Christian ones, Franck concluded that Yucatec and Mexican religion in the Americas paralleled unreformed religion, whether Jewish or Christian, in Europe. Not only did child sacrifice in the Americas correspond to Jewish practice, but "temples" in the Yucatan and in Europe were similarly adorned with gold, silver, and idolatrous images hanging on the walls.[16] Franck's theological stance on the spirit, which made possible this comparative critique, was soon judged unacceptable in the Holy Roman Empire. By 1540, Franck was condemned as a dangerous heretic by Protestant reformers as well as the Catholic church.[17]

---

der nachkumen/ von den Sünen Noel wie Sy in erdgräben mit wylden tierheüten bedeckt lange zeit gewonet haben.... (Augsburg: Raminger, 1522).

[12] Sebastian Franck, *Von dem Bawm deß wißens güts und böses* (Ulm, 1534) in *Sämtliche Werke: Kritische Ausgabe mit Kommentar,* 4 (Bern: P. Lang, 1992).

[13] Franck, *Weltbüch,* cvi[v].

[14] Franck, *Weltbüch,* xxi[v].

[15] "Heydnische tempel" and "eittel Heyden und abgötterer," cxxvi–cxxvi[v], "zauberei unnd abgötterei" cxxxiii, Franck, *Weltbüch.*

[16] Franck, *Weltbüch,* ccxxvii[v]–ccxxxii.

[17] For Franck's condemnation, Steven Ozment, *Mysticism and Dissent* (New Haven: Yale University Press, 1973), 139–67.

In comparison to Sebastian Franck, the humanist scholar Sebastian Münster negotiated the challenge of describing the world with much greater success. His *Cosmographia* initially appeared as a limited survey focusing on Europe (1544) but expanded into a compendium nearly double the length. This version, appearing in a German and a fuller Latin edition in 1550,[18] contained material excerpted from the classical canon as well as texts by Ludwig Vartoman, Johann Boemus, Polydore Vergil, Christopher Columbus, and Amerigo Vespucci dating from the first twenty years of the sixteenth century.[19] The expanded *Cosmographia* circulated widely, with multiple editions and translations into French and Italian. The original structure of the *Cosmographia* was retained in its more elaborated version: book 1 discussed cosmography and geography, followed by book 2 on western Europe from England to Italy, book 3 on the Germanies (including Bohemia), book 4 on eastern Europe and the Turks as successors to the Byzantine Empire, book 5 on Asia and the new islands of the East and West Indies, and book 6 on Africa. The 1550 Latin version of the text replicated much of Boemus's forward, including its justifications of ethnographic knowledge for the edification of the armchair or traveling reader. Münster, however, added an additional justification, made transparent in the title and prefatory pages. Münster dedicated his 1,200-plus-page description of the world's cultures to the "most invincible of emperors, Caesar Charles V," proposing that the *Cosmographia* could serve as a tool for empire to help expand and commemorate Charles's rule.[20] The title page itself displayed the book's scope in an orderly and hierarchical depiction of arms. The Holy Roman Emperor, identified through his Habsburg arms, ranked highest on the page, in a row of arms-displaying rulers representing kingdoms ranging from Scotland to Sicily. Below the independent crowns of Europe appeared a second row of the ranked spiritual and temporal princes of the Holy Roman Empire. Four troublesome military foes – Turks, Persians,

---

[18] The pre-1550 abbreviated editions were in German, with the 1544 edition numbering more than 600 pages. Karl Heinz Burmeister's *Sebastian Münster* (Basel: von Helbing & Lichenhahn, 1969), xv–xvi. Münster's German and Latin editions of 1550 contain more than 1,100 pages. The editions referenced here are the German *Cosmographei oder beschreibung*... (Basel: Heinrich Petri, 1550; facsimile Amsterdam: Theatrum Orbis Terrarum, 1968) and the first Latin edition, *Cosmographiae universalis Lib. VI* (Basel: Heinrich Petri, 1550). There was also a Latin edition in 1552. Münster died in 1552, so these editions contain his last major revisions.

[19] Münster, *Cosmographiae universalis*, [6]ᵛ. Classical authors cited include Pomponius Mela, Diodorus Siculus, Solinus, and Pliny.

[20] Münster, *Cosmographiae universalis*, 2–6ᵛ.

Tartars, and an unspecified Muslim ruler named "Sultan" – flanked the title on the right and left sides. An image of the spice-growing Indies, signified by labeled nutmeg and pepper trees, a turbaned feather-wearing Indian, and an elephant, appeared along the base of the page (Figure 23).

In both text and accompanying woodcuts, Münster focused more on sensational and outlandish information than on his stated wish that the *Cosmographia* inform the would-be world ruler. The discussions of peoples in the Americas and the Ottoman Empire emphasized cultural distance in practices rather than similitude and shied away from doctrinal issues. For the New World, Münster relied primarily on Columbus's and Vespucci's accounts of Caribbean and Brazilian peoples as uncivilized practitioners of anthropophagy, including a chapter "Canibali anthropophagi" with images of dismemberment (Figure 24).[21] He ignored the city-states of central Mexico and only briefly mentioned the Yucatan as the location of a "great city with magnificent dwellings,"[22] sidestepping discussions of religious doctrine. Almost two-thirds of Münster's section on the Turks covered the history of the expanding Ottoman Empire, followed by chapters on military organization, domestic customs (including their prohibition of images and their consequent conviction that Christians committed idolatry), administrative organization, and then religion. Within the chapter on religious matters, ostensibly centered on Turkish beliefs, he instead focused on religious institutional organization. This discussion was followed by chapters on temples and ceremonies, one doctrinal chapter on salvation, and then chapters on fasting, circumcision, justice, and funerary practices. The section on Turks concluded with the fates of Christians taken into captivity or born subjects of these Muslim people.[23]

Within this discussion, Münster acknowledged that Turkish Muslims believed in one God and recognized their descent from Abraham. He emphasized their divergence from the Old and New Testaments by reminding the reader that they followed their own prophet, Muhammad. Given Münster's interest in the sensational, his treatment of the Muslim practice of circumcision unsurprisingly underscored its disturbing distance from true faith. The age of circumcision was eight years rather than the eight days observed by Jews. While the text describes the accompanying feast and the preparation of the ox, the image is borrowed from the

[21] Münster, *Cosmographiae universalis*, 1100 and *Cosmographei*, mclxxxvi.
[22] "magna urbs cum magnificis aedibus," in Münster, *Cosmographiae universalis*, 1112; and see *Cosmographei* [mcxcii].
[23] Münster, *Cosmographiae universalis*, 956–78 and *Cosmographei*, mlxxvi–mlxxxiii.

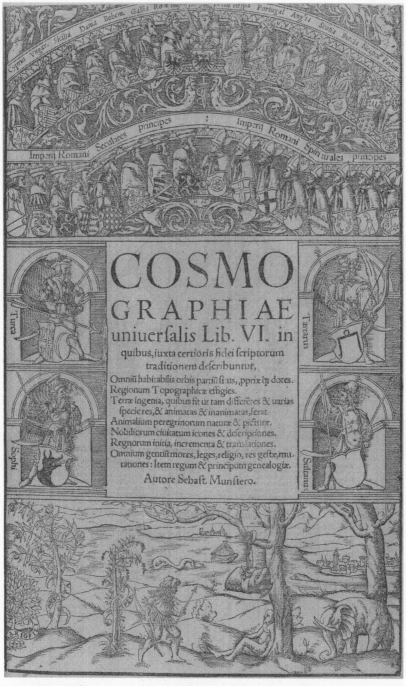

FIGURE 23. Title page, Sebastian Münster, *Cosmographiae universalis lib.*
VI ... (Basel: Heinrich Petrus, 1550). Courtesy of the John Carter Brown Library
at Brown University.

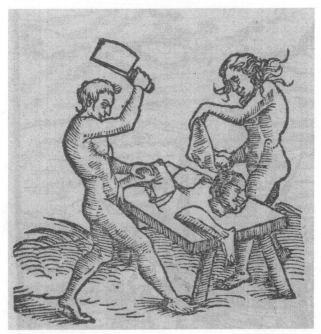

FIGURE 24. Cannibals, Sebastian Münster, *Cosmographiae universalis lib. VI...*, (Basel: Heinrich Petrus, 1550), 1100. Courtesy of the John Carter Brown Library at Brown University.

discussion of gelding in *Liber ruralium commodium*.[24] For the reader, the sensational effect of the page was to invite a comparison between human circumcision and gelding a bull (Figures 25 and 26). Münster claimed that conversion to Islam was irrevocable, presenting the act of circumcision as the moment of apostasy that could not be reversed.[25] After describing the festivities celebrating the circumcision of a voluntary Christian convert to Islam, he detailed the extreme pressures to convert faced by captive Christian men. Münster informed the reader that involuntary circumcision was meted out as punishment for speaking out against the Muslim religion.[26]

In the *Cosmographia*, circumcision was also described as a heretical eastern Christian practice. During the first half of the sixteenth century,

---

[24] Pietro de Crescenzi, *Liber ruralium commodium* (Speyer: Peter Drach, 1493), cxiii.

[25] "ut abnegata Christiana fide circumcidantur," Münster, *Cosmographiae universalis*, 977, and more fully 974–8. Also, *Cosmographei*, mlxxxi–ii.

[26] Münster, *Cosmographiae universalis*, 976–8 and *Cosmographei*, mlxxxii. In Iberia, contemporaries knew that involuntary circumcision was not practiced by Muslims.

FIGURE 25. Woodcut in chapter "On Circumcision of the Turks," Sebastian Münster, *Cosmographiae universalis lib. VI...*, Basel: (Heinrich Petrus, 1550), 974. Courtesy of the John Carter Brown Library at Brown University.

cultural descriptions of Ethiopians increasingly emphasized the distance between these peoples and Latin Christians. At the beginning of the sixteenth century, Ethiopia was the likely location of Prester John's kingdom and known to have not accepted the Council of Chalcedon's 451 position on the nature of Christ. Johann Boemus had reported on the presence of great temples, married priests, a devotion to the Apostle Thomas, and religious orders following the direction of saints Anthony, Augustine, and Macarius. Boemus's account also noted the proximity of Muslims to Ethiopia, adding that Ethiopia's western neighbor, Libya, had been peopled by "Moors."[27]

These elements were expanded in Portuguese humanist Damião de Gois's *Fides, Religio, Mores que Aethiopum sub Imperio Preciosi Ioannis* (1540),[28] which identified itself as the translation of an Ethiopian priest's

[27] Boemus, Johann, *Repertorium librorum trium de omnium gentium ritibus* (Augsburg: Wirsung, 1520), 8ᵛ–9ᵛ; Franck also notes this rejection of the Council of Chalcedon in the *Weltbüch*, vii.

[28] *Fides, Religio, Mores que Aethiopum sub Imperio Preciosi Ioannis (quem vulgo Presbyterum Ioannem vocant)* (Louvain: Rutger Rescius, 1540; reprint Lyon: Tornaesius

FIGURE 26. Gelding a young bull, Pietro de' Crescenzi, *Liber ruralium commodium* (Speyer: Drach, ca. 1493), cxiii. This item is reproduced by permission of The Huntington Library, San Marino, California.

description. Gois confirmed pre-existing understandings of Ethiopian religious practice and doctrine, adding further material and explanatory glosses to this information. According to Gois, Ethiopian practices appeared to be related to both Old Testament Solomonic rites and those of New Testament Christianity. Gois reported that Ethiopian Christians held annual baptisms in honor of the baby Jesus and practiced male and female circumcision. Accounts that the Ethiopians had practiced male

and Gazeius, 1561). For background, Elisabeth Feist Hirsch, *Damião de Gois: The Life and Thought of a Portuguese Humanist, 1502–1574* (The Hague: Martinus Nijhoff, 1967), 147–57 and Jeremy Lawrance, "The Middle Indies: Damião de Góis on Prester John and the Ethiopians," *Renaissance Studies* 6 (1992): 306–24.

circumcision dated back to Herodotus, but Gois's explanation of why they continued to do so in the present day intensified links between Ethiopian and Jewish practice. Gois dated female circumcision to the queen of Sheba's visit to Solomon, her conversion to his faith, and the conception of her heir.[29] Because the Portuguese actively cultivated ties with Ethiopians against the Ottomans and other Muslim powers in the early decades of the sixteenth century, the Ethiopians had been gingerly welcomed at the Portuguese court in 1514[30] as Christians with widely divergent rites. *Fides, Religio, Mores...* contributed to keeping the doctrinal differences behind the divergent rites vague, softening a reader's awareness of significant theological differences held by the Ethiopians, including their rejection of the Council of Chalcedon. Yet even this softened information was deemed too sensitive for some vulnerable readers: *Fides, Religio, Mores...* was prohibited in Portugal, on the grounds that it would confuse recent converts from Judaism to Christianity. The prohibition did not end its circulation; it appeared again as an appendix to a French 1561 edition of Boemus, along with descriptions of the northern lands first added in 1536 and 1542 editions.[31] As Gois acknowledged, mistaking the Ethiopian Christians for adherents to Jewish or Muslim practice was easy to do. Precisely the practices of annual baptism and the circumcision of women, which seemed to be excessive and unwarranted erroneous interpretations of the Abrahamic and Christian covenants, confirmed that the Ethiopians were Christian.[32]

Although Sebastian Münster was engaged in an ongoing dispute with Gois over the nature of proper ethnographic sources, he acknowledged his indebtedness to Gois's *Fides, Religio, Mores...* in the *Cosmographia*'s chapters on the Ethiopians. His adaptation demonstrated a keen awareness of reader interest in these circumcising Christians. Münster included Gois's details of both male and female circumcision, embellishing by describing the Ethiopians as "Moors" who did not wear clothing and were black in color. The Hebraist Münster did not explicitly invoke Jewish religion to discuss circumcising practices, as he had with the Muslims. In the 1550 version of the *Cosmographia*, Münster organized the

---

[29] Gois, 58–76.
[30] Kate Lowe, "'Representing Africans': Ambassadors and Princes from Christian Africa to Renaissance Italy and Portugal, 1402–1608," *Transactions of the Royal Historical Society*, 6th ser., 17 (2007), 107.
[31] (Lyon: Tornaesius and Gaeius, 1561); (Louvain: Franciscus Justus, 1536); and (Antwerp: Steelsius, 1542).
[32] Gois, 74–5.

FIGURE 27. Ethiopian, Sebastian Münster, *Cosmographiae universalis lib. VI...*, (Basel: Heinrich Petrus, 1550), 1145. Courtesy of the John Carter Brown Library at Brown University.

Ethiopian material so that it became the final chapter, closing with a text in "Hebraei Moderni" that Münster claimed had come from Prester John via Constantinople.[33] The entire compendium concluded with this textual description and the accompanying illustration of Ethiopians as disturbing indeterminate people, half Christian and half Jewish in religion and somehow also "Moors" in physical appearance and close association with Turkish rule (Figure 27).

---

[33] Münster, *Cosmographiae universalis*, 1145–63. The German-language *Cosmographei* does not contain the Hebrew passage, although it does discuss Ethiopians in mccxxxi–ii.

For Boemus in 1520, circumcision had been a practice of the Jews and the Egyptians from whom they had learned it. By the early 1520s, it was also a practice ascribed to idolatrous Yucatan Indians and had encouraged Peter Martyr Anglerius to conflate the peoples of the Yucatan with the stubborn Jews. By the 1550s, circumcision was known to be found east of Europe, in contemporaneous Ethiopia. The Latin church had judged it unnecessary as recently as the fifteenth-century Council of Florence; by 1540, both Reformed and papal authorities dismissed it again as a nonsensical and non-Christian practice.[34] In subsequent decades, ethnographies would associate female circumcision further with eastern Christians, who stood outside of the true Latin Christian faith. Pierre Belon du Mans's *Voyage au Levant* (1553) cited it as a practice found among both Coptic and Persian women while Andre Thevet's *Cosmographie universelle* (1575) attributed the practice to Persian, Ethiopian, and Coptic Christian women.[35] Rather than a sign of Abrahamic covenant, circumcision had, by the second half of the sixteenth century, become the failure to be truly Christian. Jacobite and Coptic churches were marked as superstitious and perhaps contaminated by Turkish or Jewish practice. By the time Thevet wrote in 1575, circumcision had become the mark not simply of unregenerate idolaters (Yucatan, Jewish, or Muslim) but other heterodox Christians: black Ethiopians and adherents of other eastern churches, churches that had, arguably, been tainted by their proximity to Islam.

While Münster popularized an estrangement from the practices and non-Christian affinities of Ethiopian and eastern Christians, other concerns dominated ethnographic texts in Iberia, where Münster's *Cosmographia* was not translated into the vernaculars. Unsurprisingly, descriptions of New World cultures were more extensive in those compendia. By the 1540s, the Aristotelian criteria for culture had been deemed insufficient. In his lectures on the Indies given in Salamanca (1539), Francisco de Vitoria acknowledged that Indians possessed attributes of civilized society but had not judged those markers of civilization to be the decisive criteria in his evaluation of them. Subsequent authors offered their solutions to the problem of how to understand and evaluate the cultures and

---

[34] Nicholas of Cusa had reminded readers of the Council of Florence's decision in *De pace fidei* (1456). David C. Steinmetz attributes the intensified 1530s-era condemnation to concerns over Sabbatarianism in "Calvin and Abraham," *Church History* 57 (1988): 443–55.

[35] Pierre Belon du Mans, *Voyage au Levant* (1553; Paris: Chandeigne, 2001), 490–2; Andre Thevet contrasts them with Turkish women, who were not circumcised, *La Cosmographie universelle* (Paris, Pierre Huillier, 1575), 75.

peoples of the New World, given those peoples' predilections for human sacrifice and idolatry.

Francisco Tamara's Castilian translation and revision of Johannes Boemus's cosmography, *El libro de las costumbres de todas las gentes del mundo, y de las indias* (1556), incorporated Castilian texts absent from Boemus.[36] Tamara did not preserve neutrality in his discussion of the Americas. He announced his intentions in his translation of Boemus's introduction, elaborating on the distinctions between cultures in which people ordered their lives through reason and those in which they did not. Possessing reason could not be separated from adherence to the Latin Church.[37] Tamara distinguished between Christians and infidels, civilized and barbarian, Spaniards and "Moors and Turks" or the impure and idolatrous.[38] Tamara's text also restructured the order of Boemus's cosmography. Boemus had followed his presentation of two theories of the world's creation (the "true" version by theologians and the "false" by older philosophers) with a discussion of cultures in three books: Africa in book one, Asia (including Christianity) in book two, and Europe in book three. Tamara inverted Boemus's order of the continents so that the book moved from most to least civilized and Christian. Europe appeared first, then Asia, and finally Africa, in which he included the Americas. For the peoples of the Americas, he highlighted the demonic influences that led them to practice human sacrifice and engage in idolatry. Only with the arrival of Christianity did they finally live as men and as Christians, free and civilized.[39]

Even as Tamara was moving toward the denigration of non-Christian practices as demonic, the Dominican Bartolomé de las Casas was producing his final authoritative work of cultural description, the *Apologética historia sumaria* (1559). Drawing on ideas of civilization and natural religion that had circulated in earlier decades, he affirmed their presence in the Indies. Las Casas began by asserting humanity's natural

---

[36] Francisco Tamara, *El libro de las costumbres de todas las gentes del mundo, y de las Indias* (Antwerp: Martin Nucio, 1556), 246–326.

[37] John Headley explores a later version of this stance in Giovanni Botero's *Relationi universali* (1591), which defined Christianity as a key foundation for the achievements of civilization. "Geography and Empire in the Late Renaissance," *RQ* 53 (2000): 1134–44.

[38] "Christianos, y no infieles: politicos, y no barbaros: Españoles, y no Moros ni Turcos, suzios ydolatras," Tamara, 4–5ᵛ.

[39] "Nunca vuo en el mundo gente en ydolatra y tan matadores y comedores de hombres, no faltava sino bever sangre humana . . . han dexada de comer hombres y de sacreficarlos, finalmente viven como hombres y como Christianos, libres, y en policia." Tamara, 289.

inclination for goodness. He then linked reason with civilization: there were three forms of *prudencia* or wisdom. Humanity began with basic reason and then acquired economic and political wisdom. For Las Casas, Mexican and Andean peoples were comparable to the peoples of Greece, Rome, and Egypt in religious worship, just government, urban development, and other markers of civilization. To support this claim, the *Apologética Historia* was structured according to Aristotle's necessary functions of a polity or state and their social orders.[40] The state necessarily included the production of food, arts, arms, revenue, care of religion or worship, and governance and justice. Society contained the necessary groups of farmers, artisans, the military, the wealthy, priests, and judges. Following Aristotle's assertion that worship was fifth in functional order, yet also first in importance,[41] Las Casas devoted the bulk of his text to the discussion of religion.

Las Casas embraced the idea of natural religion in the *Apologética Historia*, drawing on classical and patristic texts to defend religious practices of idolatry and sacrifice as virtuous and natural. Idolatry was simply the human tendency to worship, which naturally directed itself toward the objects of idolatry: celestial bodies, things occurring in nature (animals and plants), and notable humans.[42] Doctrinal parallels between the true faith of Latin Christianity and the religion practiced in the Yucatan reinforced Las Casas's belief in natural religion. Relying on Peter Martyr of Anghiera's information, Las Casas acknowledged that the people of Cozumel worshipped a cross, believed in a trinity of gods who were father, son, and holy spirit, and honored the son's virgin mother. Las Casas argued that these were signs of the Yucatan peoples' long-standing existence and their cultural development, rather than evidence of the apostle Thomas's presence in the Yucatan. He also dismissed a possible link between Yucatan and Jewish peoples based on the practice of circumcision. Instead, Las Casas cited Herodotus's assertion that the rite of circumcision had developed in multiple locations. Herodotus had argued that although the Egyptians had influenced the Syrian, Phoenician, Colchian, and Jewish peoples to adopt circumcisions, the Ethiopians had apparently developed the practice independently. Thus, the presence of circumcision in the Yucatan again indicated their relative cultural wisdom

---

[40] Bartolomé de las Casas, *Apologética Historia Sumaria*, Obras Completas, vols. 6–8 (Madrid: Alianza Editorial, 1992), esp. 6:463–7.

[41] Aristotle *Politics* 7.1328b. In her important *Religion in the Andes*, Sabine MacCormack focused on correspondences between Las Casas and other sections of *Politics* (Princeton: Princeton University Press, 1991), 211.

[42] Las Casas, 7:636–68, discussed in MacCormack, 212–25.

rather than their relationship to other peoples.[43] Idolatry and circumcision were positive signs of religious devotion.

Although Las Casas favored Egyptian, Greek, Roman, and ancient European peoples in his cultural comparisons, he saw Jewish religion as a failure of religious development. The Jews bore a strong inclination for idolatry. They learned idolatry during their Egyptian captivity and, despite the biblical commandment against it, could not abandon it. Idolatry, here negative, became innate: part of their nature and the source of all other infamies and vices. In particular, the Jews' sacrifice of their children was the reprehensible consequence of worshiping the idol Moloch. In contrast, Las Casas depicted sacrifice among the peoples of the Americas more neutrally. Las Casas even argued, based on Peter Martyr's initial discussion of capital punishment in the fourth *Decade*, that reports of human sacrifice among the people of the Yucatan were mistaken.[44]

The *Apologética Historia* was never published as Las Casas's authoritative analysis of New World culture, but large sections of his cultural evaluation did appear in the Augustinian Hieronymo Román y Zamora's *Republicas del mundo divididas in XXVII. libros*.[45] This cosmography, first published in 1575 with twenty-seven books or parts, was much broader in geographic scope. Along with his reliance on Las Casas's papers in the section on the Americas entitled the "Republic of the Indies," Román utilized *relaciones* from the reigns of Isabella, Ferdinand, and Charles, as well as the letters of Cortés and Pizarro. Following Aristotelian categories for civilized polities, Román surveyed the world's "republics" through an examination of their religious practices, structures of political organization, and social customs. The *Republicas* would explore matters "divine and human": gods, sacrifices, other religious practices, as well as matters relevant for "peace and war."[46] The *Republicas del mundo* began by invoking Augustine's Cities of God and of Man. With the creation of the world, "two cities (or to put it better) two republics began: one of God, the other of the devil," descended from Seth and Cain respectively.[47] Once Román had discussed the beginnings of human society, he turned to the different republics of the world. He divided his work and the world

---

[43] Las Casas, 7:882–3, 8:1481–3 and Herodotus, *Histories* 2:36, 2:104.

[44] Las Casas, 7:640–50, 700–3; 8:1132–7, 1480, 1583–7. Las Casas cites Psalm 106 (Vulgate 105) and Leviticus 18–20 for Moloch.

[45] Hieronymo Román y Zamora, *Republicas del mundo divididas in XXVII. libros* (Medina del Campo: Francisco del Canto, 1575).

[46] "divino y humana . . . paz y guerra" Román, (1575), I:¶7.

[47] "començaron dos pueblos (o por mejor dezir) dos republicas, la vna fue de Dios, y la otra del demonio." Román, (1575), I:4.

into two volumes and two categories: those peoples who recognized the one God in an acceptable fashion and those who did not. The first volume began with the Hebrew Republic, followed by the Christian Republic, then the peoples of the north (including Muscovy), Venice, Genoa, and concluded with additional "diverse republics" of England, Lucca, the Swiss Confederacy, and Ragusa. The second volume, discussing the *Republica Gentilica* broadly defined, consisted of the peoples who formed less perfect republics because of their religious beliefs and practices. These peoples did not hold the Old or New Testaments as their sacred texts but rather were idolaters. Found here were the Republics of the Gentiles (Greeks and Romans); the Republic of the (west) Indies; and the three separate Republics of the Muslims: the Turks, Tunis, and Fez.

In volume one, devoted to the peoples of the Old and New Testaments, Román followed Las Casas closely in his description of Jewish people. Jews honored the one true God and demonstrated their covenant with him through the practice of circumcision. Nonetheless, after being exposed to idolatry in Egypt, they themselves could not resist the draw of idolatry and consequently sacrificed children to Moloch. Along with this argument, Román also replicated Las Casas's explanation that for Jews idolatry was innate: they adored idols just as leopards had spots, or Ethiopians were dark.[48] In volume one, Román also detailed the practices of Christians, emphasizing that the Roman Church was the true form of Christianity. Other "Christian sects" practiced rites and devotions not recognized by the Catholic Church, some of which were virtuous and praiseworthy, others of which were superstitious. These Christians included Greeks, Maronites, Georgians, Ethiopians, and other eastern Christians.[49]

For each republic placed in the second volume, Román addressed their religion: gods, sacrifices, priests, ministers, temples, and festivals. Once these sacred matters had been covered, Román turned to political governance, then social customs, and finally rulers.[50] After discussing the Greeks and Romans – gentiles who had lacked the opportunity to become Christians – Román turned to the Republic of the Indies. Within that republic, Román focused primarily on the kingdoms of Peru and the more populous Mexico (now New Spain), also including Yucatan, Guatemalan, and Tlaxcalan peoples. As in his discussion of Jewish religion, Román

---

[48] Román, (1575), I: 46^v–48^v, 58–59^v.
[49] "sectas de Christianos" who held "cosas buenas y dignas de ser alabadas, por otra parte tienen tantes supersticiones," Román, (1575), I: 267, and for the Ethiopian Church 270–70^v.
[50] Román, (1575), II: ¶4^v.

followed Las Casas's lead on interpreting Indians' religious practices. As adherents of natural law, these men believed in gods and wished to offer sacrifices. Idolatry manifested itself in the three long-standing categories: celestial objects, things in nature, and famous men who were revered as gods.[51] Among those long-familiar types of idolatrous worship, Román argued that Indians tended to worship celestial bodies or animals and objects found in the natural world. Román also accepted Las Casas's conclusion that parallels between Jewish and Yucatan idolatry and human sacrifice reflected their antiquity, although idolatry was, by definition, the "maldad de los Demonios."[52] After examining the idolatry that Román saw as the heart of Indian religion, he focused on its institutional organization: temples, priests (including a supreme pontiff), nuns, lands supporting the religious institutions, astrology and a calendar, and multiple chapters on religious festivals and sacrifices. Sacrifices covered roughly half of the entire section on religion, and it is there that Román explicitly commented on Indians' belief in demons and the possession of their souls by demons.[53]

    In book two of the Republic of the Indies, Román described government, justice (both the courts and punishments meted out), laws, and books, and in book three, he addressed clothes, marriage, how to instil virtue in noble youth, funerals, and war. In the section on government, Román claimed that Moctezuma had possessed greater majesty and authority than other rulers known for their magnificence, including Prester John or the rulers of the Ottoman Empire and the successor state to Byzantium, Trebizond.[54] Román concluded the Republic of the Indies with two final chapters recounting the fall of the Mexican and Inca Empires and a list of their rulers, with Charles and Philip named as the successors to both royal houses. The downfall of the Mexican kings was precipitated by Moctezuma's miserable death at the hands of a stone-throwing subject during the siege of Tenochtitlan. The last Mexican

---

[51] "En tres maneras dividian los Indios sus dioses, vnos eran comunes: porque en cada cosa que los avian menester los llamavan, y estavavan apropriados a cosas particulares, como eran los de los panes y fructas, otros eran dioses inuentados de ellos que por ser hombres famosos los reuerenciauan y tenian por diuinos, de la manera que lo hizo el resto de la gentilidad, como queda visto a tras. Otros dioses tenian mas famosos y que eran tenidos de todo punto por diuinos: a los quales reuerenciauan y tenian assi como era al Sol y a la luna y a otros que les parecia ser cosa grande." Román (1575), 348[356]. For Román's position on natural religion, see MacCormack, 245–6.

[52] Román (1575), II: 2ᵛ.

[53] Román (1575), II: 355–80ᵛ.

[54] Román (1575), II: 382ᵛ.

king, Quahtemoc, Moctezuma's nephew, had been a "high priest of the idols" before he succeeded to the throne and was subsequently tortured to death.[55] The end of the Incas came with more ignominy. Atahualpa's downfall was brought about by a slave and translator, whose passionate attraction to one of Atahualpa's wives led him to seek Atahualpa's death. The subsequent violent deaths of three Pizarros – Francisco, Juan, and Gonzalo (the last as a traitor) – were, in Román's eyes, God's punishment for their unheroic actions.[56]

The final section of the volume on the gentiles covered the Muslim republics. The bulk of this section was the Republic of the Turks, with brief mentions of the Republica de Tunis and the Republica de Fez. Muslim republics stood contrary to true faith, residing in darkness rather than light. Through the influence of the devil, they had been drawn to error, rejecting the sacrament of baptism in favor of circumcision. Their error was made undeniable by their decision not to conform to the Jewish practice of circumcising infants, choosing instead to circumcize boys at nine or ten years of age. For Román, circumcision was nonetheless a troubling physical transformation shared by Jewish and Muslim men. Jewish men could simply walk into a mosque and announce their conversion and did not need to acquire the physical mark of circumcision before being accepted in the Turkish Republic. In contrast, Christian men had to undergo a true act of apostasy to become "Turkish," renouncing Christianity and being circumcized as adults. Whether adult captives or children given as tribute to the Ottomans, Christian men were, because of their low status in the Turkish Republic, vulnerable to the temptations of improving their circumstances through conversion. Román, like Münster, reported that Christian men in the Republic of the Turks could also be forcibly circumcized if they did not show proper respect for the Law of Mohammed as superior to the law of Christ. Although Turkish governance and military might be dauntingly and undeniably successful, Román disparaged Turkish culture in other arenas. Although they possessed some skill in metalworking, they otherwise lacked abilities in the area of mechanical arts; Román even suggested that the religious prohibition against images stemmed from their inability to produce images.[57] Román also evaluated two Muslim North African republics, Tunis and Fez. His treatment of the Republic of Tunis perhaps reflected the

---

[55] "sacerdote mayor de los ydolos", Román (1575), II: 421^v–2^v.
[56] Román (1575), II: 422^v–3^v.
[57] Román (1575) II: 252, 425–7, 432–5.

city-state's role in the symbolism of Charles V's reign. Román did not mention the 1535 conquest nor its subsequent return to Ottoman control in his history of Tunis. Instead, he emphasized the city's connections to ancient Carthage and its former governance by a Granadine Muslim under the king of Morocco before it achieved independence. He then turned to contemporary Tunis, detailing points of trade and commerce with the outside world, as well as their process for selecting a new ruler (approval by the military, theologians, priests, and magistrates) and matters of court organization.[58] Román continued this focus on topics of governance and court in his discussion of Fez. Fez, which had a close relationship with Iberia in the century after Jewish expulsion of 1492, was not subjected to heavy criticism leveled at Turkish practices. In Fez, circumcision was much more in line with the Jewish observance of the Abrahamic covenant, practiced on infants rather than young boys.[59]

Within months of its appearance, the *Republicas del mundo* provoked a negative official reaction. Although the book had been approved by both Augustinian and royal censors and given a crown license before publication, the Council of the Indies and the Inquisition objected to some of its content. These condemnations have been associated with Philip II's hostility toward Indian religion and culture, in particular information about idolatry,[60] but the book's critics were vocal about other matters. The Council of the Indies, for its part, objected to the unheroic depiction of Peru's conquest and the consequent Pizarro rebellion. Reporting on idolatry in the Republic of the Indies was not in itself problematic. When Román's revisions of the *Republicas del mundo (divididas in tres partes)* came out in 1595, the sections on religion, government, and social customs in the Republic of the Indies survived largely intact.[61]

In Román's revised text, he rearranged the work's general organization, introducing a tripartite division. The division of the world into three was not unfamiliar: older cosmographies had divided the world

---

[58] Román (1575) II: 450–1. In the *Cosmographiae universalis*, Sebastian Münster included two pages on Tunis, mentioning Charles's conquest and the subsequent right to worship gained for Christians, 1121–3.

[59] Román (1575) II: 453, and generally 451–6. The close connections between Jewish families in Fez and their converso relatives in Iberia are illustrated in Mercedes García-Arenal, *A Man of Three Worlds* (Baltimore: Johns Hopkins University Press, 2003).

[60] Román (1575), I: i^v–ii. Rolena Adorno, "Censorship and its Evasion: Jerónimo Román and Bartolomé de las Casas," *Hispania* 75 (1992): 814–27 and Georges Baudot, *Utopia and History in Mexico* (Niwot: University Press of Colorado, 1995), 490–515.

[61] Hieronymo Román y Zamora, *Republicas del mundo. Divididas en tres partes.* (Salamanca, 1595). Revisions to the text are extensive and cannot be dealt with systematically here.

into three parts (the Ptolemaic division of Africa, Asia, and Europe or, in Tamara's revision, Europe, Asia, and Africa). Yet Román's divisions were not strictly geographical, instead they amplified the religious distinctions made in his 1575 edition. He continued to maintain the broad distinction between the republics of God and the devil. In the 1595 edition, the Hebrew and Christian Republics remained together as the first volume. The republics of the devil were separated into two parts. Volume two, the Gentile Republics, was devoted exclusively to the idolatrous pagans of the classical past, the Greeks and Romans. The Christian republics that had, in 1575, followed the general Republica Christiana (loosely, the area of Catholic Europe) of volume one had been moved into a third volume. These Christian republics were the non-monarchical polities: Venice, Genoa, the Swiss Confederacy, Lucca, and Ragusa; and the insufficiently doctrinally correct: Scandinavia, (whose peoples were cited as former practitioners of human sacrifice), Muscovy,[62] Protestant England, and – a new entry for the 1595 edition – the Republic of Ethiopia. These minor republics, apparently no longer deemed suitable for the volume on the Christian Republic, were followed in the third volume by republics that were indisputably idolatrous lands: the Republic of the Indies, followed by the new entries on the Republics of the Tartars and China, and concluding with the Muslim Republics of the Turks and Fez.

In 1595, specific sections of the text ranging from the Hebrew Republic to the entire Tunisian Republic were expurgated, while most information on idolatrous practice from the 1575 edition survived censorship and editorial revision and appeared in the revised 1595 edition. Deletions centered on the discussions of religious practices and doctrines of the Hebrew and Christian Republics. Perhaps out of concern for Jewish converts in Iberia (as was the case for Gois's text), passages on the Jewish practice of circumcision as a sacrament were removed,[63] along with sections on other Jewish rites and practices that were sacraments in Christianity, such as marriage. Sections discussing Jewish texts were also deleted. In the Republic of Christians, Román deleted language neutral to sects of the "other Christians" (non-Catholics) and corrected points of doctrine and church authority.[64] The division of the *Republica Gentilica* into two volumes – past and present – implicitly placed the Republic of the Indies among the contemporary idolatrous republics. In 1575, Román

---

[62] Román (1575), I: 346^v–348^v, 357–357^v. Muscovites could be perceived as idolatrous, *Neue zeitung auß Hispania.* . . . [Nuremberg: Geyßler, 1561], Aiii.
[63] Román (1575), I: 46^v–8^v.
[64] Román (1595), I: 321–321^v; Adorno, 814–5.

had noted that Indians became Christians after the conquest of New Spain and Peru. Through its 1595 classification, the Republic of the Indies was no longer represented as a recently converted republic bearing vestiges of an idolatrous past. Rather, it appeared to be an ethnography of an idolatrous people in the here and now.

The Republic of Ethiopia was given a separate expanded entry, distinct from the general discussion of the broader Republica Christiana. The Ethiopians had been mentioned in the 1575 Republic of Christians as one of the false Christian sects whose existence necessitated a clear explanation of the "true rites" of the Catholic church. By 1595, Román no longer seemed willing to place them in the general Christian Republic at all. His expansion of ethnographic information on the Ethiopians emphasized the heterodoxy of their sacramental rituals, overturning Gois's positive interpretations of these practices. They practiced baptism annually rather than once in a lifetime. Circumcision no longer simply commemorated the baby Jesus's circumcision; it also signaled the Ethiopians' devotion to the law of Moses. Ethiopians' practice of circumcising girls was no longer a sign of faith but of their errors which extended beyond those of the Jewish and Turkish peoples. Thus the people of the Ethiopian republic were, in Román's opinion, truly renegades and apostates.[65] Román's editions of the *Republicas del mundo*, including the changes made to placate both secular and religious authorities between 1575 and 1595, underscored several trends in post-Tridentine Catholicism. The increasing importance of doctrine when assessing culture and religious practice, the tendency to note the devil's influence in idolatry outside of Latin Christian Europe or even Catholic Europe, and strategies of distancing became more evident in the second half of the sixteenth century.

In those decades, the changing stance toward the non-Latin Christian, non-European world was not simply rhetorical. The second half of this book will trace some of the shifts in practice that demonstrate strategies to demarcate differences between these peoples and those of Europe. Before turning to those examples, however, we briefly pick up the history of Nahua and other Indians envoys in Castile, left at the end of Chapter 2 in the 1540s. The Tlaxcalan embassy of 1540 had been sufficiently important that Román incorporated it into his discussion of Indian governments and the Tlaxcalan republic. He reminded the reader that the Tlaxcalan nobility's representatives had in 1540 received recognition as noble vassals and had sought to confirm their sons' rights of inheritance.[66]

---

[65] Román (1575), I: 267–70ᵛ; Román (1595): I: 321–3, 267, 270–270ᵛ, III: 100–18ᵛ.
[66] Román (1575), II: 388.

Román did not record the appearance of subsequent embassies, although these would have occurred during the decades in which he was composing the *Republicas del mundo*. As rule shifted from Charles to Philip in the 1550s, the crown and the court's lack of interest in Nahua embassies seemed to signal a devolution in the status of Nahua nobles and Indians. Abiding by new policies restricting the movements of Indians out of New Spain, the next major Tlaxcalan embassy secured a royal order in 1552 granting them permission to travel to Iberia. As noted in Chapter 2, policies in New Spain had begun reducing noble authority. By the 1560s, high-ranking noblemen increasingly ceased to become governors of their polities. The colonial Spanish administration moved to eliminate the heritability of these positions whenever possible.[67] The embassy representatives, no longer the highest-ranking noblemen of Tlaxcala but instead elected gentlemen, did receive reconfirmation of their previous privileges by the new king, Philip II, in 1562. Some Tlaxcalan nobles also received personal coats of arms. Yet their treatment at court reflected either their lesser rank or the crown's increasing disinterest in Nahua nobles. None of the Tlaxcalans were referred to by title, nor do they seem to have received any particular support from the crown.[68] Although Las Casas continued (until his death in 1566) to call for the restoration of Indian rulers who would govern under the Habsburg emperor, by the end of the century, most Nahua aristocrats had slipped from the view of Philip's court.[69] Evidence of their continued travel and petitions exists,[70] but little note seems to have been taken of them. Their symbolic place in the Habsburg polity had changed, reflecting not only the increasingly secure Iberian grip on New Spain, but also other political exigencies and conceptual shifts in Europe.

Tellingly, within Castile itself, other groups experienced a decreasing tolerance for their cultural practices during the same decades. The Muslim inhabitants of the conquered kingdom of Granada, forcibly converted by

---

[67] Charles Gibson, *The Aztecs under Spanish Rule* (Stanford: Stanford University Press, 1964), 167–72.

[68] AGI IG 427 L. 30 fols. 10v–12, IG 1963 L.9 fol. 809, Contratación 5527 l.3 fol. 25; Contratación 5788 l. 1 fols. 172ᵛ–173ᵛ; Charles Gibson, *Tlaxcala in the Sixteenth Century* (New Haven: Yale University Press, 1952), 166–8, 231. In their supplication reprinted in *Cartas de Indias* (Madrid: Hernandez, 1877), they refer to themselves as "hijos dalgos y cavalleros," 404.

[69] Hugo G. Nutini, *The Wages of Conquest: the Mexican Aristocracy in the Context of Western Aristocracies* (Ann Arbor: University of Michigan Press, 1995), 180–1; Jonathan Israel, *Race, Class and Politics in Colonial Mexico, 1610–1670* (London: Oxford University Press, 1975), 60–3.

[70] AGI Pasajeros L. 7 E3905, L. 8 E1647, L. 8 E4277.

1502 (forcible conversion in Aragon came slightly later, in 1525–1526), had become the culturally distinct moriscos. During Charles V's visit to Granada in 1526, morisco practices including the wearing of distinctive costumes, continued use of Arabic, and wedding, hygiene, and dietary customs were identified as problematic by a clerical investigatory team. Although this *junta* sought a ban on these practices, the moriscos were granted an additional forty years in which to continue these cultural practices after the payment of a significant sum (later remembered as 80,000 ducats).[71] During these years, the moriscos practiced their cultural distinction, in part through a spatial segregation from Old Christians; these were the "moros" described by Vitoria in the late 1530s as not yet fully converted to Christianity.

This period of relative coexistence ended mid-century as crown policies began reducing morisco political and economic clout in the 1550s. Both the Inquisition and regular clergy increased their religious scrutiny. When the grace period for morisco dress and use of Arabic expired in 1566, petitions from morisco leaders sought an extension, pointing out that Eastern Christians living in Jerusalem spoke Arabic and dressed in a style distinct from that of Latin Christians. The petitions and exemption were denied. Demands of religious and cultural conformity intensified and precipitated the Second Revolt of the Alpujarras (1568–1570). The revolt would end in the forcible removal of moriscos from the kingdom of Granada to other parts of Castile and Aragon. In a parallel development among formerly Jewish families who had converted to Christianity in 1492, the 1560s also witnessed an intensified effort on the crown's part to restrict their access to the highest levels of local society by enforcing purity-of-blood statutes in Old Castile.[72] Arguably, stubborn idolaters, some with tendencies so innate that they survived initial conversion to Christianity, were perceived to be culturally distinct from the true Republica Christiana.

---

[71] Enrique Soria Mesa, "De la conquista a la asimilación," *Areas* 14 (1992): 49–64; David Coleman, *Creating Christian Granada* (Ithaca: Cornell University Press, 2003).

[72] Antonio Domínguez Ortiz and Bernard Vincent, *Historia de los moriscos: Vida y tragedia de una minoría* (Madrid: Revista de Occidente, 1978); Coleman; R. Foulché-Delbosc's "Memoria de Francisco Nuñez Muley," *Revue Hispanique* 6 (1899): 204–39 is the earliest transcription, while K. Garrad's "The Original Memorial of Don Francisco Núñez" 2(1954): 199–226 includes commentary and notes. Linda Martz, "Pure Blood Statutes in Sixteenth-Century Toledo: Implementation as Opposed to Adoption," *Sefarad* LIV (1994): 83–107.

4

Boundaries and the Cultures of Diplomacy
in Central Europe

Two *Wegrayße*, published in 1531 and 1532, describe the journeys of King Ferdinand's envoys from Austria to Constantinople during the early diplomatic negotiations between Habsburg and Ottoman rulers (Figure 28). The lands that the envoys travel through and remark on are eerily empty. Shells of Christian monuments dot the landscape, and the only people they encounter while riding through the countryside are the occasional small group of armed Turks or captives destined for the slave markets. In these descriptions, styled as ambassadorial reports, formerly Christian kingdoms have become a border zone between the *Erblände* (hereditary lands) of the Habsburgs and the capital cities of their *Erbfeinde* (hereditary enemies), the Ottoman Sultans.[1] This chapter considers the construction of a cultural border zone between Habsburg and Ottoman Empires. Through an examination of this zone and the people who cross it, we will trace the evolving cultural categories of "Turk" and Christian (and the widening distance between them) during the sixteenth century.

The Border Zone

The Balkan region and the kingdom of Hungary were the major focus of Ottoman attempts to expand into Christian European lands

---

[1] *Itinerarivm Wegrayß Kün. May. potschafft/ gen Constantinopel/ züdem Türckischen keiser Soleyman. Anno XXX* (1531), Aiv^v–B^v, C–C^v. *Wegrayß/ Keyserlicher Maiestat Legation/ im.32.jar züdem Türcken geschickt/ wie und was gestalt/ sie hinein/ vnd widerumb herauß/ komen ist/....* (1532), especially Aii–Aiv.

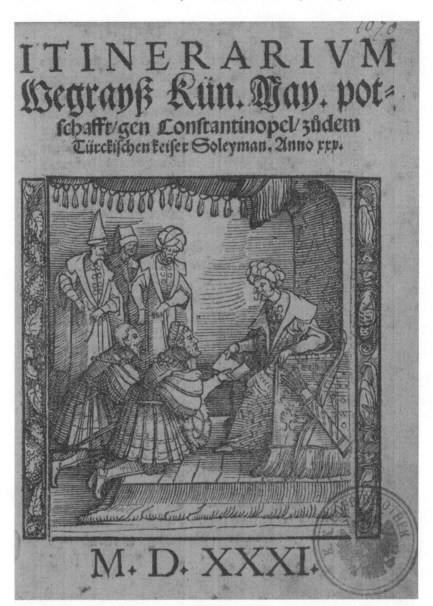

FIGURE 28. Title page, Benedict Kuripešic, *Itinerarium, Wegrayß Kün. May. potschafft gen Constantinopel zu dem Türckischen keiser Soleyman. Anno XXX.* (1531). Copyright: ÖNB Vienna, Picture Archive 48.S.11.

throughout the fifteenth century. During the century, the geographic distance between Muslim Ottoman and (Latin) Christian Habsburg regions fluctuated as Ottoman military and political influence in the Balkans waxed and waned. These Balkan territories would become the lands described as empty in the diplomatic travel accounts. During the fifteenth century, the region's stable boundary line was formed by a network of fortresses extending along the southern border of the kingdom of Hungary (which at the time included the principalities of Croatia and Slavonia and a portion of Bosnia). Serbia and Bosnia acted as buffer states to Hungary's south. Serbia bore the weight of Ottoman military and diplomatic ambitions. Serbia's subsumption into the Ottoman Empire was finally confirmed when the fortress of Belgrade (once Serbian, but the key to Hungary's defense for most of the fifteenth century) fell decisively to the Ottomans in 1521. The medieval kingdom of Hungary was quick to follow in 1526 when Ottoman forces defeated the Hungarian army at the battle of Mohács. In the subsequent rout, the king of Hungary died. The two resultant claimants for the crown of Hungary, János Zápolyai and the then-Archduke Ferdinand of Austria, divided the kingdom between them – Zápolyai received the Ottoman sultan's backing, Ferdinand the Holy Roman Emperor's. After Zápolyai's death, Hungary was further divided into Habsburg Hungary, Ottoman Hungary, and Transylvania in 1541. Habsburg Hungary extended south to include portions of Croatia and Slavonia.[2] In 1530 and 1532, when the Habsburg envoys set out for Constantinople, they moved from Habsburg Austria directly into the Balkan lands on their way to Ottoman Bosnia, avoiding heavily contested Hungarian lands along the Danube. In the German-language printed accounts of diplomatic journeys, these Slavic-speaking lands operated as an intermediary space or buffer territory between the two empires, much as they had in the fifteenth century. There was one important difference: they were no longer independent polities but instead Ottoman subject territories.

This intermediate space was not unfamiliar topography to Ferdinand's early envoys, yet they made no direct report on the changed conditions of the people now living under the dominion of "the Turk" (the Latin

---

[2] János Bak, "The Late Medieval Period, 1382–1526," 54–82 and Ferenc Szakály, "The Early Ottoman Period, Including Royal Hungary, 1526–1606," 83–99 in Peter F. Sugar, ed., *A History of Hungary* (Bloomington: Indiana University Press, 1990) and Géza Perjés, *The Fall of the Medieval Kingdom of Hungary: Mohács 1526-Buda 1541*, trans. Márió D. Fenyó (Highland Lakes: Atlantic Research and Publications, 1989).

Christian name for the ruler of the Ottoman Empire as well as the Ottoman people more generally). In each of Ferdinand's early embassies, at least one of the envoys was from the militarized zone. They were not humanists, who served as diplomats elsewhere in Europe,[3] but rather military men. One of Ferdinand's ambassadors in 1528, the Hungarian *Haiduk* Johann Hoberdanacz (Habardanecz), later attempted to assassinate Zápolyai. The 1530 ambassadors were the Croatian knight Nikolaus Jurišić and the Carniolan knight Joseph von Lamberg. Jurišić was later renowned as the commander of besieged Köszeg (Güns), who defended it during critical weeks in 1532 and thus distracted the Ottoman army from reaching Vienna.[4] In 1532, when Jurišić was occupied at Köszeg, von Lamberg was accompanied on his diplomatic mission by the Italian-born courtier, count Leonhard von Nogarola. Benedict Kuripešic (Kuripecic), attributed author of the 1531 and 1532 *Wegrayße* describing the empty Slavonian and Croatian lands, served as the embassy's Latin translator and was himself a Slavonian.[5] His depiction of a war-torn landscape, peopled only by military bands and groups of captives, contrasts with his description of the embassy's nightly stay at Turkish-held fortresses, where they were welcomed by the lord or commander of the castle and often treated to a feast.[6] The perception of the intermediary region as bleak and empty persisted during the subsequent ten years of intensive and shifting boundaries in the former Hungarian and Balkan territories. In 1542, the Croatian Tranquillus Andronicus, who held allegiances to competing rulers of Hungary during his life, described a journey through "deserta Dalmatie."[7]

---

[3] Garrett Mattingly, *Renaissance Diplomacy* (Baltimore: Penguin, 1955) and Jocelyne G. Russell, *Peacemaking in the Renaissance* (Philadelphia: University of Pennsylvania Press, 1986).

[4] Paolo Giovio, *Historiarum sui temporis, tomi secundi, pars prior* in *Opere* (Rome: Istituto Poligrafico e Zecca dello Stato, 1985) offers a contemporary encomium, 4: 213–6.

[5] *Wegrayß*, 1531, Aii^v. Marianna D. Birnbaum, *Humanists in a Shattered World: Croatian and Hungarian Latinity in the Sixteenth Century* (Columbus: Slavica, 1985) discusses Kuripešic's antecedents and the authorship of the 1532 *Wegrayß*, 263.

[6] In the example of Camergrad, "auch bey dem nachtmal wir all/ sampt den Türcken/deren vil mit uns geessen gar frölich geweßt." The next day, they saw "xx. arme leut/ellend Christen kindlin/ knäblin/ und diernlin/ so sie am yetzigen zug ungefarlich vor vi. oder vii. tagen gefanngen/ in das selbig dorff Kruschitza gebracht/..." *Itinerarivm Wegrayß* (1531), b^v–c. Contemporary diplomatic reports also describe this borderzone, e.g. HHStA Turcica, 3/1, fol. 2.

[7] Tranquillus Andronicus served the regent Lodovico Gritti, then Zápolyai, then Ferdinand. Karl Nehring, ed., *Austro-Turcica, 1541–1552* (Munich: Oldenbourg, 1995), 21.

As the embassies of 1530 and 1532 rode further into Bosnia, where Ottoman rule had been established for more than sixty years, they noted signs of devastation everywhere. Kuripešic's accounts counted ruined buildings and settlements whose destruction dated from the Ottoman conquest. After making no mention of people in his first days of travel, Kuripešic saw the people of this region as unfamiliar and chose to describe them. There were three groups of Bosnians: the Roman Christians, the Orthodox Christians, and the Turks. To Kuripešic's Slavonian eyes, all the Bosnians were culturally indistinct. Christians and Muslims looked much alike and could not be easily distinguished from each other. Their visual similarities were accompanied by cultural and religious ambiguities: the Janissaries, more loyal to the Ottomans than "true Turks" and key to Ottoman military success, were drawn from this population.[8] Kuripešic's accounts – detailed ambassadorial descriptions of travel through this space – described what can be recognized as a form of transitional or liminal space. Arnold van Gennep, in the classic anthropological definition of the neutral or transitional zone in rites of passage, characterized such frontiers as "symbolic and spatial" zones that heighten perceptions of difference or opposition between the two established territories. The traveler who "passes from one to the other finds himself physically and magico-religiously in a special situation for a certain length of time: he wavers between two worlds."[9] Beyond its ethnographic description as emptied, this territory between secure Habsburg and Ottoman control operated as a liminal zone.

Similar buffer zones existed in the late medieval period at most boundaries between Latin Christian and Muslim cultures. These frontiers were contact zones, their territory the spatial arenas where Christian and Muslim confronted each other. In the scholarly conceptualization of frontiers, and Christian-Muslim frontiers in particular, cultural encounters were often violent, as two cultures struggled for political and territorial control of a region where one group had encroached on the territory of another. Typically, a sustainable social equilibrium was established along

---

[8] "Vorgemelte Christen beyder ständ/ seind dem Türcken vast gleich bekleidt/ on allein dz die Christen ire hartragen/ und die Türcken kolbet geshoten seind/ darbey erkennt man sie von einander." *Wegrayß* 1531, Civ^v and for the Janissaries, troops formed from converts, E–Eii.

[9] Arnold van Gennep, *The Rites of Passage*, trans. M. B. Vizedom and G. L. Caffee (Chicago: University of Chicago Press, 1960), 18.

these contact zone.[10] The Iberian example of a stabilized frontier between the Kingdoms of Castile and Granada (between 1369 and 1482) would have been familiar to Ferdinand, the king of Hungary after 1526, and his Iberian advisors. There, the stabilized hostile coexistence allowed for a series of temporary truces, the exchange of people and goods across the boundary, and the development of peacekeeping.[11] The sixteenth-century Hungarian-Balkan border between Habsburgs and Ottomans developed along a similar path. Throughout the century, conflict did not disappear entirely, but shifted instead between periods of "hot" and "cold" hostility. Both sides wanted to lay claim to all of Hungary, but neither was able to fully enforce that claim (although the Ottomans certainly came closest before the stabilization of the border through the 1568 treaty).

The border was never peaceful, yet the very disputes that marked the border as violent also led to increasing interaction between the enemies. Rarely did either side mount a major offensive. Instead, both sides fortified a few important strongholds and supported them with a line of lightly defended positions from which raids and skirmishes were conducted.[12] The diplomatic minutiae in the correspondence between the two powers reveal an unceasing stream of queries, protests, and replies about treaty infractions, particularly raiding or unjust seizures of persons and property, and prisoner exchanges.[13] In turn, the day-to-day business of

---

[10]   Robert I. Burns, "The Significance of the Frontier in the Middle Ages," in Robert Bartlett and Angus MacKay, eds., *Medieval Frontier Societies* (Oxford: Oxford University Press, 1989), 307–30. Cynthia Talbot's "Inscribing the Other, Inscribing the Self: Hindu-Muslim Identities in Pre-Colonial India," *CSSH* 37:4 (1995): 692–722 investigates the identities formed at different stages of a frontier culture. For violence as part of coexistence in Spain, see David Nirenberg's *Communities of Violence* (Princeton: Princeton University Press, 1996).

[11]   José Enrique López de Coca Castañer calls this a "cold war," because neither *reconquista* nor revivals of *jihad* could allow for a true "peace" between the two cultures, in his "Institutions on the Castilian-Granadan Frontier 1369–1482," in Bartlett and MacKay, eds., *Medieval Frontier Societies* (Oxford: Oxford University Press, 1989), 127–31.

[12]   For an introduction to the border's military issues, see Perjés, chapter IV; Gunther Rothenberg, *The Austrian Military Border in Croatia, 1552–1747* (Urbana: University of Illinois Press, 1960); and Catherine W. Bracewell's *The Uskoks of Senj: Piracy, Banditry, and Holy War in the Sixteenth-century Adriatic* (Ithaca: Cornell University Press, 1992). Gábor Ágoston, "Information, ideology, and limits of imperial policy," in *The Early Modern Ottomans*, ed. Virginia Aksan and Daniel Goffman (Cambridge: Cambridge University Press, 2007) surveys the information order on the Ottoman side of this emerging border, 75–103.

[13]   The discussion here and in subsequent pages is based on Austrian HHStA section Turcica, Kartons 3, 8, 10, 16–17, 19–20, 23–30 (1533–1574), unless otherwise indicated. For other raiding reports and prisoner exchanges, see Austria Kriegsarchiv, Altefeldakten

managing the border required the development of communication routes and agreed-on structures to resolve issues. As Charles Halperin pointed out, contrasts between inflammatory rhetoric and involuntary yet pragmatic practices often existed in medieval Muslim-Christian buffer zones. What Halperin called an "ideology of silence" in Christian cultures managed the extreme contradiction between ideal rhetoric and real practice.[14] Even as the Austrian Habsburg court employed alarmist rhetoric of Christianity's impending destruction in a holy war,[15] both Habsburgs and Ottomans followed a diplomatic course of increasingly regularized border relations. Although Habsburg and Christian public propaganda did not mention cooperation and accommodation between the two enemies, there was continual traffic across and within the Hungarian and Balkan border zone. Tracing the development of diplomatic agreements between the two powers reveals the developing patterns of concern and interest along this border.

Relations between Habsburg and Ottoman courts were regularized and the border between their territories hardened through the evolving negotiations of truces and treaties. Ferdinand began to seek diplomatic relations with the Ottoman court in the spring following his disputed accession to the Hungarian throne. By April 1527, he had sent a messenger to Constantinople and received a letter from Emperor Süleyman I affirming "that ambassadors, messengers and all others are safe to travel through all my domains."[16] This was a significant first step: as Ottoman officials pointed out, Ferdinand's deceased brother-in-law Louis of Hungary had brutally mistreated the Ottoman ambassadors at his court before the 1526 defeat at Mohacs.[17] The draft instructions for Ferdinand's 1527 embassy were

---

1570–1576, fols. 1–2; Gustav Bayerle, "Turco-Hungarian Duels: Comments on a Letter of Ibrahim Agha from 1589," *Journal of Popular Culture* 16:1 (Summer 1982): 117–25.

[14] Charles J. Halperin, "The Ideology of Silence: Prejudice and Pragmatism on the Medieval Religious Frontier," *CSSH* 26:3 (1984): 442–66.

[15] Ferdinand's external correspondence highlights Süleyman's "destruicion y Ruina de nuestra fee y effusion de la sangre Cristiana." HHStA Belgien PA 6/2, fols. 22–23ᵛ. For a rejection of an oppositional notion of crusade and *convivencia*, see Norman Housley's "Frontier Societies and Crusading in the Late Middle Ages," in Benjamin Arbel, ed., *Intercultural Contacts in the Medieval Mediterranean* (London: Frank Cass, 1996), 104–19.

[16] Antal [Anton] von Gevay, ed., *Urkunden und Actenstücke zur Geschichte der Verhältnisse zwischen Österreich, Ungern und der Pforte im XVI. und XVII. Jahrhunderte* (Vienna, 1838–1842), I/1: 63–4 (1527) "quod Oratores Nunctii et omnes alii sint securi ambulare per totum dominium mee Maiestatis."

[17] These actions are detailed in *Wölcher gstalt Künigklicher Maiestet zu Hungern vnnd Behem bottschafftenn/ nemlich Herr Sigmund Weyxelberger/ vnd ein Hungerischer Herr/*

quite modest. The goal was a three-year truce in Hungary and Croatia. Even this goal proved unattainable: no truce was arranged in the next few years, and Ferdinand's 1528 embassy of Johann Hoberdanacz and Sigmund Weixelberger was placed under house arrest in Constantinople. During this period of open hostility, Ottoman forces retook Buda from Ferdinand and briefly besieged Vienna in 1529. Unable to muster committed support from his brother Charles V or the estates of the Holy Roman Empire, Ferdinand continued to send diplomatic missions to the Constantinople with instructions to offer "the Turk" a pension and to negotiate a settlement on border fortresses.[18] In 1531, a one-year truce was negotiated between the two rulers. The *Itinerarum Wegrayß*... title page, produced during 1531, depicts not only cultural difference through the splendid robes, turban, and arms of the Ottoman sultan, but also the submissiveness of the Habsburg envoys to Ottoman might (Figure 28).[19] After the Habsburgs finally mustered a significant army to defend Austria against the major Ottoman offensive in 1532, both sides agreed on a treaty in 1533. The Emperor Süleyman even sent an envoy to Vienna to witness the treaty's ratification, but the agreement itself was short-lived. Although the actual treaty has not survived, points of concern were the confirmation of Zápolyai's territory as granted by Süleyman through right of conquest, the establishment of an exact boundary between Habsburg and Ottoman-backed Hungary, and the resumption of merchant travel and business in the region.[20] This stabilized coexistence would be further developed in later longer-term peace treaties.

In 1547, as the Habsburgs were preoccupied with internal politics and the Ottomans now direct rulers of a partitioned Hungary, a five-year peace treaty was ratified by Charles V, Süleyman, and Ferdinand.[21] The treaty articles elaborated on those introduced in the 1533 treaty. Ferdinand was to pay Süleyman 30,000 gulden per year. In return, Süleyman

---

zü dem Türckischen Kayser an vnd ankommen sind/ souil vngefarlich auß vergebenlicher sag erhalten worden ist [Nuremberg: Kunigunde Hergot, 1529], aii[v].

[18] Gevay I/1:91–2 (1527); I/2: 3–28 (1529); I/3: 3–23 (1530).

[19] A truce in Hungary was arranged in the same period between Zápolyai and Ferdinand.

[20] Gevay II/1: 138–9, 153–6 (1533); also Anton C. Schaendlinger, "Der diplomatische Verkehr zwischen Österreich und der Hohen Pforte in der Regierungszeit Süleymans des Prächtigen," *Kultur des Islam*, ed. Otto Mazal, Biblos-Schriften, 113 (Vienna: Österreichische Nationalbibliothek, 1981), 95.

[21] For texts of the German and Turkish versions ratified by Süleyman, and the Latin version ratified by Ferdinand, see Ernst Petritsch's excellent "Der Habsburgisch-Osmanische Friedensvertrag des Jahres 1547," *Mitteilungen des Österreichischen Staatsarchiv* 38 (1985), 68–78.

would cease to press his claim on the remainder of the Hungary. The border was established at its current position, and peace was to be maintained along it. Along with the clarification of rights and sovereignty at the territorial line, the treaty's ratification provisos reveal further important issues on the Habsburg/Ottoman border. Süleyman wanted the terms of peace to apply to the North African border between Charles V and Süleyman as well. Even more interesting, and a point we shall return to later, Süleyman emphasized several times that piracy and raids were to stop, fugitives "whether Turk or Christian, man or woman"[22] be returned, and merchants allowed to move freely between Ottoman and Habsburg lands. Ferdinand's ratification confirmed that raiding would halt, although he had fewer stipulations. Similarly, merchants and trading were not of specific concern to him. What he did want to clarify, however, was the treatment of fugitives. Regardless of rank, all people, whether "great or small, noble or slave," should be denied refuge on whichever side of the border they fled to: "[S]uch fugitives and traitors of both parties should not be received by the other party, but returned and sent back immediately to the other party from which they fled."[23] Infringements on the treaty were a matter of contention within two years. During the following years, treaty violations were great enough to cause the house arrest of Ferdinand's envoy to Constantinople, Johann Maria Malvezzi. With this degree of friction, some years passed before the next truce was established (1559) and the peace treaty ratified (1562).[24]

In the agreements of 1559 and 1562, along with the familiar issues of tribute, borders, subject people and towns, raids, free passage of envoys, and fugitives, a new concern appeared: the issue of prisoners.[25] All unjustly seized prisoners were to be returned, and even Christian prisoners who had already sworn to give ransom were exchanged for Muslims held in Austria. This provision was further strengthened in the 1568 treaty renewed by Süleyman and Ferdinand's sons and heirs,

---

[22] "es sey ain Turckh aber Christ, ain man aber weib," Petritsch, "Friedensvertrag," 75–6.

[23] "Item quod si quis ex nostris partibus aut subditis ad partes Turcarum, aut contra ex partibus Turcarum ad nos aliquis seu magnus seu parvus seu nobilis aut servus transfugerit, quod tales transfugae et proditores utriusque partis non possint nec debeant recipi ab altera parte, sed statim et de facto reddantur et remittantur parti alteri a qua auffugerunt. . . . " Petritsch, "Friedensvertrag," 70.

[24] HHStA, Turcica 8 (1549); published letters of Süleyman to Ferdinand are in Anton C. Schaendlinger, *Osmanisch-Türkische Dokumente aus dem Haus-, Hof–und Staatsarchiv zu Wien* (Vienna: Österreichischen Akademie der Wissenschaften, 1983), 1:20–3; HHStA Turcica 16/1, fol. 147^{v}.

[25] Schaendlinger, *Osmanisch-Türkische Dokumente*, 1:59–65, 67–74.

Selim II and Maximilian II. In this agreement, all prisoners with no arranged ransoms were to be set free immediately. Further, the sale or purchase of prisoners was forbidden.[26]

As these evolving sixteenth-century treaty negotiations reveal, both sides wanted to regularize the passage of people in this Hungarian and Balkan borderland. Whether it be restricting the movements of fugitives, or protecting the persons of merchants, border residents, and soldiers, the two states sought to establish rules of conduct toward people who could and would cross this border zone. Initially, some of these people – nobles from the border zone – were called on by the Habsburg court to travel across this border as diplomatic envoys. Most of the other cultural go-betweens across this border were categories of people discussed in the various treaty negotiations. Merchants, often identified as Italian or Jewish, made agreements with Ottoman officials and continued trading throughout the period. Fugitives from Christianity could reemerge as Ottoman subjects engaged in the business of their new state. Captives, either military or civilian, could be ransomed, converted, enslaved, or escapees to their homelands. As detailed in the following pages, these people were recognized for their abilities to cross linguistic and cultural barriers. Yet even as they were needed to facilitate the diplomatic and economic exchanges of the borderland, their very ability to cross between Habsburg and Ottoman worlds was viewed with suspicion. These go-betweens across the geographic border between Habsburg and Ottoman, and the explanations for their acceptance and rejection, helped shape the nature of an evolving cultural border in the region.

After the Ottomans conquered Constantinople in 1453, Christian and Jewish merchants and traders who depended on trade with territories east of the Mediterranean faced the prospect of either losing access to those routes or acknowledging a new Muslim ruler. Some groups quickly made trade agreements recognizing the sovereignty of the Ottomans in the former Byzantium. Of the Latin Christians, the Venetians and the Ragusans were the notable examples. The Venetians' very favorable treaty was established eleven months after Constantinople's fall, granting them trading rights and a resident ambassador (the *bailo*) in the city as they had previously maintained under Byzantine rule.[27] Visiting western

---

[26] This clause was adopted as well in the treaty of 1606. Gustav Bayerle, "The Compromise at Zsitvatorok," *Archivum Ottomanorum* VI (1980), 19.

[27] For Venetian relations with the Ottomans, see Eric Dursteler, *Venetians in Constantinople: Nation, Identity, and Coexistence in the Early Modern Mediterranean* (Baltimore: Johns Hopkins University Press, 2006) and Franz Babinger, *Mehmed the Conqueror and his Time*, trans. Ralph Manheim (Princeton: Princeton University Press, 1978), Books 2 and

European ambassadors did not hesitate to use these merchants as go-betweens. Embassies to Constantinople were politically volatile and physically dangerous – ambassadors could be and often were placed under house arrest and threatened with execution. The non-Muslim merchant had invaluable connections that facilitated ambassadors' missions. The merchants arranged audiences with members of the Ottoman court, ransomed prisoners, and acted as interpreters of both language and custom.[28] Italian, Greek, and Jewish intercessors in Constantinople were familiar agents for the western European courts.[29]

Yet merchants held an ambiguous status in the eyes of the Habsburg court, for "it is impossible to be both a lord and a merchant."[30] Further complicating matters, uninterrupted merchant activities in the area benefited the Ottoman, not Habsburg, economy. As a group, merchants had chosen of their own volition to cooperate with the Muslim *Erbfeind*. In Habsburg eyes, the Venetians and Ragusans had been disturbingly quick to make trade agreements with the new Muslim rulers in Constantinople for the purpose of making a profit.[31] The close familiarity and economic connections of Venetian merchants and the Turks were well known. For example, Felix Faber's well-known account of a pilgrimage to Jerusalem and Egypt in 1483 not only began with a trip to Venice – the departure point for most voyages to the eastern Mediterranean – but also described the integrated presence of Venetians in various Muslim cities.[32]

---

6. For the Ragusan case, see HHStA Span. DK 2/29 fol. 9-9ᵛ; N.H. Biegman, "Ragusan Spying for the Ottoman Empire," *Belleten* 27 (1963): 237–9 and his monograph *The Turco-Ragusan Relationship* (The Hague: Mouton, 1967).

[28] See Gevay, for example II/1:29–47 (1533); HHStA Rom. Correspondenz 13/10a 24/8/1551; Hans Dernschwam, *Hans Dernschwams Tagebuch*, ed. Franz Babinger (Munich: Duncker & Humblot, 1923), 1:140–8, 274; and Hermann Kellenbenz, *Die Fugger in Spanien und Portugal bis 1560* (Munich: E. Vogel, 1990), 352 for examples of the ransom trade.

[29] HHStA 10/10, fol. 1; HKA Reichsakten 174a, fols. 72–75ᵛ, 92–102 mention Italian, Greek, and Jewish translators. Also Nehring 249, 488. For a more extensive look at one Macedonian translator/merchant who was recruited for Habsburg service, see Josef Žontar, "Michael Cernović, Geheimagent Ferdinands I. und Maximilians II., und seine Berichterstattung," *Mitteilungen des Österreichischen Staatsarchivs* 24 (1971):169–222.

[30] "Esse autem dominum et mercatorem impossibile est." Gevay, II/2:38 (1534).

[31] The Venetians' and Ragusans' "eternal peace treaties" with profitable merchant protections were advertised in pamphlets such as *Ein Summari der Turckischen Botschafft werbung/ an die Herrschafft zu Venedig / in Welscher sprach beschehen/ sampt des Venedischen Senats gegeben antwort.* [Nuremberg: Johann Petreius, 1537] and *Newe Zeyttung von dem Tyrannen des Türckischen Keysers Haubtman....* [1542], aiiii.

[32] Felix Faber, *Eigentliche beschreibung der hin vnnd wider farth zu dem Heyligen Landt gen Jerusalem vnd furter durch die grosse Wüsteney zu dem Heiligen Berge Horeb Sinay/....* [1556].

Despite Venetian-Ottoman competition and even war over the control of
the islands between these empires, the subsequent peace treaties allowed
the Ottoman fleet passage through Venetian waters and increased control over the Adriatic.[33] By 1508, when the League of Cambrai was
formed, the anti-Venetian league allies could speak of the Venetians as
"merchants of human blood, traitors to the Christian faith, [who] have
tacitly partitioned the world with the Turks. . . . "[34] Venetians, "untrue"
to their faith and often blamed for the increased Turkish presence in
the Mediterranean,[35] might pressure other merchants to assist the Turks.
Such arrangements could be turned to the benefit of Latin Christendom
if the merchant passed on his hard-earned information, as exemplified
in the 1523 *Haimliche Anschleg/ vnd fürnemun des Türckischen Kaysers*
(wann er Rodis eroberte) wider die Cristen vnd Christliche Lender rc.
Vnd anders mer durch die gefangen Türcken so von Möran gen Görtz
gefürt/ Newlich bekant vnd gegeoffenbart worden.rc. In this news pamphlet, information about the Ottoman military as well as Süleyman's
intentions, his alliances with the Venetians, and his person are presented
in the form of questions posed to one of these merchants. Preceding
the interrogation account, the author includes the story of how the
merchant was commissioned to convey Turkish envoys by a Venetian
official.[36]

These close relations between Ottoman state and merchants were not
exclusive to citizens of Italian states. Dealing with the non-Christian
world was part and parcel of successful merchants' activities. These deal-
ings could be open or secret, benign or injurious to Christian concerns.
In practice, merchants could ransom prisoners in Constantinople, as they
possessed the connections and the necessary reserves of money or credit
to pay ransoms or emancipations.[37] Yet they profited from the charitable

---

[33] The Venetians and Ottomans were at war from 1463 to 1479.

[34] Quoted in William Bouwsma, *Venice and the Defense of Republican Liberty* (Berkeley:
University of California Press, 1968), 98.

[35] *Türckenbiechlin, Ain Nutzlich Gesprech oder Underrede etlicher personen* [1522], Civ*.

[36] *Haimliche Anschleg/ vnd fürnemunb des Türckischen Kaysers (wann er Rodis eroberte)*
wider die Cristen vnd Christliche Lender rc. Vnd anders mer durch die gefangen Türcken
so von Möran gen Görtz gefürt/ Newlich bekant vnd gegeoffenbart worden.rc. (Augsburg: Heinrich Steiner, 1523), aii–aiii*.

[37] "Diser Jacob fugger ist ain solich Kauffman gewesen, der sein hanndl nit allain in der
Cristenhait, sonnder pey turggen, Juden vnd haidn gehebt," Georg Kirchmair, *Georg*
Kirchmair's Denkwürdigkeiten seiner Zeit (1519–1553), FRA, 1:1, 475. Also, HHStA
Span. DK 3/53, fol. 338 and *Türckenbiechlin*, diii–diii*.

and Christian activity. Matters did not improve when one of these merchants, the half-Venetian and half-Greek Lodovico Gritti, became one of the most powerful men in Constantinople in the late 1520s. He converted to Islam and became one of Süleyman's ministers. In the eyes of the western European observers, he never lost the taint of his merchant (and bastard) status. Another Italian convert in service to the Ottomans disparaged Gritti as sybaritic and untrustworthy on the grounds of his base birth: "he cannot forget his nature."[38] The 1534 news of his murder in Hungary, where he had been sent by Süleyman as a representative, was met with pleasure in Austria as an appropriate fate for such a grasping man.

Members of Jewish communities comprised another group of cultural and linguistic intermediaries in the Mediterranean and eastern Europe. During the second half of the fifteenth century, Jewish physicians established themselves as court doctors and diplomatic negotiators in both Muslim (Persian and Ottoman) and Christian courts (Italian and Polish, although the courts of the Iberian kingdoms had also been part of this tradition in the earlier medieval period). The international connections between Jewish communities throughout Europe and the Middle East allowed them to move between kingdoms and territories relatively easily, and their positions of access and trust as rulers' personal physicians gave them credibility as diplomats. Extant descriptions of these men reveal just how intertwined their professional functions were.[39] Isaac Bey began his diplomatic career after leaving Iberia, serving as an interpreter for a Venetian envoy of the Persian court in 1471. A doctor, he became court physician and then personal physician of the Persian ruler Uzun Hassan and was sent on missions to Hungary and several other courts. Isaac Bey eventually settled down in Poland to serve the royal Jagiellon family, finally becoming the personal doctor of King Sigismund.[40] Iacopo of Gaeta (Ya'qub Pasha) served at Mehmed II's court as physician from

---

[38] "Ipse naturam suam non potest oblivioni tradere." Gevay II/2:38. For a profile of Gritti, Ferenc Szakály, *Lodovico Gritti in Hungary, 1529–1534* (Budapest: Akademiai Kiadó, 1995).

[39] Lajos Tardy cites the courts of Uzun Hassan and Matthias Corvinus as evidence that the personal physician was the customary fifteenth-century envoy in *Beyond the Ottoman Empire. 14th–16th Century Hungarian Diplomacy in the East*, trans. János Boris (Szeged, 1978), 62–6. Robert Jütte surveys the roles of Jewish doctors in "Contacts at the Bedside: Jewish Physicians and Their Christian Patients," *In and Out of the Ghetto*, ed. R. Po-Chia Hsia and Hartmut Lehman (Cambridge: Cambridge University Press, 1995), 137–50.

[40] Tardy, *Beyond the Ottoman Empire*, 62–70.

at least 1452 until Mehmed's death and as a diplomatic assistant from 1466, particularly in Venetian affairs.[41]

Under Süleyman, Jewish court physicians continued to be active in diplomacy between the Ottoman court and Christian powers. Particularly in the first decades of his reign, Süleyman's closest councilors and advisors consisted of individuals like these, who could cross this line between the public world and the imperial household with its restricted access. Moses Hamon, son and father of other court physicians serving the Ottoman family, played a role in settling the Ottoman-Venetian peace treaty of 1540.[42] Perhaps the best-known Jewish court physician in the sixteenth century, Solomon Ashkenazi, left the Italian peninsula to serve as Sigismund II's court physician at Krakow, then attended the first vezir Sokollu in Constantinople under Süleyman and then Selim II. His successes as a diplomatic negotiator depended on his role as physician at these courts: Ashkenazi was the attending physician of not only the vezir Sokollu, but also the Venetian bailo. He could move easily between their households even during times of public diplomatic strain between Venice and the Porte. Through this connection, Ashkenazi and a hand-picked translator were able to draft a treaty between the two powers (signed in March 1573). He later used his Polish connections to help determine the election of the next Polish king in 1574–1575. In Constantinople, Ashkenazi provided links beyond the first vezir and other Latin Christian representatives' households: he was also the physician of the Austrian Habsburg ambassador Albert Wyss.[43]

Yet even as Jewish physicians were valued for diplomatic relations between Ottoman, Polish, and Venetian courts, they do not appear to have been regularly employed for interactions between Ottomans and Habsburg courts in central Europe during much of the sixteenth century (certainly not until the end of Ferdinand I's reign). Undoubtedly, this partially reflects the absence of Jewish communities in Austria. Jews had been expelled in waves that began in the early fifteenth century (Vienna in

---

[41] Bernard Lewis, "The Privilege Granted by Mehmed II to His Physician," *Bulletin of the School of Oriental and African Studies* XIV 3(1952): 550–63.

[42] Leslie Peirce, *The Imperial Harem: Women and Sovereignty in the Ottoman Empire* (Oxford: Oxford University Press, 1993), 75 and Uriel Heyd, "Moses Hamon, chief Jewish physician to Sultan Süleyman the Magnificent," *Oriens* 16 (1963): 152–70.

[43] Benjamin Arbel, *Trading Nations: Jews and Venetians in the Early Modern Eastern Mediterranean* (Leiden, New York: Brill, 1995), 78–86 and HKA, Reichsakten 174a, fols. 73, 97.

1421) and were concluded by the beginning of the sixteenth century. Ferdinand regarded Jewish communities with disfavor, supporting policies to drive them out of Bohemia and Moravia (although these policies were reversed under his son Maximilian II).[44] In Hungary, anti-Jewish and anti-foreign-merchant sentiments had risen together as recently as 1525, when the persecution of the Jewish court treasurer Emericus Fortunatus escalated into a pogrom against Jews, Croatians, the Fuggers, and other foreigners in Buda.[45] Habsburg opponents in the Holy Roman Empire did send Jewish envoys to the Ottoman court. Ferdinand's ambassador reported in 1531 that the "Duke of Saxony and his Lutherans" had sent an ambassador to Süleyman who was also a Jew, raising the specter of unholy alliances in Habsburg minds.[46]

Anti-Jewish sentiments grew in the sixteenth century. In the years immediately following the Turkish defeat of Hungary in 1526, Hungarian Jews were perceived as hostile to the Turks. One account of the Turkish siege of Buda stated that:

[T]he Jews and some burgers that remained in the city stood guard and had previously reinforced some gates . . . the Jews of Ofen had greatly feared for their persons and their goods, on account of which their streets were barricaded with a special wall and they courageously intended to resist [the Turks].[47]

Another casualty report stated that only 20 out of 4,500 Jews survived the conflict.[48] Yet rumors spread that they had welcomed the Turks into other

---

[44] Although heir to a Castile absent Jews, Charles V did accept the presence of Jewish communities in the Holy Roman Empire, in response to their support of his authority. However, he did not encourage them to return to areas from which they had been expelled. For an overview of Jewish migration and rulers' policies toward Jewish communities, see Jonathan I. Israel, *European Jewry in the Age of Mercantilism 1550–1750*, rev. ed. (Oxford: Oxford University Press, 1989), 5–50.

[45] Birnbaum, 71–2.

[46] "el duque de saxonia con sus luteranos hauia embiado alla su embaxador/ que a su parecer era vn ebreo . . . " HHStA Span DK 1/10, fol. 1.

[47] "die Jüden unnd [e]ttliche bürger so inn der statt bliben waren stelleten sich zue der wehr unnd haben zůvor ettliche Thor vermaüren lassen. . . . aber die Juden zue offen haben sich ires leib und guetts vor dem Turkhen hart geforcht, deßhalben ir gassen so mit ainer besonnderen maür umbfanngen gespert unnd sich dapffer wehren wellen . . . " ÖNB, CVP 8614 "Das sibendt unnd letste Büech dises meines Oesterreichischen Ehrenwerkhs Welliches das ganntzherrlich leben mit allen löblichen und ritterlichen thaten des Allerkhünenisten Theürischen Khaiesers Ertzhertzogen zue Oesterreich," 352.

[48] *Hernach volgt des Blüthundts/ der sych nennedt ein Türckischen Keiser/ gethaten/ so er vnd die seinen/ nach eroberung der schlacht/ auff den xxviii. tag Augusti nechstuergangen geschehen/* . . . , 1526, ai[v] claimed that only 20 out of 4,500 Jewish residents survived.

towns and, in subsequent years, that they were close allies (along with some Greeks) of the Turkish advisor Gritti.[49] The evidence of perceived prosperity for Jews living under Ottoman protection in both Hungary and the Levantine did not reassure the suspicious. As Jews moved into the international trade once dominated by Venetians, hostility towards them increased. (Even several of the court physicians, Moses Hamon and Solomon Ashkenazi, had well-known mercantile connections.)[50] Mistrust of Hungarian Jews, let alone Levantine Jews subject to the Turks, extended to Jews who simply wished to cross the border. Jews traveling on business could be seized and imprisoned, and even their safe-conduct passes ignored.[51] On the seas, Ottoman-subject Jewish merchants and their goods could be classified as legitimate targets.[52] Jews were perceived to be active not only as merchants, but also as attacking enemies. In popular pamphlets and diplomatic reports from the 1530s, Jews were reported to be corsairs allied with Muslims against the Christians as well as captains of ships in the Ottoman fleet.[53] These reports added to the increasingly antagonistic rhetoric against Jews as spies of the Turks and enemies of Christianity, which flourished in the middle decades of the sixteenth century.

Perhaps reflecting the unviability of merchants or Jewish physicians as diplomatic go-betweens, in the later part of his reign Süleyman favored another group that already played an important role in establishing policies and treaties with Latin Christendom – his interpreters. The presence of his interpreters is evident throughout the diplomatic exchanges between Ottoman and Habsburg courts. They acted as official translators or dragomen for Habsburg envoys' meetings with vezirs and the sultan. They translated the continual flow of diplomatic papers. Contemporary reports and explanations of disruptions in the flow of negotiation, either through clashes between envoy and translators or shifts in translators' position in court politics, make it clear how crucial these translators were

---

[49] Heinrich Kretschmayr, "Ludovico Gritti," *AÖG* 83 (1897), 82.

[50] Arbel, 15–18.

[51] For example, the 1563 exchange of two captive knights for Salomon from Buda in Turcica 17/5, fols. 100–3, and the imprisonment of Moises Kauffman of Buda, Turcica 25/2, fols. 89–89a and Turcica 26/1, fols. 242–3.

[52] HHStA Rom Corres. 14 (1558), 157.

[53] "Juden Corsaro," *Ein Summari der Turckischen Botschafft werbung*, 4; *Römischer Keyserlicher Maiestat Christenlichste Kriegs Rüstung wider die vnglaubigen/ anzug in Hispanien vnd Sardinien/ Ankunfft in Africa/ vnd eroberung des Ports zu Thunisi im monat junio Anno 1535. Aus Teutschen/ Italianischen vnd Frantzosichen schrifften vnd abtrucken fleissig ausgezogen*, iiii; HHStA Belgien PA 28/2 fols. 1–2ᵛ.

in mediating between vezir and Habsburg envoy. Süleyman and his successor Selim employed converted Christians in the positions of both chief translator and court translator. Of the three known chief translators, the two with known antecedents (Yunus and Ibrahim) were originally Greek and Polish Christians. Of the seven lower-ranking translators, the four with known antecedents were also converts to Islam, but from countries with which the Ottomans were at war: Hungary, Austria, or Germany (Mahmud, Murad, Ferhad, and Ali the younger).[54]

Süleyman's administration, both bureaucratic and military, contained many subjects who were converts to Islam.[55] The Habsburgs were fully aware of the preponderance of such "renegades" both in Süleyman's court and in his military. They regularly deplored Ottoman military superiority, attributing the Ottoman army's success in large part to its formerly Christian troops. In their diplomatic missives, they were also careful to identify converted officials accordingly. The issue was tricky to negotiate: renegades were "disavowed Christians" who had abandoned their faith, yet an Ottoman soldier or courtier could have become a renegade through several different routes. A person could be an opportunistic Christian who converted to Islam for the advantages to be gained as a Muslim; they could have been sent from the Balkan borderlands as part of the child tax placed on Slavic Christians; or they could be captured as booty (either as a bystander or as a combatant) during a borderland skirmish and sold into slavery, converting to survive.

The extent to which the physical and spiritual dangers of captivity excused or explained a distasteful familiarity with the Turk is evident in the Habsburg court's opinions of the converts. Ferdinand and his ambassadors dealt with and even presented gifts and money to the translators who were voluntary renegades, but rarely trusted them.[56] The exception was the renegade who had begun his career either as enslaved or as a prisoner-of-war.

---

[54] Josef Matuz, "Die Pfortendolmetscher zur Herrschaftszeit Süleymans des Prächtigen," *Südost-Forschungen* 34 (1975): 26–60; Ferenc Szakály and Lajos Tardy, "Auf der Suche nach einem aus Ungarn stammenden Dolmetscher des Sultans," *Osmanistik – Turkologie – Diplomatik. Festgabe an Josef Matuz*, eds. Christa Fragner und Klaus Schwarz, Islamkundliche Untersuchungen, 150 (Berlin: Klaus Schwarz Verlag, 1992).

[55] For the possibilities and limits of this strategy, see Peirce, *Imperial Harem* and Ebru Turan, "Voices of Opposition in the Reign of Sultan Süleyman," in *Studies on Istanbul and Beyond*, ed. R. G. Ousterhout (Philadelphia: University of Pennsylvania Museum of Archaeology and Anthropology, 2007), 23–35.

[56] Examples include HHStA Turcica 16/1, fol. 38; Venedig Berichte 12, fol. 3; and throughout Nehring.

Captivity, enslavement, escape, and release were common phenomena along the Habsburg-Ottoman border. With the fragmentation of Hungary after the death of its king and most of its nobles in 1526, an era of Ottoman incursions into Austria began. Although there are no exact figures for the number of captives taken in the early decades of hostility between Habsburg and Ottoman empires, there were daily or weekly incidents of villages raided and captives (both military and non-military) taken. Indeed, selling and ransoming prisoners were lucrative sources of income in this border zone, particularly for the Ottomans. Captives wrote to Ferdinand's court, pleading for assistance: as one unfortunate began his petition, "I am wretched and a captive in the hands of the Turks."[57] In the second half of the century, both sides were spurred to diplomatic negotiation by their desire to exchange captives. Some prisoners did return outside of official negotiations – year after year, Ferdinand's account books record a continual trickle of knights and other soldiers returning from captivity. Occasionally the crown granted a pension to an escaped man in recognition of "suffering in Turkish captivity."[58] Soldiers appeared at the Habsburg court after being freed or in the process of raising money to pay their ransoms; common practice allowed soldiers to post bail and then depart to raise their own or their fellows' ransoms. Ferdinand felt some responsibility for them, personally granting a small sum of money to each knight. Apparently, the soldiers then moved on toward their homelands. This form of charity was also practiced outside the Habsburg court. In southern Austria, small towns contributed what they could to such worthy causes. Cities such as Vienna held collections to help pay for soldiers' ransoms and support other men and women returning from many years' captivity. Imperial cities in the Holy Roman Empire gave the soldiers alms, and towns they passed through regarded them as

---

[57] Sergij Vilfan, "Die wirtschaftlichen Auswirkungen der Türkenkriege aus der Sicht der Ranzionierungen, der Steuern und der Preisbewegung" in *Die Auswirkungen der Türkenkriege*, hrsg. Othmar Pickl, Grazer Forschungen zur Wirtschafts– und Sozialgeschichte (Graz, 1971), 177–99. For the economic importance of ransom in wars generally, see Maurice H. Keen, *The Laws of War in the Late Middle Ages* (London: Routledge & Kegan Paul, 1965), "Chapter X: The Law of Ransom." The ransom economy in the western Mediterranean, flourishing several decades later, is in Ellen Friedman, *Spanish Captives in North Africa in the Early Modern Age* (Madison: University of Wisconsin Press, 1983) and Bartholomé Bennassar and Lucile Bennassar, *Les chrétiens d'Allah* (Paris: Perrin, 1989). "Ego miser et captivus, in manibus turcarum..." HHStA Turcica 16/1, fol. 133.

[58] HKA Hofzahlamtsbücher, 1–30 (1543–1576). For the year 1543, see vol. 1, fols. 270–277^v, 280^v. HKA Gedenkbuch 109, fol. 61–61^v.

sources of news about the true conditions on the Hungarian front and in "Turkish captivity."[59] After the disastrous Hungarian defeat in 1526 and the border zone's shift to the edge of Habsburg lands, public perceptions of Christian captives were framed not only by numerous sermons or orations and printed narratives, but also by the tangible relicts of that condition.

Citizens' alms giving to the unfortunate returning captives was fueled by their understanding the harrowing nature of captivity. In the years after the battle of Mohács in 1526, Georgius of Hungary's depiction of captivity among the civilized Turks, onerous primarily because of the religious temptations presented by Islam, would be overtaken by more incendiary descriptions of the physical dangers present in a war zone. In October 1529, the siege of Vienna brought home to all of the Holy Roman Empire how volatile the region was. Justus Jonas, a close ally of Luther, later recalled the moment when the extent of Ottoman military ambition registered among the Protestant reformers. Traveling with Luther and Philip Melancthon between Gotha and Eisenach, they heard the news of the siege:

Still nobody wanted to believe that the Turk was in Austria, or that it could be possible that such a great army might be found before Vienna. . . . The praiseworthy city Vienna knows now well that it didn't see the paper Turkish hats of a carnival play, but was visited by Süleyman's army. There have been books written before and after this, which warned and cautioned, but what good are they?[60]

The siege of Vienna caused both Luther and Erasmus to modulate their stances on the "Turkish peril." The Turk could no longer simply stand as an inspiration for the reform of Latin Christianity or for the resolution of conflict between Rome and the reformers. Interpretations of the Turks as a moral punishment of Christianity continued to find adherents, but

[59] Vilfan, 184–5. Vienna, Stadt- und Landesarchiv, OKAR 90 (1557), fol. 21; 95 (1562), fols. 109^v–116^v; Ulm, Ratsprotokolle 24 (1559), fol. 275^v; StAN, Stadtrechnungsbelege II 1526–30, 1531–4.

[60] "es noch nicht gleuben wolten/ das der Türcke jnn Osterreich were/ oder das es jmer müglich sein könte/ mit so grosser rüstung/ sich vor Wien finden zu lassen. . . . Die löbliche stad Wien/ weis nu wol/ das sie nicht papiren Türcken hütte/ jnn einem fastnacht spiel gesehen/ sondern das sie von Solimani kriegs volck besuchet ist/ Es sind bücher zuuor vnd her nach geschrieben/ welche gewarnet vnd vermanet/ aber was hilffets." *Vrsprung des Turkischen Reichs/ bis auff den itzigen Solyman/ durch D. Paulum Jouium/ Bischoff Nucerin an Keiserliche Maistat/ Carolum V . . . / Verdeutschet durch Justus Jonam,* [1538], Yii. This was perhaps a bit disingenous of the reformed party, as the Ottomans had raided in southern Austria in the previous decades.

now people in the Holy Roman Empire were also offered justifications for defending themselves against the Turkish invaders.

Luther intensifed his attacks on erroneous religion through the newly prominent figure of the captive. Luther had introduced the language of captivity to describe the sacraments' imprisonment in a Babylonian Captivity by Rome, in his influential 1520 pamphlet *Von der Babylonischen Gefengknuß der Kirchen.* Luther's 1529 pamphlets employed the example of Christian captives in the Ottoman Empire largely to inspire adherents of religious reform to endure the papacy's assaults. His calls for steadfast faith under pressure were given a vivid directness in the figure of the Christian enduring Turkish captivity. They also allowed readers to focus enmity or anxiety on a distant foe of true Christianity. In the pre-siege *Vom Kriege*, Luther argued that living under the Turks was difficult because the Turks prohibited the public preaching of Christianity or any condemnations of Islam. Without the "living bread for souls," Christians would find the "free fleshly ways" of the Turks irresistable.[61] Writing a few months later, after the siege, Luther reassured the reader that, for the good Christian, death was only bodily and led to eternal life, whereas Turks (and implicitly others who followed religious error) went to hell. Thus, being hacked to death, speared on hedgestakes, or exposed to "italian and sodomite immorality" were only transitory sufferings.[62] As a prisoner of an ungodly person, one's duty was to maintain true belief. Luther used gender to underscore the relative powerlessness of Christians: Turks were the men and Christians the women. Yet being feminized or sexually violated did not justify passivity. The Jews had figured as the women to the Babylonians' men, but the Jews had engaged in converting the Babylonians.[63] Although Luther's concerns remained primarily on matters internal to Latin Christendom, other authors applied the metaphor of the Babylonian captivity without qualification to unfortunate Christians in Balkan and Hungarian lands conquered by the Ottomans.[64] Their tactic was reinforced by vivid printed images of captive Christians.

---

[61] "Denn sie mangeln des lebendigen brodts der seelen und sehen das frey fleischlich wesen der Türcken und müssen sich wol also zu yhn gesellen." Luther, *Vom Kriege wider die Türcken* (1529), WA 30(2): 120–1.

[62] "Welsch und Sodomisch unkeuscheit," Luther, *Heerpredigt wider den Türken* (1529), WA 30(2):, 191, also 177–8.

[63] Luther, *Heerpredigt*, WA 30 (2):191–2.

[64] By 1531, the *Itinerarivm Wegrayß* described the suffering of the Balkan peoples as their Babylonian captivity, Eii.

The 1529 siege of Vienna had inspired a flurry of pamphlets describing the battle and the two military hosts. In the next several years of intensified military conflict, artists produced woodcut series presenting the Ottoman military train in an ethnographic mode. Sultan Süleyman, Ibrahim Paşa, and different types of military troops (including cavalry and infantry) were depicted with their costumes, armament, and accompanying descriptive identifying verses. The Turkish military train series contained vivid images of Christian captives, included woodcuts of Christians being dragged off into captivity by Turkish soldiers, who marched with spitted babies still embellishing their lances or staked on hedgestakes as Luther described (Figure 29).[65] These woodcut series had precedents in Maximilian I's *Triumphzug* and close parallels in German soldier series from the 1520s. Reflecting the subsequent conflict with the Ottomans, a 1532 composite woodcut of a German army train with Turkish prisoners and symbols of death updated the *Triumphzug* tradition. Both the German and Turkish soldier series have been attributed to Hans Sebald Beham, Erhard Schön, and Niklas Stör. All three were Nuremberg artists, and Beham and Schön at least were dedicated to the cause of religious reform. German soldier woodcuts are generally thought to have been created for secular consumers; the target consumer for these images of the Turkish army may have been the same.[66] Notably, the representations of the Turkish army were being produced in Nuremberg even as the city refused to support the Habsburg call for funding and troops to defend the eastern border of the Holy Roman Empire from the Turks. The years immediately after the siege of Vienna, then, saw an uneasy tension between the reformers' messages of internal reform rather than military support and the practice, in the commercial realm, of popularizing images of the siege's victims.

Dangers to the captive body, which Luther had dismissed as not important, received heightened attention from other reformers in the years following the siege. Justus Jonas elaborated on Luther's 1529 themes of apocalypticism and the horrors of captivity in his 1530 *Das siebend*

---

[65] Max Geisberg, *The German Single-Leaf Woodcut, 1500–1550*, rev. and ed. Walter Strauss (New York: Hacker Books, 1974), IV: 1192, 1194, 1339–41 and Walter Sturminger, *Bibliographie und Ikonographie der Türckenbelagerungen Wiens* (Gräz: H. Böhlau, 1955), 3–59.

[66] J.R. Hale, "The Soldier in German Graphic Art of the Renaissance," *Journal of Interdisciplinary History* XVII (1986): 85–114; Keith Moxey, *Peasants, Warriors, and Wives: Popular Imagery in the Reformation* (Chicago: University of Chicago Press, 1989), ch. 4, especially 72–83.

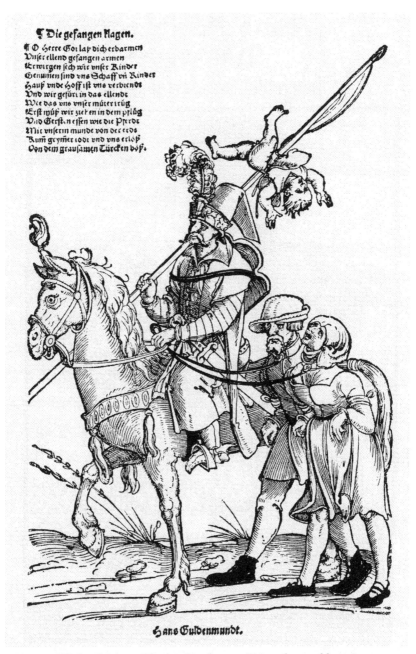

FIGURE 29. Erhard Schön, *The captives lament [Die gefangen klagen]*, ca. 1532. Max Geisberg, *The German Single-Leaf Woodcut*, vol. 4 (New York: Hacker, 1974), G1242.

Capitel Danielis/ von des Türcken Gottes lesterung vnd schrecklicher morderey...through a comparison of the Ottoman and other empires.[67] Any reservation of judgment or admiration of Turkish practices despite their heterodoxy was absent from Jonas's writing. Jonas stated unequivocally that the Turkish people failed to follow God, honor, or natural law, and that the Ottoman Empire was the creation of the devil.[68] Jonas also explicitly associated the Turks with the apocalypse-heralding Red Jews. Although Turks were not "born Jews," their adoption of Jewish customs and wisdom, however admixed, caused them to become this dangerous other kind of Jew.[69] Having addressed the coming end-time, Jonas turned to life in captivity and the horrors faced by Christians living under Turkish rule. The first horrors were those familiar from Georgius of Hungary, but made less palatable by Jonas's definition of Turkish culture and religion as lacking virtue. The attrition of the Christian population under Turkish rule had two causes in Jonas's eyes: the child tax placed on Christian subjects and the weakening of Christianity due to the prohibition against criticizing Islam. Evidence that the Turks lacked natural law lay in their willingness to violate the laws of warfare: they captured or killed women, children, and the ill or elderly; in the conquest of Constantinople, they raped women and girls and publicly hacked members of the Byzantine ruling family to pieces. People were sold naked like cattle (apparently an additional violation of natural law) in markets.[70] Through these actions, Jonas argued, the Turks were civilizationally lower than classical Greeks or Romans: they lacked philosophy and orderly *Policey*. This deficiency of order was not confined to wartime situations. Another sign of this, according to Jonas, was that Turks failed to embrace the institution of monogamous marriage (choosing instead to have multiple women). Jonas assured the reader that this rejection of social organization was common

[67] Justus Jonas, *Das siebend Capitel Danielis, von des Türcken Gottes lesterung vnd schrecklicher morderey*.... (Wittenberg, [1530]). For a discussion of Luther's apocalypticism and the Turks, see Heiko Oberman, *The Roots of Antisemitism in the Age of Renaissance and Reformation* (Philadelphia: Fortress Press, 1984), 116–17, 121–2; and Mark U. Edwards, Jr., *Luther's Last Battles* (Ithaca: Cornell University Press, 1983), 97–114, 141–2.

[68] Jonas, *Das siebend Capitel Danielis*, aiv^v.

[69] Jonas, *Das siebend Capitel Danielis*, diii–div^v. Andrew Gow notes the conflation of Red Jews with Turks, via Luther's identification of Gog and Magog with the Turk, beginning in 1529. *The Red Jews: Anti-Semitism in an Apocalyptic Age*, 1200–1600 (Leiden: Brill, 1995), 155–9.

[70] Jonas, *Das siebend Capitel Danielis*, f-fiii^v. Nancy Bisaha, *Creating East and West: Renaissance Humanists and the Ottoman Turks* (Philadelphia: University of Pennsylvania Press, 2004) analyzes fifteenth-century accounts, 63–9.

to many heresies.[71] Marriage's importance as a determinant of civilized people and true belief also served to reinforce reformed Christianity's embrace of monogamy as the preferred state for most individuals, including clerics.

Reformer Johannes Brenz continued Jonas's rhetoric in his more alarmist 1537 pamphlet on the dangers of the Turks. Along with a reprise of apocalyptic predictions, Brenz included the association of Turks with Red Jews. He charged that Turks violated natural law because of their horrific treatment of noncombatants in the aftermath of a successful siege, when they raped and killed women and children. Including Jonas's account of the Byzantine Empress's and imperial daughters' deaths after the siege of Constantinople, Brenz added another story in his effort to rally military support for the Turkish front. He recounted the story of a Rhodian mother who killed her young sons to spare them the "shameful abuse" of sexual assault, according to Brenz a vice which was popular among the Turks.[72]

The year 1541 saw the formal annexation of Ottoman-controlled Hungary by the Ottoman Empire. Luther's discussion of the Turkish threat that year encorporated an escalation of rhetoric even as he continued to focus on the problems of Christian faith within Christendom. The *Vermahnung zum Gebet wider den Türcken* begins with an assessment of "papist darkness and idolatry."[73] His language became more belligerent even as he intensified his use of the Turk to attack unreformed Christianity. Both were destructive to order and governance within the household, the city, and the church.[74] Along with the pairing of Pope and Turk, scatological references to the devil ("Teufelsdreck") increased. These parallels established, Luther also spelled out for the reader how Christian society was destroyed in captivity: familes were torn apart and women physically abused.[75] The years 1541–1542 also saw the reprinting of Luther's 1529 pamphlets on the Turks. *Vom Kriege wider die Türken* was reprinted once and *Heerpredigt wider den Türken*, with additional

---

[71] "Dann der Turck acht keiner kunst odder Philosophi / wie doch die Heiden geacht haben/ Richt auch kein ordenliche policey an." Jonas, *Das sibende Capitel Danielis*, fiii^v, and also fiii.

[72] Brenz, *Wie sich Prediger und Leien halten sollen*, ... (Wittenberg: Rhaw, 1537), A4^v–C2.

[73] "Bebstliche finsternis und abgotterey." Martin Luther, *Vermahnung zum Gebet wider den Türken* (1541), WA 51:585–6.

[74] "Summa, da ist nicht anders, denn Haus, Stad und Kirchen regiment verstören, beide, im Bapstum und Türckey," *Vermahnung*, WA 51:621.

[75] *Vermahnung*, WA 51:585–625, esp. 620–2.

sensational detail, four times.[76] Luther's correspondence over the next few years revealed him to be consciously concerned about the threat of the Turkish military, yet he did not throw his efforts into rallying the Holy Roman Empire's military forces. Instead, he continued his tactic of explicitly linking unreformed Christians and Muslims. In Luther's prologue to fellow reformer Erasmus Alberus's *Der Barfusser Münche Eulenspiegel und Alcoran* (1542), adherents of papal Christianity and the Turks were directly comparable. Alberus described the Franciscan *Liber conformitatum* as the *Alcoran* of the Franciscans in which they committed the same errors that the Muslims had by elevating "Idol Francis" ("Abgott Francis"), like Muhammad, to a position of greater importance than Christ's. This "blindness" was a divine punishment shared by "Heathens/ Jews/ Turks/ Pope."[77]

Reformer Heinrich Knaust's May 1542 pamphlet elaborated on both Turkish violence and religious error, understood by him as deviance. His detailing of the violent Turkish "bloodhound"[78] is familiar: Turks robbed, burned, and killed the young and old, women and men. Their wartime barbarity included spearing children. Knaust was also concerned about Christian doctrine and the Ottomans' efforts to lure young Christians away from the faith of their birth and convert them to Islam. For Knaust, Islam's creation from the confused beliefs of true Christians, Jews, and heretical Arians had allowed for the renewal and concentration of all the devil's diffuse sowing of heresies. In the pamphlet, he detailed each heresy now concentrated in Islam. Doctrinal heresies on the nature of the Trinity and Christ and practices like regular ablutions to wash away sin were listed along with the names of previously condemned heresies that had encorporated these errors. Another type of heresy involved forms of licentiousness that Knaust found depraved: taking multiple wives, marrying nonbelievers, and the fourteenth heresy of sodomy which "the Qur'an openly states is not a sin."[79] While the pamphlet focused on the religious

---

[76] F. Cohrs and A. Goetze, "Introduction to "Vom Kriege wider die Türken"," *WA* 30(2): 98 and "Introduction to "Heerpredigt wider den Türken"," *WA* 30(2): 153.

[77] "Heiden/ Juden/ Türcken/ Bapst." Erasmus Alberus, *Der Barfusser Münche....* (Wittenberg: Hans Luft, 1542), Aiii, and *ii–**ii^v, Bii, Biv^v, Ci–i^v.

[78] Heinrich Knaust, *Von geringem herkommen/ schentlichem leben/...Machomets / und seiner verdamlichen vnd Gotßlesterischen Ler* (1542). The metaphor of the bloodhound can be found the *Hernach volgt des Blüthundts*; Luther, *Heerpredigt*, WA 30 (2):191; Jonas, *Das siebend Capitel Danielis*, fii–fii^v; Brenz, Cii; and Knaust, Bi.

[79] "Sodomitschen und stummen Sünde/ spricht das sey kain Sünde / wie inn seynem Alchoran offenbar stehet." Knaust, Aii, Bii^v–Biii, Diii–Div^v.

errors of Islam, the title page image reminded the reader of the crucial context in which these errors are confronted. The woodcut depicts
captivity through a scene in which the Ottoman Emperor speaks to a
bound man. From these accounts of captivity, it was only a short step
to Sebastian Münster's descriptions in the 1550 *Cosmographia*. Münster
described, in sensationalist detail, the various sexual perils that awaited
the captive in the Ottoman Empire: conversion and circumcision under
pressure, castration for particularly attractive boys and concubinage for
the particularly attractive girls, and the sexual assault of young boys.[80]

By 1542–1543, Luther concentrated more directly on Turkish religious
authority and the evaluation of doctrinal errors. In the previous decades,
reformers had, like other Christians, understood Islam as the concatena-
tion and revival of older heresies. The text of the Augsburg Confession
(1530), for example, had been careful to repudiate Islam's position on
the Trinity along with other anti-Trinitarian stances[81] in an effort, presumably, to deflect charges of like heresy levied against the Confession's
adherents. Luther also demonstrated an interest in educating the public about Islam's errors, being careful to eliminate possible association
between reformed Christianity and Islam in light of their shared repudiation of iconophilism.[82] His first effort had been the 1530 reprint of
Georgius of Hungary's *Tractatus*, discussed in Chapter 1. In the late
1530s and early 1540s, the Wittenberg reformers produced a body of
texts on Turkish culture, history, and religion that would help differentiate themselves from Islam. In 1537, Philip Melancthon introduced a Latin
edition of Paolo Giovio's history of the Ottomans, and a German translation by Justus Jonas quickly followed.[83] In 1542–1543, Luther actively
worked on the production of texts explaining Islam's doctrinal errors to
reformed Christians. He produced a translation of Riccoldo da Monte
croce's *Confutatio Alcorani* (1542) that cast Islam in a significantly more
negative light than Georgius's *Tractatus*.[84] Both Luther and Melancthon
wrote introductions to Theodor Bibliander's 1543 Latin Qur'an (based

---

[80] Captives faced, among other perils, "sceleratissimae libidinis" and "contra naturam &
ante naturam libidine saevit," Münster, *Cosmographiae universalis* (Basel: Petri, 1550),
977.

[81] *Confessio odder Bekantnus des Glaubens etlicher Fürsten vnd Stedte: Uberantwort
Keiserlicher Maeistat: zu Augsburg* (Wittenberg: Georg Rhaw, 1531), Aaii, Aaiiiiᵛ.

[82] Luther, *Vom Kriege*, WA 30(2):128.

[83] D. Clemen, "Introduction to *Vorwart zu dem Libellus de ritu et moribus Turcorum*,"
WA 30(2): 200.

[84] Hartmut Bobzin evaluates the translation briefly in "'A Treasury of Heresies': Christian
polemics against the Koran," *The Qur'an as Text*, ed. Stefan Wild (Leiden: Brill, 1996),

on Robert of Ketton's translation). Luther has been credited with persuading the Basel city council to allow its publication, despite the council's prior ban on it. Sebastian Münster, writing as a supporter of the ban, argued that the book possessed "no truth, no piety, no decency."[85] Luther concurred that the book was shameful and full of lies and fables, but he argued that it should be published nonetheless so that more people could learn for themselves that the Qur'an was contrary to Christianity.[86] According to Luther, the study of Jewish rites and customs through Jewish texts allowed the Christian reader to evaluate them against true faith and practice. Now that the errors of the "defenders of the idolatrous papacy," Jews, Anabaptists, and Michael Servetus had all been exposed, it was time to do the same for Islam.[87]

In his foreword to the Qur'an, Luther framed the need for a Latin translation of the Qur'an in terms of natural religion. All civilized people, Luther conceded, made sacrifices and felt the need to worship. Although worshiping idolatrous objects was thus comprehensible, it was still unacceptable because the devil had prevented the Jews from recognizing Christ as the son of God after Christ's resurrection. For Latin Christians, this failure had led, indirectly, to the creation of Islam. Luther characterized Muslims as erroneous in both doctrine and practice: they slandered Christ, recognized a foolish prophet, invented "crude" rites, and "lacerate their own bodies and those of infants" (presumably a reference to circumcision, although echoing idolatrous sacrifices in the New World). These errors had to be refuted. Luther also asserted that Jews, Muslims, and papists were idolatrous. Here the word extended beyond simple worship of images; a few paragraphs later Luther acknowledged that Muslims did not tolerate images. Luther also compared the Turks to the non-Christian Jews and *ethnici* in their shared failure to follow the prophets and apostles appropriately. Returning to Daniel and the condition of captivity, Luther reminded the reader that the Babylonian captives served as the model for converting Muslims to true faith.[88]

167–9. A prior vernacular German version of the Qur'an exists as *Alchoran* (Strasbourg: Schott, 1540).

[85] Münster, with Wolfgang Wyssenburg and Jakob Truckenbrot: "kein warheit, kein fromheit, kein erberkeit," Karl Hagenbach, "Luther und der Koran vor dem Rathe zu Basel," *Beiträge zur vaterländischen Geschichte* 9 (1870), 311.

[86] Luther, "wie gar ein verflucht, schendlich, verzweifelt buch es sey, voller lugen, fabeln und aller grewel," in Hagenbach, 299.

[87] Luther, "Vorrede zu Theodor Biblianders Koranausgabe," WA 53: 569–72.

[88] "lacerant sua et infantium corpora," "Vorrede...Koranausgabe," 570–1.

With the publication of the Qur'an and its refutations, in 1542–1543, Luther and his circle ceased to work toward the dissemination of knowledge about Islam or the Turks. Luther died several years later, and larger political concerns dominated Protestant circles in the subsequent decades. The Smalkaldic war and its aftermath focused energy on political and religious concerns internal to the Holy Roman Empire. With the official Peace of Augsburg in 1555, guaranteeing religious tolerance to adherents of the Augsburg Confession, reformers ceased to use the language of present or impending captivity as a veiled description of their own condition. Their investigations of Islam and Turkish history seem to have waned as their energies turned to building confessions, institutional churches, and Protestant states. They did not forget Constantinople and the Ottoman Empire, but in the 1550s their interest was in the Orthodox Church and exploring the possibilities of reunification. Even as the Protestant reformers abandoned their interest in Islam, an emphasis on captivity and its role in the production of knowledge about the Ottomans emerged in a very different place: Ferdinand's court in Austria, a court still committed to Rome and Catholicism.

Ferdinand charged the clergy at the Habsburg court and in Vienna to preach against the Turk as a common enemy of Christendom. Clerics showed little interest in Muslim doctrine, emphasizing instead the physical brutalities suffered by prisoners and all subjugated Christians.[89] Perhaps the best-known preacher was Friderich Nausea, bishop of Vienna from 1541 to 1552. Nausea's sermons contained the familiar physical horrors of the Turk, who raped wives, virgins, and nuns, slaughtered adolescents, abused boys in moral turpitude, and defiled churches with excrement.[90] His student, Urban of Gurk, preaching in Vienna from 1552 to 1568, drew on his own experience as a former captive in his sermons. From the pulpit and in print, Urban of Gurk directed his flock to consider the horrible lot of these prisoners: "the misery, distress, difficult prison and brutal servitude, the hard and despicable work, the intolerable hunger and need, the knocks and blows, torment and pain, that the poor miserable imprisoned Christians under this tyranny must endure."[91]

[89] The development of this rhetoric by bishops of Vienna and court preachers has been traced by Emil Knappe, "Die Geschichte zur Kulturgeschichte einer Stadt während der Türkenzeit" (Ph.D dissertation, University of Vienna, 1949), 17–66.

[90] Friedrich Nausea, *Friderici Nauseae Blancicampiani,... Evangelicae veritatis Homiliarum Centuriae quatuor* (Cologne: Peter Quentell, 1540), cxxxv–cxxvi^v.

[91] Urban Sagstetter of Gurk was himself briefly captured as a child during the 1529 siege of Vienna. "dann ich selbs in meiner Kindthait in seinen Tyrannischen henden gewesen/

Other former captives sought the Habsburg crown's support. The escaped prisoner and author Bartolomej Georgijević dedicated his *Türckey oder von yetziger Türcken kirchen gepräng*... (1545) to a Habsburg court official. The pamphlet, based on Georgijević's own experiences during thirteen years in captivity,[92] became very popular. Sebastian Münster circulated its contents further when sections of the pamphlet, including Georgijević's information on the festivities of circumcision, appeared in the *Cosmographia*'s cultural description of the Turks.[93]

Georgijević's subsequent *Pro Fide Christiana cum Turca Disputationis habitae*... (1548), addressed to Maximilian, moved away from the experience of captivity to the religious knowledge that the author had gained there. Georgijević's stance on Islam was far from Georgius of Hungary's of sixty years past – Georgijević defined Islam as a sect with perverse doctrine. In the *Pro Fide*, Georgijević interpreted a Turkish prophecy about the balance of power between the Ottoman state and Christendom, explained the Muslim rejection of the Christian Trinity and other points of doctrinal difference, and provided a Turkish-language version of the Lord's Prayer, the Ave Maria, and the Credo.[94] In his explication of the prophecy, he described the current prosperity of Turkish culture (as evidenced by its flourishing building projects, agriculture, and families) but foretold its eventual decline. He also addressed two sections of the pamphlet to Christian leaders: he chastised leaders of the Church for their moral negligence and urged secular rulers to unite against the Turk and not forget to ally with common enemies of the Turk outside of Latin Christendom – Prester John as Emperor of India and the kings of Persia and Georgia.[95] Addressing his texts to members of the Habsburg court, Georgijević may have been attempting to establish himself as a Turkish authority at court through both the content of the pamphlet and

---

da er mich meines alters ongefehrlich im dritten oder vierdten Jar meiner lieben Eltern beraubt/..." and "das ellend/ der jamer/ die schwer gefencknuß vnd viehische dienstbarkeit/ die harte vnd verachteste arbait/ der vnleidliche hunger vnd not/ die schleg vnd straich/ marter vnd pein/ so die arme ellende gefangene Christen vndter disem Tyrannen gedulden müssen/" Urban of Gurk, *Gaistliche Kriegsrüstung/ Das ist/ Christliche Buss vnnd Trostpredigen* (Vienna: Caspar Stainhofer, 1567), γ iii, civ–civ^v.

92 *Türckey oder von yetziger Türcken kirchen gepräng*..., trans. Joannes Herold (Basel: And. Cratander, 1545), 222.

93 *Türckey oder von yetziger Türcken kirchen gepräng*..., 174; Münster, *Cosmographiae Universalis*, 974.

94 *Pro Fide*, bii^v–ciii^v.

95 *Pro Fide*, fii^v–fiv.

the demonstration of his linguistic prowess. He carefully demonstrated his command of language in his annotated translation of the prophecy.[96]

Former prisoners who had risen to prominence in Vienna such as Georgijević and Urban emphasized that knowledge of Turkish allowed the unfortunate Christian to survive. In his chronicle of Turkey, Georgijević provided both Turkish and Slavic or "Windisch" language primers. A Turkish vocabulary list and conversational guide would aid the captive in his physical survival and allow travelers to identify themselves as merchants headed to Constantinople. The text also taught its possessor how, in Slavic, to claim to be Venetian. A Slavic or "Windisch" Lord's Prayer, Ave Maria, and Credo would enable the captive to reach out to the conquered and enslaved Christians from the Balkan border zone in shared belief.[97] Urban of Gurk also perceived language to be a central part of the captive's experience and problem. In a text discussing the danger of the Turk, he introduced the section on the prisoner as a problem of language: their captors are "a people whose language you don't know, thus you will not understand or hear what they say." Speaking with your enemy allowed you to negotiate "so that you can ask him either to preserve your life or for leniency in captivity."[98] Language, in the eyes of these former captives, allowed for the survival of body and faith.

After the 1529 siege of Vienna, the Austrian Habsburg and the Ottoman courts began to work toward direct negotiation with each other. Despite the pressing need for a peace or boundary treaty and for the exchange of hostages and prisoners taken in the continual border raids, diplomatic negotiation proved challenging for the Habsburgs. Until Ferdinand raised a significant military force, he had difficulties getting the Ottoman Sultan Süleyman to treat him as a significant power in the region. Süleyman was much more interested in Charles V's rank and authority, and initially signaled to Ferdinand that he saw him only as the "king of Vienna." Embarrassingly, in 1529, Ferdinand was forced to admit to Süleyman the inadequacy of his court. He could not respond in a timely fashion to Süleyman's letters and proposals because he had no available

---

[96] *Pro Fide*, particularly d–div^v. Georgijević paid for publication, addressed one section to Maximilian, and eventually presented him with a copy. See title page and g^v of ÖNB copy 19.L.41.

[97] *Türckey oder von yetziger Türcken kirchen*, 196–202, 222–6.

[98] "[e]in Volck dessen sprach du nicht kennest/ vnd nicht verstehen oder vernemen wirst/ was sie reden. . . . /in entweder vmb frißtung des lebens/ oder vm milterung der gefengknuß bitten kan" in Urban of Gurk, Siv^v.

translator of Turkish.[99] Admitting this inadequacy was tantamount to admitting that Ferdinand's court lacked magnificence, importance, and erudition at a time when Süleyman's court was an acknowledged center of wealth and splendor. Not only did this lack reflect poorly on the Austrian Habsburg court in the continual symbolic rivalry between courts; it hindered diplomatic negotiation itself.[100] Although the Sultan and his ministers often included a translation for the recipients, Ferdinand and his ministers preferred not to rely on the Ottoman court translation for important treaty points.[101]

The problem was, in part, that of finding a culturally suitable linguistic go-between. From the early days of Ferdinand's negotiations with the Ottomans, prisoners of war acted as translators and go-betweens. During the siege of Vienna in 1529, the Ottomans sent "four *einspennig* (low rank) knights previously captured" to tell the city commanders that their resistance was hopeless.[102] The imprisoned knights' service as couriers followed established practice in Latin Christendom.[103] Ferdinand first solved his translation problem similarly, using a Turkish captive, but the solution was only a stopgap measure. Ferdinand's reliance on the Turkish captive as a translator underscored his rejection of that other existing translator option – the Jewish or Venetian merchants who had ties or businesses in Constantinople. The difficulties of such translators were highlighted when an Italian translator was revealed as a spy in 1532.[104]

Within a few years, Ferdinand found translators more to his liking. Three knights in Ferdinand's retinue in 1539 were described as possessing the ability to translate Turkish documents.[105] By 1541, when the direct

99 Gevay I/3:23 15 Juli 1529. For the steps taken to alleviate the situation, see Gevay I/2:76 23 February 1529 "ad nos celerrime mittat qui linguam Turcicam calleat legereque et scribere ac per lingue alterius idioma referre sciat, . . . "

100 For the issue of language and diplomacy, see Jocelyne G. Russell, *Diplomats at Work: Three Renaissance Studies* (Wolfeboro Falls: Alan Sutton, 1992), chapter 1 – "Language: a barrier or a gateway?"

101 E.g. "Eur Mt: Türkische Tulmätsch darüber befragt (werden) ob ain misverstanndt oder aquinacation aus den Turkischen wortten . . . getzogen werden könnde." HHStA Turcica 17/2, fol. 22ᵛ.

102 "vier einspennig knecht so sie vormals gefangen," *Des Turcken Erschreckliche belagerung / vnd Abschiedt der Stat Wien. 1529* [o.O, 1529], aii.

103 Keen, *The Laws of War*, 160.

104 Keen, 160. For the Turkish captive, Gevay I/2:51 (1528); and the spy is discussed in *Nuntiaturberichte aus Deutschland I*, supplement 2 (Tübingen: Niemeyer, 1969), 376.

105 HHStA Hofstaaten, Hofstaatsverzeichnisse 181/16, fols. 14–15.

Ottoman presence in Hungary led to a more pressing need for treaty negotiations between Ottoman and Austrian courts, these translators' special duties were recognized formally through the creation of a new court position – resident Turkish translator. The translators' salaries and clothing and horse allowances continued to reflect their knightly status. The duties of the translators required unusual skills, and the men were rewarded accordingly. The chief translator, Hans or Johann Spiegel, was honored in 1544 with a further improvement of his arms and nobility (a *Wappensbesserung*). The patent of nobility explained the route by which "Johan Gaudier, called Spiegel, the Turkish and Persian interpreter"[106] had learned those languages. Within that explanation lay the reason Ferdinand valued him so highly. Spiegel had submitted to learning Turkish and Persian languages well during many years of captivity among the Turkish enemies of Christianity. Then, after his captivity was ended, he had served not only Ferdinand but also the Holy Roman Empire as a translator and interpreter in negotiations and correspondence. The patent then praised the knight's probity and dedication. Spiegel continued to serve Ferdinand as a courtier and as the highest-ranked Turkish translator at the Austrian court for the next thirty years.[107] Evidence exists that Spiegel turned his knowledge against his former captors beyond diplomatic translation; he also translated a chronicle from Turkish into German to make more information about the enemy available.[108]

Ferdinand retained other knights as adjunct translators. These knights were a fixed part of the Austrian court, generally serving at least ten years each in the capacity of Turkish translator.[109] Occasionally one

---

[106] "Fideli nobis dilecto Joanni Gaudier, Spiegel appellato, Turcicae et Persaen Lingqe Interpreti nostro Gratia Regia.... Joannes Spiegel per pluro annos in captivitate apud Chrīam nominis hostes Thurcas existens turcicam et persianicam lingam veluti hemo gratious et industrius [....] lo qui [.... scribere] ita dedieris, ut deinde ab ea captivitate auxilio eliberatus non tantum nobis sed etiam Sacro Romano Imperio et ser.mo domini nostri Austrie..." AVA Adelstand Prag 23 Feb. 1544, 2–4.

[107] HKA Hofzahlamtsbücher 1543, 1545–9, 1553–4, 1556–8, 1560, 1566–70. For an analysis of Spiegel's linguistic abilities, see Petritsch, "Die Wiener Turkologie," in *Osmanistik – Turkologie – Diplomatik. Festgabe an Josef Matuz*, hrsg. Christa Fragner und Klaus Schwarz (Berlin: Klaus Schwarz Verlag, 1992), 25–33.

[108] *Chronica oder Acta von der Türckischen Tyrannen herkommen/ vnd gefürten kriegen/ aus Türckischer Sprachen vordeutschet. Vorhin nie in Druck ausgangen* (Frankfurt an der Oder: Johan Eichorn, 1567). For the text's relationship to Ferdinand's court, Joannes Leunclavius, *Annales Sultanorum Othmanidarum* (Frankfurt a. M.: Wechel, 1587), *ii–*iv*.

[109] Account books indicate that Hatterl served at least from 1543–4, Drachschütz 1560–74, and Gentsch 1560–8.

would be sent to the Hungarian front to assist Habsburg generals there, but one or two were always in residence with Ferdinand. Of two non-German translators little record exists beyond their names, but the three other German translators were eventually rewarded as Spiegel had been – with patents of nobility. Peter Hätterl and Lukas Drachschütz were given more distinguished arms, and Sigmund Gentsch was raised to noble status at around the time he began to serve as a Turkish translator. Their patents of nobility reveal a consistent pattern for the knightly Turkish translator. Each served willingly and obediently "first as Ferdinand's soldier in Hungary in the war against the common Christian hereditary enemy, the Turk, who held the soldier in long imprisonment. And now," each patent continued, "he serves as Turkish translator in the imperial court."[110] These periods of imprisonment under the Ottomans could be lengthy; Sigmund Gentsch was imprisoned thirty-two years before returning to Austria. Each patent made it clear that the knights' knowledge of Turkish was a consequence of military service to the Habsburgs. As the case of Sigmund Gentsch suggests, nobility was not a prerequisite for service as a court translator – these men's experiences as soldiers and as imprisoned Christians who had gained knowledge crucial to Habsburg interests ennobled them. They had not sought to learn Turkish for financial profit like merchants, but rather had learned Turkish as a necessary consequence of surviving captivity. These patents of nobility observed that once survival no longer demanded it, the translators' continued use of Turkish and Persian demonstrated particular devotion to Ferdinand and the empire. These men constituted a trustworthy and honorable group of translators who were handsomely rewarded for their continued use of the language of "Christianity's hereditary enemy" in the service of ruler and empire.

Through the decades-long developing rhetoric of prisoners' suffering, the Austrian court's translators were understood as admirable. Captivity, as described by pamphlet authors and reported by former prisoners, was, by the middle of the sixteenth century, a physical ordeal. As such, the captive's suffering and travails harkened back to early Christian hagiographies and in the sixteenth century, martyrdom for true faith had a place in

---

[110] "Aüch die angenemen getrewen gehorsamen und willigen dienste so Er uns Erstlich Inn hüngern als ein Kriegsman wider gemaner Christenhait Erbfeind den Turgen von denen [e]r dan gefangen und ab 32 Jar Inn der Turggeÿ gefenklich enthalten worden..." AVA Adelsakten. Sigmund Gentsch 1561 [21 July]. For very similar wording, but an imprisonment of "ettlich Jar," see AVA Adelsakten Lucas Drachschütz Wappensverbesserung and Peter Hatterl's grant, HKA Familien Akten H69, fols. 2-3^v.

all the confessions.[111] As a near-martyr, a captive's knowledge of Turkish marked his suffering and spiritual pilgrimage, his reduction to a physically tortured being unable to communicate and his eventual return from that state.[112]

The received understandings of the physical and spiritual dangers of captivity help explain the Habsburg court's opinions of the Turkish translators serving at the Ottoman court. Those renegades who had begun life as captives were regarded with compassion. Such a person's conversion would have occurred in the context of pain and suffering, and was, in Habsburg eyes, in some measure coerced. The translator Mahmud, born Sebold von Pibrach, was such a renegade. One of Ferdinand's noble envoys wrote approvingly that "Mahmud... translated for us each time and spoke and conducted himself well. God knows his heart."[113] Ferdinand and other Latin Christian monarchs received him as an envoy in their courts and frequently presented him with gifts to demonstrate their appreciation of such envoys.[114] Prisoner-of-war renegades were not only intelligible to Christians west of the Ottoman Empire; they could also still aid Christendom with occasional intelligence reports. Mahmud himself was believed to provide counterintelligence for the Habsburgs.[115] The crux of the matter lay in intent. Unlike greedy merchants or opportunistic courtiers, be they Italians, Poles, Slavs, Greeks, Germans, or Jews, the enslaved captive could not avoid contact with Turkish language and

---

[111] For discussions of the pain of medieval ordeal and early modern torture, Talal Asad's "Pain and Truth in Medieval Christian Ritual," in *Genealogies of Religion* (Baltimore: Johns Hopkins University Press, 1993) and for early Christian martyrdom, Judith Perkins, *The Suffering Self* (London: Routledge, 1995). For the sixteenth century, Michel de Certeau discusses the hero in travel literature and hagiography, *The Writing of History*, trans. Tom Conley (New York: Columbia University Press, 1988), chapters 5 and 7; and Brad Gregory compares martyrdom in different confessions in *Salvation at Stake* (Cambridge: Harvard University Press, 1999).

[112] For parallels with modern experiences of pain and language, Elaine Scarry, *The Body in Pain* (Oxford: Oxford University Press, 1985).

[113] "Sein Namen was Machmut, (Der ist zw Wienn geborn, aines Khramer Sun, Jacoben von Pibrach, Sein Tauffnamen was Sebold)... der vnns Jeder zeyt gedolmätscht hat. Redt vnnd erzaigt sich guet. Got wesste sein hertz." *Selbst-Biographie Siegmvnds Freiherrn von Herberstein*, ed. Theodor g. von Karajan, FRA, 1:1, 315a–317a; Petritsch, "Friedensvertrag"; Pál Ács, "Tarjumans Mahmud and Murad," *Europa und die Türken in der Renaissance*, ed. B. Guthmüller and W. Kühlmann (Tübingen: Niemeyer, 2000), 307–16; Tijana Krstić, "Illuminated by the Light of Islam and the Glory of the Ottoman Sultanate," *CSSH* 51(2009): 35–63.

[114] HHStA Turcica 8/1, fol. 168–70, 16/1, fol. 104, 30/6, fols. 209–210.

[115] Renegade Faik, Gevay II/2:82–3. HHStA Turcica 26/1, fols. 21–22; Turcica 27/4, fol. 64; Turcica 30/1 fol. 48.

Ottoman culture. Imprisoned while attempting to fulfill his Christian duty to repel the *Erbfeind*, he could choose to learn Turkish as a means to survive and maybe escape the experience. The adoption of a pagan language or even what was considered a heretical faith, Islam, under duress was understandable. In the case of Ferdinand's translator-courtiers, it made them and their knowledge honorable, and in the case of the prisoner-renegades, it made their false spiritual step forgivable.

Ferdinand's decision to develop a staff of former military captives as Turkish translators had important ramifications. Unlike Süleyman's translator renegades who voluntarily embraced life in a different religion and culture, the "Turkish translators" at Ferdinand's court did not return to the Ottoman Empire as active diplomatic mediators. The men who would become his favored translators were fundamentally alienated from the Ottomans. Given that the Hungarian and Ottoman courts had exchanged diplomatic envoys regularly throughout the 1510s and 1520s, Ferdinand's 1529 lack of a Turkish translator is suggestive. He either chose to exclude and ignore previous mediators, or they were allied with his rival for the throne of Hungary, Zápolyai. Zápolyai's influence on Ferdinand's diplomatic strategies was significant during the fifteen years they struggled for control of Hungary. Ferdinand's initial embassy to the Ottoman court in 1528 had been prompted by the knowledge that Zápolyai had already sent a successful one.[116]

Ferdinand's early envoys, with their print-media *wegrayße* and their Balkan and Hungarian roots, expanded public perceptions of foreignness and unfamiliarity in the Balkan and Hungarian territories. After establishing a description of the border zone in print, these first envoys were replaced in their roles of shaping representation of the Turks by a group of authors emphasizing captivity. These authors, including former captives, solidified the rhetoric of estrangement during the second half of the sixteenth century. By the beginning of Maximilian II's reign, Hungary and the Balkans had a new cultural geography. The boundary was still a war zone, now mediated by treaties, ritualized challenges, raids, and skirmishes. The groups of merchants and Jews who had traveled through this zone had been consistently discouraged. Now, soldiers, captives, and slaves were visible as they traveled across this land. After fifty

---

[116] In *Newe zeytung von Keyserlicher Mayestat/ vnd von Franckreych/ Auch von vil andern Fürsten vnd Steten Welscher vnd Teütscher Nation/ geschehen im Jar. MD.XXviii* [Nuremberg: Georg Wachter, 1528], Ferdinand's embassy is depicted as a response, Aiii–Aiii^v.

years of military border contact, to read and speak Turkish was a sign that you had crossed into the culturally liminal and increasingly alien zone and returned. The prisoner, returned from a liminal experience, could be accepted in Christian society. This cultural perception of the prisoner as transmitter of knowledge about an unfamiliar, un-Christian culture became more widespread in the sixteenth century. Even as it was being established for the Turkish case, this figure appeared in New World ethnographies. One of the first German-language accounts of a German in the New World was also one of the first vernacular accounts of a Christian man alone in an Indian culture.[117] In the *Warhaftig/ Historia und Beschreibung eyner Landt-/schafft der Wilden Nacketen Grimmigen Menschfressen*..., Hans Staden both narrated his suffering at the hands of fierce Tupinamba cannibals and provided the reader with a catalog of the cultural and linguistic knowledge he gained during this time of captivity.[118] Such sixteenth-century captivity narratives framed the new ethnographies of cultural separation.

[117] Another account, Alvar Nuñez Cabeza de Vaca's *La Relacíon*, appeared in Castilian. It was published first in 1542 and then again in 1555, and recounts the experiences of the expedition's remnants.
[118] (Marburg, 1557).

5

Imperial Authority in an Era of Confessions

On November 23, 1562, a man identified as the "Turkish ambassador" rode to the city of Frankfurt am Main with more than thirty retainers, forty-some horses, and six camels. It was late, past two in the night, when he and his train reached the city; the city gates were shut. Holy Roman Emperor Ferdinand I ordered the gates opened so that the Turkish envoy, Ibrahim Bey, could witness the election of Ferdinand's son Maximilian as King of the Romans the next day. On November 27, Ibrahim Bey was granted a public audience with Ferdinand and Maximilian, during which he extended the congratulations of Emperor Süleyman, presented a draft peace treaty approved by the Ottoman court, publicized the release of three Castilian nobles who had been prisoners in Constantinople, and requested the freedom of Turkish captives held in Austria. Ibrahim then presented Ferdinand with two crystalline dishes, a horse, and four camels. In another audience after the coronation ceremony, he gave the new King Maximilian the other two camels, along with a horse, a dog, a bow and quiver of arrows, and four pikes. After the festivities in Frankfurt concluded, Ferdinand accepted the treaty and Ibrahim began his homeward journey to Constantinople.

By 1562, the Habsburg power could no longer be conceptualized as it had been during the preceding half-century. The family was no longer headed by Charles, the universal monarch under whom all territories and peoples would dwell. With the election of Ferdinand's son as King of the Romans rather than Charles's, the separation of the Habsburgs into Austrian and Spanish branches became likely, although not irrevocably determined. That same year, Philip II arranged with his Austrian relatives to have his nephews and potential heirs, Maximilian's sons, sent to the Iberian court for their secular and religious education.[1] In the events and descriptions of the 1562 election, we can trace the Habsburgs' efforts to negotiate and reinscribe their symbolic authority in a newly multiconfessional Holy Roman Empire. During the previous half-century, Latin Christian perceptions of Ottoman culture, government, and religion had been shifting as estrangement from Turkish culture and the peoples of the Ottoman empire grew. Ibrahim's very presence in Frankfurt contributed to an Austrian Habsburg strategy, even as voices of dissent interpreted the election and embassy more critically. The varied propaganda of this Austrian-Ottoman diplomatic exchange all supported a cultural distancing between the Habsburg and Ottoman empires which exoticized the eastern empire.[2]

During a two-week period from the end of November to the beginning of December, Ferdinand I oversaw his eldest son Maximilian's election and coronation as King of the Romans. These ceremonies were enacted and witnessed by the assembled princes and notables of the empire, along with envoys of the papacy, the Spanish kingdoms, France, and Poland. This succession had been the subject of much maneuvering and dispute: with dynastic succession and primogeniture not yet formally established in the Holy Roman Empire, many candidacies were possible. Candidates had ranged from Charles's son Philip to members of other electoral houses like the Wettins. Charles and Ferdinand had themselves wrangled over the question of succession at the imperial diet of 1550–1551, with their sister Mary trying to broker an agreement between them.[3] The debates had been confessional as well as dynastic: the Peace of Augsburg was only seven years old in 1562, and religious differences remained a volatile matter. Maximilian's Protestant leanings were well known in the Holy Roman Empire: he had been known to refuse to participate in public

---

[1] *Die Korrespondenz der Kaiser mit ihren Gesandten in Spanien,* ed. Friedrich Edelmayer (Vienna: Verlag für Geschichte und Politik, 1997), 1: 38–40; for some of the tutorial arrangements, see HHStA Span. DK 6/118, fol. 122.

[2] This analysis of Ibrahim Bey's embassy was developed in Carina L. Johnson, "Negotiating the Exotic: Aztec and Ottoman culture in Habsburg Europe, 1500–1590" (PhD dissertation, University of California at Berkeley, 2000). The subject has been treated recently by Harriet Rudolph, "Türkische Gesandtschaften ins Reich am Beginn der Neuzeit..." in *Das osmanische Reich und die Habsburgermonarchie,* Marlene Kurz et al., eds. (Vienna: Oldenbourg, 2005), 295–314.

[3] Paula Fichtner, *Ferdinand I of Austria: the Politics of Dynasticism in the Age of the Reformation* (Boulder: East European Monographs, 1982), 168–70.

Catholic religious ceremonies and he was committed to communion in both kinds.[4]

The widely held perception that Maximilian was a crypto-Protestant may have helped make him palatable to the Protestant electors, but religious tensions were openly visible in the ceremonies of election and coronation. The three non-Habsburg secular electors were all Protestants; the three archbishop-electors were not. Even as the electors began assembling for the election, their membership changed: the archbishop-elector of Cologne died and the Holy Roman election waited on the election of his successor and the new archbishop's arrival in Frankfurt. At the election ceremony itself in St. Bartholomew's Church, the Protestant electors demonstrated their religious loyalties. When the bishop of Würzburg began to celebrate mass, the three Protestant Electors moved to avoid participating in it. Doctrinal distinctions between the Protestant Electors (Frederick III of Wittelsbach was Calvinist, August of Saxony and Joachim II of Brandenburg Lutheran) were symbolically underscored by their reported behavior during the mass. All three left the conclave, the Palatine Elector Frederick moving far into the choir while the Electors of Saxony and Brandenburg did not. When the mass was over, all three then rejoined the electors' conclave. All three secular electors did participate in the other ceremonies, holding the imperial orb, sword, and scepter respectively as the ceremonies of election prescribed. At the coronation six days later, the Elector Palatine once again removed himself from attending or hearing the coronation mass. Such symbolic protestations of faith were not new: Protestant electors had refused to celebrate Catholic feast days during earlier imperial diets, while Charles and Ferdinand had refused to attend the reformed masses held upon their ceremonial entrances to Nuremberg. The electors of the Palatinate and Saxony further questioned whether the oath to uphold the authority of the papal see should remain part of the coronation ceremony, with the elector of Brandenburg stepping in to placate them.[5] Protests did not remain in the ceremonial realm:

---

4 Fichtner explores Maximilian's positions in *Ferdinand I*, 246–53 and *Emperor Maximilian II* (New Haven: Yale University Press, 2001), 35–44; cf. Viktor Bibl, "Zur Frage der religiösen Haltung Kaiser Maximilians II," *AÖG* 106 (1918): 289–425.

5 Hans Habersack, *Die Krönungen Maximilians II. zum König von Böhmen, Römischen König und König von Ungarn (1562/63) nach der Beschreibung des Hans Habersack, ediert nach CVP 7890*, ed. Friedrich Edelmayer et al., *FRA* 1:13 (Vienna: Österreichische Akademie der Wissenschaften, 1990), 156–8, 168; Rosemarie Aulinger, *Das Bild des Reichstages im 16. Jahrhundert* (Göttingen: Vandenhoeck & Ruprecht, 1980) 301–3; *Nuntiatur berichte aus Deutschland, 1560–1572* II.3 (Vienna: Carl Gerold's sohn, 1903), 152–3.

the second day after the election, the Protestant electors met with Ferdinand to express their unhappiness with the third session of the Council of Trent.[6]

On the other side of the religious divide, Catholic concerns also required delicate compromises. Both the papacy and Emperor Ferdinand had deep reservations about Maximilian's faith, and relations between Ferdinand and the papacy were not particularly warm. In 1558, Ferdinand had snubbed the papacy and Pope Paul IV by declining to be crowned Holy Roman Emperor in Italy. Before Maximilian's election could go forward, Ferdinand had to reconcile the new pope Pius IV to his son and his son to the Roman church. Through careful negotiation, Ferdinand arranged for a papal dispensation from Pius IV, which permitted Maximilian to receive communion in both kinds at his coronations. In response, Maximilian agreed in the spring of 1562 to remain in the Catholic faith. This promise removed Ferdinand's concern about his son's election and made it possible to proceed with the ceremonies and their associated masses. Until the imperial election was secured in favor of Maximilian rather than a Protestant prince, the papacy was careful not to inflame Protestant sentiments. Through Maximilian's agreement to remain Catholic, papal apprehensions about the election of a sufficiently Catholic king seemed assuaged, and even further diminished when Maximilian sent an envoy to Rome immediately after his election. Maximilian's cooperation with the papacy would remain, however, largely tacit and passive rather than active.[7]

The decision to crown Maximilian at Frankfurt, rather than at Aachen as his father, uncle, and great-grandfather had been, may have reflected a further religious compromise. In 1562, Frankfurt was confessionally mixed: the rights of Lutheran Protestants and Catholics to worship were guaranteed by the Peace of Augsburg.[8] In contrast, Aachen was legally Catholic. The traditional coronation at Aachen was imbued with ceremonial practices repugnant to Protestants, and it has been argued that the relocation of the coronation to Frankfurt allowed it to take a

---

[6] Habersack, 162.

[7] Paula Sutter Fichtner, "The Disobedience of the Obedient: Ferdinand I and the Papacy 1555–1564," *SCJ* XI (1980): 25–34; *Nuntiatur berichte*, II.3: 112–53; and Fichtner, *Maximilian II*.

[8] Sigrid Jahns, "Frankfurt am Main im Zeitalter der Reformation (1500–1555)," in *Frankfurt am Main: die Geschichte der Stadt in neun Beiträgen*, ed. Frankfurter Historischen Kommission (Sigmaringen: Thorbecke, 1991), 198–203.

desacralized form.[9] Whether or not the ceremony in Frankfurt, with its mass and royal regalia, was fully desacralized, Maximilian would prefer less divisive, non-religiously orthodox forms of spectacular display to symbolize his sovereignty throughout his reign.[10]

The appearance of the Turkish embassy party fit the category of non-religiously orthodox or at least non-confessional display well. To the members of the electoral diet assembled at Frankfurt, Ibrahim Bey's appearance was extraordinary: the Turkish ambassador represented an implacable foe, come to make peace. Long-standing military and political clamoring had raised the awareness of the Turkish threat in the Holy Roman Empire. For forty years, the Habsburgs had agitated about the danger at the Holy Roman Empire's southeastern border. The 1547 Ottoman-Habsburg peace treaty had established that Emperor Süleyman would cease pressing his claim to Habsburg Hungary, in exchange for the payment of 30,000 gulden per year.[11] The resulting peace diminished the threat of conquest but had been marked by perennial skirmishes and attacks on civilians along the Hungarian and Croatian borders. Both sides were dissatisfied with the treaty and, after it expired, representatives of the Habsburg court were sent to Constantinople to negotiate more favorable terms. Habsburg envoys spent the subsequent ten years attempting to do so. When the Habsburg and Ottoman diplomats finally reached an agreement in 1562, Ibrahim Bey was dispatched by Süleyman's grand vezir along with the Habsburg ambassador, humanist Ogier Ghiselin de Busbecq, to carry the hard-negotiated peace treaty to Ferdinand for ratification.

No Turkish notable had appeared in the Germanys north of the Alps since the beginning of the sixteenth century. In 1473–1475, Bayezid, the exiled brother of Ottoman Emperor Mehmed II, had traveled throughout the Holy Roman Empire as a member of Emperor Frederick III's court. Baptized as Calixtus, he was touted by the Habsburgs as Emperor Bayezid, the rightful Ottoman ruler. Through his presence, the Habsburgs implicitly claimed to have a check or counterbalance to the Turkish threat

9 Winfried Dotzauer, "Die Ausformung der frühneuzeitlichen deutschen Thronerhebung," *AKG* 68 (1986): 25–80; Heinz Duchhardt, *Protestantisches Kaisertum und Altes Reich* (Wiesbaden: Franz Steiner, 1977), esp. 52–69.

10 Margit Altfahrt, 'Die politische Propaganda für Maximilian II," *Mitteilungen des Instituts für Österreichische Geschichtsforschung* 88(1980): 283–312, 89(1981): 53–92.

11 Ernst Petritsch, "Der Habsburgisch-Osmanische Friedensvertrag des Jahres 1547," *Mitteilungen des Österreichischen Staatsarchiv* 38 (1985): 68–78.

of sultan Mehmed II. Calixtus reinforced his Turkishness at times, dressing on some ceremonial occasions in Turkish clothes and turban. After 1475, Calixtus's visibility diminished. He spent most of his time in Austria, although he did travel with Maximilian I to several south German imperial cities in 1491 before dying in 1496. A few Turkish embassies had traveled to Austria: one embassy had appeared, complete with camels, in the 1480s, and other envoys had crossed from Hungary into Austria during the 1530s.[12] Representatives of a different eastern empire had been present at a gathering of the Imperial Estates in 1524. Persian envoys had appeared at the imperial diet in Nuremberg, the same diet that had seen the arrival of regalia from Moctezuma's realm. Observers at Frankfurt in 1562 made no explicit reference to the previous Persian visitor, although Ferdinand may well have remembered the Persian envoy's impact at the diet for which he had first served as Charles's *Statthalter*. The Persian had been notably lacking in ceremonial magnificence. He had appeared in the closing days of the diet, looking so shabby and sick that his identity was accepted only after he had been recognized by a bishop in the papal nuncio's train. The envoy carried a letter proposing an alliance with Charles V and the Persian shah, but because no one at the diet could read the Persian-language letter, the envoy and missive were forwarded to Rome.[13]

Unlike that uninspiring envoy of 1524, Ibrahim Bey's appearance in Frankfurt was deliberately fashioned to be splendid. The Habsburgs were involved in engineering his arrival and appearance. Once Busbecq and Ibrahim arrived in Vienna with their draft treaty, Busbecq wrote to Ferdinand, asking whether Ibrahim should remain in Vienna or proceed north with some or all of his companions. Waiting in Vienna was unappealing, and Busbecq was anxious to continue on to Frankfurt. Busbecq proposed

---

[12] Calixtus's death was largely unremarked. Franz Babinger, "'Bajezid Osman' (Calixtus Ottomanus), ein Vorläufer und Gegenspieler Dschem-Sultans," *La Nouvelle Clio* 3 (1951): 349–88. For Maximilian I and Calixtus, see Hermann Wiesflecker, *Maximilian I* (Munich: Oldenbourg, 1971), 1:399–400. Another defeated Ottoman prince, Djem, retreated to Christian Europe in 1482 after his brother Bajezid II established his rule over the Ottoman Empire. He remained outside the Holy Roman Empire, under the control of the Knights of St. John, the papacy, and the king of France, until his death in 1495. V.L. Ménage, "The Mission of an Ottoman Secret Agent in France in 1486," *Journal of the Royal Asiatic Society of Great Britain and Ireland* (1965), 112–13. For the Turkish embassy to Wiener Neustadt in 1487 and another to Vienna in 1533, see Karl Teply, "Türkische Gesandtschaften nach Wien (1488–1792)," *Österreich in Geschichte und Literatur* 20 (1976): 14–32.

[13] Carl Eduard Förstemann, *Neues Urkundenbuch zur Geschichte der evangelischen Kirchen-Reformation* (1841, reprint Hildesheim: Georg Olms, 1976), 177–8.

to Emperor Ferdinand that bringing Ibrahim to Maximilian's coronation would achieve two objectives. Ibrahim, who reported directly to the grand vezir, Ali Pasha, at Constantinople, would be impressed by the German cities, people, and resources. More importantly, Busbecq argued, in view of Ottoman intelligence about the Holy Roman Empire's religious divisions and its consequent military weakness, the display of electoral unity at Maximilian's coronation would belie that assessment. Similarly, the appearance of an Ottoman ambassador at the election would promote Ferdinand's reputation in the Holy Roman Empire. Ferdinand concurred and ordered that the Turkish Orator be brought to Frankfurt.[14]

The logistics of bringing the Turkish party through the Holy Roman Empire to Frankfurt were then carefully considered. Not only Ferdinand, but also his sons, the Archdukes Ferdinand (*Statthalter* of Bohemia) and Charles (in Austria when Busbecq and Ibrahim Bey appeared), were involved in arranging the group's progress. It was agreed that they would travel from Vienna to Linz, through Bohemia (and Prague) to Bamberg, Würzburg, and finally to Frankfurt.[15] Along the way, subjects in Austria, Bohemia, and southern German lands would all have the opportunity to witness Ibrahim's passage. The visual splendor of the group was magnified: Ibrahim and the other members of the Turkish party were outfitted in garments of a lord and his retinue.[16] Word of Ibrahim's travel through the empire preceded the party: in one response to the news, the city councillors of Nuremberg heralded the Turkish embassy as a sign of hope for all "Christianity and the German Nation."[17]

The size of Ibrahim's retinue had to be calibrated carefully: a noble's status in ceremonial processions was measured by the size of his escort, yet too large a party of Turks on horseback might inspire anxiety. Busbecq estimated that an accompaniment of twelve Christian knights would be

---

[14] HHStA Turcica 16/2, fol. 131, fols. 147–149ᵛ. Hofkammerarchiv (HKA), Reichsakten 190a, fols. 67–68. Busbecq repeated the arguments of fols. 147–48ᵛ in his published account of his embassy, *Augerii Gislenii Busbequii D. Legationis Turcicae Epistolae quatuor* (1589, Frankfurt: Andrea Wechel, Claud. Marnius, Ioannis Aubrius, 1595), IV:296–7. For Busbecq's career, Zweder von Martels, "On His Majesty's Service. Augerius Busbequius, Courtier and Diplomat of Maximilian II," in *Kaiser Maximilian II. Kultur und Politik im 16. Jahrhundert* eds. Friedrich Edelmayer and Alfred Kohler, (Vienna: Verlag für Geschichte und Politik, 1992), 169–81.

[15] HHStA Turcica 16/2, fols. 146, 149–149ᵛ, 166–7ᵛ; HKA, Reichsakten 190a, fols. 69–80ᵛ; Busbecq, IV:297.

[16] HKA, Reichsakten 190a, fol. 101–101ᵛ. StAN, SIL 134 no. 24, "Verzaichnus des Actus der iüngst am 24. Novemberis ervolgter glückseliger Election...," fol. 1ᵛ.

[17] StAN, SIL 134 no. 24, fol. 1–1ᵛ.

needed to allay the fears of the German people, who were unaccustomed to seeing Turks in their lands.[18] The posture of military defense was adopted by cities along the route of the Turkish party. Upon entering cities, Ibrahim and his retinue would be met by assembled burghers, armed in a show of strength that was traditional for important entries. In Vienna, for example, eight hundred burghers received the embassy in full armor, remaining on the streets for the entire day.[19] In Frankfurt, the potential threat of thirty-plus men from the Ottoman Empire was also evident in their reception. When the Turkish ambassador came to the city gates in the dead of night requesting entrance, the Elector of Saxony was consulted about whether the party should be granted admission. The elector deferred the decision to Emperor Ferdinand and ordered that a group of Frankfurt burghers should arm themselves. After Ferdinand sent his command that Ibrahim be admitted, this contingent of armed citizens of Frankfurt escorted the ambassador from the gate to his lodging. Busbecq later made much of the fact that, according to custom, the gates were supposed to remain closed throughout the following day of the election ceremony. Only the importance of Ibrahim, he claimed, had caused them to be opened.[20]

The spectacle of the Turkish ambassador's presence at the election was intended to impress both the German and Turkish audiences with the strength of a Habsburg-led Holy Roman Empire. To ensure this dual effect, in which Germans viewed the Turks and the Turks viewed the Germans, the Turkish ambassador and his retainers watched events from a well-located building on the day of election, and again on the coronation day. From there, he could observe all of the day's activities from an unobstructed vantage point.[21] Accounts of these events asserted that Ibrahim saw the panoply as a united assemblage of the Holy Roman Empire and its allied Christian princes, whether Protestant or Catholic.

---

[18] HHStA Turcica 16/2, fol. 145, 17 October 1562. In 1563, treaty negotiations dictated that groups of Turks traveled from Vienna to the border and back with protective escorts. HKA, Reichsakten 190a, fols. 136–40.

[19] Vienna, Stadt- und Landesarchiv, Oberkammeramtsrechnungen 95, fols. 65ᵛ–67 (October 5).

[20] Busbecq, IV: 297–8.

[21] Michael Beuther, *Ordenliche Verzeychniß/ welcher gestalt/ die Erwehlung unnd Krönung/ des Allerdurchleuchtigsten Großmächtigsten Fürsten und Herrn/ Herrn Maximilian/ Römischen unnd zu Böheym Königs etc. zu Franckfurt am Main/ im Wintermonat nähestverschienen 1562 jars/ geschehen. Mit vermeldunge etlicher sonst fürnehmer sachen und Händel/ so sich darneben/ durch ankunfft eyner Türckischen Bottschaffte/....* (Frankfurt am Main: David Zöpffeln, 1563), Iivᵛ, Mii[i]ᵛ.

Paul Pfintzing's account of the proceedings, addressed to Philip II's son Prince Carlos, emphasized the concord and support for "universal tranquility of Christianity" by all assembled, Catholics and Protestants in a degree of unity not seen for forty years.[22] This effect was highly desirable, especially given that Süleyman was believed to be alert to confessional divisions in order to exploit them to the Ottoman Empire's advantage. Of course, Ibrahim's view of the proceedings also allowed him to be seen by many of the important witnessing dignitaries, both from within and outside the Holy Roman Empire.

Efforts to turn the Turkish ambassador's presence at Frankfurt into a visible triumph of diplomacy seem to have been successful. A flurry of manuscript and printed accounts circulated about Maximilian II's election and coronation, with the attendance of the Turkish embassy featured prominently in many. Some authors and texts targeted specific audiences. The manuscript account *Beschreybung kayser Maximilians des anndern römischen, hungerischen und behaimischen kunigclichen crönungen, wie dieselben der zait nach aufainannder gevolgt sein* was directed toward a Habsburg family readership. Presentation copies of the manuscript were made for various important Habsburg members: Maximilian, his brother Archduke Ferdinand, his son the future Rudolf II, and his brother-in-law Duke Albrecht V of Bavaria all received copies. The manuscript was written by Hans Habersack, a longtime attendant of the Habsburg family. Habersack had served as an advisor and court secretary to Archduke Ferdinand and Emperor Ferdinand; he had also fought in Hungary against Ottoman forces in the 1550s. Perhaps with an eye toward his Habsburg audience, Habersack concentrated on the details of the three kingly ceremonies of election and coronation in Bohemia, the Holy Roman Empire, and Hungary, as well as the actions of the assembled electors, princes, and other notables.[23] Pamphlets printed in the imperial cities of Frankfurt, Cologne, Nuremberg, Strasbourg, and Augsburg quickly appeared, some within a month of the events. Most of the pamphlets were anonymous, although several bore authors' names. One lengthy account was composed by Michael Beuther, a humanist and student of Melancthon, whose pamphlet seemed directed at the patrician

---

[22] "Tranquillidad universal de la Christianidad," Paul Pfintzing, *Relacion particular y sumaria de la manera que el serenissimo muy alto y muy Poderoso Principe, Maximiliano segundo deste nombre, Rey de Romanos y de Bohemia, fue Coronado* . . . 1562, ÖNB, CVP 8251, fols. 31-2.

[23] Habersack, 39-42, 87-9.

and burgher urban elite of the imperial cities. A version was authored by Laurentius Fuchs of Pirna, who dedicated another pamphlet to officials at the court of Saxony.[24] In the printed accounts, the Turkish ambassador's presence was often highlighted in a subtitle and was the sole subject of at least one pamphlet.[25] The pamphlets detailed the size of Ibrahim Bey's retinue, sometimes naming its members, their Hungarian cities of residence (Ofen, Pécs/Fünfkirchen), and the numbers of horses and attendants, in the format used to list the retinues of other lords at these imperial gatherings. Perhaps reflecting the diplomatic and symbolic importance of Ibrahim Bey's embassy, the manuscripts and pamphlets also included information about the new treaty brought for ratification to Ferdinand, Ibrahim's audience with Ferdinand and Maximilian, and listed the gifts brought by Ibrahim and presented by him to the emperor and the new King of the Romans.

The texts' representations of the embassy, sometimes diverging and sometimes agreeing in detail and focus, reveal a range of perspectives on Ibrahim's reception as an envoy. Habersack concluded his description of the audience by commenting that such a fine presentation had been previously inconceivable in the German lands.[26] With his interest focused on the political dynamics of the three elections and coronations, Habersack downplayed the drama of Ibrahim's middle-of-the-night appearance on the eve of the election. For Habersack, the first arrival "very late in the night"[27] was that of the new archbishop and elector of Cologne, urgently awaited so that a full roster of voting electors would participate in the election. Ibrahim's arrival was merely the second of the night. For the pamphlet authors, it was Ibrahim's arrival that attracted attention. As

---

[24] Michael Beuther's account included details of the Frankfurt elite; Adam and Nicolaus Heyden, *De Electione et Inauguratione Maximiliani Austrii II. Rom. Regis, Francofurti ad Moenum, Anno 1562* (Frankfurt am Main: Georg Corvinus (Raab), Sigismund Feyerabend, the heirs of Wygand Gallus, 1563); *Warhafftige Beschreibung/ welcher gestalt die königkliche wirde Maximilian . . .* (Frankfurt am Main: Georg Corvinus (Raab), Sigismund Feyerabend, the heirs of Wygand Gallus, 1563); Laurentius Fuchs, *Kurtze Beschreibung der Königlichen Wirden und Magistrat Ampt . . .* (1563).

[25] *Anbringen Türkischer Legation/ Ebrahimi Strotschii/ gebornen Polecken/ . . .* (Nuremberg: Johann vom Berg und Ulrich Newber, 1562); see also the eight-leaf woodcut by Jost Amman. For a catalog of other pamphlets, see Carl Göllner, *Turcica* II (Bucharest: Academy, 1968), 91–101.

[26] "Welliche audientz lennger dann ain stundt gewehrt, und ist zwar dises ain schöner und solcher actus gewesen, dergleichen man vormals in teutschen lannden geschehen zu sein nit gedennckht," Habersack, 166.

[27] " . . . gar spatt in die nacht." Habersack, 155.

Michael Beuther commented critically (placing Ibrahim's arrival an hour later than the time described in other accounts), Ibrahim's lateness made him seem more "offensive" and reflected poorly on him and his Turkish sovereign. Beuther suggested that the party was unwilling to be scrutinized in a daytime procession, as foreign ambassadors to Constantinople were forced to be.[28] Some of the pamphlets also seemed critical of the embassy's rush to arrive at the election and coronation and present themselves, noting that it had caused some of the camels to become weak and sickly.[29]

Beyond the facts of arrival, the accounts diverged in their descriptions of Ibrahim's cultural identity as signaled during the treaty presentation. Hans Habersack referred continually to Ibrahim as the unnamed "türggisch pottschaffter," underscoring his Turkishness and high status as ambassador.[30] He also emphasized Ibrahim's Turkish manners at the formal reception, stating that Ibrahim bowed in the Turkish custom. In the anonymous *Warhafftige Beschreibung/ welcher gestalt . . .* , along with Ibrahim Bey's Turkish manners, an attribution of Turkishness was applied to the physical treaty itself. The document from Süleyman was described in terms that highlight its material splendor and unfamiliarity: a "Turkish letter" written on noticeably beautiful paper, bearing a tughra illuminated with gold, small colored figures, and seals impressed with Turkish letters, housed in a green velvet case and tied with silk cords.[31] Habersack also stated that Ibrahim presented the treaty and Süleyman's address to Ferdinand in Turkish and that, in response, Ferdinand's own Turkish translator rendered the speech into German.[32] Habersack's description of the translation reinforced an impression of Ibrahim's cultural and linguistic distance and the Habsburg court's able translation skills, yet the Habsburgs and their diplomatic advisors knew that Ibrahim was a relatively high-placed court translator at the Ottoman

---

[28] Beuther, Hii[v] -Hiii. Beuther was in Frankfurt as a historiographer, according to *Franckfurter ankunfft/ oder verzaichnuß aller Potentaten/ Chur vnd Fürsten/ Gaistlichen vnd Weltlichen/ Bischofen/ Prelaten/ Thummherrn/ Grafen/ Freyherrn/ dero von der Ritterschafft/ Bottschafften vnd Stenden/ Doctorn vnd Geleerten etc. . . . die auff der Roem. Kün. May. Waal vnd Kroenung zu Franckfurt am Mayn personlich erschinen vnd gewesen seind*, (Augsburg: Philipp Ulhart), Giii.

[29] Fuchs, *Kurtze Beschreibung*, K; *Anbringen*, Aiii[v]; and Beuther, Kiii[v].

[30] Habersack 155, 162; with the imperial chancellery following suit in HHStA, Reichskanzlerei Wahl- und Krönungs Akten 5, fols. 374[v]–375.

[31] *Wahrhafftige Beschreibung*, Lii.

[32] Habersack, 162–6 and *Warhafftige Beschreibung/ . . . Maximilian*, K[v].

court, with significant linguistic skills of his own.[33] Habersack's description of Ibrahim also elided other information about Ibrahim's identity, information disseminated in the pamphlets. The pamphlets named the envoy "Ibrahim, that is Abraham Strotzky, born Polish."[34] In other words, Ibrahim was a Polish renegade. The absence of any redemptive information of military capture would suggest to the reader that Ibrahim was a voluntary renegade. At least one pamphlet also reported in its title that, not unsurprisingly for a Pole, Ibrahim spoke "Slavonic," not Turkish.[35] The pamphlets, then, offered information that problematized Habersack's simple presentation of a Turkish envoy acknowledging Habsburg status and triumph. Ibrahim was not the only renegade in the Turkish embassy: Laurentius Fuchs noted that the orator of the "Pascha of Buden" was a German renegade from Schmiedeberg in electoral Saxony. His conversion to Islam would have hit close to home for regional readers, as Schmiedeberg was relatively near Fuchs's Pirna.[36] Whether cast in a positive or negative light, the texts present Ibrahim and his party as Turkish officials, who were Muslim by birth or by choice. In doing so, Habersack and the pamphlets' authors all emphasized the distance and difference between Ottoman and Habsburg and between Muslim and Christian cultures.

The challenge of dealing with an apparently voluntary renegade who had abandoned Christianity for Islam also contextualized Ibrahim's presentation of a treaty point awaiting finalization. The language used in some of the pamphlets to explain this condition remind the reader of the charged confessional context for these events. The proffered treaty included an Ottoman request that Turkish prisoners from the border zone be freed. These prisoners, some men and a Turkish woman who was the wife of a minor official, were being held in Austria.[37] According

---

[33] HHStA Turcica 16/3, fols. 37^v, 44r, 186–186^v and HKA Reichsakten 190a, fol. 122^v.

[34] "Ebrahim/ das ist Abraham Strotzky/ eyn geborner Polack," Beuther, Hii^v; Ibrahim is similarly identified in Heyden, *De Electione . . .* , Dii^v; Fuchs, *Kurtze Beschreibung*, Jiii^v; *Anbringen Türkische Legation*, Aiii^v; and *Warhafftige Beschreibung/ . . . Maximilian*, Hiii. Ibrahim's family name was given as Strotsch, Strozzini, or Stadius.

[35] *Anbringen Türkische Legation/ Ebrahimi Strotischii/ gebornen Polecken/ . . . in Schlavonischer sprach. . . .* (1562).

[36] Fuchs, *Kurtze Beschreibung*, Liv.

[37] HHStA, Turcica 16/3, fols. 79–81; Turcica 17/5, fol. 95. At roughly the same time period, French negotiations over French captives were stalled over the question of returning several converted Turkish women in Catherine de Medici's household. (Catherine de Medici had included Moorish and Turkish women in her retinue when she first came

to Beuther and a Nuremberg account, Ibrahim's speech invoked, as a justification for this release, the request for mercy by allowing these Ottoman subjects to return to their lands and freedom of their *Religion* or practice of religion, presumably Islam.[38] As a show of good faith and for a substantial ransom, the Ottomans had released several high-ranking Iberian nobles, including a field general, Don Alvaro de Sande. These men had been defeated at the battle of Djerba in 1560, captured either in battle or in a failed escape from the subsequent siege, and imprisoned near Constantinople. Sande himself was known in the Holy Roman Empire, having fought for the Habsburgs many times, perhaps most memorably for German observers at Mühlberg during the Smalkaldic War.[39] These men's release was a diplomatic triumph for Busbecq and represented a shift in relations between the Latin Christians and the Ottoman court. French envoys had previously requested the three men's ransom on behalf of Philip II, but their request had been turned down by the Ottomans. Instead, Busbecq, the agent of an often diplomatically ignored Ferdinand, had arranged their ransom. Ferdinand's success in gaining the release of the Iberian nobles underscored his new position as emperor and, at least by seniority of age, the head of the Habsburg family. Seeking to make this shift in power to the Austrian branch of the family more palatable, Paul Pfintzing's account of the events, written to Prince Carlos at the Castilian court, emphasized that Busbecq was Flemish, and thus really Philip's subject.[40] The Habsburgs were slow to reciprocate by freeing their Turkish prisoners, despite continued complaints from officials in Buda and Ibrahim Bey himself. Finally, with Ferdinand's own Hungarian nobles

---

to France in 1533.) Susan Skilliter, "Catherine de' Medici's Turkish Ladies-in-Waiting: A Dilemma in Franco-Ottoman Diplomatic Relations," *Turcica VII* (1975): 188–204. Turkish women seem to have been able to convert to Christianity more easily and unnoticed. See Archivo Municipal Seville, Seccion Tercero Tomo 11, no. 45 (1550s) for evidence of such women at the Castilian court.

[38] Beuther, Kii[v] and *Anbringen*, Aii[v]. In contrast, Habersack makes no mention of this argument.

[39] Huberto Foglietta, *Vida de Don Alvaro de Sande* (Madrid: 1962), 101–26. Foglietta also details Alvaro de Sande's service to the Habsburgs in Tunis, Bohemia, Italy, and Djerba. For Sande's earlier correspondence with Ferdinand, see HHStA Span. DK 2/32, fols. 1–3.

[40] Busbecq, IV: 226–8, 230–1, and 270–4 for more retrospective details; Alfonso Ulloa, *Vita del potentissimo e christianiss. Imperatore Ferdinando Primo* (Venice: Camillo and Francesco Franceschini, 1565); CDIE 98: 211–2, 223 and 101: 55–74 for the perspectives of Philip II's agent; and Pfintzing, fol. 17[v].

still held "in cruel imprisonment" as they reminded in their frequent letters from Constantinople, this treaty point was eventually settled.[41]

Differences of opinion about the envoy's status as a born or renegade Turk, and the merit of an appeal to free Muslim prisoners on grounds of their *Religion*, might reflect confessional or political tensions within the Holy Roman Empire. Other aspects of the embassy and audience description were described very similarly by all the authors, suggesting a shared underlying understanding.

All accounts of the audience emphasize that Ibrahim Bey presented gifts (*"Geschencken"*) from Emperor Süleyman to Emperor Ferdinand and his newly elected successor, King Maximilian.[42] After many rather poorly received and unsuccessful Habsburg embassies traveling to Constantinople, it is no wonder that the accounts were unanimous in their promotion of the gift-giving reception ceremony as an act recognizing the Holy Roman Emperor's importance. Even the forms of the gifts would have seemed transparent and comprehensible to Latin Christian viewers. European and other Mediterranean rulers shared mutually intelligible diplomatic gift-giving practices, within a range of gifts signifying diplomatic esteem.[43] The honor of the ambassador and the value of the gifts were important signals to the receiving court about how they were regarded by the gift-giving sovereign. (Thus Habersack's tactic to proclaim the importance of Ibrahim and remain silent about his renegade identity.) In a counterexample, a Spanish envoy to Constantinople and his diplomatic messages met with a poor reception in Constantinople, attributed by onlookers to his failure to bring a gift and his status as a recent former captive.[44] Ferdinand might occasionally make excuses for not sending suitable gifts with envoys, but in general he and his ambassadors incorporated gift giving in their attempts to smooth ragged diplomatic relations between the courts. This tactic was laid out by the then-interim envoy Johann Maria Malvezzi, who suggested in 1545 that instead of insufficient sums of money, Ferdinand should send gifts of pure

---

[41] HHStA, Turcica 17/1, fols. 34, 39ᵛ, 43ᵛ, 49; 17/5, fols. 95–9ᵛ. Also *Korrespondenz der Kaiser*, ed. Edelmayer, 206–7.

[42] *Warhafftige Beschreibung/... Maximilian*, title page.

[43] Figure 28. *Wegrayß / Keyserlicher Maiestat Legation / im.32.jar zü dem Türcken geschickt/....* (1532). Also Konrad Dilger, *Untersuchungen zur Geschichte des Osmanischen Hofzeremoniells im 15. und 16. Jahrhundert* (Munich: Trofenik, 1967) 96–104, who suggests that Ottoman sultans preferred to present ceremonial robes and money.

[44] Salomon Schweigger, *Ein Newe Reyssbeschreibung auss Teutschland nach Constantinopel und Jerusalem* (Nuremberg: Johann Lantzenberger, 1608; facs. Graz: Akademische Druck u. Verlagsanstalt, 1964), 87.

gold that would not exceed 5,000 ducats. Malvezzi was sufficiently cognizant of the politics of gift giving and family politics in Constantinople to suggest further that, along with the gifts from king to emperor, Ferdinand's wife Anna give Mihrimah, Süleyman's daughter and grand vezir Rustem's wife, a gift valued between 300 and 500 ducats.[45]

In the Holy Roman Empire, the display of sumptuous treasure had continued in a somewhat modified form. Some sacral treasure was melted down and some simply not displayed publicly in 1530s, 1540s, and 1550s, during the decades after the Reformation's repudiation of sumptuous display. Recyclable and convertible secular treasure of plate retained its currency as ceremonial gifts for both Catholic rulers and more reform-minded cities. For example, in 1562, the Nuremberg city council gave Maximilian and his wife Maria a silver dish valued at 252 gulden to honor their coronation as King and Queen of Bohemia.[46] In the pamphlets covering the Frankfurt events, plate was noted as a sign of the coronation feast's magnificence.[47] Ferdinand gave and received plate regularly in the middle decades of the century. The circulation of plate onward to resolve financial pressures was sometimes immediate: in several instances, Ferdinand received silver plate from his subjects in Hungarian Transylvania, only to send it on to Constantinople in a matter of months.[48] In contrast, Ibrahim Bey's gift transcended the idiom of plate; he offered two valuable crystal or alabaster dishes, adorned with jewels, which could not themselves be converted into specie. Instead, Habsburg court sources offered genealogies for the stone dishes to increase their value. Habersack asserted that a queen of Persia had previously possessed them, while Pfintzing made a claim of prior Byzantine imperial ownership. Fuchs and an anonymous author described them as "splendid."[49]

Along with the dishes, the envoy presented Ferdinand with four camels and a horse. After Maximilian's coronation, the new king also received two camels and a horse. Turkish horses were highly esteemed in Latin

---

[45] Karl Nehring, ed., *Austro-Turcica, 1541–1552* (Munich: Oldenbourg, 1995) 59–69; "Munus sit aliquid de auro puro, fabricatum ita tamen quod, omnibus computatis artificium cum auro...," 57.

[46] "schenck dem Behemischen konig und künigin zu ad kronüng," StAN, Stadtrechnungs-belege II, 1562/63 nr. 12.

[47] Beuther, Miv^v–Ni^v and Fuchs, *Kurtze Beschreibung*, Hiv^v, Jii.

[48] Wendelin Boeheim, "Urkunden und Regesten aus der K.K. Hofbibliothek," *JKSW* 7 (1888): cxi (no. 4870). For other examples of plate gifts, HKA, Reichsakten 174a, fols. 26^v, 33.

[49] Habersack, 166; Pfintzing, fol. 19; Fuchs, *Kurtze Beschreibung*, K; *Warhafftige Beschreibung... Maximilian*, Jii.

Christendom, but camels were a richly evocative animal to gift the Holy Roman Emperor. They were the pack and riding animals known to be used throughout Islam, a part of the Muslim territories' military and economic success.[50] Culturally, they served as symbols of Muslim strength, yet beyond pragmatic contemporary concerns, camels also evoked even more unfamiliar lands to the east of Europe, including the lands of the biblical magi. As such, they had appeared in the background of paintings of the Adoration of the Magi,[51] a very popular theme in late-fifteenth- and early-sixteenth-century art. By the beginning of the sixteenth century, the identification of the magi with the non-familiar, non-European world was accomplished in part through depictions of the third king. The third king often physically appeared to be from sub-Saharan Africa or Levantine Asia, and, with the discovery of the Americas, very occasionally from the west Indies.[52] With the Reformation critique of religious images, paintings of the three magi followed the trend of other religious art and descended into decades of obscurity in much of the Holy Roman Empire. Nonetheless, the magi were utilized as pageant symbols on ceremonial occasions in Catholic territories as late as 1550, when the Gonzagas dressed as the magi gave presents to Prince Philip upon his entry into Milan.[53] Ibrahim's appearance, with gifts in the form of precious dishware and an entourage of camels, echoed this iconography.

---

[50] For example, *Des Turckischen Keysers Heerzug vnd vörnem widder die Christen* (Erfurt: 1531), bii^v; *Warhafftige newe zeitung von dem Türcken / welliche eyn gefangner Türck zü Wien / auff die fragsstuck . . .* (1532), Aiv; and Jan Cornelisz Vermeyen's cartoon for *March to Rada* (circa 1546–1550), one of his Conquest of Tunis tapestry series, Inv. No. GG 2046, Vienna, Kunsthistorisches Museum. See Konrad Gesner, *Conradi Gesneri medici Tigurini historiae animalium Lib. I de quadrupedibus viviparis* (Zürich: Christoph Froschauer, 1551), 171 and in the German translation, *Thierbuch*, trans. Conrad Forer (Zürich: Christoph Froschauer, 1563), xcvi^v and xcv–xcvii for camel capabilities.

[51] An example of the magi with camel train is Nuremberg-based Hans Süss von Kulmbach's *Adoration of the Magi* (1511) Inv. No. 596a Berlin, Staatliche Museen, Gemäldegalerie. For Italian art, Claudia Lazzaro, "Animals as Cultural Signs," in *Reframing the Renaissance*, ed. Claire Farago (New Haven: Yale University Press, 1995), 222.

[52] For a survey of this theme, see Richard Trexler, *The Journey of the Magi* (Princeton: Princeton University Press, 1997), 76–123; Jean Devisse and Michel Mollat, *The Image of the Black in Western Art* 2:2, trans. William Granger Ryan (Lausanne: Office du Livre, 1979), 134–42, 161–86; Castilian examples in Chandler Post, *A History of Spanish Painting* (Cambridge, M.A.: Harvard University Press, 1947) 9:118, 210, 323, 332, 419, 458, 599; and central European examples are Inv. Nos. 184, 245, 358, Cologne, Wallraf-Richartz-Museum. See the museum's *Die Gemälde der Altdeutschen Meister* (Cologne: Gutenberg, 1939).

[53] Trexler, *Journey of the Magi*, 163.

Although the invocation of the magi may have been unintentional, the camels' appearance among Ibrahim's gifts was not. Busbecq had orchestrated their presence in Frankfurt. The camels had been acquired by Busbecq himself in the Ottoman Empire, although in Frankfurt they were presented by Ibrahim as gifts of his sovereign.[54] Why, then, the effort, whether conscious or unconscious, to present gifts of exotic animals in this diplomatic spectacle?

Possessing the natural world through a menagerie of animals from far-flung geographic areas had become an idiom of magnificence in late-fifteenth-century Europe. In Rome, animals from beyond the bounds of Europe could symbolize the pope's position as successor both to St. Peter and to the ancient Roman Empire. There, references to the magi were fairly conscious: such animals also appeared in Florentine ceremonial enactments of the magi adoring the Christ Child. The Portuguese, with their new trade empire on the coasts of Africa and India, also adopted this strategy of spectacle through the possession of exotic animals. Their menageries contained secular meanings of geographic expansion, although their imperial ideology included strong Christian components. In Lisbon, the royal court was filled with "gifts" from kings of India such as elephants, camels, and smaller creatures.[55] In the first decades of the sixteenth century, the Portuguese king Manuel had famously given the papacy lavish presents from India, including an elephant and a rhinoceros. In an embassy from sovereign to new pope, the Portuguese declared their new discoveries – laying claim to them, boasting of them before ambassadors of other kingdoms, and honoring the pope with gifts of animals demonstrating the geographic expansion of Portugal's reach.[56] The ruler's menagerie was a Mediterranean rather than an exclusively Christian strategy: Süleyman and his successor Selim II both kept splendid collections of live animals.[57]

Maximilian had experimented with exotic animals as declarations of magnificence in the decade before his election as King of the Romans.

---

[54] Busbecq, III: 130–4.
[55] Luis F. R. Thomaz, "L'idée impériale manuéline" in *Découverte, le Portugal et l'Europe*, ed. J. Aubin (Paris: Touzot, 1990); Hieronymus Münzer, *Viaje por España y Portugal en los años 1494 y 1495*, trans. Julio Puyol (Madrid: (1924), 107–9; Lazzaro, 219–22.
[56] See Sanjay Subrahmanyam, *The Career and Legend of Vasco da Gama*. The late-fifteenth-century Egyptian caliphs also chose to evoke biblical gift giving in their presentations to the papacy. Silvio Bedini, "The Papal Pachyderms," *Proceedings of the American Philosophical Society* 125 (1981): 75–90.
[57] *Wegrayß* (1532) and Schweigger, 129. Cortés's admiration of Moctezuma's menagerie in his second letter can be placed in this context.

In 1551, Maximilian had returned from the Iberian peninsula, where he had served as Charles V's regent. His service in Castile had been designed in part to clear the way for his cousin Philip's tour through Italy and the Holy Roman Empire (1548–1549), as Charles maneuvered for his son to succeed Ferdinand as King of the Romans. When Charles finally agreed that his son-in-law and nephew Maximilian could return to central Europe, Maximilian sought to reassert his claim as the ablest candidate for election despite a relative shortage of funds. He and his wife Maria progressed through Austria to Vienna with an elephant in their entourage. Like the elephant sent to the papacy, Maximilian's elephant had been a gift from the rulers of Portugal, in this case Joao III and Catherine (Maximilian's cousin and aunt). The spectacle of its progress through Austria generated much comment before it settled in Vienna and then died a few years later.[58] Like the elephant, Ibrahim Bey's camels played their part as exotic animals in a spectacle of Maximilian's magnificence before disappearing from documentary record.[59]

Maximilian actively maintained a collection of non-European beasts after his election, although neither Maximilian's father nor his uncle had maintained a menagerie as a form of imperial display. The occasion of his elections to kingship in Bohemia, the Holy Roman Empire, and Hungary prompted the Portuguese crown to send Maximilian a second elephant from Portugal in 1563. At least one Cologne observer interpreted this splendid gift instead as from Philip, head of one branch of the Habsburgs, to Ferdinand, head of the other. This elephant lived for more than a decade, maintained in an imperial menagerie outside of Vienna along with a tiger and several leopards. Visiting notables were taken to view the menagerie, just as a previous generation might have been invited to

---

[58] Almudena Pérez de Tudela and Annemarie Jordan Gschwend, "Luxury Goods for Royal Collectors," *JKMW* 3 (2001), 15–17. For the elephant's passage through Austria and its effects on cultural topography, see Peter Franz Kramml, "Der Erste Elefant in Österreich (1552) und die Geschichte des Salzburger 'Elefantenhauses' in der Sigmund-Haffnergasse," *Salzburg Archiv* 4 (1987): 49–70. I thank Michael Milway for this reference. After the elephant's death, its Indian origin caused Sebastian Huetstocker, a councillor and sometime-mayor of Vienna (1549–50, 1553–5), to have a chair fashioned from some of its bones. For a commemorative medal, see Georg Habich, ed. *Deutschen Schaumünzen des XVI Jahrhunderts* 2:1 (Munich: Bruckmann, 1929), no. 2369. This elephant is reputed to have been named Süleyman, but this is evidently a later convention in the secondary literature. Hilda Lietzmann, *Das Neugebäude in Wien* (Munich: Deutscher Kunstverlag, 1987), 29, 33–4.

[59] There is a lacuna in Habsburg household accounts during the relevant years.

view the imperial relics at Nuremberg.[60] For Maximilian's generation, menageries expressed imperial magnificence without stirring questions or debates on confessionally based understandings of sacrality. In the diminished scope of empire in the generation after Charles V's abdication, it allowed for physical possession of the world without the actual sovereignty of universal empire. Rather than a court attended by many peoples from throughout the world, Maximilian could display animals from the far-flung regions of the world. The camels referenced the world beyond Christian Europe, the Roman Empire of antiquity, or the rich overland trade routes to India. Ostensibly gifts of Süleyman, they offered an alternative symbolism of the King of the Romans' power.

Because the camels also functioned as instruments of war and as a symbol of Ottoman superiority, they could be linked to the confessional-era challenges of symbolizing imperial authority. Older symbols of imperial authority – Charlemagne's regalia (crown, scepter, orb, sword and robes of Charlemagne, saint and Holy Roman Emperor) – had been categorized with other relics, most notably a section of the holy lance, in pre-Reformation descriptions of the imperial relics housed in Nuremberg. At Charles's 1520 coronation in Aachen as King of the Romans, an account sent back to the Castilian court could describe the regalia in sacral terms: Charles was dressed and crowned in the regalia of "Emperor Charles the Great, venerated and canonized as a saint."[61] As events in Nuremberg in 1524 exemplified, the religious veneration of the imperial treasure as relics was repudiated by the imperial subjects assembled there. In 1531, city leaders from Nuremberg had again carried the imperial regalia to Ferdinand's coronation in Aachen, but printed accounts made little mention of it. Herald Paul Pesl named the insignia and clothing of Charles the Great as "the *caleas*, sandals, alb, stole, and other old imperial ornament and clothing" to be used in the coronation, while a pamphlet from Leipzig noted the objects brought from Nuremberg as "the kingly clothing."[62]

---

[60] Hermann Weinsberg, *Das Buch Weinsberg. Kölner Denkwürdigkeiten aus dem 16. Jahrhundert* (Leipzig: Alphons Dürr, 1887) 2:127. Donald F. Lach, "Asian Elephants in Renaissance Europe," *Journal of Asian History* 1 (1967): 168–71. HKA, Hof-zahlamtsbücher,21, fol. 689; 24, fol. 157ᵛ; 25, fols. 355ᵛ–6.

[61] "Emperor carlo magno venerado y canonizado como sancto," HHStA Span.Varia 1/ i, fol. 8.

[62] "Kayser Karls des grossen/ Insignia unndt klaidunng/ wie dann von alter im hey. Reich herkommen/ als nemblich Caleas/ Sandalea/ Albn/ Stola/ und annder allt Kayserliche Ornament und klaider (So die verordente von Nueremberg dahin gebracht)" *Warhafftyge und aigentliche verzaichnüs.../ sambt seiner Kayser. Maiestat Brueders*

In 1562, with the coronation relocation from Aachen – a city associated with Charlemagne – to Frankfurt, symbolic links between the coronation and Charlemagne might have waned; yet they did not.

As noted in Chapter 3, with the Protestant repudiation of relics, the imperial regalia had lost symbolic valence. The election of 1562 marked a Habsburg attempt to reinvest the regalia with a new form of cultural value or density, one that refocused attention on the coronation mantle. The coronation mantle had been a rather unremarkable object in the regalia and relics of Charlemagne. In 1562, Ferdinand ordered the city councillors of Nuremberg to bring all of the imperial regalia (crown, scepter, orb, sword, and the other objects) to Frankfurt for his son's coronation.[63] Many of the princes gathered in Frankfurt were Protestant and the authority of Charlemagne's robes could no longer depend on his sainthood. Habersack's detailed discussion of the coronation ceremony described Charlemagne as historical Holy Roman Emperor rather than saint. Charlemagne's prior possession of scepter, orb crown, and clothes was noted, and Maximilian's seat was identified as symbolizing Charlemagne's throne.[64] In the Frankfurt city records, the Nuremberg treasures were reduced to the regalian "kingly crown."[65] Sixteenth-century printed texts promoted Charlesmagne's life and valor: Einhard's *Life of Charlemagne* had appeared in a 1521 edition, drawing an explicit connection between Charlemagne (Charles I) and the newly crowned Charles V through a pair of portraits on the title page. The *Life*, reprinted in 1561 and 1562 prior to Maximilian's election and coronation, offered a blueprint of military campaigns and the reception of gifts honoring his singular magnificence: Charlemagne had received an elephant from the King of Persia, identified as ruler of all the east (*orient*) except India.[66] A

Künig Ferdinanden rc. Wegnemen... Election des Roe. Künigs... unnd die Croenung zü Aach.... [Vienna: Singriener, 1531], D-Diii^v, here Diii and the Leipzig pamphlet *Krönung Königlicher Maiestat/ welche volpracht ist zu Ach am eylfften tag Januarii ymm M.D.xxxi* [1531] simply summarizes the materials as "das Königliche klayd", a^v. StAN, Krönungsakten Nr. 5, fol. 1.

63 StAN, SIL 134, no. 23.

64 Habersack, 169–70.

65 "küniglich Crone" Frankfurt Stadtarchiv, Ratsprotokolle 1562–63, fol. 64; "Kö. Cron" FSA Bürgermeisterbuch 1562–63, fol. 160^v, in discussions of an appropriate reception for the regalia's Nuremberg escort, expected on November 26 or 27.

66 Einhard, *Vita et gesta Caroli magni* (Cologne: 1521), A2, 20, 100–2; *Annales Regvm Francorvm... Item Caroli Cognomento Magni....* (Cologne: 1561) and (Cologne, 1562). For Charlemagne's gift exchange, Leslie Brubaker, "The Elephant and the Ark," *Dumbarton Oaks Papers* 58 (2004): 175–6.

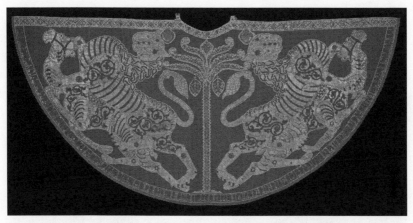

FIGURE 30. Coronation Mantle, 1133/1134. Kunsthistorisches Museum, Vienna.

historic Charlemagne in 1562 infused the regalia with genealogical importance but arguably would not have fully compensated for the diminution
of its sacral meanings in the 1520s.

After the coronation ceremony on November 30, Maximilian or some
of his court officials explored a new layer of meaning for the imperial
robes, one that might further reinvigorate their symbolic capital. The
Nuremberg city councillors who brought the imperial regalia to and from
Frankfurt documented the effort. In their detailed report of the coronation
and travel expenses, the Nuremberg city representatives explained that
their return from the coronation had been delayed due to the intervention
of the new King Maximilian. As they prepared to pack up the regalia in
its traveling trunk, the chief court translator came to their quarters and
informed them that Maximilian had become interested in the coronation
mantle. He had noticed (presumably during the coronation ceremony)
that the coronation mantle – a semi-circular red cloak heavily decorated
with gold designs – had some "chaldean and syrian" letters embroidered
on it. Maximilian ordered the Nurembergers to let his translators examine
the mantle to explicate the script's meaning (although in the end they
were not particularly successful).[67] The mantle depicted two lions, in
mirror image, each triumphantly crouching on a prone camel, and was
bordered with a Kufic Arabic script (Figure 30). The mantle had received
little comment in the coronations before 1562, but in light of Ibrahim's
enacted gifting of the camels, its imagery would have been compelling.

[67] StAN, SIL 134 no. 23, unfoliated bundle letter of December 1, fol. 1ᵛ.

Maximilian probably would not have seen it previously, because in then-existing representations of the regalia (such as Albrecht Dürer's portraits), the mantle decorations were obscured. Older woodcuts, such as those in the 1487 relic book, depict the lions on the mantle but not the camels (Figure 20).[68]

From 1562 on, the coronation mantle would be described in records as containing this "syrian, chaldean, and arabic" script and the figures of lions dominating camels.[69] Whether these figures were understood as prophetic or commemorative, the mantle depicted supremacy over Muslim culture. The new significance of the imperial mantle, a Muslim gift whose full message was as yet literally unreadable, built on the symbolism created by Ibrahim's Turkish embassy and its gifts.[70] It did not replace the mantle's significance as the clothing of the Emperor Charlemagne, but offered an additional military resignification. Maximilian's interest in the imperial relics apparently was stimulated by his coronation: a few years later, Maximilian made efforts to appropriate the imperial relics. In response to his inquiry, the city of Nuremberg replied that the relics would remain in the city.[71]

Along with the Frankfurt election authors' common descriptions of treaty, audience, and gift giving, some also described a specific incident within the audience. In Ibrahim's audience with Ferdinand before the princes of the empire, he made a show of acknowledging the event that had assembled them all: the peaceful succession of Ferdinand's son in his own lifetime. Descriptions of this incident offered vivid details of

---

[68] See Albrecht Dürer's sketch and portrait of Charlemagne, H. Tietze and E. Tietze-Conrat, *Kristische Verzeichnis der Werke Albrecht Dürers* II:1 (Basel and Leipzig: Holbein, 1937), 60–1, 76–7, 212–13, 229. Two woodcuts depicting the mantle are *Wie das hochwirdigist Auch kaiserlich heiligthum... Nüremberg* (Nuremberg: P. Vischer, 1487) and the fragment in Campbell Dodgson's "A Woodcut Illustrating the Relics of the Holy Roman Empire," *The Burlington Magazine* 30 (1917): 97.

[69] StAN, Krönungsakten Nr. 5, fol. 25; the SIL 134 no. 23, 1562 report documents the camels as "untergedrückt." In an inventory of 1562, the mantle appeared much higher on the list of items, standing third after the crown and orb.

[70] A sustained chain of records does not exist, although by the eighteenth century, a triumphal reading of imperial strength and victory over Muslim foes was in place, reinforced by a translation of the script that claimed the mantle was a tribute from a Muslim lord to the Holy Roman Emperor. See Christoph Gottlieb von Murr, *Beschreibung der vornehmsten Merkwürdigen in des H. R. Reichs freyen Stadt Nürnberg und auf der hohen Schule zu Altdorf* (Nuremberg: Johann Eberhard, 1778), 237–55. The mantle had been produced by Muslim silkworkers in 1133/34 (528) in the royal workshops of Roger II, King of Sicily, and commented on the reign's prosperity and peace.

[71] "die reliquien so die von nirnberg haben sainden nit versetzt worden sondern perpetinert worden." HHStA Familien-Akten 88, Tagebuch Maximilian II, April 1567, fol. 84ᵛ.

gestures and speech. Ibrahim asked Ferdinand which of the assembled princes was his prince and heir. Ferdinand pointed with his finger to his son, Maximilian, who was seated at his left hand. Ibrahim then bowed to the son and wished him a happy life and a peaceful succession. He then added that with such an auspicious given name, the son could only become greater than the father (playing on the relationship between Maximilian and *maximus*).[72]

For the informed sixteenth-century Latin Christian reader, such comments would have evoked thoughts about dynastic matters in the Ottoman Empire. Süleyman was known to be aging. He had outlived Charles V, and Habsburg advisors in Latin Christendom argued that the threat of immediate Ottoman aggression was low because of Süleyman's advanced age and waning health. Latin Christians also had gained some understanding of the open succession practiced within the house of Osman as a family history of fratricides, patricides, and even filicides. In histories circulating in Habsburg Europe, Süleyman was thought to have committed the "shocking and cruel deed" of executing his oldest son Mustapha after suspecting him of conspiracy. The histories blamed Süleyman's wife Hürrem for this death of Süleyman's son by another woman. The execution led Mustapha's devoted younger half brother, Jihangir, to kill himself in despair over his brother's death.[73] This execution of one son was followed by another a decade later: after Süleyman's son Bayezid and Selim fought over the succession, Bayezid was forced to retreat to Persia. Süleyman sent agents to Persia to kill him and his sons, Süleyman's grandsons.[74] Indeed, it was this filicide that precipitated the proposed treaty settlement of 1562. With Bayezid no longer a threat to the east, Busbecq was persuaded by Ottoman court officials that no better treaty terms would be forthcoming and that he should accept those proffered.[75] These deaths were not the first reported as executions and murders within the family of Osman: Selim I, Süleyman's father, was said to have killed his father and his brothers in a combined patricide-fratricide. The trope of violent and uncertain succession in the Ottoman house would soon be reinforced by the accounts of a glut of

---

[72] Beuther, Kiii; *Anbringen*, Aiii.

[73] "der Erschrecklichen vnd grewlichen that," *Wie der Türckisch Tyrann Soleyman/ der itzung regiert/ seinen eltesten Son Mustapha/....* (Wittenberg, 1556), Bi[v], also Diii[v]-Div; Theodore Spandounes, *On the origin of the Ottoman Emperors* (1538), ed. and trans. Donald M. Nicol (Cambridge: Cambridge University Press, 1997) 27, 32, 53, 64.

[74] Busbecq, III: 178-81; IV: 274, 278-81.

[75] Busbecq, IV: 235, 283-7 and CDIE 98: 298-9.

family deaths: in 1575, news circulated that the new Emperor Murad had secured his own succession through not one but five fratricides of his younger brothers, whose mothers killed themselves out of grief.[76] The violent consequences of Ottoman succession, known to many readers in 1562, encouraged reflection on the differences between the militarily and economically powerful Ottoman Empire and their own Holy Roman Empire, with its deep religious divisions but newly secured peaceful succession.

The tension between the admirable military and political success of the Ottoman state and an increasingly negative depiction of Ottoman cultural practices has been located in the discourses of tyranny developed in Venetian diplomatic accounts from the 1570s. As admiration turned to revulsion, the seventeenth-century trope of the Oriental despot gradually emerged. In the last thirty years of the sixteenth century, representations of the cruel Turk intensified; Ottomans were increasingly depicted as greedy, ignoble, and venal in their governance and family life, as well as in the early charges of unnatural behavior during the aftermath of military sieges.[77] The 1562 embassy, predating this intensification of the despotic trope, was itself a complex site of knowledge formation in which cultural interpretations of the Turk were reinforced or reshaped, intentionally and unintentionally. The Ottoman embassy was portrayed with a focus on difference rather than cultural comparability, a difference that supported Habsburg political assertions. Ibrahim Bey was a Muslim, perhaps acknowledged as a renegade but so immersed in Turkish culture and language that he appeared unfamiliar. His ceremonial gestures occurred in idioms unfamiliar to Latin Christianity, even as his material splendor and gifts reminded of a rich and mythic Levant. Yet in Süleyman's violent dispatching of his own children and grandchildren, the Ottoman ruler was already seen to be removed from the sensibilities of paternal protectiveness. These varied characterizations recurred in travel narratives by Habsburg diplomats and their attendants who journeyed to Constantinople during the next three decades.[78]

---

[76] *Newe zeittung vnnd gründtliche Beschreibung/ Von des Türckischen Keysers absterben/....* (1575), Aii^v–Aiii.

[77] Lucette Valensi, *The Birth of the Despot: Venice and the Sublime Porte*, trans. Arthur Denner (Ithaca: Cornell University Press, 1993), 23, 31–7, 69–77.

[78] See Busbecq's own letters, published in 1592, Salomon Schweigger's account of the 1577 embassy published in 1608, and Reinhold Lubenau's manuscript of his travel in 1587 that was completed by 1628. Lubenau even included a chapter on family dynamics, "Turkish Tirannie in genere," in *Beschreibung der reisen des Reinhold Lubenau*, ed. W. Sahm (Königsburg I. Pr.: Beyer, 1912–20), 287.

In the years after Ibrahim Bey's 1562 journey, diplomacy across the Ottoman-Austrian border became more regular. The Austrian Habsburgs were granted permission to establish a permanent embassy, with its associated improved status, in Constantinople. With the exception of a brief militarily aggressive testing phase from 1564 to 1566, during the years when Maximilian II became Holy Roman Emperor and Süleyman's son Selim II succeeded as *padishah*, diplomatic exchange proceeded relatively smoothly. Diplomatic embassies traveled to Constantinople in most years and a few other Ottoman envoys and renegades would travel to Vienna over the decades. In 1565, Hidayet Aga, envoy of the peace-oriented Arslan Pasha of Ofen, remained in Vienna for several months while his Habsburg counterpart traveled to Constantinople.[79] In the 1570s after Ibrahim's death, the high-ranking interpreter, Ottoman court official, and renegade Mahmud Bey[80] traveled to Prague on a diplomatic mission. After a reversal of the usual military outcomes through the Ottoman defeat at the Battle of Lepanto, an Ottoman official brought gifts and ransom to the victorious Habsburg commander, Don Juan of Austria.[81]

Amid all their enthusiasm to interpret the Turkish presence at Frankfurt triumphantly, the Habsburg family and court propagandists had hidden some less appealing information from the gathered estates and readers. The terms of the new peace treaty brought by the envoy Ibrahim left much to be desired. Despite years of determined negotiation by Habsburg ambassadors, the terms did not vary significantly from the heartily disliked treaty of 1547. The Ottoman Emperor required the continuation of the annual 30,000 gulden payment in exchange for ceasing to press their claim on Habsburg territories in Hungary. Since 1547, the Habsburgs had sought to obscure the nature of this payment so that it was not understood as a tribute, but as something else. In the 1547 treaty, the Ottoman and Habsburg versions of the treaty both named the 30,000 ducats a payment of money. When Ferdinand disseminated the treaty terms to Hungarian magnates, the word *pecuniam* had been

[79] Alfred Sitte, "Tsausch Hedajets Aufenthalt in Wien (1565)," *AKG* 6 (1908): 192–201; Karl Vocelka, "Eine türkische Botschaft in Wien 1565," *Beiträge zur neueren Geschichte Österreichs*, ed. Heinrich Fichtenau and Erich Zöllner (Vienna: Böhlau, 1974), 102–14; Josef Zontar, "Michael Cernović, Geheimagent Ferdinands I. und Maximilians II. und seine Berichterstattung," *Mitteilungen des Österreichischen Staatsarchivs* 24 (1971): 169–222.

[80] Both Ibrahim and Mahmud held the court title of *müteferrika*. HHStA Turcica 26/4, 133–4 and Turcica 30/5, fols. 48–50.

[81] HHStA Venedig, Berichte Karton 12/1572, pamphlet *Epinicium* (Angelo, 1571), b; Rom Varia, 5/Lepanto, fols. 81–4, 5/(1571), fol. 21.

replaced with *"munus honestum et honorarium"* (honor-gift and hono-rarium). The term *munus honorarium* or *Ehrengeschenk* would be used henceforth in all official Habsburg papers. The Ottomans and their trans-lators would adopt this distinction, employing Turkish words for present (which they translated using the Italian "present" as well) when they began to describe this sum of money more concretely in 1565.[82] Although the Habsburg crown kept silent about the renewed payments at the tri-umphal treaty ratification in November 1562, it would have to address the unpleasant task of raising the money for the *Ehrengeschenk* the following year.

This tension over the honorable gift and its implications of subordi-nation was increasingly problematized by observers after Maximilian II's death in 1576. Salomon Schweigger, who served as a preacher for the Habsburg ambassador to Constantinople in 1577, later claimed that a blatant conceptual deception was at play. He himself chose, he said, to call the payment a *present*, because a tribute would be shameful and the German people should take up arms if such tribute were occurring. But, he explained, the Ottomans openly called the present "a *Charatsch*, which means a tax or tribute," as though it were a payment from subject Christians.[83] Although this criticism of the gift as shameful was echoed by other observers,[84] the payment could not be eliminated, and in fact reemerged as a precipitant of the "long war" between Ottomans and the Holy Roman Empire at the end of the century.[85]

In the short term during the sixteenth century, Ferdinand and Maxi-milian II responded to their inability or reluctance to meet the payment in part by systematizing and escalating the gift giving that accompanied the tribute embassies to Constantinople. To find an impressive gift for a Muslim ruler required a certain ingenuity, given that Christian relics or costumes of knightly orders dedicated to the defense of Christian-ity were not an option. The Habsburgs turned to elaborate mechanical clocks as a solution to their desire to impress the Ottoman court favor-ably. During the middle decades of the sixteenth century, the demand

---

[82] For Ferdinand's alteration of the 1547 treaty, I have relied on Ernst Dieter Petritsch's "Tribute oder Ehrengeschenk?" *Archiv und Forschung*, ed. Elisabeth Springer and Leopold Kammerhofer (Vienna: Verlag für Geschichte und Politik, 1993), 54–8.
[83] "einen Charatsch, das heißt 'ein Schatzung oder Tribut'." Schweigger, 64–5.
[84] Lubenau, I:200–1.
[85] For the Pasha of Buda's increasing dissatisfaction with the timeliness of the payment in 1590–1593, see Gustav Bayerle, *Ottoman Diplomacy in Hungary* (Bloomington: Indiana University Press, 1972).

in the Ottoman Empire for European clocks became well known.[86] The Habsburgs responded to this interest in 1541, directly after Ottoman forces had retaken Buda and declared the majority of Hungary to be a province in the Ottoman Empire. At this difficult juncture, Ferdinand sent diplomatic negotiators to Constantinople with an elaborate silver mechanical clock and planetarium that had been constructed for Ferdinand's grandfather, Emperor Maximilian I, according to his specifications.[87] The French, having established an alliance with the Ottoman Empire and a regular embassy in Constantinople, were quick to follow suit and began to gift Süleyman and members of his court with clocks.[88] Ferdinand, however, initially seemed to reserve clocks for important diplomatic moments. The next call for clocks came in 1548, the first payment year after an Austria-Ottoman treaty had been concluded in 1547. "The Turk," wrote Habsburg ambassador Gerhard Veltwyck, "is extremely delighted by mechanical arts, of which the best are German."[89] In preparation for bringing the 1548 tribute money to Constantinople, the envoy Justus de Argento sought out four clocks and included a clockmaker along with a translator in his newly caparisoned retinue.[90] In 1559, the year of a new truce to negotiate a treaty, Ferdinand sent a clock fashioned as a tower on the back of an elephant.[91]

With the ratification of this new peace treaty in 1562, Habsburg clocks became annual diplomatic gifts. Beginning in 1563, Habsburg administrative records reveal clocks' regular use as a second ceremonial gift type, joining the stand-by silver goblet or cup.[92] In 1563, Habsburgs agents purchased fifteen silver, gilded *doppelpokaln* and six clocks in Augsburg

---

[86] In the early 1530s, at least one miniature Venetian clock was brought to Constantinople and sold to Emperor Süleyman. Otto Kurz, *European Clocks and Watches in the Near East* (London: The Warburg Institute, 1975), 22. Correspondence in *Austro-Turcica*, ed. Nehring, records the grand vezir Rustem Pasha's requests for a clockmaker in the late 1540s, 189, 209.

[87] This first gift does not appear in Ferdinand's diplomatic or *Hofkammer* archives, according to Gottfried Mraz in "Die Rolle der Uhrwerke in der kaiserlichen Türkenverehrung im 16. Jahrhundert," Klaus Maurice and Otto Mayr, ed. *Die Welt als Uhr: Deutsche Uhren und Automaten, 1550–1650* (Munich: Bayerisches Nationalmuseum, 1980), 43–4. Paolo Giovio recorded this 1541 gift in his *Historiarum sui temporis libri* (1577), in *Opere* (Rome: Istituto Poligrafico e Zecca dello Stato, 1985) 5:47–8.

[88] Kurz documents French clocks as gifts beginning in 1543, 24–5.

[89] Nehring, 196.

[90] HKA Reichsakten 190, fols. 14ᵛ–26.

[91] Busbecq, III: 208.

[92] Turcica 23/1, fol. 36–36ᵛ; HKA, Reichsakten 190, fols. 111–14, esp. 112–112ᵛ; 161–4.

and Munich as presents for the Ottoman court,[93] a tactic followed again in 1566.[94] The year 1567 followed a humiliating defeat of Habsburg forces in Hungary,[95] during which not even Süleyman's death had prevented Ottoman troops from taking over the fortress of Szigeth. From this year onward, the Habsburgs seemed to no longer differentiate completely between the presents and the sums of money required by treaty, treating both as obligatory.[96] Both objects and money were considered regular costs of the annual embassy to Constantinople, necessary to keep the peace and guarantee the lives of the ambassadors. The increase in diplomatic gifts rather than cash payments suited the Habsburgs, who had persisted in calling their payments presents rather than tribute, as if all gifts were entrance ceremony gifts of plate filled with coins.[97] In Constantinople, Habsburg observers noted that the two types of payments were received differently. Unlike the payment of money, gifts of clocks and plate were presented publicly.[98]

The costs were not inconsiderable, as seen in the accounts of the 1567 embassy. The crown agent Georg Ilsung, Landvogt von Schwaben, acquired forty-one silver pieces[99] and ten clocks in Augsburg, in purchases totaling more than 6,100 gulden. The two most expensive clocks were intended for Emperor Selim, and the next two for Pashas Mehmed and Pertav. The final list of gifts totaled more than 85,900 gulden with money payments, silver plate, and clocks to the Ottoman emperor, the grand vezir and other vezirs (six in total in 1567), other officials, regional

---

93 HHStA Turcica 17/4, fol. 16.

94 For the 1566 purchase of a 38 fl. clock made by Hanns Runckel, see HKA Hofzahlamts-buch 21: 47. Clockmaking established itself as a distinct trade apart from metal-smithing in the mid-sixteenth century. Hermann Kellenbenz, "Wirtschaftsleben der Blütezeit," *Geschichte der Stadt Augsburg*, ed. Gunter Gottlieb et al. (Stuttgart: Konrad Theiss, 1984), 262. For a prosopographical history of the sixteenth- and early-seventeenth-century clockmaker trade, see Maximilian Bobinger, *Kunstuhrmacher in Alt-Augsburg* (Augsburg: Hans Rösler, 1969).

95 Maximilian II's short war of 1565–6 is discussed in Eduard Wertheimer, "Der Geschichte des Türkenkrieges Maximilians II. 1565–1566," *AÖG* 53 (1875): 43–102.

96 "eius munus illud triginta millium [sic] Ducatorum una cum viginti inauratis scÿphis seu cuppis duplicatis ac duobus uel tribus horologÿs," Maximilian's instructions, HHStA Turcica 23/1, fol. 80–80ᵛ. This approximates, but does not completely follow, his ambassador in Constantinople's advice. For Wyss's advice, Mraz p. 46. For 1570–1571, HHStA Turcica 23/4, fols. 137–138ᵛ.

97 For gifts of coin-filled plate, see HKA Reichsakten 190, fol. 112.

98 See Lubenau, II: 10.

99 The goldsmiths were Hannß Flickher, Martin Marquart, and Ulrich Meringer, with total sums more than 5,200 gulden, Mraz, 46.

governors along the way to Constantinople, and two important translators (including Ibrahim Bey) in Constantinople. Further costs, including outfitting the embassy (for 6,377 gulden) pushed the expense of the embassy to more than 98,200 gulden.[100] The Turkish *Ehrengeschenck* remained just as costly during the rest of Maximilian II's reign. In the years 1570–1576, the total present (objects and money) outlays ranged between 80,000–90,000 gulden, with silverware and clocks accounting for between a tenth and an eighth of the total value.[101] After 1568, Maximilian II included a salaried clockmaker at his court, who began to produce the smaller clocks, valued at around 35 gulden, for gifts to the Ottoman court.[102]

Clocks are valued higher than silver plate in the account books: their numbers were limited and their recipients restricted to only the highest-ranking Ottoman officials. Yet their cost was lower: a lower-ranking official might receive a silver or gilded plate valued at more than 100 gulden but a clock valued at about 35 gulden.[103] According to Schweigger, they were not convertible, so their value was not in the precious metals of their construction. Lubenau explained their desirability in the possibilities of innovation: each clock could have a new form.[104] A clock designed for the demands of the Turkish tribute might, for example, take the form of the intended recipient.[105] The value of innovation was testified to by the

[100] Augsburg Stadtarchiv (StA), Handwerkerakten, Uhrmacher Akten, fols. 135–6. The clockmakers were Daniel Lotter, Caspar Buschman, Hanns Chunat, Master Mathis Stoßwender, Simon Fridrich, Hannß Zeller, Erasmus Piernprunder, and Master Georg Zurn. In all, ten pieces costing 949 gulden, Reichsakten 190, fols. 340–54. Reichsakten, fols. 288–93. Lotter and Zeller's clocks were intended for the Ottoman Emperor, Mehmed Pasha received one made by Buchman, and Pertav Pasha the masterwork by Chunat. fols. 290ᵛ–91.

[101] HKA Reichsakten 190, fol. 526–6ᵛ.

[102] Gerhard Emmoser relocated to Augsburg in 1563, joining the court in Vienna in 1566 and joined by Martin de Bel Campo in 1575. Kurz, p. 31. Among the clocks Emmoser produced were two for Ibrahim Bey. HKA Hofzahlamtsbücher 23:89, 93ᵛ, 324ᵛ, 24: 247; 25:454, 497ᵛ, 558; 27:334, 28:352 for 1574 lists his pay with other artists; 29: 528–528ᵛ; 30: 420. In 1569, Emmoser produced three and purchased nine clocks of similar value (~116 gulden and ~267 gulden). HKA Hofzahlamtsbücher 23: 93ᵛ, 24: 658, 467. In the 1580s, clocks became a gift exchanged among members of the Habsburg family. See Pérez de Tudela and Jordan Gschwend, "Luxury Goods."

[103] Examples are in HKA Reichsakten 190, fols. 288–93, 349–52.

[104] Schweigger, 61–2 and Lubenau, I: 200–1.

[105] Thomas Steiger made a clock in the form of Achmat Bassa, for him, in 1570–1571, HHStA Turcica 23/4, fols. 137–8ᵛ.

crown official Ilsung, who petitioned the Augsburg clockmaker's guild on behalf of a clockmaker who was making a clock "which perhaps no-one, or few here, could make."[106] With clocks, the Habsburgs may have believed that they had found a payment that both satisfied the Ottoman court's demand for payment and their own desire to give a gift rather than a tribute. The value of the gift lay in the addition of mechanical skill. Although indisputably secular rather than sacred, the clock had mimicked the relic in one regard: it possessed a value that lay outside its materials.

Amid all this annual flurry of clock preparation, the question of why Ottomans did not simply make their own clocks was not addressed explicitly. As noted in Introduction to Part II, Experiments of Exclusion, Hieronymo Román had asserted in 1575 that Ottomans were not particularly skilled in the mechanical arts, yet his corollary had been that they did possess some ability in metalworking. Busbecq's letters noted that the Turks used water clocks to tell the time during the day, particularly the calls to prayer. He had also reported that the Ottomans' inability to keep track of time at night without spring-driven clocks led to confusion between moonrise and sunrise, which upset his travels until his Turkish escort began to rely on Busbecq's clocks.[107] He contrasted what he defined as their general interest in importing technological inventions with their refusal to adopt public clocks or printing. These rejections, according to Busbecq, stemmed from their fear that the authority of their ancient rites would be undermined by these technologies.[108] As with Busbecq's description of their attitude toward paper, he presented these ideas as superstitious sentiments. The explanations offered to Latin Christian readers allowed them to appreciate their own freedom from superstition and skill at technological innovation.

After this first "success" of European automation, clocks would become gifts for diplomatic embassies to China, Persia, and India. Over

---

[106] "Des filleicht kainer, oder weinig alhie machen khindten." StA Handwerkerakten, Uhrmachern I, fol. 135..For the role of the Habsburg tribute purchases in guild matters, see StA Handwerkerakten, Uhrmachern I, Jacob Marquard, fols. 135–46, Hans Runckhel, fols. 125–30; also Bobinger 45–6; Volker Himmelein, "Uhren und wissenschaftliche Instrumente," *Welt im Umbruch: Augsburg zwischen Renaissance und Barock* (Augsburg: Augsburger Druck- und Verlagshaus, 1980) 2:55–7, 434–48; and Helmut W. Seling, "Silberhandel und Goldschmiedekunst in Augsburg im 16. Jahrhundert," *Welt im Umbruch* (Augsburg: Augsburger Druck- und Verlagshaus, 1981) 3: 162–70.

[107] Busbecq, I: 27–9.
[108] Busbecq, I: 169–70.

time, they would be touted as a symbol of European scientific superiority.[109] Yet the Habsburgs had offered clocks to the Ottomans from a position of significant political and military weakness rather than domination.[110] The Habsburgs were engaged in a scrambling search for conceptual and tactical responses to Ottoman strength. In the propaganda of 1562, the Habsburgs and other Latin Christian observers had promoted a cultural distancing between the Holy Roman and Ottoman Empire, between Muslim and Christian, that exoticized the world east of Latin Christendom.

Equally if not more important was the need to locate the authority and symbolism of imperial sovereignty in a confessionally divided Holy Roman Empire. The ceremonies of coronation in 1562 had been literally mapped onto a new space – Frankfurt. At Maximilian's first imperial diet of 1566, customary confessionally-specific ceremonies were also eliminated. He and his court would continue experimenting with non-confessional strategies that evoked Roman antiquity or the need for unity in the face of the Turkish threat. In Maximilian's 1563 post-coronation entry into Vienna, the classical symbolism of the triumphal arches, used to mark Charles V's and Philip II's entries in the 1540s, was employed. An Austrian arch reminded all of the 1529 siege of Vienna, and a Bohemian arch was decorated with a rhinoceros and an elephant, as well as personifications of the Bohemian lands. A Roman arch gestured toward global empire, topped by a globe and with spandrel victories holding inscriptions "De Indis" and "De Saracenis," that likely commemorated Charles V's older triumphs. Nonetheless, the focus of the arch's iconography was a genealogy of Habsburg emperors. Under Maximilian, the imperial court's cultural production expressed a "middle way" of irenicism. Its new projects emphasized confessional conciliation and a unifying pan-European imperialism harkening back to the Roman Empire.[111]

---

[109] David Landes, *Revolution in Time* (Cambridge, MA: Harvard University Press, 1983), 101; Kurz, 62–3.

[110] Edward Said, *Orientalism* (New York: Vintage, 1978), 40–73 characterized this pre-eighteenth-century development of the "vocabulary available to talk about the east" as a period of implacability rather than anxious adaption.

[111] Margit Altfahrt, "Propaganda," 53–92; Josef Wünsch, ed., *Der Einzug Kaiser Maximilians II in Wien 1563* (Vienna: Brzezowsky, 1914); Howard Louthan, *The Quest for Compromise: Peace-makers in Counter-Reformation Vienna* (Cambridge: Cambridge University Press, 1997), especially 35–46, 79; Karl Rudolf, "Die Kunstbestrebungen Kaiser Maximilians II. im Spannungsfeld zwischen Madrid und Wien" *JKSW* 2nd ser. 55 (1995); Thomas DaCosta Kaufmann, *The Mastery of Nature* (Princeton: Princeton University Press, 1993).

Authors evoking the empires of the classical world were careful to exclude activities deemed un-Christian frivolity. A description of the Viennese entry explained the Christian significance of the wine fountains. A history of the Turks published in 1563, the year after the election, was prefaced by a discussion of Maximilian's election and more sober festivities in contrast to "heathen pomp." The history explained that it was translating the account into German to help people prepare for military conflict.[112] The Ottoman Empire continued to serve as the ominous and unifying threat in whose face the religiously divided people of Christian Europe must unite under their emperor. In 1567, Laurentius Fuchs, author of an election and coronation pamphlet, heralded the unifier of the empire as the military leader Christianus. Despite Fuchs's close connections to the Saxon electoral court, he identified Christianus as Emperor Maximilian II. Fuchs called for Christian unity against the Turk, "child of the devil," without demanding doctrinal orthodoxy. Similarly, Maximilian's former military general, Lazarus von Schwendi, cited the example of Emperor Constantine's peaceful toleration of pagan worship (for decades after his conversion to Christianity) in his early-1570s treatises on the necessity of promoting or accepting religious tolerance among Christians in the Holy Roman Empire. Perhaps reflecting the absence of sacral authority, Schwendi also called for Maximilian to base his authority on his fair governance.[113]

Maximilian's interest in artifacts and knowledge from Asia Minor and the Ottoman Empire would continue throughout his reign. With the defense of the Habsburg lands in mind, he supported Hugo Blotius's project to make information about Turkish culture in the imperial libraries accessible.[114] Maximilian's councillor Hieronymus Beck supported the production of material about the Turk. Immediately after the

---

[112] Heinrich Müller *Türkisch Historien....* (Frankfurt am Main, 1563),)(ii-*iiᵛ.

[113] Laurentius Fuchs, *Kurtzer vnnd klarer Unterricht/ von des Türkischen Tyrannen Gewalt/ Namen vnd Lendern/ Vnnd wie die Gegenwehre wider den Türcken/ Christlich sol fürgenomen werden* (Dresden: M. Stöckel, 1567), d–eᵛ; Frauenholz, Eugen von. ed. *Des Lazarus von Schwendi. Denkschrift über die politische lage des Deutschen Reiches von 1574* (Munich: Beck, 1939), 31–7; and the 1570 text in Maximilian Lanzinner, "Die Denkschrift des Lazarus Schwendi zur Reichspolitik," *Zeitschrift für historische Forschung*, suppl. 3 (1987): 154, 162–5.

[114] Blotius's first catalog was of the Turcica, drawn from the imperial and other libraries. Louthan, 75. A surprising range of information about Turkish culture might be utilized for military aims. One plan to smuggle explosives on board Turkish galleys depended on knowing that some food was off-limits to Muslims but not Christian galley-slaves. David C. Goodman, *Power and Penury* (Cambridge: Cambridge University Press, 1988), 131–2.

ignominious failure of the Habsburg offensive in Hungary in 1567, Hans Spiegel would produce his translation of a Turkish chronicle at Beck's instigation and at least one other chronicle of captivity, by Georg Huzthi, was dedicated to Beck.[115] Not all familiarity with Turkish culture was intended to fuel an imperial unity through hostility toward an aggressive enemy: Maximilian's new summer palace was built on the purported site of Suleiman's tent during the 1529 siege and arguably included Muslim design elements.[116] In the search for ways to unify a doctrinally divided empire without reference to the Americas, the attention of Maximilian's court turned increasingly away from the New World, the domain of the Iberian Habsburgs, and toward the Turks. Frankfurt, then, can be seen as an experiment in offering a new symbolism for Habsburg sovereignty and power.

The imperial diet of 1566, called amid Maximilian's brief military offensive against the Ottomans, initiated an increase in empire-wide support for military funding along the Habsburg-Ottoman border. Yet after that offensive ended in defeat and stalemate, the imperial estates and imperial circles did not lose their enthusiasm for the Turkish tax. They funded the military efforts along the border at comparable rates from 1576 to 1592, during the reign of Maximilian's son Rudolf II. In 1592, another imperial diet at the beginning of the "Turkish war" (1592–1606) continued financial support for an imperial military response to the Ottomans.[117] Groundbreaking scholarship on this era emphasized growing perceptions of the Turkish threat during the last third of the century. The majority of this anti-Turkish political propaganda was produced during the war and in the immediate prelude to it in the 1590s.[118] Events at Frankfurt in 1562 and Maximilian's complicated responses, whether sustained or fragmentary, reveal more variegated perceptions of the Ottomans during most of the second half of the sixteenth century.

---

[115] Johann Gaudier, *Chronica oder Acta von der Türckischen Tyrannen herkommen* (Frankfurt an der Oder: Eichorn, 1567), aiii^v. Georg Huszthi, "Descriptio peregrinationis," *Starine* 13 (1881): 1–38, here 2. Beck then moved, in 1569, from a position as president of the treasury to high provisioner of the army in Hungary. Fichtner, *Maximilian II*, 82.

[116] Hilda Lietzmann identified this spatial connection, as well as the arguably Muslim design elements in *Neugebäude*, 11–23, 181–3, 198–9; also Louthan, 43–6.

[117] Winfried Schulze, *Reich und Türkengefahr im späten 16. Jahrhundert* (Munich: C.H. Beck, 1978). Schulze argued that the commitment to funding Habsburg military projects in Hungary was tied to increased awareness of the Turkish threat.

[118] Schulze; Karl Vocelka, *Die Politische Propaganda Kaiser Rudolfs II. (1576–1612)* (Vienna: Österreichische Akademie der Wissenschaften, 1980).

Eschewing confessionally charged symbols of authority, Maximilian and then Rudolf, in the first half of his reign, focused instead on the signs of a classical Roman Empire,[119] ignoring confessional issues as a means of overcoming internal tensions. In these decades, the Ottomans were more unfamiliar and more exotic, but not necessarily more frightening. Rather than fear alone, a regard for the exotic built a stronger image of the Roman emperor who held commanded respect (and camels, if not elephants) from empires to the east.

[119] Kaufmann, *Mastery of Nature*.

6

Collecting Idolatry and the Emergence of the Exotic

The second half of the sixteenth century marked the emergence of the *Kunstkammer* and the encyclopedic collection. In the Habsburg territories, people at many different social ranks – emperors, secular and ecclesiastical princes, urban patricians, well-to-do merchants, and humanist scholars – all collected material objects as representations of the wider world.[1] The values and purposes behind these representations reflected differing ambitions: to display scholarship, wealth, or symbolic and sovereign power. In a legacy from the earlier treasury, princes sought to express their magnificence and thus their power and right to rule through extensive and wide-ranging collections.[2]

Treasuries in the medieval era had proclaimed material magnificence, their relics and reliquaries had served as signs of accrued sacral authority. Awareness of these sacrally valuable collections had been promoted

---

[1] Julius von Schlosser, *Die Kunst- und Wunderkammern der Spätrenaissance* (Leipzig: Klinkhardt & Biermann, 1908); Elizabeth Scheicher, *Die Kunst- und Wunderkammern der Habsburger* (Vienna: Molden, 1979); José Miguel Morán and Fernando Checa, *El Coleccionismo en España. De la cámara de maravillas a la galería de pinturas* (Madrid: Cátedra, 1985); Thomas DaCosta Kaufmann, "From Treasury to Museum: The Collections of the Austrian Habsburgs," in John Elsner and Roger Cardinal, ed., *The Cultures of Collecting* (Cambridge: Harvard University Press, 1994); Oliver Impey and Arthur MacGregor, ed., *The Origins of Museums: the Cabinet of Curiosities in Sixteenth- and Seventeenth-Century Europe* (Oxford: Clarendon Press, 1985); Paula Findlen's *Possessing Nature: Museums, Collecting, and Scientific Culture in Early Modern Europe* (Berkeley: University of California Press, 1994); and more recently, Pamela Smith and Paula Findlen, ed., *Merchants and Marvels* (New York: Routledge, 2002); the substantial literature on non-noble Central European collections is too large to address here.

[2] Thomas DaCosta Kaufmann, *Mastery of Nature* (Princeton: Princeton University Press, 1993), 174–91.

through itemized descriptions (circulating, for example, as relic books) and the fairs and pilgrimages associated with their exhibition. Medieval rulers publicly supported these sacral treasuries, making explicit their patronage of these magnificent displays.[3] With the status of relics and sacral objects called into question during the early decades of the sixteenth century, the relative importance of secular treasure grew. Rulers expanded their non-sacral treasure through ever-larger art and antiquities collections, valued for more than their convertibility to specie. Princely collections gained importance during the last three decades of the century in this reconstituted form. Collecting served as an arena for princes to vie with one another in constructing the most impressive symbolic microcosm of the world. Amid other items, both natural (*naturalia*) and man-made (*artificialia*), Indian and Turkish objects gained a noted place in these collections. Their evolving categorizations in Habsburg and other princely collections reveal shifts in organizing principles. By the end of the sixteenth century, collections instantiated reformulated understandings of extra-European cultures and hierarchical cultural evaluation.

In Chapter 3, the reception of Aztec treasure in Europe and its initial dispersion to Habsburg treasuries in Castile, the Low Countries, and Austria were linked to pressing questions of imperial symbolic authority and financial solvency. In Castile, such liquidations of royal treasure had occurred at the beginning of the century with Queen Isabella of Castile's treasure and continued through Philip II's early reign. Philip II melted down the imperial crowns of his grandfather Maximilian I and his father Charles V in 1562, after it was widely recognized that his cousin and brother-in-law Maximilian would be elected King of the Romans rather than Philip.[4] Much gold and silver treasure from the Americas and Europe was melted down to finance Habsburg territorial and military ambitions in the mid-1530s.[5] In the same decade, the featherwork

---

[3] The Habsburg emperors and princes restricted access to their treasuries through Rudolf II's reign. As with imperial regalia viewings in Nuremberg, diplomats and visiting nobles were granted collection viewings. Court artists and their associates were also permitted to view the collection for study. Kaufmann, "From Treasury to Museum," 143–5.

[4] Antonio de la Torre, ed., *Testamentaría de Isabel la Católica* (Valladolid: 1968). For Philip's decision to melt down these crowns, Pedro de Madrazo, "Über Krönungsinsignien und Staatsgewänder Maximilian I. und Karl V. und ihr Schicksal in Spanien," *JKSW* 9 (1889): 446–64; and context, Regine Jorzick, *Herrschaftssymbolik und Staat* (Vienna: Verl. für Geschichte und Politik, 1998), 78–98.

[5] Martin de Salinas, *El emperador Carlos V y su corte segun las cartas de Don Martin de Salinas...* (Madrid: Fortanet, 1903), 648; *Corpus Documental de Carlos V*, ed. Manuel Fernández Alvarez (Salamanca: Universidad de Salamanca, 1973) I: 459.

treasure of crowns, shields, and priestly robes and military decorations slipped from notice in Habsburg collections. A few new pieces were added after a quashed Peruvian rebellion, but without much comment. Some efforts were made to value the featherwork ecclesiastical vestments and images of saints created by Christian Mexicans, but these, too, were not sustained.[6] Evidence from the mid-century decades is sketchy but suggests that treasuries continued to be shaped by the exigencies of rule and diplomacy.

Charles V's collection of precious objects continued to reflect its early-sixteenth-century origins. When the emperor's goods were inventoried after his death in 1558, their organization and categorization followed pre-existing patterns for royal treasure in Castile and the Holy Roman Empire.[7] The familiar categories of sacral and secular valuables were all present. Religious treasure included liturgical objects for conducting worship, relics, and devotional paintings, whereas secular treasure included gold, silver, jewels, tableware (often of gold or silver), other decorations, sumptuous and ordinary clothing, secular paintings, books, and other precious crafted goods. Although the bulk of the inventoried treasure consisted of these well-established forms, objects from the Americas and North Africa still had a valued place among them.[8] Both the capture of Tunis and the discovery and conquest of the west Indies had ranked in the list of Charles's most important achievements, commemorated in artistic projects intended to illustrate his successes.[9] Accordingly, these accomplishments beyond Europe were reinscribed in descriptions of

---

[6] Pedro de la Gasca presented featherwork to Ferdinand in February 1554 along with a manuscript, *Descripción del Perú*, about Peru and Gonzalo Pizarro's rebellion, which Pedro de la Gasca had been sent to Peru as governor to quash. He was made bishop of Palencia upon his return to Iberia. HHStA Span. Hofkorr. 1/4, fols. 104–105ᵛ. De la Gasca described the featherwork as an example of the ingenious skill of the Indians. Bartolomé de Las Casas provided Old Testament support for valuing featherwork in the *Apologética Historia Sumaria* (Madrid: Alianza, 1992) 7:592–3. Alessandra Russo discusses these uses and evaluations in "Plumes of Sacrifice," *Res* 42 (2002): 227–49.

[7] *Testamentaría*, ed. A. de la Torre; Archduchess Margaret's holdings in 1499 and 1523–1530 in Rudolf Beer, "Acten, Regesten und Inventare aus dem Archivo General zu Simancas," *JKSW* 12 (1891), cx–cxxiii; and Heinrich Zimerman, "Urkunden und Regesten aus dem k. u. k. Haus-Hof- und Staats-Archiv in Wien," *JKSW* 3 (1885), xciii–cxxiii; and Ferdinand's holdings up to 1527 in ÖNB, Codex 7871.

[8] For Charles's collection as transitional in its final years, see Morán and Checa, *El Coleccionismo en España*, chapters 3 and 4.

[9] These conquests were iconographically prominent in the second half of Charles's reign. Particular examples include a military campaign series drawn by Maarten van Heemskerk and copied in Hieronymus Cock's engravings (1556) and related cherrywood reliefs (ca. 1560–1565), Inv. No. 3944–5, 3947–9, 3980–1, 3985–6, Kunsthistorisches Museum,

Charles's treasure holdings after his death. Jewels and ceremonial robes from "Tunéz" and "las Indias" appeared immediately after the categories of sacral treasure from the royal chapel, gifts from the pope, sacral treasure formerly owned by Charles's mother, and altarpieces. In the inventory, objects from his tributary non-European states of Tunis and the (west) Indies were kept in separate subsections. He possessed "goods that were from the king of Tunis" and "Jewels originating in the Indies, from the island of Peru."[10] Some of this treasure was still understood to signify sovereignty: in 1563, one "crown or collar" of the King of Tunis was placed in an inventory category of imperial crowns and regalia.[11] More limited evidence available for Charles's brother Ferdinand suggests that he also continued to organize his collections as a treasury (*Schatzkammer*) during his lifetime.[12] Both were steadfast Catholics, but as confessional strife and critiques of relics as idolatrous intensified, neither Charles nor Ferdinand seems to have focused on rescuing collections of relics or reliquaries threatened by iconoclastic subjects.[13]

Charles's collections remained centered on treasure from the territories under his control, including non-European lands. After Charles's death and Philip II's inheritance of Castile, Aragon, and the Low Countries, Ferdinand I's and Maximilian II's collections began to reflect these Austrian Habsburgs' rule of royal Hungary. Maintaining a military border with the Ottomans led to expanded holdings of Turkish objects. In two partial inventories of 1568 – a *Nachlass* of Ferdinand I and a *Kammerinventar* of Maximilian II – Turkish-made objects were scattered throughout the

Vienna, see *Katalog der Sammlung für Plastik und Kunstgewerbe*, Part II (Vienna: Kunsthistorisches Museum, 1966), 73–4; see also Emperor Matthias's *Nachlaßinventar* in Hans von Voltelini, "Urkunden und Regesten...," *JKSW* 20 (1899), cxiv.

10 "los bienes que fueron del rey de Tunez" and "Joyas provenientes de las Indias, de la isla del Perú," AGS Casas y Sitios Reales Leg. 72, unfoliated, 1559 inventory by Alonso de Baeça. Another inventory from 1555 is in AGS, Contadurías Generales, Legajo 1145, fol. 3 and partially reprinted in Beer, *JKSW* 12 (1891), cliii–clvii, see also clxx–clxxii. Paz Cabello's "Los Inventarios de Objetos Incas Pertenecientes a Carlos V," *Anales del Museo de América* 2 (1994) lists inventories of treasures from Peru, including robes of state, that arrived in Castile several years after Charles had ordered the melting of treasure from the Indies and specifically Peru, 33, 44–6.

11 Beer, *JKSW* 12 (1891), clxxix–clxxxvii.

12 Wendelin Boeheim, "Urkunden und Regesten aus der K.K. Hofbibliothek," *JKSW* 7 (1888): xcvi–c and Karl Rudolf, "Die Kunstbestrebungen Kaiser Maximilians II. im Spannungsfeld zwischen Madrid und Wien," *JKSW* ser. 2, 55 (1995): 165–256.

13 For the shift in patrician commissions away from religious art after 1525, Jeffrey Chipps Smith, "The Transformations of Patrician Tastes in Renaissance Nuremberg," in *New Perspectives on the Art of Renaissance Nuremberg*, ed. Jeffrey Chipps Smith (Austin: University of Texas Press, 1985), 83–100.

categories of jewelry, ornaments, garments, and various weapons. Both Ferdinand's and Maximilian's inventories included items from diplomatic exchanges with the Ottomans. During Ogier de Busbecq's years of diplomatic negotiations in Constantinople, he had sent Ferdinand a cup and Maximilian two Persian carpets,[14] and Maximilian owned at least one piece of gilded plate intended for the Turkish tribute. The Governor-general (Paša) of Ofen [Buda], with whom Maximilian conducted many border negotiations, had sent nine "Turkish objects."[15] Diplomatic gift exchanges with other sovereigns also merited recognition: Maximilian's inventory identified gifts from Prince Constantine of Russia, King Henry II of France, and Emperor Charles V, as well as the pope, and electors or other nobles from the empire. Retaining other regalian elements of the early-sixteenth-century treasury, Maximilian II's inventory highlighted his coronation crowns and a lidded goblet previously possessed by St. Stephen of Hungary.[16] After Maximilian II's death in 1576, his brothers Archdukes Ferdinand and Charles continued collecting for several more decades. Given their more limited scopes of authority within the dynasty, their collections did not replicate their brother's and father's emphasis on objects commemorating diplomatic exchange or sovereignty. The structures of their collection inventories suggest that, instead, the developing principles of the *Kunstkammer* were employed.[17]

Princely collections in the form of *Kunstkammern*, showcasing an encyclopedic range of material possessions, rather than *Schatzkammern*, showcasing sacral and secular treasuries, emerged in the last third of the sixteenth century. Samuel Quiccheberg's 1565 description of an ideal collection or *Kunstkammer*, promoted a universal organizing structure for it. The ideal collection should represent the world in an encyclopedic manner, to demonstrate princely mastery of that world. Quiccheberg, the

---

[14] "herr Bußbeckh aus der Türckhey," Rudolf, "Kunstbestrebungen," 252 (no. 192), 242 (no. 332).

[15] "Etliche Türckische Sachen so der Pascha von Offen verert." Rudolf, "Kunstbestrebungen," 247 (nos. 508–16). See *Die Korrespondenz Maximilians II.*, ed. Viktor Bibl (Vienna: Holzhausen, 1916) 1: 38–40, 50, 60, 148, 223, 259–60; HHStA Turcica 16 and 17.

[16] Rudolf, "Kunstbestrebungen," 232 (no. 27), 234 (no. 73), 236 (nos. 135–6, 146), 242 (no. 324), 245 (nos. 447, 449), 238 (no. 190); and Hans von Voltelini, "Urkunden und Regesten aus dem k.u.k Haus-, Hof- und Staats-Archiv in Wien," *JKSW* 13 (1892), xci–civ.

[17] In Archduke Charles's inventory, some gifts were still noted. They were mostly military trophies or mechanical devices from lower-ranking people, reflecting Charles's border zone responsibilities. Heinrich Zimerman, "Urkunden, Acten und Regesten aus dem Archiv des K.K. Ministeriums des Innern," *JKSW* 7 (1888), xxi, xvii–xxxiii.

Bavarian Wittelsbach court historiographer,[18] sidestepped confessional issues in this first printed programmatic discussion. Emphasizing both texts and material objects, Quiccheberg's ideal collection or "universal theater" encompassed a library, workshops, and material sections. The library should house books classified by the subjects of human knowledge: Theology, Law, Medicine, History, Philosophy (including Magic), Mathematics (including Astrology), Philology (including military matters, architecture, and agriculture), Sacred and Profane Poetry, Music, and Grammar.[19] The craft workshops, a pharmacy, and a smithy would be complemented by a collection of exemplary objects. The material collection (*artificialia* and *naturalia*) itself should include images and sculptures depicting sacred and profane subjects. Quiccheberg reserved a section of the collection for ancient and new statues of spirits (*numina*), whether made of stone, wood, clay, or bronze. He remained silent on whether to value these statues as religious or artistic examples. Quiccheberg also incorporated the study of "foreign" or "exotic" peoples (*exterarum nationum* and *gentium peregrinarum*) into the encyclopedic plan. He encouraged the collection of information about foreign peoples' mores, culture, and products both military (arms) and domestic (clothing). Mexica feather arts were listed as a notable material used to make foreign peoples' clothing, without any mention of their extraordinary aesthetic value.[20] Quiccheberg's separation of the category of "foreign peoples" and objects from those of European Christians was an innovation, even as he recodified many ethnographic categories long present in travel narratives. One category, however, was absent: *religio*, the practice of religion. Although Quiccheberg's organizational structures revealed heightened interest in extra-Europeans, he remained silent about how or whether to collect these peoples' religious paraphernalia or objects.

In inventories dating from the 1590s, Archduke Charles's and Ferdinand's collections reflect the principles of the expansive *Kunstkammer*. The archdukes continued the Austrian Habsburg interest in Turkish objects begun by their father and brother, but they focused on the material culture of the Ottomans as one of Quiccheberg's exotic peoples. Rather than symbols of sovereignty, the archdukes focused their

---

[18] *Franckfurter ankunfft/ oder verzaichnuß aller Potentaten/ Chur vnd Fürsten/... / Doctorn vnd Geleerten etc.... die personlich erschinen vnd gewesen seind* (Augsburg: Ulhart, 1562), Giii.

[19] Samuel Quiccheberg, *Inscriptiones, vel tituli theatri amplissimi* (Munich: 1565), ciii^v.

[20] Quiccheberg, aii–aiv, ciii^v–fiii.

collecting on military and domestic objects as the products of Turkish and Indian cultures and signs of material rather than territorial possession. Acquisition and display of such cultural goods had practical military and symbolic values. Turks and Indians were, in Quiccheberg's terms, *nationes exterae*, whose craftsmanship should be acquired and displayed; Turkish and Indian cultural goods met the criterion of skillful workmanship for *artificialia*. Their societies were civilized, according to this criterion, although there is no effort to value them as distinct cultures. Charles's and Ferdinand's archducal *Kunstkammern* grouped together a range of *artificialia* from cultures understood as at least somewhat civilized societies, including the bellicose Turks, Tartars, and Muscovites.

Archduke Charles governed Inner Austria and defended the Holy Roman Empire's southeast border with the Ottomans. His collection inventory, compiled after his death in 1590, demonstrated these responsibilities. Turkish goods and war booty comprise the majority of objects with a cultural provenance, some of which had been acquired in military confrontations.[21] Charles also owned a few Hungarian, Tartar, Polish, and Indian weapons, cloth, or domestic items, in accordance with Quiccheberg's encouragement to collect the materials of exotic nations. Among the domestic items, Turkish carpets were particularly valued; after Charles's death, family members sought to acquire them.[22]

The extensive descriptions of Archduke Ferdinand's collection document a strong interest in Turkish material culture. Ferdinand even had a space designated the "Turkish chamber."[23] Lists of jeweled and ornamental treasure (*"clainoter"*) in 1569, 1571–1572, and 1577 all sporadically mentioned Turkish objects. His 1583 and 1596 armory inventories incorporated the arms and armor of famous men, including many Latin Christian rulers, the Emperor Süleyman, and a ruler identified as the King of Cuba. They also identified armor and weapons by land of origin (Turkish, German, Hungarian, and Roman, among others) and sometimes grouped the arms accordingly. Particularly prized pieces hung on

---

[21] For Charles's interest in Turkish banners as war-booty , see HHStA Turcica 27/1, fols. 129–34ᵛ. For the display of Turkish booty as spectacle in this era, see Karl Vocelka, *Die Politische Propaganda Kaiser Rudolfs II. (1576–1612)* (Vienna: Österreichische Akademie der Wissenschaften, 1980), 275–9.

[22] Zimerman, *JKSW* 7, xvii–xxxiii. For interest in Turkish carpets, Leonie von Wilckens, "Oriental Carpets in the German Speaking Countries and the Netherlands," *Oriental Carpet and Textile Studies* 2 (1986): 139–50.

[23] The *Türkenkammerl*, Elisabeth Scheicher, "The Collection of Archduke Ferdinand II at Schloss Ambras," in *The Origins of Museums*, ed. Impey and MacGregor, 29.

the armory walls; Turkish arms dominated the walls, with a sprinkling of objects identified as Hungarian, Muscovite, Moorish, and English.[24] Mixing of cultures was evident throughout the *Kunstkammer*, rather than a strict arrangement by cultural origin. For example, the combined category of "Hungarian and Muscovite saddles"[25] reinforced the two cultures' reputations as eastern nomadic horse-riding peoples. Both were perceived as culturally and geographically too close to the bellicose and Christianity-resistant Tartars, vulnerable to cultural or religious influence.[26] In a similar conflation, war trophies with geneaologies such as "Turkish armor given by Lazarus von Schwendi" were mostly Turkish in origin but also included one German, two Indian, two Hungarian, and more than six Muscovite items.[27]

In Archduke Ferdinand's 1596 inventory, the *Kunstkammer* chamber itself contained objects invested with extra-European authority. This chamber held symbolically authoritative objects: an ivory scepter embellished with Turkish lettering, a sword and ducal hat from the pope. One case in the room contained "things made of feathers," but the feather ornaments were almost all without Indian or Mexican identification, and instead the few with cultural affiliation were named "Moorish." Among these undifferentiated feather objects was a red feather shield, no longer a symbol of Castilian victory in Mexico but rather an example of artisan skill. The assignation of Moorish origin to other Mexican artifacts occurred throughout the collection: one weapon was identified, according to its contemporary attached note, as the Indian axe of the Moorish king[28] (glossed in later inventories as Moctezuma). Jumbled in the first

[24] Boeheim, *JKSW* 7 (1888): cxxxi–cxlii, cli–clxiii; clxix–clxxix; clxxxix–ccxviii; and cclxxi–clxxiv; especially cciii, ccvii–ix, ccx–ccxi, and cclxxi.

[25] Boeheim, *JKSW* 7 (1888): ccxxvi, clxxvi–cclxxix. In Sebastian Münster's *Cosmographia universalis*... (Basel: Heinrich Petri, 1550), Tartars descended from nomadic Scythians, Huns from Tartars, and Muscovites were influenced by Sarmatian cultures (both European and Asian), 855–8, 887, 909–13. Later conflations between Slavic and Hungarian cultures have been examined in Larry Wolff, *Inventing Eastern Europe* (Stanford: Stanford University Press, 1994), chapter 7.

[26] For example, HHStA Span. DK 3/68, fols. 8–8ᵛ; Johann Boemus, *Repertorium... omnium gentium* (Augsburg: Wirsung, 1520); Münster, *Cosmographia universalis*... 1059–64

[27] Boeheim, *JKSW* 7 (1888): cclxxiv–cclxxix. For Schwendi's military activities, see Paula Fichtner, *Maximilian II* (New Haven: Yale University Press, 2001), 121–34.

[28] *JKSW* 7 (1888): ccxvi–ccxviii, ccxciii–ccxciv, ccciii–cccix, for other featherwork, ccxxxvii and for the "Moorish" king's axe, ccciv. Karl Nowotny's *Mexikanische Kostbarkeiten aus Kunstkammern der Renaissance im Museum für Völkerkunde Wien und in der Nationalbibliothek Wien* (Vienna: Museum für Völkerkunde, 1960).

compartment of a special *Variocasten* were small objects of foreign origin: Turkish, Muscovite, and Indian artifacts, others uncertainly either
Turkish or Hungarian, and still others valued for their incorporation of
extra-European materials rather than artistry. These shifts suggest that
value was increasingly detached from cultural association. Such objects
did not symbolize a specific people's skills as a mark of civilization, but
rather stood as exemplars of a mechanical art. These archducal collections generally adhered to Quiccheberg's categories, particularly those
for extra-European material objects.

Habsburg interest in religiously neutral cultural projects, especially that
of Maximilian II, has encouraged interpretations of the late-sixteenth-
century collection as the pursuit of universal knowledge that could bridge
confessional divides.[29] Quiccheberg's elision of religious issues could be
considered such an attempt. However, for sixteenth-century cultural production, religious tensions proved inescapable. As doctrinal debates generated more narrow determinations of theological orthodoxy, practices
and beliefs were understood not as points in a field of humankind's struggle to comprehend the divine, but as true or false. Charges of idolatry,
as a metonym of false belief, flew in multiple directions during the Reformation era. Catholic veneration of sacred images and relics, as well as
their devotion to saints, had prompted early reformers' accusations of
idolatry. Catholics had responded by reaffirming the value of their own
religious practices involving images and objects of worship.[30]

By 1563, when the Council of Trent issued a decree on images and
relics, Protestants had been attacking the practices and beliefs of the
unreformed Church as idolatrous for four decades. They rejected the cult
of the saints and the veneration of relics and images as superstitious error.
John Calvin had reinvigorated early Reformation-era claims in the 1540s,
arguing that relics, images, and other idolatrous objects were dangerous
to those in their physical presence.[31] Alert to the increasing number of

---

[29] R.J.W. Evans, *Rudolf II and His World* (Oxford: Oxford University Press, 1973), 176–
83, 243–9; Eliška Fučíková, "The Collection of Rudolf II at Prague," in *The Origins
of Museums*, ed. Oliver Impey and Arthur MacGregor, 47–53; and the assessment by
Kaufmann, *The Mastery of Nature*, 174–94, 293–312.

[30] Catholic rebuttals predate the Council of Trent. See Johannes Faber, *Opera* (Cologne:
Quentell, 1537–9); and Christian Hecht, *Katholische Bildertheologie im Zeitalter von
Gegenreformation und Barock* (Berlin: Gebr. Mann, 1997) for Nicolas of Herborn's
work on images. Also, Lee Wandel, *Voracious Idols and Violent Hands* (Cambridge:
Cambridge University Press, 1995), 39–49.

[31] Carlos Eire, *War against the Idols* (Cambridge: Cambridge University Press, 1986),
197–213, 225–33.

iconoclastic acts occurring in France during 1561–1562, the French delegation to Trent had pressed the council for a declaration on images and relics.[32] With the Council of Trent's December 1563 decree on relics and images, the Catholic Church affirmed a key doctrinal distinction between themselves and other Christians. Catholic veneration of sacred images and relics, as well as invocation of saints, was reaffirmed as distinct from wrongful acts of superstition. Catholics were reminded that idolaters' superstitious error was locating the divine within images themselves.[33] Examples of historical acts of idolatry committed in antiquity by Gentiles were provided even as the Tridentine decree remained silent about Old Testament worship of idols. Despite this decree, Calvinist-inspired iconoclasm erupted less than three years later in the Netherlands, where it was linked to political rebellion.[34] The Catholic Church did not retreat in the wake of these attacks, continuing to embrace images and the cult of saints as true religious practice and turning to contrast their own religion with those of demonically inspired societies that did practice idolatry.

After the conclusion of Trent, Catholic theologians began to position their defenses of devotional images against Protestant charges of idolatry. Initially, these authors showed little interest in cultures beyond Europe: their attention was firmly focused on Europe and Protestant threats. From 1559 through the 1560s, Lutheran theologians had produced the multivolume *Centuries*, detailing the history of the true church, to establish the long-standing precedents for their positions, including their position on idolatry. This chronological documentation of heresy and orthodoxy had been supported in its early days by Maximilian II, who had given the *Centuries* researchers access to the imperial library. Soon after 1563, however, Catholic authors began refuting the first *Centuries*. In Nicholas Harpsfield's 1566 *Dialogi sex contra summi pontificatus, monasticae vitae, sanctorum, sacrarum imaginum oppugnatores, et pseudomartyres*, cultures and religion outside Europe were mentioned only to underscore

---

[32] Hubert Jedin, *Geschichte des Konzils von Trent*, IV/2 (Freiburg: Verlag Herder, 1975), 165–6.

[33] H. J. Schroeder, ed., *Canons and Decrees of the Council of Trent* (B. Herder: St. Louis, (1941), Latin text, 483–5, and English translation, 215–7.

[34] For events of 1566, Eire, 279–282 and Andrew Pettegree, *Emden and the Dutch Revolt* (Oxford: Clarendon Press, 1992), 115–32. Episodes of iconoclasm also occurred in 1590s, during the establishment of Calvinist polities in the Germanies. For the Reformation and images more broadly, see Hans Belting, *Likeness and Presence* (Chicago: University of Chicago Press, 1994); David Freedberg, *The Power of Images* (Chicago: University of Chicago Press, 1989); Sergiusz Michalski, *The Reformation and the Visual Arts* (London: Routledge, 1993); and Joseph Koerner, *The Reformation of the Image* (Chicago: University of Chicago Press, 2004).

the active presence of saints throughout the world or the church's missionary vigor.[35] More polemical defenses of Catholicism, such as Georg Eder's 1573 *Evangelische Inquisition*, which was vigorously suppressed by Maximilian II, argued that heathens (*ethnici*) were preferable to faithless Protestant heretics.[36]

In the 1580s, Jesuit theologian Robert Bellarmine's *De controversiis fidei christianae* became a favored theological reference for Counter-Reformation writers. In 1576, Bellarmine proposed a plan for this major theological counterattack against a half-century of Protestant arguments. Bellarmine had just taken up the chair in controversial theology at the Roman College and, like Harpsfield, he employed a historical survey of the church to dismiss Protestant attacks. For some 600 years, he argued, the devil had been inspiring people to heresy. Protestants were just the latest group to assault papal authority, grace and free will, and the veneration and invocation of saints, relics, and sacred images. These demonically inspired religious fallacies demanded urgent resolution and were to be the focus of the *De controversiis fidei christianae*, appearing in three parts in 1586, 1588, and 1593. The 1588 installment addressed the cult of saints, relics, and the proper use of devotional images.[37] Perhaps reflecting his experiences at Louvain during the early 1570s, Bellarmine identified the principal troublemaking heretics as Calvin and his followers, whose critique of images had inspired iconoclasm in France and the Low Countries during the preceding decade. Bellarmine defended the Tridentine decree on images by citing biblical sources extensively. He rarely mentioned non-Christian (*ethnici*) idolaters but did cite them to distinguish between polytheistic idolaters and Catholic monotheists. One sign of the orthodoxy of Catholic images, then, was their representation of one god in contrast to idolatrous images that represented many gods.[38] Bellarmine's

---

[35] Fichtner, *Emperor Maximilian II*, 39; Alan Copus [Nicholas Harpsfield], *Dialogi sex contra summi pontificatus....* (Antwerp: Christopher Plantin, 1566), esp. 384–7, 780–3. He cited John of Damascus and the Second Council of Nicaea to support his discussion.

[36] Georg Eder, *Evangelische Inquisition wahrer und falscher Religion* (1574), 84ᵛ. For context, Howard Louthan, *The Quest for Compromise* (Cambridge: Cambridge University Press, 1997), 127–9 and Elaine Fulton, *Catholic Belief and Survival in Late Sixteenth-Century Vienna* (Aldershot: Ashgate, 2007).

[37] For an example of Bellarmine's prominence, see Johann-Baptista Fickler, *Replica wider das ander uberhaufft/ falsch/....* (München: Adam Berg, 1592), 49, 102–9; Robert Bellarmine, *Opera Omnia*, ed. Justin Fèvre, (Frankfurt a. M.: Minerva, 1965), 1:60–61, 3: 199–266.

[38] Robert W. Richgels discusses Bellarmine's targets in "The Pattern of Controversy in a Counter-Reformation Classic," *SCJ* 11 (1980): 3–15; Bellarmine, *Opera Omnia*, 3:190–253, especially 236–40, 7:489–503. For biographical details, James Brodrick, *Robert Bellarmine* (Westminster: The Newman Press, 1961), 51–63.

attention to scriptural evidence for the correct use of images, as well as the materials that religious images could correctly be made of, did not persuade Protestants.

Protestant iconomachia had, by the time Bellarmine penned his rebuttal, wrecked lasting changes in the material world. Churches of western and central Europe were transformed by reforming iconoclasts, who stripped sacred spaces bare of adornment. In the arena of post-Tridentine Catholic and Protestant polemics, charges of idolatry were not limited to intangible theology or tangible church decoration; they extended to other objects. Some Protestants argued that all images, including Greek and Roman sculpture, were dangerous even if desacralized, because a beautiful statue might well promote idolatry. Catholic responses explained to the pious worshipper as well as the artist how they could view sacred and profane images virtuously.[39] For both Protestant and Catholic, religious and non-Christian figurative art required an understanding of what constituted an appropriate non-religious image and what constituted an idol. In the wake of the Reformation's polarizing rhetoric and actions, collections became confessionalized.

In 1587, Gabriel Kaltemarckt offered a Protestant Lutheran aesthetic and organizational scheme for the Saxon Wettin collection. The visual arts, along with music, were given to humans by God. These arts were both particularly suited for use in religious worship and easily corrupted for idolatrous purposes. Kaltemarckt illustrated this point by detailing the errors of others. Catholics and heathen Romans and Greeks produced idols, and Muslims and radical reformers refused any role for the visual arts and thus ignored their divinely supported purposes. For Kaltemarckt, charges of false religion and the abuse of images excluded non-Lutheran Christians as well as non-Christians from using images appropriately. He also emphasized the deep divisions between different reformed parties, repudiating "zealot" Protestants by equating them with Muslims. Only Kaltemarckt and followers of the Augsburg Confession practiced true Christian religion and the correct use of art. "Just as no people under the sun (except for the orthodox Christian church) has a thorough understanding of God, so too the right use of sculptures and paintings is

39 Johannes Molanus, *De picturis et imaginibus sacris* (Louvain: Hieronymus Wellaeus, 1570); David Freedberg, "Johannes Molanus on Provocative Paintings," *JWCI* 34 (1971), 229–33; Cardinal Gabriele Paleotti, *De imaginibus sacris et profanis* (Ingolstadt, 1594), 66–89; Pamela M. Jones, "Art Theory as Ideology," in *Reframing the Renaissance*, ed. Claire Farago (New Haven: Yale University Press, 1995), 127–39; and Hecht, 302–12.

confined to the true religion."⁴⁰ The actual Wettin *Kunstkammer*, inventoried the same year that Kaltemarckt wrote this text, took an even more cautious approach to images. It focused on tools, measuring instruments, and artisanal masterpieces.⁴¹ Comparing the Protestant Wettin collection and contemporaneous Catholic collections of Habsburg and Wittelsbach princes reveals that confessionally based doctrines on images and idolatry also shaped the content and organization of Catholic collections.

The collections of sovereigns Philip II of Spain (inventoried in 1598), the Bavarian Wittelsbachs (inventoried in 1598), and Emperor Rudolf II (inventoried in 1607–1611) contained material objects categorized not as images of deities or figures of living or mortal creatures, but as idols. The early-sixteenth-century treasuries of Charles V and Ferdinand I had housed some of this sculpture and metalwork, where it had been described as bearing figures of humans or animals. The mid-century collection of Ferdinand's son, Maximilian II, had not identified extra-European material objects as idolatrous or even as containing depictions of gods. In the collection of non-ruling Archduke Ferdinand, objects representing a diversity of religions were stored together in a chest: relics of St. Dominic and a piece of wood miraculously transformed into stone when under a farmer's iconoclastic attack were housed with greenstone idols, a heathen or idolaters' altar, instruments of circumcision, and objects described as animal heads and a figure of a woman formerly worshipped by idolaters.⁴² In contrast to this mix of material relicts, the collections of Philip, the Wittelsbachs, and Rudolf connected idolatry to cultures beyond Europe and kept such objects far from Christian relics.

If the princely *Kunstkammer* can provide a window into later-sixteenth-century conceptualizations or reconceptualizations of the world, its peoples, and its histories, the redefinition of objects as idols in Catholic collections at the end of the century is noteworthy. Although early-sixteenth-century Habsburgs and later-sixteenth-century Protestant princes might not have collected idols, post-Tridentine Catholic princes did. Bellarmine had not taken the step of locating the true idolater in

---

⁴⁰ "Das / gleich wie kein Volck under der Sonnen (aus-/serhalb der rechten christlichen Kirchen.) nichts / gründlichs von Gott weis, also ist auch der/ rechte gebrauch der Bilder und Gemehle, al-/lein bei rechter Religion zufinden, ... " Kaltemarckt's text and translation in Barbara Gutfleisch and Joachim Menzhausen, "'How a Kunstkammer should be Formed'," *Journal of the History of Collections* 1 (1989), 8–9.

⁴¹ Joachim Menzhausen, "Elector Augustus's Kunstkammer," in *The Origins of Museums*, ed. O. Impey and A. MacGregor, 69–74.

⁴² Boeheim, *JKSW* 7 (1888), ccxcv, ccxxxvii.

time or space, but other post-Tridentine Catholic authors would do so, in texts and in collections.

Catholics like Bellarmine had argued that idolatrous images were produced by non-Christian cultures; exemplary statues would demonstrate their point. In so doing, Catholics displaced Protestant charges of idolatry onto what Catholics saw as their proper focus. In the second half of the sixteenth century, ethnographic texts increasingly emphasized the presence of idolatry as a central aspect of culture and religion in the Indies. Tamara's 1554 adaption of Boemus had expanded the ethnography to include a section on the Indies, the devil's busy activities there, and the resultant religious practices. Hieronymo Román's 1575 *Republicas del mundo* made available, in one volume, the myriad forms of idolatrous practice in the west Indies, although for Román, idolatry had been rooted out by missionary efforts. Censorship on other issues curtailed this edition's circulation, but its descriptions of Indian idolatry (which Román judged more prevalent among the Inca than among the Indians of New Spain) was retained in the more successful 1595 edition. For Román, ethnography or cultural description had remained the overarching goal of his project. Even in the reworked 1595 form of the text, which separated the world into three books and three categories, attributes of civilization (and religion) organized his material: first were Jews and Christians, second the ancient Greeks and Romans, and third the contemporary idolatrous peoples (Indians, Chinese, and Tartars), heterodox Christians, and Muslims.

In contrast, Román's contemporary, José de Acosta, placed idolatry first and foremost in his evaluations of people. Tacit comparison between the religious practices of the peoples in the Indies and the Christians and Jews who had formed a covenant with God was not of interest to the Jesuit Acosta. While recognizing that the Indians had some understanding of a divine creator (among other gods), Acosta explicitly dismissed the idea that Indians were Jewish or followed the Law of Moses in any form. Acosta justified his evaluation by contradicting earlier ethnographic observations of circumcision. Jews, he argued, were defined by their circumcision and, in contrast to the Ethiopians, no Indians were circumcised.[43]

---

[43] José de Acosta, *Historia Natural y Moral de las Indias* (1590), in *Obras de P. José de Acosta*, BAE 73 (Madrid: Atlas, 1954), Dedication and Prologue to Books 5–7 and Book 5/1–6, 139–47. Recent summaries of Acosta's thought and career are Anthony Pagden, *The Fall of Natural Man* (Cambridge: Cambridge University Press, 1982), 149–200; Sabine MacCormack, *Religion in the Andes* (Princeton: Princeton University Press,

In *De procuranda Indorum salute*, dedicated to Philip II, and *Historia natural y moral de las Indias*, dedicated to Philip's daughter and advisor Isabel Clara Eugenia, Acosta retained Las Casas's strategy of comparing the cultural traits of non-Christian peoples from the present day and antiquity. While never denying the particularities of non-Christian cultures, Acosta argued that commonalities between cultures were important for categorizing the world's peoples. Societies with equivalent levels of government organization and religion would also maintain certain cultural practices, such as devotion to ceremonies, belief in superstitions, and dressing in similar forms of clothing.[44] Well-developed idolatry, with priests and temples as signs of institutional organization, was usually found in the most "civilized" of these non-Christian cultures.[45] In such ranked equivalencies, we can see Acosta's model of cultural hierarchy being constructed. Religious error, present by definition among these polytheistic-minded peoples, was no longer a Lascasasian sign of a society's striving toward God. Error was wrong; problematically, it was also prevalent in the Americas. For Catholic thinkers in the 1580s, the project of eliminating idolatry in the Americas was still tied to concerns about the proliferating Protestant heresy and the numbers of false believers in the world. In the 1530s, Franciscan missionaries had heralded the missionary opportunities of the New World as consolation for souls lost to the Protestant Germans.[46] In the post-Tridentine era, Valentinus Fricius's expansion of Diego de Valadés in the *Yndianischer Religionstandt der gantzen newen Welt* framed missionary successes (and martyrdoms) among the Indian idolaters in the shadow of European confessional strife.[47]

Acosta's analysis of idolatry relied on John of Damascus and the Book of Wisdom even as he elaborated on those sources. In *De procuranda*

1991), 264–80; and D.A. Brading, *The First America* (Cambridge: Cambridge University Press, 1991), 184–95.

[44] Acosta, *Historia Natural y Moral*, 1/23, 36–7 and 6/11, 191–2.

[45] José de Acosta, *De Natura Novi Orbis libri duo et de Promulgatione Evangelii apud Barbaros sive, de procuranda indorum salute* (Salamanca: Foquel, 1589) 5/9–10: 513–26.

[46] Nicolas Herborn, *Epitome de inventer nuper India...* (1532) and Pedro de Gante, "Epistola alia eiusdem argumenti" in *Chronica compendiosissima ab exordio mundi* (Antwerp: Simon Cock, 1534), 124–7.

[47] The dedication to Archduke Matthias was made with specific reference to the religious wars in the Netherlands (Ingolstadt: Wolfgang Eder, 1587). Louthan discusses Matthias's attempts to become involved as an irenicist governor there in the 1570s, 143–54. Matthias owned two copies of the text at his death. Voltelini, *JKSW* 20 (1899), l.

Indorum salute (1588), wrongful objects of worship had all once physically existed. Acosta explained the three forms of idolatry through examples from antiquity: Chaldeans worshiped celestial bodies, signs, and
elements; Greeks worshiped the dead as gods; and Egyptians worshiped
animals and inanimate things like rocks.[48] Acosta also argued that idolatry was a disease, inherited in mother's milk and nurtured by culture. The
heritability of idolatry meant that converts in the New World could never
become full members of the Christian church, remaining neophytes barred
from the priesthood. Seven years after *De procuranda*'s composition, the
Third Church Council of Lima (1583), with Acosta as advisor, adopted
this argument and declared that Indians should be assigned permanent
neophyte status.[49] By 1588, when Acosta completed the *Historia natural
y moral de la Indias* (1590), the devil rather than culture had become idolatry's nurturer, although the eradication of this new causal agent was no
more certain. The three previously cataloged forms of idolatry – worship
of nature, of animals, and of the dead – were declared present in the Americas as well as in the classical past, and were supplemented by another.
The fourth form of idolatry, found in the Book of Wisdom, was the
worship of objects made by human hands. Such pieces of human invention included "statues of wood, stone, or gold, like those of Mercury or
Pallas... which represent nothing."[50] Although Acosta did not make any
further direct comment on this fourth form of idolatry, its focus on the
problem of graven images had a distinctively Tridentine resonance. Further, by arguing that Indian religious errors lay solely in the imagination
and not in mistaking natural signs or past heroes, Acosta magnified the
role of the devil and the danger of idolatrous error. In the *Historia natural y moral*, Acosta explicated the devil's active role in driving Indians

---

[48] Acosta, *De procuranda*, 5/9:514–6. MacCormack explores this theme in *Religion*,
265–6.

[49] "Illud magis cogitandum est haereditarium esse impietatis morbum, qui ab ipsis matrum
visceribus ingenitus, ipso uberum lacte nutritus, paterno & domestico exemplo con-
firmatus,..." Acosta, *De procuranda* 5/9:517; 5/10–11:519–29. For an interpretation
of Acosta's position as relatively inclusive, see Osvaldo Pardo, *Mexican Catholicism:
Nahua Rituals and Christian Saints in Sixteenth-Century Mexico* (Ann Arbor: University
of Michigan Press, 2004), 145–56; and for parallel exclusions by the Mexican Council,
see Stafford Poole, "The Declining Image of the Indian among Churchmen in Sixteenth-
Century New Spain" in *Indian-Religious Relations in Colonial Spanish America*, ed.
Susan E. Ramírez, (Syracuse: Syracuse University Press, 1989), 11–19.

[50] "estatuas de palo, o de piedra o de oro, como de Mercurio o Palas, que... ni es nada,
ni fué nada." Acosta, *Historia*, 5/2, 141.

to worship falsely, concluding with extensive advice on how to combat such demonic influences.

In the same year that the *Historia natural y moral* was published, Bellarmine had also highlighted the devil's role in guiding Jews and heathens to make objects and worship them as idols.[51] Although Bellarmine did not offer a hierarchy of non-Christian cultures in his *De controversiis*, he shared with Acosta the tendency to conflate such cultures. In Counter-Reformation discourse, the devil's temptation was understood as a sign of cultural weakness common to non-Christians. Other authors found it unnecessary to make temporal distinctions in their comparisons. For example, Lorenzo Pignoria's 1615 revision of a manual of the deities of Greek, Roman, and Egyptian antiquity integrated the gods of Mexico and Japan into the text.[52] There, idolatrous religion could be comfortably located either in time or space outside the boundaries of sixteenth-century Europe; the idea that sincere, if limited, faith could be found in antiquity and in the far-flung corners of the contemporary world had been rejected. Instead, the idea of progress from an undifferentiated idolatrous state to one of true religion and proper veneration of images was found throughout Counter-Reformation polemics. (With their fear of images, Protestant and Muslim "heretics" had fallen off the path of progress.) The material presence of idols in Counter-Reformation collections, then, must also be read through this shift to cultural hierarchy and conflation. True idols signaled the distance between Catholic European religion and that of demonically inspired cultures.

After the closing of the Council of Trent in 1563, Philip II had actively worked to improve religious faith and practice in his empire, both in Iberia and the Americas. In Iberia, he supported the Tridentine reform of clerical institutions, promoted the cult of saints, collected relics avidly from throughout the Habsburg territories, and restricted the flow of unauthorized religious writing.[53] In the Americas, Philip II and the Council of the

---

[51] Bellarmine, *Opera Omnia*, 3:202–18.

[52] Vincenzo Cartari, with supplement by Lorenzo Pignoria, *le vere e nove imagini de gli dei delli antichi* [1615] (Padua: Tozzi, 1626). Sabine MacCormack explores Cartari's project in "Limits of Understanding: Perceptions of Greco-Roman and Amerindian Paganism in Early Modern Europe," in *America in European Consciousness, 1493–1750*, ed. Karen Kupperman (Chapel Hill: University of North Carolina Press, 1995), 87–93.

[53] William Christian, Jr., *Local Religion in Sixteenth-Century Spain* (Princeton: Princeton University Press, 1981), 126–46. For Philip II's religious efforts and their relationship to Habsburg authority, see Marie Tanner, *The Last Descendant of Aeneas* (New Haven: Yale University Press, 1993), 143, 215–21; Carlos Eire, *From Madrid to Purgatory* (Cambridge: Cambridge University Press, 1995), 255–313; and Guy Lazure, "Possessing

Indies rejected Lascasian investigative approaches to Indian knowledges and moved to curtail inquiries into Indian religion and culture during the 1570s. In 1577, the seizure of all known texts on the subject, including the monumental works of Franciscan Bernardino de Sahagún, was ordered. Philip's ban on knowledge about the Indies explicitly mentioned the "interpretation of idols" as a motivation for suppressing information. Around this time, a few "idols" began to be cataloged in Castile: Diego Hurtado de Mendoza's collection contained three gold figures designated as idols, and in 1581, Anselm Stöckl's travel pass out of Castile noted that he carried two "little idols from India" for delivery to Duke Wilhelm V of Bavaria's collections.[54] Philip did not engage in these efforts simply to further Tridentine reforms; he also directed these efforts to bolster the symbolism of Habsburg autonomy. In building the Escorial, Philip intended it to serve as a palace, Habsburg mausoleum, and reliquary shrine for relics rescued from the impious.[55]

Philip's treasury collection at the Escorial, inventoried after his death in 1598, followed the pattern of an older Habsburg generation in many ways. The contents and categories of his inventory resembled that of his father Charles quite closely. His religious and devotional treasures were itemized first, followed by categories of books, precious jewels, worked gold and silver, household furnishings from a variety of precious materials, plate, arms, coins, mechanical devices, musical instruments, paintings and images, and other artwork.[56] The geographical scope of Philip's collection, like his father's, reflected his territorial ambitions and claims. The non-European contents consisted almost exclusively of objects from west and east India, authority over the former inherited from Charles and over the latter through the annexation of Portugal in 1580. In contrast to the numerous Indian objects, Philip II's collection held only a few

the Sacred: Monarchy and Identity in Philip II's Relic Collection at the Escorial," *RQ* 60 (2007):58–93.

54 " idolillos de la india," R. Foulche-Doelbosch, "Un point conteste de la vie de don Diego Hurtado de Mendoza," *Revue Hispanique* 2 (1895): 290–303, here 295. Almudena Pérez de Tudela and Annemarie Jordan Gschwend, "Luxury Goods for Royal Collectors," *JKMW* 3 (2001), 55.

55 Georges Baudot, *Utopia and History in Mexico* (Niwot: University Press of Colorado, 1995), 490–515.

56 F. J. Sánchez Cantón, ed., *Inventarios Reales: Bienes Muebles que Pertenecieron a Felipe II*, 1–2 (Madrid: 1956–9) and, in the Escorial, *Inventario de las alhajas, pinturas y objetos…donados por Felipe II al Monasterio de El Escorial (1571–1598)*, ed. Julián Zarco Cuevas (Madrid: 1930). These inventories do not include objects placed in the royal armory. See Moran and Checa, *El Coleccionismo*, chapters 5–8, Fernando Checa Cremades, *Felipe II, Mecenas de las Artes* (Madrid: Nerea, 1992).

Muslim treasures. Several items of morisco clothing and some old astro-
labes were the only pieces in his collection from his formerly Muslim
Iberian peoples.[57] He had no Turkish objects identified as diplomatic
gifts or trophies from military victories, and the only Turkish pieces
in the collection were some short blades (short scimitars, daggers, and
knives).[58] Through his territorial claims to the Philippines and the expansion of trade routes from the Americas to China, Philip also acquired a
significant number of Asian goods. These were valued both as precious
commodities and as symbols of the wished-for next Iberian conquest.[59]

In 1598, Philip's collection generally sustained his own ban on representations of Indian religions and cultures. Instead of artifacts made in the
Indies that represented their makers' cultures, he collected objects constructed from "Indian" materials of balsam, coconut, various woods, and
elephant skins, all worked into European forms.[60] Philip seemed largely
uninterested in objects crafted by non-European people, the major exception being the unreplicable porcelain. The other striking exception to
this tendency toward European manufacture was Philip's Inca treasure,
which included items identified as idols. In the face of the ban on religious
material and idols, the provenance of the Inca treasure offers a possible
explanation for their continued inclusion in the treasury. By 1598, many
material objects from the original 1532 conquest had been melted down,
and most that remained were no longer valued as symbols of the conquest. What Philip treasured, instead, were newer pieces symbolizing
Habsburg triumphs sent to him by Francisco de Toledo, his viceroy in
Peru from 1569 to 1581. Toledo had sent twelve "little idols" found
in Inca houses, a silver idol of a *xeme*, and symbols of governance: the
"coronation insignia" of the ultimate and penultimate Incas "Guanacar"
and Atahualpa and feather ornaments identified as symbols of obedience from the "yndios sanchos." During Toledo's tenure, he had enacted
sweeping organizational reforms, reinvigorated the search for idolatry
among the Andean Indians, and finally captured the last outpost of non-
Christian Inca rule, along with the "rebel" Inca (Tupac Amaru) himself.

---

[57] Sánchez Cantón, 2: 435–6, 309–29; nos. 5526, 5535–7, 5539, 4680, 4706, 4741.

[58] Sánchez Cantón, 2: 157–62; nos. 3440, 3445, 3449–57, 3459, 3468, 3471.

[59] See Pérez de Tudela and Jordan Gschwend, "Luxury Goods" and Karl Rudolf, "Exotica
bei Karl V., Philip II. und in der Kunstkammer Rudolfs II," *JKMW* 3 (2001): 173–203.
In the last decade of Philip's reign, numerous plans to conquer China were being hatched
in Madrid. C.R. Boxer, "Portuguese and Spanish Projects for the Conquest of Southeast
Asia, 1580–1600," *Journal of Asian History* 3 (1968), 132.

[60] Sánchez Cantón.

The Inca treasures sent by Toledo, then, symbolized recent victories for Christian faith and Castilian political and religious domination in Peru. They were classified as the first part of a category of "extraordinary objects" ("cosas extrahordinarias"), along with Indian objects associated with idolatrous worship or the Inca. A few other idols were dispersed through the collection in more convertible categories, with weight and monetary value listed for their planned sale. In a 1601 description of the collection, the worship of these idols was attributed to Satan's works.[61]

Unlike Philip II, the Bavarian Wittelsbachs and Emperor Rudolf II held no direct sovereignty over peoples, whether Christians or idolaters, in the world outside of Europe. The Wittelsbach dukes Albrecht V and Wilhelm V embarked on an ambitious program of art patronage and Catholic religious revival in their territories during the last decades of the sixteenth century. They were extremely committed to the project of the Counter-Reformation; the expansion of their own authority was invested in their promotion of Catholicism in Bavaria. They supported religious instruction, and their symbolic efforts focused on monumental building projects (particularly major churches) and a *Kunstkammer* designed for relatively wide access.[62] Their collection inventories closely followed Quiccheberg's model of a microcosmic world over which a prince demonstrated his symbolic mastery, yet these collections encompassed not only arms and clothing of "exotic peoples," but also devotional objects and idols.

A portion of that Bavarian *Kunstkammer* was inventoried in 1598 by court historiographer Johann Baptista Fickler. The inventory sorted objects into categories of materials and forms of daily practice. Material categories included brass, shell, wood, leather, ivory, porcelain, ironwork,

---

[61] Note that the Caribbean term "xeme" was applied more broadly to American deities in sixteenth-century Europe. These objects are Sánchez Cantón, 2: 332–52, 77–8, 252; nos. 2172, 3057, 4134, 4759–60, 4763, 4765, 4860. The category also included an earthenware bowl valued by the Sanchos Indians, 2: 270–1; no. 4312 and several objects lacking a cultural provenance. For idols outside the *cosas extrahordinarias* category, see 1: 274–6, 347–50; nos. 2171, 2180–1, 2633, 2638–9 and 2643–4. Franz Unterkircher, ed., "Hieremias Gundlach: Nova Hispaniae Regnorum Descriptio," *JKSW* 56 (1960): 186–7.

[62] Wolfgang Braunfels, "Cuius Regio Eius Ars," in *Wittelsbach und Bayern*, ed. Hubert Gläser, vol. II:1, Um Glauben und Reich: Kurfürst Maximilian I (Munich: Hirmer, 1980), 133–40; Jeffrey Chipps Smith, *Sensuous Worship* (Princeton: Princeton University Press, 2002); J. Stockbauer, *Die Kunstbestrebungen am Bayerische Hofe unter Herzog Albert V. und seinem Nachfolger Wilhelm V* (Vienna: Braumüller, 1874); and Lorenz Seelig, "The Munich *Kunstkammer*, 1565–1807," in *The Origins of Museums*, ed. Impey and MacGregor, 76–89.

and feathers.[63] In this post-Tridentine reformed Catholic Wittelsbach inventory, Fickler placed non-Christian religious objects and equipment together. Jewish instruments of circumcision and worship, for example, were found next to religious objects from both east and west Indies. Several Indian priests' masks and head-coverings, a Muslim "tract" (probably the Qur'an), and idols "that the unbelievers pray to and revere... [that] looked more like a devil than a man" were all present, displaying their devilish aspects. These were "the idols of Mexico" that would be noted by Pignoria.[64] These idolatrous objects of false religions were not accidental remainders of old treasuries. Rather, the Wittelsbachs actively sought such pieces to expand their collection, with examples that revealed the devil's inspiration in the west Indies.[65]

The collections shared other tendencies with Habsburg princely collections. Regalian objects were also collected. Fickler listed an "Indian Scepter" made from ebony and ivory, two Indian "umbrellas" (understood as signs of lordship in India), and robes of Moorish or Turkish lords.[66] The collection displayed the artifacts of non-Christian cultures from the past (Greek, Egyptian, Roman) and present (Turkish and Indian). Just as in Archduke Ferdinand's collection, "Turkish" and "Indian" objects were commingled on the tables or placed next to each other.[67] Even as some objects were gaining multiple or confusing cultural origins, others were losing their cultural identity, become simply examples of artificialia or *kunst*.[68] Histories of possession also added value to objects. As one supplier wrote: "I have a bowl made of precious

---

[63] *Inventarium oder Beschreibung aller deren Stuckh und sachen frembder und Inhaimischer bekanter und unbekanter seltzamer und verwunderlicher ding...* The inventory, extant in two manuscript copies, Bayerisches Staatsbibliothek (BStB) cgm 2133 and cgm 2134, was compiled by Fickler. The MS cgm 2134 is cited (See Tables 3, 4, 5, 16, 17, 27 for materials).

[64] BStB, cgm 2134 (Tables 3–4), fols. 14–19ᵛ; 133–134ᵛ, esp. "daselbst von denn unglaubigen angebettet und geehret worden... sollich bildt sihel mehr ainem Teüfl als Menschen gleich," fol. 134ᵛ (no. 1618). Pignoria, 555.

[65] For princely involvement in acquisitions, see Bayerisches Hauptstaatsarchiv (BStA), KaA, 4855 *Libri Antiquitatum* V; BStB, cgm 2134, fol. 133ᵛ (no. 1606), fol. 134 (no. 1615) "Eine Indianischer Götz einem Teüfl gleich."

[66] BStB, cgm 2134, fol. 133 (no. 1600), fol. 134ᵛ, (no. 1619), fol. 150.

[67] For commingled objects, BStB, cgm 2134, (Tables 10, 14, 33), fols. 37–45ᵛ, 86ᵛ–89, 139–143ᵛ. For adjacent items, BStB, cgm 2134, (Tables 26 and 27, 29 and 30); Table next to Table 33, fol. 145–145ᵛ.

[68] See, for example, BStB, cgm Table 12 (no. 843), fol. 75 for a Mixtec ring no longer described as such by 1598, instead simply identified as a ring. For its origin, see Detlef Heikamp, "Mexikanische Altertümer aus süddeutschen Kunstkammern," *Pantheon* 28 (1970), 213–4.

stone, which one hundred and forty-five years ago a king of Tunis used as his regular drinking-goblet...noone knows from what material it is made."[69] Military trophies and artifacts were prized: clothing worn by Francis I when captured at the battle of Pavia, two Turkish sabers captured at Lepanto, and a military challenge sent from the Turkish Emperor Süleyman to Ferdinand I were collected.[70] History added to an object's value, and some histories seem to have been embellished in consequence. The majority of symbolic objects with designated extra-European provenance, however, symbolized idolatry and pagan religion.

The Wittelsbachs acquired many of their objects through dealers and collectors, in contrast to the Habsburgs' acquisitions through tribute, diplomatic missions, and war spoils. Perhaps recognizing that their collection was not grounded in the symbolism of sovereignty, and in keeping with their strong Counter-Reformation commitments, the Catholic Wittelsbachs actively expanded the religious components of their treasure holdings. In the Wittelsbach collection, the display of idolatrous objects could be contrasted with the renewed veneration of true relics. The Wittelsbachs energetically collected relics and reliquaries from locations throughout the Protestant areas of the Holy Roman Empire, establishing Bavaria as a haven for Catholicism in the face of the crypto-Protestantism and open Protestantism found in the Holy Roman Emperor's hereditary lands. The Wittelsbachs even sought custodianship of the imperial relics, arguing that Protestant Nurembergers neglected them, and that they should be guarded by true Christians rather than the heretical Protestants.[71] Christian relics were not placed in the same part of the collection as the non-Christian religious objects; objects in the two categories were physically separated from each other.[72] The collection overall, then, represented idolatry and pagan religion in distinction from the Catholic faith's relics and cult of saints. Through the separate locations of true and false religious objects, the viewer would easily absorb the

---

[69] "hab Ich ein schale von edlen gestein beÿ mir, welche vor 145 Jaren ein khönig von Tunnis zum gewohnlichen trinkhgeschirr gebraucht...niemand der wissen khund von was materÿ die gemacht seÿ." BStA, KaA 4855, fols. 60–1.

[70] BStB, cgm 2134, fol. 120–120ᵛ.

[71] Uwe Müller, "Herzog Wilhelm V. und das Reichsheiltum," *MVGN* 72 (1985): 117–29; *Der Schatz vom Heiligen Berg Andechs* (Munich: Kloster Andechs, 1967), 74–5; *Um Glauben und Reich*, ed. H. Glaser, II:2, 225–47. BStA, GR Fasz 513, Nr. 65a.

[72] Samuel Klingensmith, *The Utility of Splendor* (Chicago: University of Chicago Press, 1993), 29.

Counter-Reformation message that Catholic and non-Christian images and art were categorically different. The Wittelsbachs, anxious to demonstrate their leading role in the religious revival of the Counter-Reformation, could collect idols as examples of the devil's work, as part of a project to symbolically represent and to advance the church's triumph over the devil. The Wittelsbachs' own propagandistic public art commissions incorporated the iconography of a battle between good and evil. The façade design of their new monumental Munich church, St. Michael's, featured a large bronze statue of the Archangel Michael pinning a grotesque Lucifer with a cross. In a religious play performed as part of the festivities surrounding the church's consecration, Michael battled Lucifer's agents – sins, vices, Protestants, and, in several acts, different forms of idolatry and pagan gods beloved by classical Roman rulers – in order to help the peoples of the New World and the erring Eastern Christians find the path to true, Catholic religion.[73]

Fickler's work with the Wittelsbach collection began after 1592, but no pre-1598 inventory exists to establish the degree to which Fickler's innovations influenced the collection's organizational scheme. Nonetheless, Fickler's published texts suggest that he was keenly alert to the religious dangers of possessing idols. His pamphlets reveal a deep engagement with the issues of images, relics, and the religious reform. A lay legal scholar, Fickler devoted his life and work to promoting the Counter-Reformation cause. He had attended the third session of the Council of Trent as a delegate of the Archbishop of Salzburg. Even at Trent in 1563, Fickler had participated in shaping perceptions of Turkish culture to central European readers, publishing a version of the letters from Süleyman to Ferdinand carried by the envoy Ibrahim to Frankfurt.[74] After studying law in Italy and solidifying connections with Counter-Reformation figures active in the Holy Roman Empire, Fickler established his position as a legal scholar with a *Theologia Juridica, seu ius civile theologicum*..., which called straying Christians back to the true Catholic Church.[75] He subsequently published aggressive vernacular rebuttals of Protestant doctrinal attacks on the veneration of the Virgin Mary and the saints and on

[73] Jeffrey Chipps Smith, *Sensuous Worship*, 57–75; *Triumph und Frewdenfest, zu Ehren dem Heiligen Ertzengel Michael* (Munich, 1597), A3ᵛ–C3ᵛ.
[74] *Literae Sultani Sulemanni Turcarum Imp. Missae Constantinopoli ad Ferd*.... (Passau, [1563]), aii–aiiᵛ.
[75] Josef Steinruck, *Johann Baptist Fickler* (Münster: Aschendorff, 1965). Fickler, *Theologia Juridica* (Dillingen: Sebaldus Mayer, 1575).

the Catholic use of images. Fickler's determination to refute his opponents or at least win over the reading public continued after his move from the ecclesiastical Salzburg court to the ducal Bavarian court.[76] In his polemical works, Fickler illustrated true religion through cultural comparison: he drew contrasts between Jewish uses of images or pagan worship of goddesses and Catholic veneration of the Virgin Mary. By the 1590s, Fickler's rebuttals contained conflated rejections of the "heathen, Jewish, Turks, and other unbelievers, as well as the Protestants [Heyden / Juden / Türcken / oder andern Unglaubigen / als bey den Evangelischen]." Their religious texts (Koran, Talmud, vernacular bibles) were all tools of the devil, and thus easily conflated with one another. He also elaborated his critiques of Protestant Christianity and Islam by directly comparing the adherents of the Augsburg Confession and Turkish Muslims.[77] Fickler's pamphlet rhetoric paralleled his inventory of the Wittelsbach collection, in which idolatrous objects were interchangeable but also infused with the demonic.

The first inventory of Rudolf II's collection, dating from 1607–1611, reveals a similar interest in collected, conflated idolatrous religious paraphernalia distinct from Catholic objects. This inventory separated Catholic religious images and the rest of the *Kunstkammer* collection both conceptually and materially, excluding most Catholic religious images from the inventory. An exception was Mexican featherwork depicting religious images, including one of the Archangel Michael defeating the devil. Rudolf's relationship to the Counter-Reformation was less straightforward than that of the Wittelsbachs. His cultural patronage, particularly in his early years, had focused on the search for overarching cosmological order or occult knowledge, avoiding doctrinal debates between the confessions. His more balanced early religious patronage included Protestants and Catholics, ended in 1599 when Rudolf allowed a consequential Counter-Reformation presence to establish itself at his court in Prague. After 1599, Rudolf did not abandon his occult investigations, which relied on non-Christian knowledges, even as his support

---

[76] Fickler's texts include *Censur oder Urtheil* (Ingoldstadt: David Sartorius, 1583); *Anderer und Dritter Theil* (Ingolstadt: David Sartorius, 1585); *Spongia Contra Praedicantum* (Ingolstadt: David Sartorius, 1585); *Rettung der Concilien Catholischen Glaubens...* (Ingolstadt: Wolfgang Eder, 1590); and *Replica* in 1592.

[77] Fickler, *Rettung*, 45, 90–5; *Replica*, 124; *Historische Erzehlungen/ Einer lang verdeckten heymischen/ vnd gemeyner Kirchen gefährlicher That* (Munich: Adam Berg, 1592), 8–13.

of Counter-Reformation thinkers grew stronger during the remainder of his rule.[78]

In Rudolf's first collection inventory, Quiccheberg's categories can be found along with a few non-Christian religious objects and idols. False gods appear scattered among Indian religious objects as "Egyptian idols." Rudolf was certainly interested in Egyptian artifacts for occult study, but their position among the Indian objects conflated cultures of extra-European pagans.[79] In the post-Tridentine era, Egypt was widely understood to have been responsible for bringing idolatry, along with some arts of civilization, to Greece and Rome and thus to Europe.[80] Egyptian idols also continued to symbolize the triumphal arrival of Christianity and the end of superstition; in the apocryphal story of Christ's life, idols cracked and toppled in the presence of the Christ Child when the Holy Family entered into Egypt. The multiple meanings of the idols as "Egyptian" or pagan were significant for two of Rudolf's interests: the Counter-Reformation triumphal church and occult investigations. By 1607, Rudolf was convinced of his own lack of salvation even as he supported a polemical Counter-Reformation church. He refused the Eucharist and increasingly explored pagan and occult knowledges to the neglect of his political rule.[81] Although Rudolf's personal religious state may have been far distant from those of the Wittelsbachs, the contrast between idolatrous cultures and the true Catholic Church could be valuable for his own explorations of hidden universal knowledge. In Rudolf's collection, the symbolic value of such items seems to have been located

---

[78] Rotraud Bauer and Herbert Haupt, ed., "Das Kunstkammerinventar Kaiser Rudolf II, 1607–1611," *JKSW* n.s. 72 (1976). Rudolf II's collection drew on those of family members, including select portions of his sister Elisabeth's collection (her east Indian objects and ornate devotional objects, with the odd mechanical device, carved-agate dish, and a copy of Fricius's *Religionstandt*). He also acquired his uncle Archduke Ferdinand's feather ornaments. Hans von Voltelini, ed., "Urkunden und Regesten aus dem k. u. k. Haus- Hof- und Staats-Archiv in Wien," *JKSW* 15 (1894): no. 12158, cxx–cxxi; Kaufmann, *Mastery*, 136–50 and Evans, *Rudolf II*, 89–91.

[79] Bauer and Haupt, 32–4, 43, 93, 102, 123.

[80] Anthony Grafton, *Joseph Scaliger*, vol. 2 (Oxford: Oxford University Press, 1993); Eric Iversen, *The Myth of Egypt and its Hieroglyphs* (Princeton: Princeton University Press, 1993); Walter Mignolo, *The Darker Side of the Renaissance* (Ann Arbor: University of Michigan Press, 1995); Gutfleisch and Menzhausen, 15. For the early-seventeenth-century tendency to derive the false gods of Mexico and Japan from Egypt, see MacCormack "Limits of Understanding," 88.

[81] R.J.W. Evans, *The Making of the Habsburg Monarchy, 1550–1700* (Oxford: Oxford University Press, 1979), 32–7 and Evans, *Rudolf II*, 85–92, 196–242.

in their representation of distance, not as examples of other religious practices.

As traced through the subsequent inventories of Rudolf's collection, made in 1619 and 1621 during the initial years of the Thirty Years' War, the diminution of the feather treasure's cultural valency was more explicit. The first imperial inventory (1607–1611) of Rudolf's collection contained a few feather cloaks and objects. Although some might have been ornaments of the Aztec Empire, their cultural provenance had been lost. The meager descriptions were devoid of extra-European symbolic meanings. The second inventory of Rudolf's collection, that of 1619, was ordered by Protestant nobles to facilitate the efficient sale of Rudolf's collection for costs associated with their seizure of power. The inventory suggests that feather objects had lost any sacral, regalian, or triumphal symbolism, as well as any aesthetic value, for these objects were seldom listed and had no monetary price. Among the few sculptures of non-Christian origins, male and female figures were valued in terms of their gold, silver, and other precious materials. Only one was identified as a *göczen* (idol), suggesting that for these Protestant officials, non-Christian idols held little relevance. In the third inventory of 1621, conducted after Catholic forces had regained control of Prague, these feather objects were identified as without value and housed in a box of "mean things."[82] In these first years of the Thirty Years' War, no faction was inclined to value the triumphs of Habsburg conquests overseas.

In collections of the Counter-Reformation Wittelsbachs and Rudolf II, contemporary extra-European idols were evidence of the distance between their own Catholic and non-Christian religions and cultures. For the Counter-Reformation papacy, idolatrous cultures became similarly distant. Although in the early sixteenth century, the papacy had supported Platonic investigations of religion, classical knowledge, and art, the display of classical images had been rejected mid-century because of their idolatrous nature.[83] Counter-Reformation popes Gregory XIII and Sixtus V (1572–1590) transformed Counter-Reformation Rome into

---

[82] Jan Morávek, *Nově Objevený Inventář....* (Prague, (1937), 2, 24, 30; "schlecten sachen," Heinrich Zimmerman, "Das Inventar der Prager Schatz- und Kunstkammer vom 6. Dezember 1621," *JKSW* 25 (1905): xx, and generally xiii–li; Beket Bukovinska, "The Kunstkammer of Rudolf II," in *Rudolf II and Prague: the Court and the City*, ed. Eliška Fučíková (London: Thames and Hudson, 1997), 199–208.

[83] Ingrid Rowland, *The Culture of the High Renaissance* (Cambridge: Cambridge University Press, 1998); Francis Haskell and Nicholas Penny, *Taste and the Antique* (New Haven: Yale University Press, 1981), 14–5; Hecht, *Katholische Bildertheologie*.

a material symbol of Catholic vigor. This new Rome touted its Christian triumph over pagan antiquity, extolling its victory over antiquity's "Empire of Satan." Newly installed monuments such as obelisks symbolized the Church's triumph over idolatrous religion and culture.[84] The important distinction to be made, heard, and seen was between the Counter-Reformation church and the demonic idols of pagans and heretics.

By 1600, Catholic authorities had reached a new consensus on material objects. With the refutation of Protestant criticisms, sensually sacred Baroque churches could be built, and pagan idols could be housed in collections that were microcosms of the world. Rather than placing the Catholic viewer at risk of misunderstanding the nature of images, pagan idols illustrated the distance between non-Christians and Catholics. The 1563 Tridentine decree encouraged Catholics to do more than flatly deny Protestant accusations of idolatry or produce Counter-Reformation art against Protestant iconoclasm. Counter-Reformation thinkers like Acosta and Fickler displaced Protestant charges by redefining idolatrous cultures as safely past or, if contemporaneous, safely located beyond Europe. In collections, Catholic Europeans could contemplate the devil's power to inspire superstitious faith and worship, as well as the folly of Protestants.

These lessons about idolatry were popularized through widely circulating catechisms designed to re-Catholicize Central Europe and guide practice in Iberia. Georg Eder and Jesuit Peter Canisius's catechisms illustrated true religion's veneration of saints and use of images through the counterexample of heathens, who adored false gods. Fellow Jesuit Bellarmine produced more detailed popular catechisms (two formats from 1597 and 1598 were translated into multiple vernaculars).[85] He promoted the distance between true Christians and false sects, conflating "the false religions of pagans, Muslims, Jews, and heretics." This

---

[84] Frederick McGinness, *Right Thinking and Sacred Oratory in Counter-Reformation Rome* (Princeton: Princeton University Press, 1995), 152, 179–83; Anthony Grafton, "The Ancient City Restored" in *Rome Reborn* (Washington D.C.: Library of Congress, 1993), 112–23; Domenico Fontana, *Della Trasportatione* (Rome: Domenico Basa, 1590); Eric Iversen, *Obelisks in Exile* (Copenhagen: Gad, 1968), 1:29–44, 51–4, 62–4.

[85] Georg Eder, *Catechismus Catholicus qui antea quidem ex decreto Concilii Tridentini,...* (Cologne: Gervins Calenius, 1569), 305–8; Peter Canisius, *Parvus Catechismus Catholicorum* (Vienna: [Gulielmus Sulienus], 1559), 18ᵛ–19 and, after the close of Trent, *Catechismus Catholicus* (Ingolstadt: Wolfgang Eder, 1583), 23–4; and Bellarmine, *Außführliche Erklärung Christlicher Catholischer Lehr* (Augsburg: Christoph Mang, 1607), 141–9. For the Bellarmine catechism's popularity, Brodrick, 153–5.

catechism also reminded the reader that false gods could appear in natural forms as celestial objects, animals, and dead men, but also, more idolatrously, as images made of gold, silver, wood, or stone that were inspired by the "hellish devil."[86] From the Council of Trent's closing to the end of the century, extra-European religions and culture became woven together both conceptually and materially into a category of falsity and denigrated difference located in the world outside of Europe.

The fixing of idolatry was a significant outcome of this Reformation-era nexus of material object and theology. If religious comparison began in a search to understand the unfamiliar during the early decades of the sixteenth century, it ended with idolatrous peoples in a collective and collected ethnographic category at the century's close, with consequences beyond religion. The conflated position of Turkish and Indian culture in these collections illuminated their new associations and epistemological position in Europe. A blurrily defined category of people emerged, "civilized" yet undeniably and irredeemably idolatrous, and therefore less than Christian Europe.

Some elements of this categorical mixing had descriptive precedents. During the sixteenth century, the names "Indian," "Moor," and "Turk" were used somewhat generally. The descriptive category of "the Indies" had covered a broad geographic expanse from India to the Americas, while after 1517, Moors and Turks were members of the same Ottoman state. Old Christian Castilians worried that the expansion of the Ottoman Empire might well be the ambition of the peoples they suspected were crypto-Muslims resident in Spain and they often referred to the "Moors and Turks" together. Once the Portuguese began reporting on their adventures in east India, the presence of Moors there, alongside Christians and other people, became popularized, and the naming of people from the Indian subcontinent as Moors solidified.[87] In the second half of the century, the terms and cultural categories Turk and Moor, as well as Moor and east or west Indian, were increasingly conflated, growing more comparable and indistinguishable.[88] These elisions of difference appeared

---

[86] "von allen falschen Secten der Heyden/ Türcken/ Juden/ und Ketzer," Bellarmine, *Außführliche Erklärung*, 11, 142.

[87] Sanjay Subrahmanyam, *The Career and Legend of Vasco da Gama* (Cambridge: Cambridge University Press, 1997), chapter 3 passim.

[88] The use of "Moorish" for "Indian" has been noted by several modern scholars, but only as a corrective. The epistemological underpinnings of this practice have not been extensively discussed. For example, see Ferdinand Anders, "Der Federkasten der Ambraser Kunstkammer," *JKSW* 61 n.s. 25 (1965): 119–132.

not only in the descriptions of cultural goods described in this chapter, but also in the easy transference of Reconquista iconography to Spanish America, including the "Moor-Christian" plays enacted by Christian Indians and the general colonial Spanish transformation of St. James from *"Matamoros"* (Moor-killer) to *"Mataindios"* (Indian-killer).[89]

Initial tendencies to group the products of these cultures together could be seen in the inventories of Charles V's possessions after his death in 1558. A few objects from the other extra-European culture were mixed in with materials from either Tunis or the Indies. Descriptions reveal geographic or cultural indiscriminancy: objects known to be from the Indies were nonetheless described as "morisca" in color, a sword from Majorca listed among the "swords from the Indies," a large alloy medal depicting the "Great Turk" was stored with other medallions and pieces of money from the Indies, and two porcelain jars rounded out the category "more things from the Indies" ("mas cosas de Yndias") – that is, the west Indies of America.[90] Similarly, in the partial inventory of Ferdinand I's collection, the last seven entries were a jumble of Turkish and Indian objects.[91] The archducal, ducal, and Rudolfine collection elaborated this practice of conflation, placing together Muscovite and Indian objects, Turkish and Indian weapons. Cultural attributes became mixed within an object, too; an Indian shield could have Turkish script running along its border, and a card game might be Turkish or Indian.[92]

As in the Bavarian *"rariorten"* and the jumbled *"variocasten"* of the Habsburgs, the "rare" cultural goods from the idolatrous yet complex societies bordering Habsburg Europe took their new form as exotic. This proto-ethnographic representation of exotic culture was marked out for princes and scholars through trophy weapons signifying violent encounters, luxury trade goods or raw materials, and idols that underscored these cultures' unrepentant inability to embrace true Christianity.

---

[89] This theme is developed in Richard Trexler, "We Think, They Act: Clerical Readings of Missionary Theatre in 16th Century Mexico" in *Church and Community, 1200–1600* (Rome: Edizione di storia e letteratura, 1987), 575–613; Patricia Lopes Don "Carnivals, Triumphs, and Rain Gods in the New World" *Colonial Latin American Review* 6 (1997): 17–40; Irene Silverblatt, "Political Memories and Colonizing Symbols: Santiago and the Mountain Gods of Colonial Peru" in *Rethinking History and Myth*, ed. Jonathan D. Hill (Urbana: University of Illinois Press, 1988), 174–94. Exemplifying the interchange of "Moor" and "Turk", a fiesta at Tordesillas in 1550 enacted the battle of Rhodes as one between Moors and Christians. HHStA, Span. DK 2/34, fols. 76–79ᵛ.

[90] Cabello, 53, 59–60.

[91] Rudolf, "Kunstbestrebungen," 253 (nos. 222–8).

[92] Bauer and Haupt, 66, 70.

FIGURE 31. Ostrich-egg lidded goblet. Clement Kicklinger, Augsburg, 1570/ 1575. Kunsthistorisches Museum, Vienna.

FIGURE 32. Coconut goblet. Augsburg, second half of the 16th century. Kunst-historisches Museum, Vienna.

Mexican feather ornaments appeared only as playful symbols of rule in festivities, worn when Duke Wilhelm and Archduke Ferdinand dressed as "Moors" in the festivities marking Wilhelm's marriage to Renata of Lorraine, or adorning Ferdinand's horse in the procession of his second marriage in 1582.[93]

It has been argued that the "new worlds" were seen through the lens of pagan antiquity.[94] Yet rather than occurring quickly and automatically upon first encounter, the process of codifying Indians and Turks as a conflated foreign, exotic (*extera*) cultures took place over decades. Rather than a simple domestication, the category of "exotic" had, in a sense, to be defined and excluded from princely collections and ethnographies of strange peoples or imperfect Christians. Several late-sixteenth-century German lidded goblets, designed for princely *Kunstkammern* by craftsman in Augsburg, reveal just how mixed understandings of these civilized yet non-Christian peoples could become.[95] They are constructed of raw materials from beyond Europe (an ostrich egg and a coconut), which made them rare and valuable for their materials alone (Figure 31 and Figure 32). Exotic men support both bowls. At first glance, they are simply Nubians from the classical Roman world, wearing the body armor of antiquity. On closer inspection, however, the men wear feather ornaments on their heads, armor, and legs. They are not symbols of the past, but rather a general extra-European present. They are Moorish Indians or Indian "Blackamoors"[96] – exotic and no longer sufficiently civilized, they would become the ubiquitous symbol of the Americas in seventeenth-century images.

---

93 Hanns Wagner, *Kurtze doch gegründet beschreibung... gehalten Hochzeitlichen Ehren Fests. Im 1568. jar.* (Munich: Adam Berg, 1568), Giii–Gv[v] and Anders, "Federkasten," 123–8.

94 Michael Ryan's insightful and early "Assimilating New Worlds," *CSSH* 23 (1981) proposes this argument, as well as the process of "domestication," 523.

95 Inv. Nos. KK 897 and KK 914 are in the Sammlungen für Plastik und Kunstgewerbe, Kunsthistorisches Museum, Vienna. Ernst Kris, ed. *Goldschmiedearbeiten des Mittelalters, der Renaissance und des Barock* (Vienna: Schroll, 1932) I:40, 52.

96 For a depiction of the *"Schwarzmohr"* or "blackamoor" identified as such, see Wallhanging Inv. No. V466, 1571, Museum für Kunsthandwerk, Grassi Museum Leipzig.

Conclusion

Categorical Denials

Inclusionary conceptions of the world's peoples and exclusionary denigrations of heterodox Christians and non-Christians had existed in tension with each other long before the sixteenth century. With the coming of the Protestant and Catholic Reformations, the balance between these different understandings shifted significantly. Latin Christendom splintered over disagreements about whether some practices were dangerously superstitious or merely adiaphoric and about whether some doctrines were true or false. Catholics and Protestants worked to define faith and consequent true religious practice, in part so that the lines between their own confessions and those of the erroneous were comprehensible to all. Adherence to correct religious doctrine became not just the crowning but the pre-eminent and necessary evaluative category of a culture or people. By the end of the sixteenth century, the conjuncture of these developments and of European engagements with the Aztec and Ottoman empires resulted in the definition of non-Christians as well as heterodox Christians as unredeemed and perhaps unredeemable. As such, they were denied the status of civilized peoples.

During the Reformation, when different Christian interpretations of the mass or forms of prayer inspired opponents to charge each other with cannibalism or idolatry, the practices of religion such as circumcision and sacrifice to idols could no longer be considered signs of worship or covenant. Martin Luther explicitly noted the new concept of *religio* in his *Von den Consiliis und Kirchen* (1539).[1] *Religio*, he wrote, no longer referred to strictures of practice such as the Law of Moses (and

---

[1] *WA* 50: 509–653.

circumcision) or the rules of monastic orders, but rather to true faith. He drew on examples of idolatrous Jews and Egyptians and their "blood sacrifice" to describe practices that had been irretrievably misguided. Religious difference and ethnographic description would no longer be measures of human creativity inspired by the divine, but methods of determining cultural hierarchy.

For humanist scholars, courtiers, and diplomats, European encounters with the Aztec and Ottoman empires involved not only ideas and evaluations of religious practice, but also more tangible experiences. From the early decades through the close of the sixteenth century, these extra-European peoples and their material objects also helped create cultural value, and in turn had their significance shaped by cultural currents within Europe. Habsburg commitments to universal empire embodied at their Iberian court and, later, to the evocation of Roman or Carolingian-era imperial tributes at the Holy Roman imperial court, provided roles as esteemed envoys for extra-European peoples. Similarly, in the early sixteenth century, there was space to incorporate extra-European objects from the Aztec Empire into material categories of inalienable treasure, as symbols of regalian and perhaps even sacral authority for Habsburg viewers. During the early Reformation, Latin Christians widely repudiated material sacrality, and in decades with steep military costs, gold and silver treasure was reformed into specie. Nor could featherwork maintain its value as treasure based on its artistry, as Mexican craftsmanship was increasingly devalued. Feather treasures would eventually lose even their value as alienable or saleable objects. Feather-crowned and skirted American Indians became little more than symbols of a primitive continent in seventeenth-century representations of the world.

With sacral display eliminated as a unifying proclamation of legitimacy for rulers, the elite in the Habsburg empire drew on other possibilities, some experimental, some long-lasting. The princely collection proved to be one of the most enduring once idolatry was located outside of Europe in time and space. The construction of dazzlingly sensual baroque monuments was another. The Holy Roman Empire's competition with the Ottoman Empire over which was the true heir of the Roman Empire encouraged the use of Roman triumphal iconography, the collection of its artifactual past, and the conceptual relocation of the Ottomans as a people separated from the heritage of Rome by their exotic cultural distance. Even the post-Tridentine development of absolutist theories of divinely supported monarchy served to replace the late-medieval numinous quality of relics.

The Habsburg empire, produced through the person of Charles V and sustained during the next generations, employed symbolic categories through which to understand, display, and promote legitimacy and authority. These developments were intertwined with the pragmatic politics of sixteenth-century empire building. The Habsburg empire was, in crucial ways, singular. The French and English empires were latecomers, emerging after European evaluations of extra-European cultures had already been formed by a century of cultural production. Although both would engage in defining the evolving categories of civilized European and non-civilized extra-European during subsequent centuries, the definitive categorization of extra-Europeans as uncivilized predated those empires. The Portuguese empire, in contrast, developed before that of the Habsburgs. Not surprisingly, symbolic strategies similar to those of the Habsburgs were supported at the fifteenth- and early-sixteenth-century Portuguese court, with its vision of an expansive and inclusionary empire. Nobles from west Africa were welcomed as representatives of subject crowns. Exotic animals from India were lauded as magnificent gifts not seen in Europe since the era of Christ's birth. Full conversion to Christianity, including the entrance of Kongolese nobles into the higher ranks of the church, was encouraged. If the Portuguese were innovators of cultural meanings for extra-Europeans in Europe, the Habsburgs' significantly more extensive European territories allowed them a much broader cultural field of influence and engagement. This broader field also had forced the Habsburgs to respond more directly to the Reformation's challenges, as the confessionally divided Holy Roman Empire became a central arena for reformed attacks on material sacrality and the scope of sovereign authority.

The Portuguese and the Habsburg empires differed in meaningful ways, perhaps most evidently in their different bases of productive wealth, through control of trade and land, respectively. During the first half-century of New World expansion, Portuguese inclusionary strategies did not seem to extend to their territories in Brazil. In contrast to the Portuguese, who engaged in trade and resource extraction with the non-city-dwelling Tupí peoples, Castilians in New Spain and Peru sought to rule as the successor state to older empires. Another, geographic difference was evident in the two empires' engagements with powerful empires east of Iberia. While the Portuguese gained footholds in a far-off Indian Ocean basin and beyond through alliance, trade, and armed conflict, the Habsburg borders were directly vulnerable to an Ottoman Empire that half-encircled the Habsburg empire south and east of Castile and Aragon,

Naples and Sicily, Croatia and Hungary. As a consequence of this territorial boundary, the Habsburg court could not simply allow geographic
distance to diminish the military or political power and symbolic force
of the Ottoman Empire, an option available to the Portuguese crown
in relation to Indian or Chinese rulers. The Habsburgs needed to pro-
mulgate understandings of their authority in relation to this much more
powerful neighbor, and sought to do so in the sixteenth century through
strategies of distancing and denigrating the Ottomans as uncivilized. Yet
even with these differences, the Portuguese court, like those of the Habsburgs, ceased to employ tactics of imperial inclusivity during the second
half of the sixteenth century.[2] Arguably, this exclusion extended from the
Reformation-era condemnation of false practice and faith and the consequent denial of a classification as civilized for extra-European subjects.

The sixteenth-century treatment of Nicholas of Cusa's *De pace fidei*
and its inclusionary religious dialogue illustrates the European-wide
transformation in cultural evaluation and the conceptual hierarchization of peoples. Johannes Kymeus, a reformer in the Wittenberg circle,
printed an ostensible German translation of Cusanus's *De pace fidei* in
1538, *Des Bapsts Hercules/ wider die Deutdschen*. In Kymeus's version,
the text no longer offered a dialogue between the representatives of seventeen peoples and the divine or apostolic voice. It retained only frag-
ments of the one dialogue between the Tartar and Paul. In his translation
of Cusanus's argument in *De pace fidei*, Kymeus inverted much of its
conclusion. Although love, which Kymeus defined as belief in Christ,
remained the true fulfillment of God's law, Cusanus's acceptance of a
diversity of ceremonies and rites to inspire faith was deleted and replaced
with a rejection of ceremonies and laws as useless at best.[3] The previous year, Kymeus had repudiated Anabaptists as heretical pawns of the
devil, in part by conflating their refusal to baptize children with Jewish
circumcision and child sacrifice. He listed Indian brahmins, Syrian magi,

---

[2] Ivana Elbl, "Prestige Considerations and the Changing Interest of the Portuguese Crown
in Sub-Saharan Atlantic Africa, 1444–1580," *Portuguese Studies Review* 10/2 (2002):
15–36; Luis Filipe F.R. Thomaz, "Factions, Interests and Messianism: the Politics of Portuguese Expansion in the East, 1500–1521," *Indian Economic and Social History Review*
28 (1991): 97–109; and, for recent surveys of Portuguese imperialism, Sanjay Subrahmanyam, "Holding the World in Balance: The Connected Histories of the Iberian Overseas Empires, 1500–1640," *American Historical Review* 112 (2007): 1359–85 and A.J.R.
Russell-Wood, "Settlement, Colonization, and Integration in the Portuguese-Influenced
World, 1415–1570," *Portuguese Studies Review* 15 (2007): 1–35.

[3] (Wittenberg, Georg Rhaw, 1538), Hiii^v–J^v.

Greek philosophers, and Turkish or Papist monks[4] – all types of wise men valued by thinkers like Cusanus or Ficino – as false holy men and agents of the devil. By the end of the sixteenth century, Bellarmine's synthetic defense of Catholic doctrine skipped discussion of *De pace fidei* in favor of other works by Cusanus. When jurist Jean Bodin wrote the *Colloquium heptaplomeres de rerum sublimium arcanis abditis* in the early 1590s, the gathering of learned men would be much reduced in number. Rather than Cusanus's seventeen, there were seven representatives who gathered in the Venetian home of their Catholic host, a collector of antiquities, ethnographies, and *naturalia* from around the world.[5] In the wide-ranging conversation, West Indians were discussed as peoples mired in idolatry. The scholars eventually concluded that they would not discuss religion again, for the debate left them each convinced of his own religion's truth and the importance of harmony among themselves. The Muslim who joined in the debates was de-exoticized and familiar, as he was a convert from Catholicism and bore an Italianate surname. In contrast, no peoples from the west or east Indies were participants in the colloquium about the sublime. While attitudes of cultural and religious superiority were not a given for Christian Europeans in 1453 or 1500, strategies of denigration had worked to form this category of excluded exotic during the course of the sixteenth century.

---

[4] *Ein Alt Christlich Concilium/ fur zwelff hundert jaren zu Gangra...wider die hoch genante heiligkeit der Mönchen vnd Widerteuffer* included an introduction by Luther (Wittenberg: Klug, 1537), Gii, Jii–Jii[v].

[5] The seven participants were a natural philosopher, a skeptic, a Jew, a Muslim, a Catholic, a Lutheran, and a Reformed Protestant (1857, reprint Frommann: Stuttgart, 1966). See Marion Leathers Kuntz's essays on the *Colloquium* in *Venice, Myth and Utopian Thought in the Sixteenth Century* (Aldershot: Ashgate, 1999).

Bibliography

Primary Sources

Archival / Manuscript / Museum Collections

Austria
Allgemeines Verwaltungsarchiv, Vienna (AVA)
Adelsakten

Haus-, Hof-, und Staatsarchiv, Vienna (HHStA)
Belgien
    PA 6, 25, 28
Handschriften
    Blau 192, Marcos de Nica [1538]
Hausarchiv
    Familien-Akten 88
    Hofsachen 97, 98, 103, 104
Hofarchiv
    OMeA SR Hofstaatsverzeichnisse 181/16
Reichsarchiv
    Reichskanzlerei Wahl- und KrönungsAkten 5
Staatenabt.
    Rom Correspondenz 13, 14; Varia 1, 5
    Spanien Diplomatische Korrespondenz (DK) 1/1, 4, 6, 7, 8, 10–13, 15, 16;
        2/21, 22, 24, 29, 30, 31, 33–36, 37; 3/39–50, 53, 62, 66, 67, 68; 6/117–118
    Spanien HofKorrespondenz 1, 2; Varia 1–4
    Turcica (now Türkei I) 2/1; 3/1, 5; 8/1, 3, 4; 10/2, 3; 16/1, 2, 3, 4; 17/1, 2, 3,
        4, 5; 19; 20; 23/1, 2, 3, 4, 5; 24; 25/1, 2, 4; 26/1, 4; 27/1, 2, 3, 4, 5; 28/1, 2,
        3, 4, 5; 29/2, 3, 4; 30/1, 2, 4, 5, 6
    Venedig, Berichte 11, 12 /1572
Staatskanzlei
    Wissenschaft, Kunst, und Literatur 1, 5, 9, 10

269

Hofkammerarchiv, Vienna (HKA)
Familien Akte H69
Gedenkbuch 109
Hofzahlamtsbücher 1–30 (1543–1576)
Reichsakten 174a, 190, 190a

Kriegsarchiv, Vienna
Altefeldakten 1570–1576

Stadt- und Landesarchiv, Vienna
Oberkammeramtsrechnungen (OKAR) Books 90, 91, 95

Österreichische Nationalbibliothek, Vienna (ÖNB)

CVP 3614: Johann Jacob Fugger. *Das sibendt unnd letste Büech dises meines Oesterreichischen Ehrenwerkhs Welliches das ganntzherrlich leben mit allen löblichen und ritterlichen thaten des Allerkhünenisten Theürischen Khaisers Ertzhertzogen zue Oesterreich*, [copy from 1598].
CVP 5542: Alonso de Santa Cruz. *Islario general de todos . . . partes 3 &4.*
CVP 7195: Alonso de Santa Cruz. *Historia de las islas meridionales et occidentales.*
CVP 7871
CVP 8251: Paul Pfintzing de Henffenfelt. *Relacion particular y sumaria de la manera que el serenissimo muy alto y muy Poderoso Principe, Maximiliano segundo deste nombre, Rey de Romanos y de Bohemia, fue coronado . . . 1562.*
Codex Vindobonensis S.N. 1600

Kunsthistorisches Museum, Vienna
Inv. Nos. GG 2046; KK 897, 914, 3944, 3945, 3947, 3948, 3949, 3980, 3981, 3985, 3986

Germany
Augsburg, Stadtarchiv (StA)
Handwerkerakten 342, Uhrmachern 1

Bayerisches Hauptstaatsarchiv (BStA)
GR Fasz 513, Nr. 65a
Kurbayern Äußeres Archiv (KaA), 4851–4855 Libri Antiquitatum I-V

Bayerische Staatsbibliothek (BSB)
CGM 2133, 2134. Johann-Baptista Fickler. *Inventarium oder Beschreibung aller deren Stuckh und sachen frembder und Inhaimischer bekanter und unbekanter seltzamer und verwunderlicher ding So auf Ir Fürst.lh: Durch. Hertzogen in Baÿrn rc. Kunstcamer zu sehen und zu finden ist.*

Frankfurt-am-Main Stadtarchiv (FSA)
Burgermeisterbücher (1562)
Ratsprotokolle 1562–1563

Leipzig, Grassi Museum/ Museum für Kunsthandwerk
Inv. No. V466, 1571

Nuremberg, Burg
Springinklee, Hans. Ceiling (Modern restoration), Emperor's reception room.

Nuremberg, Staatsarchiv (StAN)
Krönungsakten 1, 4, 5, 6
Ratsbücher 12
Ratsverlässe (des Inneren Rats) No. 699, 701
Losungsamt, Akten S. I, L. (SIL) 131, no. 22; 134, no. 1, 19, 23, 24, 26
Stadtrechnungsbelege 1515–1526
Stadtrechnungsbelege II, 1562–1563
Amts- und Standbücher 316:Schenckbuch

Trier, Stadtbibliothek
Codex 1374/140 4°

Ulm, Stadtarchiv
Ratsprotokolle 24

Spain
Archivo General de Indias, Seville (AGI)
Contratación 4675; 5527 l. 3; 5788 l. 1

Indiferente General (IG) 420/ Libro (L.) 8, L. 9; 421/ L. 11; 422/ L.15, L.16, L.17;
423/ L. 19; 425/ L. 23, L. 24; 427/ L. 30; 737; 1085/ L. 1575, L. 1576; 1961/
L. 1, L. 2, L.3; 1962/ L.2, L.4, L. 6; 1963/ L. 6, L. 7, L.8, L.9

Justicia 218, no. 2, r. 3

M.P. – Escudos 77, 78

Pasajeros L. 4, 7, 8

Patronato 74 n. 1 r. 13; 122 n. 1, r. 13; 180 r. 84–85, 86, 88; 188 r. 6; 245 r. 10,
14, 25; 275 r. 41; 1748 leg. 55 n. 3 r. 4; 2460 leg. 93 n. 4 r. 4; 3097 leg. 40 r. 4

Quito 89; 211

Archivo General de Simancas, Simancas (AGS)
Casas y Sitios Reales, Legajo 72

Archivo Municipal, Seville
Seccion Tercero, Tomo 11, no. 45

Printed Materials

Acosta, José de. *De Natura Novi Orbis Libri duo, et de Promulgatione Evangelii
apud Barbaros, sive de procuranda indorum salute*. Salamanca: Foquel, 1589.
_____. *Historia Natural y Moral de las Indias (1590)*. In *Obras de P. José de
Acosta*. BAE 73. Madrid: Atlas, 1954.
*Ain christlich gedechtnüß der betrüebten Christen in der Türckey gefangen/ im
Papier thon*. 1532.
*Ain über Schönlesen/ Von den Wilden rauhen menchen der nachkumen/ von
den Sünen Noe/ wie Sy in erdgräben mit wylden tierheüten bedeckt lange*

zeit gewonet haben und wie Sy nachmalen heüser gezimert Hiemat auch Augspurg.... [Augsburg: Melchior, Raminger 1522].

Alberti, Leon Battista. *On the Art of Building in Ten Books.* Translated by Joseph Rykwert and Robert Tavernor. Cambridge, MA: MIT Press, 1988.

[Alberus, Erasmus]. *Der Barfusser Münche Eulenspiegel und Alcoran mit einer Vorrede D. Martini Luther.* Wittenberg: Hans Luft, 1542.

Alchoran. Das ist/ des Mahometischen Gesatzbüchs/ und Türckischen Aberglaubens ynnhalt/ vnd ablänung. Strasbourg: Hans Schott, 1540.

Aleander, Girolamo. *Acta academiae Lovaniensis.* [Basel: Cratander, 1520].

Anbringen Türkische Legation/ Ebrahimi Strotischii/ gebornen Polecken/ welche er vor Key. Maye. Roemischem Koenig/ . . . in Schlavonischer sprach.... Nuremberg: Berg und Newber, 1562.

Anzaygendt Newtzeyttung/ wie es aigendtlich herren/ unnd mitt der schlacht vor Pavia. [Augsburg: Johann Schönsperger, 1525].

Aspland, Alfred, ed. *The Triumphs of the Emperor Maximilian I.* Manchester: Holbein Society, 1873.

Auß Ratschlage Herren Erasmi von Roterdam/ die Türcken zubekriegen/ Der ursprung vnnd alle geschichten der selbigen gegen Römische Keyser vnnd gemeyne Christenheyt/ Von anbeginn des Türckischen namenn/ nach der kürtze new verteutscht. Kriegs rüstung vnd behendigkeit der Türcken/ durch Sabellicum beschriben im ix. büch Enneadis. x. Türckisch vnd Machometisch Glaub Gesatz/ Chronic/ Gotsdienst/ Ceremonien/ allegbräuch/ Ordnungen/ Disciplinen/ in Kriegs vnnd Fridens zeiten. Die Zehen Nationen vnnd Secten der Christenheit/ Des gleich wie mechtig ein iede/ Vnnd worinnen sie Glaubens halb nit übereinkommen. [Egenolff, 1531].

Auszug aines Brieffs, wie ainer, so in der Türckey wonhafft, seinem Freund in dise Land geschriben, vnnd angezaigt, was das Türckisch Regiment vnd wesen sey. 1526.

Baader, J. ed. "Einreiten des Erzherzogs Ferdinand zu Nuremberg im Jahre 1521." *Anzeiger für Kunde der deutschen Vorzeit* N.F. 16 (1869): 93–102, 125–30, 157–64.

Bauer, Rotraud and Herbert Haupt, eds. "Das Kunstkammerinventar Kaiser Rudolfs II., 1607–1611." *JKSW* n.s. 72 (1976).

Bauer, Wilhelm, Robert Lacroix, Christiane Thomas, Herwig Wolfram, eds. *Die Korrespondenz Ferdinands I.* Veröffentlichungen der Kommission für neuere Geschichte Österreichs 11, 30–31, 58. Vienna: Holzhausen, 1912–1977.

Beer, Rudolf. "Acten, Regesten und Inventare aus dem Archivo General zu Simancas." *JKSW* 12 (1891): xci–cciv.

Bellarmine, Robert. *Außführliche Erklärung Christlicher Catholischer Lehr.* Augsburg: Christoph Mang, 1607.

———. *Opera Omnia.* Edited by Justin Fèvre. Vols. 1, 3, 7. Frankfurt a. M.: Minerva, 1965.

Belon du Mans, Pierre. *Voyage au Levant.* 1553. Paris: Chandeigne, 2001.

Beschreibung des Thourniers vnd kampfspiels, so auf ankunfft Keys. Maiest. sampt dem Prinzen auf Hispanien, zu Bintz gehalten des 24 tags Augusti An. 1549.... [Cologne: Mameranus, 1550].

Beuther, Michael. *Ordenliche Verzeychniß/ welcher gestalt/ die Erwehlung unnd Krönung/ des Allerdurchleuchtigsten Großmächtigsten Fürsten und Herrn/*

Herrn Maximilian/ Römischen unnd zu Böheym Königs etc. zu Franckfurt am Main/ im Wintermonat nähestverschienen 1562 jars/ geschehen. Mit vermeldunge etlicher sonst fürnehmer sachen und Händel/ so sich darneben/ durch ankunfft eyner Türckischen Bottschaffte/ und in andere wege haben verlauffen und zugetragen. Frankfurt a. M.: David Zöpffeln, 1563.

Bibl, Viktor, ed. *Die Korrespondenz Maximilians II.* Veröffentlichungen der Kommission für Neuere Geschichte Österreichs 14, 16. Vienna: Holzhausen, 1916–1922.

Bildnisse viler zum theyle von uralten/ zum theyle von newlichern zeitern her/ Kriegs und anderer Weltlicher Hänndel halben/ bei Christen unnd Unchristen gewesener berühmter Keyser . . . dieselbige Paulus Jovius/ vor weilen Bischoff von Nocera/ durch allerley gelegenheyt zusammen gebracht. . . . Basel: Peter Perna, 1582.

Bodenstein von Karlstadt, Andreas. *Von abthieung der Bylder.* Basel, 1522.

———. *Von abtuhung der Bylder.* Wittenberg: Schyrlentz, 1522.

Bodin, Jean. *Colloquium heptaplomeres de rerum sublimium arcanis abditis.* 1857. Reprint, Stuttgart: Frommann, 1966.

Boeheim, Wendelin, ed. "Urkunden und Regesten aus der K.K. Hofbibliothek." *JKSW* 7 (1888): xci–cccxiv.

Boemus, Johann. *Mores, leges et ritus omnium gentium.* Lyon: Tornaesius and Gazeius, 1561.

———. *Omnium gentium mores.* Louvain: Franciscus Justus, 1536.

———. *Omnium gentium mores.* Antwerp: Steelsius, 1542.

———. *Repertorium librorum trium de omnium gentium ritibus.* Augsburg: Wirsung, 1520.

Bonaventura. *Das Leben unsers erledigers Jesu Christi.* Nuremberg: Johannes Stücks, 1514.

Bordone, Benedetto. *Libro di Benedetto Bordone nel qual si ragiona de tutte l'Isole del mondo.* Venice: Nicolò Zoppino, 1528.

Bottschafft des Groszmechtigsten Konigs David aus dem grossen und hohen Morenland/ den man gemeinlich nennet priester Johann an Babst Clemens den Siebenden/ zu Bononia vorhort in offnem Consistorio am xxix. tag Januarii Anno. 1533. Ein Sendbrieff des Königs von Portugal an Babst Clement den sibenden. Ein Sendbrieff des Morenkönigs an König Emanuel von Portugal. Ein Sendbrieff des Morenkönigs an König Johann von Portugal . . . Ein Sendbrieff des Bischoffs der grossen stadt Temixtitan in der Newen erfunden welt/ an die Väter parfusser Ordens . . . zu Tolosa in Franckreich vorsamlet. 1532. Dresden: Wolffgang Stöckel, 1533.

Brenz, Johannes. *Wie sich Prediger und Leien halten sollen,* . . . Wittenberg: Rhaw, 1537.

Breydenbach, Bernhard von. *Peregrinatio in terram sanctam,* 1486.

Busbecq, Ogier Ghiselin de. *Augerii Gislenii Busbequii D. Legationis Turcicae Epistolae quatuor.* 1589. Reprint Frankfurt a. M.: Andrea Wechel, Claud. Marnius, Ioannis Aubrius, 1595.

Cabeza de Vaca, Alvar Nuñez. *Naufragios.* Madrid: Cátedra, 1989.

Calvete de Estrella, Juan Cristobal. *El felicissimo viaje del muy alto y muy poderoso principe don Phelippe.* Antwerp: 1552.

Canisius, Peter. *Catechismus Catholicus.* Ingolstadt: Wolfgang Eder, 1583.

———. *Parvus Catechismus Catholicorum.* Vienna: [Gulielmus Sulienus], 1559.
Cartari, Vincenzo. Supplement by Lorenzo Pignoria. *Le vere e nove imagini de gli dei delli antichi* [1615]. Padua: Tozzi, 1626.
Cartas de Indias. Madrid: Hernandez, 1877.
Cartas de Relación de la conquista de la Nueva España: Codex Vindobonensis S.N. 1600. Facsimile. Graz: Akademische Druck, 1960.
Chronica/ Abconterfayung vnd entwerffung der Türckey. Augsburg: Steiner, 1530.
Chronica/ Beschreibung und gemeyne anzeyte/ vonn aller Wellt herkommen. Frankfurt: C. Egenolff, 1535.
Colección de documentos inéditos, para la historia de España. 113 vols. Madrid, 1842–1895. Reprint, Vaduz: Kraus, 1966.
Colección de documentos inéditos, relativos al descubrimiento, conquista y organización de las antiguas posesiones españolas de América y Oceanía, sacados de los archivos del reino y muy especialmente del de Indias. 42 vols. Madrid: Real Academia de la Historia, 1864–1884.
Colección de documentos inéditos relativos al descubrimiento, conquista y organización de las antiguas posesiones españolas de ultramar. 25 vols. Madrid: Rivadeneyra, 1885–1932.
Confessio odder Bekantnus des Glaubens etlicher Fürsten vnd Stedte: Uberantwort Keiserlicher Maeistat: zu Augsburg. Wittenberg: Georg Rhaw, 1531.
Copey etlicher brieff so auß Hispania kummen seindt/ anzaygent die eygenschafft des/ Newen Lands/ so newlich von Kay. May. Armadi auff dem newen Mör gefunden ist worden/ durch die Hispanier. 1535.
Copey eynes brieffes so miser Johann Baptista de Grimaldo/ seynem vettern Ansaaldo de Grimaldo/ vnnd andern Edlen gen Genua auß Hyspanien zuᵒgeschribenn hat. M.D.XXiX. [Nuremberg: Kunigunde Hergot, 1529].
Copey unnd lautter Abschrifft ains warhafftigen Sandbrieffs/ wie der Türckisch Kayser Solyman/ disen seinen yetzt gegenwürtigen Anzug wider die Christenhait geordnet/ von Constantinopel außgezogen/ vnd gen Kriechischen Weissenburgk ankomen ist/ wie volgt. [1532].
Copey vnd lautter Abschrifft eins warhafftigen Sendbrieffs/ wie der Türckisch Kayser Solyman/ disen sein yetzt gegenwürtigen Anzug wider die Christenhait geordnet.... [1532].
Copia de vna littera del Re de Portagallo mandata al Re de Castella del viaggio y successi de India. Rome: Besicken, 1505.
Copus, Alan [Nicholas Harpsfield]. *Dialogi sex contra summi pontificatus....* Antwerp: Christopher Plantin, 1566.
Cortés, Hernán. *Carta de relacion embiada a su majestad del emperador nuestro señor por el capitan general de la nueva spaña llamado Fernando Cortes.* Seville: Cromberger, 1522.
———. *Carta de relacion embiada a su majestad del emperador nuestro señor por el Capitan general de la Nueva España.* 2 ed. Zaragoza: George Coci, 1523.
———. *De Insulis Nuper Inventis Ferdinandi Cortesii ad Carolum V. Rom. Imperatorem Narrationes....* Cologne: Birckmann, 1532.
———. *Les coutrees des iles et des paysages, trouves et conquis par le capitaine.* Anvers, 1522.

————. *Praeclara Ferdinandi. Cortesii de Nova Maris Oceani Hyspania Narratio Sacratissimo. ac Invictissimo Carolo Romanorum Imperatori.* . . . Nuremberg: Peypus, 1524.

Crescenzi, Pietro de. *Liber ruralium commodium.* Speyer: Peter Drach, 1493.

Das Wiener Heiligthumbuch. Vienna: M. Heuperger, 1502.

Der krieg zwischen dem groszmechtigen propheten Sophi/ Turcken vnnd dem Sol- dan/ alle die ding die do geschehen seyndt in auffgang der sonnen rc. hat kundt gethan ein Christen Kauffman wonend zu Alexandria/ vnserm aller heiligsten vater dem Babst Im iar. 1517.

Der Schatz vom Heiligen Berg-Andechs. Munich: Kloster Andechs, 1967.

Dernschwam, Hans. *Hans Dernschwams Tagebuch.* Ed. Franz Babinger. Studien zur Fugger-Geschichte, 7. Munich: Duncker & Humblot, 1923.

Des Turcken Erschreckliche belagerung / vnd Abschiedt der Stat Wien. 1529 [1529].

Des Turckischen Keysers Heerzug vnd vörnem widder die Christen. Erfurt: 1531.

Deutsche Reichstagsakten. Ed. Adolf Wrede. 2nd se. Jüngere Reihe. Vols. 2–4: 1520/21; 1522/23; 1523/24. Gotha: Perthes, 1900–1905.

Díaz del Castillo, Bernal. *Historia verdadera de la conquista de la Nueva España.* Edited by Miguel Leon-Portilla. Madrid: Historia 16, 1985.

Die abschrifft auß dem Original so der Turck sampt dem könig von Cathey vnd Persien allen Christlichen stenden des Römischen Reychs geschryben haben. [Nuremberg]: Friedrich Peypus, 1526.

Die belägerung der Stat Wien Osterreich/ von dem aller grausamesten Tyrannen vnd verderber der Christenhait dem Turckischen Kayser/ genandt Sultan Soli- mayn/ Nemlich beschehen/ im Monat Septembris des Newvndzwayntzigsten [1529].

Die Chroniken der deutschen Städte vom 14. bis ins 16. Jahrhundert. Vol. 3. Leipzig: S. Hirzel, 1864. Reprint, Göttingen: Vandenhoeck and Ruprecht, 1961.

Die Chroniken der deutschen Städte vom 14. bis ins 16. Jahrhundert. Vol. 11. Leipzig: S. Hirzel, 1874.

Die Kunstsammlung des Paulus Praun: Die Inventare von 1616 und 1719. Edited by Stadtarchiv Nürnberg. Quellen zur Geschichte und Kultur der Stadt Nürnberg 25. Nuremberg: Verlag des Stadtrats zu Nürnberg, 1994.

Die Ritterlich und lobwürdig reiß des gestrengen vnd über all ander weyt erfar- nen Ritters vnd landtfarers/ herren Ludowico Vartomans von Bolonia. Sagend von den landen / Egypto/ Syria/ von beiden Arabia Persia/ India vnd Ethiopia/ von den gestalten / sitten/ vnd dero menschen leben vnd glauben. Auch von manigerley thieren/ vöglen vnd vil andern in den selben landen seltzamen wun- derbarlichen sachen. Das alles er selbs erfaren vnd in eygner person gesehen hat. Strasbourg: Joannes Knoblock, 1516.

Die Stend des hailegen Römischen Reichs/ mit sampt aller Churfürsten und Fürsten gaistlichen und weltlichen mit iren Titeln/ und geschikten Potschafftn/ so zu Augsburg in der Kayserlichen Raichstatt. Augsburg: [Silvan Otmar], 1518.

Dise figur anzaigt vns das volck und insel. . . . Augsburg, 1505.

Diss Hernachgetrucktes wirdig Heyltum: ist funden worden / Im hohen altar im Thumbezu Trier [1512].

Doesborch, Jan van. *De Novo Mondo*. Facsimile, edited by M.E. Kronenberg. The Hague: Martinus Nijhoff, 1927.

Duca de Albische Pardon. *Welches ist/ Ein General oder allgemeine gnad und verzeihung/ so die Königlich Maiestat auß Hispanien in disem 1570 Jar hat lassen Publicieren und außruffen/ belangend die empörung/ so sich in nechst vergangen jaren in Niderlanden zugetragen rc. Auß Frantzösischer Sprach trewlich verdeutscht*. 1570.

Dürer, Albrecht. *Schriftlicher Nachlass*. Edited by Hans Rupprich. Vol. 1. Berlin: Deutscher Verein für Kunstwissenschaft, 1956.

Edelmayer, Friedrich, ed. *Die Korrespondenz der Kaiser mit ihren Gesandten in Spanien*. Vol. 1. Vienna: Verlag für Geschichte und Politik, 1997.

Eder, Georg. *Catechismus Catholicus qui antea quidem ex decreto Concilii Tridentini*, ... Cologne: Gervins Calenius, 1569.

―――. *Evangelische Inquisition wahrer und falscher Religion*. 1574.

"Ehrenpforte des Kaisers Maximilian I." *Jahrbuch der Kunsthistorischen Sammlungen des Allerhöchsten Kaiserhauses*. Sonderband IV. 1883.

Ein außzug ettlicher sendbrieff dem durchleüchtigisten großmechtigisten Fürsten und Herren Herren Carl römischen und Hyspanischen König rc. unserm gndedigen hern durch ire verordent Hauptleut/ von wegen einer newgefunden Inseln/ derselben gelegenheit und inwonder sitten und gewonheit inhatend vor kurtvershinen tagen zugesandt. ... [Peypus: Nuremberg, 1520].

Ein kurtz Christenlich vnterricht des grossen irrthumbs/ so im heiligthüm zü eren gehalten/ das dan nach gemainem gebrauch der abgötterey gantz gleich ist. D. Jacobus Strauß zu Eysenach in Doringen Ecclesia stes. [Erfürt: Michael Büchführer] 1523.

Ein kurtzer bericht vber die recht warhafftig Contrafactur/ Türckischer belegerung der Stat Wien/ wie dieselbig anzusehen vnd zuuersteen sey/ welche zu rhüm/ preyß/ lob vnd eer gantzem Römiscchem Reich/ Gemeyner Ritterschafft/ vnd in sonderheyt einem Erbern Rath der statt Nürmberg/ durch Niclaus Meldeman yetzt verfertigt/ getrückt vnd außgangen ist. [1529].

Ein missif oder sendbrieff newer zeytung/ betreffendt ein fryd/ zwysschen dem Allerdurchleuchtigisten großmechtigisten Fürsten vnnd herrn/ herrn Ferdinandus Röm. Kö. rc. vnnd dem Türckyschen Keyser / Außgangen zu Cracaw/ di 18. May. 1533 jar. gar schön vnd kurtzweylig zu lesen. Newe zeyttyng von einer wunderbarlichen Insel/ welche yetz durch des Königs von Portugals Schyffart ist gefunden worden. 1533. jar. [1533].

Ein newe Zeitung/ wie des Künigs auß Portugals Schiffleut eynen grossen mann haben zü wegen bracht/ heißt Christian groß India/ wie er sich vermähelt hat/ mit eyner Junckfrawen/ die Christenheyt Europa genant/ würdt sein leyb mit seynen glidern im anfang schimpfflich beschriben/ aber zü letst Christenlich außgelegt. Auch wie die Junckfraw die Christenheyt Europa im werde kinder geberen/ vnd inn eyner kurtzen zeyt auff wachssen/ vnd im helffen kriegen wider den Türcken vnd alle vnglaubigen. [1546].

Ein schöne Newe zeytung so Kayserlich Mayestet auß India yetz nemlich zu(o)kommen seind. Gar hüpsch von den Newen ynseln/ vnd von yrem sytten gar kurtzweylig züleesen. [Augsburg: Melchior Ramminger] 1522.

Ein Sermon von der Abgötterey/ durch den Pawern/ der weder schreyben noch lesen kan. 1524.

Ein Summari der Türckischen Botschafft werbung/ an die Herrschafft zu Venedig/ in Welscher sprach beschehen/ sampt des Venedischen Senats gegeben antwort.

Copia eins brieffs dem Cardinal von Neapolis zugeschickt/ inhaltend die anzal der Türckischen Armada vnd kriegßvolcks zu roß vnd fu(o)ß wider Italien. [Nuremberg: Johann. Petreius] 1537.

Ein warhafftiger tractat wie man das hochwirdig heiligthüm verkündt und geweist in der heiligen stadt Trier im thün.... [1512].

Einhard. *Annales Regvm Francorvm, Pipini, Carlomagni, et Lodovici....* Cologne, 1561.

———. *Annales Regvm Francorvm, Pipini, Carlomagni, et Lodovici....* Cologne, 1562.

———. *Vita et gesta Caroli magni.* Cologne, 1521.

"Einritt Ferdinand I." *Anzeiger für Kunde der deutschen Vorzeit* 16 (1869):161–2.

Erasmus, Desiderius. *Collected Works of Erasmus*, vol. 64. Toronto: University of Toronto Press, 2005.

———. *Dulce bellum inexpertis* [1515 ed.]. Opera Omnia 2:7. Amsterdam: Elsevier, 1999.

———. *Vltissima consvltatio de bello tvrcis inferendo, et obiter enarratvs Psalmvs XXVIII.* Opera Omnia 5:3. North Holland: Elsevier, 1986.

Eyn sermon gepredigt vom Pawren zu Werdt// bey Nürmberg/ am Sonntag vor Faßnacht/ von dem freyen willen des mennschen/auch von anrüffung der hailigen. 1524.

Faber, Felix. *Eigentliche beschreibung der hin vnnd wider farth zu dem Heyligen Landt gen Jerusalem vnd furter durch die grosse Wüsteneyzu demHeiligen Berge Horeb Sinay/....* [1556].

Faber, Johannes. *Opera.* Cologne: Quentell, 1537–9.

Federmann, Nicolas. *Indianische Historia.* Hagenau: Sigmund Bund, 1557.

Fernández Alvarez, Manuel, ed. *Corpus Documental de Carlos V.* 5 vols. Salamanca: Universidad de Salamanca, 1973–1981.

Fernández de Oviedo y Valdés, Gonzalo. *Historia general y natural de las Indias*, vol. 3. Madrid: Real Academia de la Historia, 1855.

———. *Libro de Camara Real del Principe Don Juan e Offiçios de su Casa e serviçio ordinario.* Madrid: Sociedad de Bibliófilos Españoles, 1870.

Ficino, Marsilio. *Liber de cristiana religione* [Florence: Nicolaus Laurentius Alamus, 1476].

Fickler, Johann-Baptista. *Anderer und Dritter Theil.* Ingolstadt: David Sartorius, 1585.

———. *Censur oder Urtheil.* Ingoldstadt: David Sartorius, 1583.

———. *Historische Erzehlungen....* Munich: Adam Berg, 1592.

———. *Literae Sultani Sulemanni Turcarum Imp. Missae Constantinopoli ad Ferd....* Passau: [1563].

———. *Replica wider das ander uberhaufft/ falsch/....* Munich: Adam Berg, 1592.

———. *Rettung der Concilien Catholischen Glaubens...* Ingolstadt: Wolfgang Eder, 1590.

———. *Spongia Contra Praedicantum.* Ingolstadt: David Sartorius, 1585.

———. *Theologia Juridica.* Dillingen: Sebaldus Mayer, 1575.

Foglietta, Huberto. *Vida de Don Alvaro de Sande.* Madrid: 1962.

Fontana, Domenico. *Della Trasportatione.* Rome: Domenico Basa, 1590.

Förstemann, Carl Eduard. *Neues Urkundenbuch zur Geschichte der evangelischen Kirchen-Reformation.* 1841. Reprint, Hildesheim: Georg Olms, 1976.

Foulché-Delbosc, R. "Memoria de Francisco Nuñez Muley." *Revue Hispanique* 6 (1899): 204–39.

Franck, Sebastian. *Auß Rathschlage Herren Erasmi von Roterdam/ die Türcken zubekriegen....* [Egenolff, 1531].

———. *Chronica unnd Beschreibung.* Augsburg: Steiner, 1530.

———. *Chronica unnd Beschreibung.* 2nd ed. Augsburg: Steiner, 1530.

———. *Chronica unnd Beschreibung.* 3rd ed. Augsburg: Steiner, 1531.

———. *Chronica unnd Beschreibung der Türckey mit eyner vorrhed d. Martini Lutheri.* 1530. Facsimile in *Chronica unnd Beschreibung der Türckey,* ed. Carl Göllner, 1–106. Schriften zur Landeskunde Siebenbürgens 6. Vienna: Böhlau, 1983.

———. *Chronica, Zeytbuch vnd geschychtbibel.* Strasbourg: Beck, 1531.

———. *Germaniae Chronicon.* Augsburg: Weissenhorn and Steiner, 1538.

———. "Von dem Bawm deß wißens güts und böses" (Ulm, 1534). *Sämtliche Werke: Kritische Ausgabe mit Kommentar,* vol. 4. Bern: P. Lang, 1992.

———. *Weltbuch.* Tübingen: 1534.

Franckfurter ankunfft/ oder verzaichnuß aller Potentaten/ Chur vnd Fürsten/ Gaistlichen vnd Weltlichen/ Bischofen/ Prelaten/ Thummherrn/ Grafen/ Freyherrn/ dero von der Ritterschafft/ Bottschafften vnd Stenden/ Doctorn vnd Geleerten etc.... die auff der Röm. Kün. May. Waal vnd Krönung zu Franckfurt am Mayn personlich erschinen vnd gewesen seind. Augsburg: Ulhart [1562/1563].

Frauenholz, Eugen von. ed. *Des Lazarus von Schwendi. Denkschrift über die politische lage des Deutschen Reiches von 1574.* Munich: Beck, 1939.

Fricius, Valentinus. *Yndianischer Religionstandt der gantzen newen Welt/ beider Indien gegen Auff und Nidergang der Sonnen.* Ingolstadt: Wolfgang Eder, 1587.

Fries, Laurentius. *Underweisung vnd vßlegunge der Cartha Marina oder die mercarten/ darm man sehen mag/ wa einer in der welt sy/ vnd wa ein ytlich land/ wasser vnd stet ligen/ als in den büchlin angezögt vnd in der charten züsehen.* Strasbourg: Grüninger, 1530.

———. *Uslegung der mercarthen oder Cartha Marina Darin man sehen mag/ wo einer in der wellt sey/ vnd wo ein yetlich Landt/ Wasser vnd Stadt gelegen ist. Das alles in dem büchlin züfinden.* Strasbourg: Grüninger, 1527.

Fuchs, Laurentius. *Kurtze Beschreibung der Königlichen Wirden und Magistrat Ampt.* 1563.

———. *Kurtzer vnnd klarer Unterricht/ von des Türkischen Tyrannen Gewalt/ Namen vnd Lendern/ Vnnd wie die Gegenwehre wider den Türcken/ Christlich sol fürgenomen werden.* Dresden: M. Stöckel, 1567.

Garrad, K. "The Original Memorial of Don Francisco Núñez Muley." *Atlante* 2 (1954): 199–226.

Gasca, Pedro de la. *Descripción del Perú*. Reprint, edited by Josep M. Barnadas. Cuzco: CBC, 1998.

Gattinara, Mercurino Arborio di. "Historia vite et gestorum per dominum magnum cancellarium." Edited by Carlo Bornate. *Miscellanea di storia italiana* 48, 3rd ser. 17 (1915): 231–585.

Gaudier, Johann. *Chronica oder Acta von der Türckischen Tyrannen herkommen/ vnd gefu'rten kriegen/ aus Türckischer Sprachen vordeutschet. Vorhin nie in Druck ausgangen*. Frankfort an der Oder: Johan Eichorn, 1567.

Geiler von Kaysersberg, Johann. *Die Emeis*. Strasbourg: Johann Grüninger, 1516.

Geisberg, Max. *The German Single-Leaf Woodcut, 1500–1550*. Revised and edited by Walter Strauss. New York: Hacker Books, 1974.

Gengenbach, Pamphilus. *Diss ist ein iemerliche clag uber die Todtenfresser*. Augsburg: Steiner, 1522.

Georgijević, Bartholomeus. *Pro Fide Christiana cum Turca Disputationis habitae*. Vienna: Haeredes Syngreniis, 1548.

————. *Türckey Oder Von yetziger Türcken kirchen gepräng*. [Basel: Cratander, 1545] Translated by Johannes Herold. Facsimile in *Chronica unnd Beschreibung der Türckey*, edited by Carl Göllner, 165–228. Schriften zur Landeskunde Siebenbürgens, vol. 6. Vienna: Böhlau, 1983.

Georgius de Hungaria. *Arithmeticae summa tripartita* [1499], Facsimile, edited by A.J.E.M. Smeur. Nieuwkoop: B. de Graaf, 1965.

————. *Tractatus de moribus, condicionibus et nequicia turcorum*. Edited by Reinhard Klockow. Schriften zur Landeskunde Siebenbürgens 15. Vienna: Böhlau, 1993.

Geschichts beschreybung/ Unsers aller gnedigist[.] Herrn/ des Rö. Kayser Carls des fünfften Belehnung umb das Hochloblich Ertzherzogthum Osterreich/... durch Kai/ Mai. Brüder/ Künig Ferdinand... [1530].

Gesner, Konrad. *Conradi Gesneri medici Tigurini historiae animalium Lib. I de quadrupedibus viviparis*. Zürich: Christoph Froschauer, 1551.

————. *Thierbuch*. Translated by Conrad Forer. Zürich: Christoph Froschauer, 1563.

Gevay, Antal von, ed. *Urkunden und Actenstücke zur Geschichte der Verhältnisse zwischen Österreich, Ungern und der Pforte im XVI. und XVII. Jahrhunderte*. Vols. I-III. Vienna, 1838–1842.

Giovio, Paolo. *Historiarum sui temporis libri. Opera*, vols. 4–5. Rome: Poligrafico dello Stato. 1985.

Gois, Damião de. *Fides, Religio, Mores que Aethiopum sub Imperio Preciosi Ioannis (quem vulgo Presbyterum Ioannem vocant)*. Louvain: Rutger Rescius, 1540. Reprint Lyon: Tornaesius und Gazeius, 1561.

Grynaeus, Simon. *Novus orbis regionum ac insularum veteribus incognitarum*. Paris: Jehan Petit, 1532.

Gutfleisch, Barbara and Joachim Menzhausen. "'How a Kunstkammer should be Formed': Gabriel Kaltemarckt's advice to Christian I of Saxony on the formation of an art collection, 1587." *Journal of the History of Collections* 1 (1989): 3–32.

Habersack, Hans. *Die Krönungen Maximilians II. zum König von Böhmen, Römischen König und König von Ungern (1562/63) nach der Beschreibung des Hans Habersack, ediert nach CVP 7890.* Edited by Friedrich Edelmayer, Leopold Kammerhofer, Martin C. Mandlmayr, Walter Prenner, and Karl Vocelka. *FRA,* I:13. Vienna: Österreichische Akademie der Wissenschaften, 1990.

Habitus Praecipuorum Populorum, Tam Virorum Quam foeminarum Singulari arte depicti. Trachtenbuch: Darin fast allerley und der fürnembsten Nationen/ die heutigs tag bekandt sein/ Kleidungen/ beyde wie es bey Manns und Weibspersonen gebreuchlich/ mit allem vleiß abgerissen sein/ sehre lustig und kurtzweilig zusehen. Nuremberg: Hans Weigel, 1577.

Haimliche Anschleg/ vnd fürnemung des Türckischen Kaysers (wann er Rodis eroberte) wider die Cristen vnd Christliche Lender rc. Vnd anders mer durch die gefangen Türcken so von M öran gen Görtz gefürt / Newlich bekant vnd gegeoffenbart worden.rc. Augsburg: Haynrich Stayner, 1523.

Henry, Avril. *Biblia Pauperum. A Facsimile and Edition.* Ithaca: Cornell University Press, 1987.

Herberstein, Sigmund Freiherr von. *Selbst-Biographie Siegmvnds Freiherrn von Heberstein.* Ed. Theodor von Karajan. *FRA,* I:1. Vienna, 1860.

Hernach volgt des Blüthundts/ der sych nennedt ein Türckischen Keiser/ gethaten / so er vnd die seinen/ nach eroberung der schlacht/ auff den xxviii. tag Augusti nechstuergangen geschehen/ an vnsern mitbrüdern der Ungrischen lantschafften gantz unmenschlich triben hat/ und noh teglichs tüt. 1526.

Herr, Michael. *Die Newe Welt.* Strasbourg: Georg Ulrich von Andla, 1534.

Heyden, Adam and Nicolaus Heyden. *De Electione et Inauguratione Maximiliani Austrii II. Rom. Regis, Francofurti ad Moenum, Anno 1562.* Frankfurt a. M.: Georg Raab, Sigismund Feyerabend, the heirs of Wygand Gallus, 1563.

Huszthi, Georg. "Descriptio peregrinationis." *Starine* 13 (1881): 1–38.

In disem puechlein ist verzaichent das hochwirdig heyligtum so man In der loblichen stat Wienn.... [Vienna: Joh. Winterburger, 1502].

In disem puchlein stet vertzeichet das hochwirdig heiltum ... zu Bamberg. Nuremberg: Hans Mair, 1493.

In dißem büchlin würt vil wirdigs heyltumbs so üm sant Mathiis zü Trier. [1513].

Jonas, Justus. *Das siebend Capitel Danielis, von des Türcken Gottes lesterung vnd schrecklicher morderey....* Wittenberg, [1530].

————. *Vrsprung des Turkischen Reichs/ bis auff den itzigen Solyman/ durch D. Paulum Jouium/ Bischoff Nucerin an Keiserliche Maistat/ Carolum V ... /* [1538].

Keyserlicher Maiestat eroberung des Königreychs Thunisi.... Nuremberg, 1535.

Kirchmair, Georg. *Georg Kirchmair's Denkwürdigkeiten seiner Zeit (1519–1553). FRA,* I: 1. Vienna, 1860.

Klarwill, Victor, ed. *Fugger-Zeitungen.* Vienna: Rikola, 1923.

Knaust, Heinrich. *Von geringem herkommen/ schentlichem leben/ ... Machomets / und seiner verdamlichen vnd Gotßlesterischen Ler.* 1542.

Köbel, Jakob. *Dialogus libertatis ecclesiastice defensorius cum Imperatorum sanctionibus.* Oppenheim, 1516.

———. *Glaubliche Offenbarung/ wie vil fürtreffenlicher Reych vnd Kayserthumb auff erdtrich gewesen/ wa das Römisch Reich herkomm/ ayß was ursach es zü den Edeln Teutschen verändert wordenn sey. Auch von der Erwölung/ Salbung/ Weyhung/ Crönung rc. Eins Römischen Kunigs vnd Kaisers/ vnd von andern Kaiserlichen herrlichaiten/ vnnd ordenungen/ findestu inn disem bu'chlein zü eeren dem großmechtigsten Carolo dem fünfften Röm. Kay. angezaygt.* Augsburg: Steiner, 1532.

Konetzke, Richard. *Colección de documentos para la historia de la formación social de Hispano-América 1493–1810.* Madrid: CSIC, 1953.

Krása, Miloslav, Josef Polišensky, and Peter Ratkoš, ed. *The Voyages of Discovery in the Bratislava Manuscript Lyc. 515/8 (Codex Bratislavensis).* Prague: Charles University, 1986.

Krönung Königlicher Maiestat/ welche volpracht ist zu Ach am eylfften tag Januarii ymm M.D.xxxi. [1531].

Kuripešic, Benedict. *Itinerarivm Wegrayß Kün. May. potschafft/ gen Constantinopel/ zu(o)dem Türckischen keiser Soleyman. Anno XXX.* 1531.

Kymeus, Johannes. *Des Bapsts Hercules/ wider die Deutdschen.* Wittenberg: Georg Rhaw, 1538.

———. *Ein Alt Christlich Concilium fur zwelff hundert jaren zu Gangra . . . wider die hoch genante heiligkeit der Mönchen vnd Widerteuffer.* Wittenberg: Klug, 1537.

La conquista del Peru, llamada la nueva Castilla. Seville: 1534.

La tryumphante Entree de Charles Prince des Espagnes en Bruges 1515. Facsimile with introduction by Sydney Anglo. New York: Johnson, 1973.

Lanz, Karl, ed. *Correspondenz des Kaisers Karl V. Aus dem königlichen Archiv und der Bibliotheque de Bourgogne zu Brüssel.* 3 vols. Leipzig, 1844–1846. Reprint, Frankfurt a. M.: Minerva, 1966.

Lanzinner, Maximilian. "Die Denkschrift des Lazarus Schwendi zur Reichspolitik." *Zeitschrift für historische Forschung.* suppl. 3 (1987): 141–85.

Las Casas, Bartolomé de. *Apologética Historia Sumaria*, Obras Completas, vols. 6–8. Madrid: Alianza Editorial, 1992.

Leunclavius, Joannes. *Annales Sultanorum Othmanidarum.* Frankfurt a. M.: Wechel, 1587.

Libro Primero de Cabildos de Lima. Vol. 3: Documentos. Lima, 1888.

Lichtenberger, Johannes. *Prognosticatio.* Ulm, 1488.

Lockhart, James, ed. and trans. *We People Here: Nahuatl Accounts of the Conquest of Mexico.* Repertorium Columbianum 1. Berkeley: University of California Press, 1993.

López de Gómara, Francisco. *Annales del Emperador Carlos Quinto.* Edited by R.B. Merriman. Oxford: Clarendon Press, 1912.

———. *La istoria de la conquista de Mexico.* Zaragoza, 1552.

Lubenau, Reinhold. *Beschreibung der reisen des Reinhold Lubenau.* Ed. W. Sahm. Königsburg I. Pr.: Beyer, 1912–20.

Luther, Martin. *D. Martin Luthers Werke. Kritische Gesamtausgabe.* Abt. 1: Werke. Weimar: Böhlau, 1883–1920. Reprint, Graz: Akademische Druck-u. Verlagsanstalt, 1966.

———. *D. Martin Luthers Werke. Kritische Gesamtausgabe.* Abt. 4 Briefwechsel Weimar: Böhlau, 1930–85.

Maur, Hartmann. *Coronatio Invictissimi Caroli Hispanarum Regis Catholici in Romanorum Regem.* Nuremberg: Friedrich Peypus, 1523.

Meditations on the Life of Christ. Translated by Isa Ragusa and Rosalie B. Green. Princeton: Princeton University Press, 1961.

Michelant, M. "Inventaire des vaisselles, joyaux, tapisseries, peintures, manuscrits, etc., de Margurerite d'Autriche ... 9 juillet 1523" *Compte Rendu des Séances de la Commission Royale d'Histoire* 3rd series 12 (1871): 5–78, 83–136.

Mihailović, Konstantin. *Memoirs of a Jannissary.* Translated by Benjamin Stolz, Michigan Slavic Translations, no. 3. Ann Arbor: University of Michigan, 1975.

Molanus, Johannes. *De picturis et imaginibus sacris.* Louvain: Hieronymus Wellaeus, 1570.

Morávek, Jan, ed. *Nově Objevený Inventář Rudolfinských Sbírek Na Hradě Pražském.* Prague, 1937.

Müller, Heinrich. *Türkisch Historien. Von der Türcken Ankunfft, Regierung, Königen vnd Keysern, Kriegen ... vnd Sigen, wider Cristen vnd Heiden....* Frankfurt a. M., 1563.

Müllner, Johannes. *Die Annalen der Reichstadt Nürnberg von 1623.* Edited by Gerhard Hirschmann. Nuremberg: Verlag des Stadtrats zu Nürnberg, 1984.

———. *Die Annalen der Reichstadt Nürnberg von 1623.* Part III. Edited by Michael Diefenbacher. Nuremberg: Verlag des Stadtarchiv Nürnberg, 2003.

Muñoz Camargo, Diego. *Descripción de la ciudad y provincia de Tlaxcala.* Relaciones Geográficas del Siglo XVI: Tlaxcala vol.1. Ed. René Acuña. Mexico: Universidad Autonoma de Mexico, 1986.

Münster, Sebastian. *Cosmographei oder beschreibung....* Basel: Heinrich Petri, 1550. Facsimile, Amsterdam: Theatrum Orbis Terrarum, 1968.

———. *Cosmographiae universalis Lib. VI....* Basel: Heinrich Petri, 1550.

Münzer, Hieronymus. *Viaje por España y Portugal en los años 1494 y 1495.* Trans. Julio Puyol. Madrid: 1924.

Murr, Christoph Gottlieb von. *Beschreibung der vornehmsten Merkwürdigen in des H. R. Reichs freyen Stadt Nürnberg und auf der hohen Schule zu Altdorf.* Nuremberg: Johann Eberhard, 1778.

Nausea, Friedrich. *Friderici Nauseae Blancicampiani, ... Evangelicae veritatis Homiliarum Centurae tres, nuper excusae.* Cologne: Peter Quentell, 1532.

———. *Friderici Nauseae Blancicampiani, Sacra Theologiae & L. L. Imp. p. doctoris, in clytae Viennensis ecclesiae coadiutoris ... [Homilies].* Cologne: Peter Quentell, 1540.

Navagero, Andrea. *Viaje a España de Magnifico Señor Andres Navagero (1524–1526). Embajador de la Republica de Venecia ante el Emperador Carlos V.* Translated by Jose Maria Alonso Gamo. Valencia: Castalia, 1951.

Nehring, Karl, ed. *Austro-Turcica, 1541–1552.* Südosteuropäische Arbeiten 95. Munich: Oldenbourg, 1995.

Neue zeitung auß Hispania.... [Nuremberg: Geyßler, 1561].

New zeytung auß Ungern des datum stehet zu Wienn am andern tag des Weynmonats M.D.xxvii. [1527].

New zeytung. Die Schlacht des Turckischen Kesers mit Ludovico etwan König zu Ungern geschehen am tag Johannis entheuptung. Item des Türcken feyndtsbrieff/ König Ludouico zugesandt vor der schlacht. Item eyn kleglicher Sendbrieff so die Vngern dem König im Polen zugeschickt/ nach der schlacht. Item etzlich naw getzeyten aus Polen. New zeytung vom Babst zu Rome am xxvii. tag Septembris geschehen. 1526.

Newe zeittung vnnd gründtliche Beschreibung/ Von des Türckischen Keysers absterben/ vnnd des Newen ankunfft. . . . 1575.

Newe zeittung. von demlande. das die Sponier funden haben ym 1521. iare genant Iucantan. Newe zeittung von Prußla/ von Kay: Ma: hofe. 18 Martze. 1522.

Newe zceyt von des Turcken halben von Offen geschrieben. [Erfurt: Michael Maler, 1522].

Newe zeyttung aus Polen/ von wunderlichen geschichten/ ynn Polen Vngern vnd Behemen/ auch von andern landen. Newe zeytung von Rom Venedig vnd Frantzosen. [1527].

Newe Zeyttung von dem Tyrannen des Türckischen Keysers Haubtman. . . . [1542].

Newe Zeyttung von Kayserlicher maiestat/ von dem Türcken/ und von dem grossen Sophi/ rc. Auß Venedig gen Augspurg geschriben. 1535.

Newe Zeyttung Welcher massem römishe Kayserliche Mayestat/ im jüngstvershynen monatt Junio/ von Sardinia auß gehen Aphrican geschifft. 1535.

Newe Zeytung Aus dem Niderlandt. Auss Rom. Aus Neapolis. Auss der Newenstat Auß Oesterreych. 1523.

Newe Zeytung aus Hispanien vnd Italien. Mense Februario. 1534. [Nuremberg: Petreius, 1534].

Newe zeytung von Keyserlicher Mayestat/ vnd von Künig von Franckreych/ Auch von vil andern Fürsten vnd Steten Welscher vnd Teütscher Nation/ geschehen im Jar. M.D.XXviii. Von der Schatzung die Keyserliche Mayestat gefordert oder angeleget hat alle seyner Geystligkeyt. Schatzung des Künigs von Franckreych aller Geystligkeyt. Newe zeyttung von Graff Hans Weyda auß Hungern/ hat ein grosse legation durch.XXVI. die er bey sich gehabt hat/ an den Türcken gesandt/ vnd des Türcken antwort darneben/ geschehen zu(o) Betaw im Jar M.D.XXviii. Newe zeyttung vom Hertzog von Gellern/ vnnd Bischoff von Uterich/ Geschehen am.xix. tag des monats May/ im Jar M.D.XXviii. [Nuremberg]: Georg Wachter 1528.

Nicholas of Cusa, Nicolai de Cusa opera omnia: iussu et auctoritate Academiae Litterarum Heidelbergensis ad codicum fidem edita. Leipzig, Hamburg: Felix Meiner, 1932–.

Nicolas of Herborn. Epitome de inventis nuper Indiae populis idololatris ad fidem Christi, atque adeo Ecclesiam Catholicam convertendis. Cologne: Birckmann, 1532.

Nola, Ruberto de. Libro de cozina. Toledo: Ramon de Petras, 1525.

Nouvelles certaines des Isles du Peru. Lyon, 1534. Translated by Raul Porras Barrenechea, Las Relaciones Primitivas de la Conquista del Peru. Lima: 1967.

Nuntiaturberichte aus Deutschland, 1533–1559. I, supplement 2. Tübingen: Niemeyer, 1969.

Nuntiaturberichte aus Deutschland, 1560–1572. II/3. Vienna: Carl Gerold's sohn, 1903.

Nürnberg, Jörg von. *Ayn Tractat von den Türck*. Facsimile in *Chronica unnd Beschreibung der Türckey*, ed. Carl Göllner, 107–200. Schriften zur Landeskunde Siebenbürgens 6. Vienna: Böhlau, 1983.

Osiander, Andreas. "Ain einfürung in den passion, in der karwochen durch den prediger zü sant Lorentzen in Nürnberg gepredigt, 1524." *Gesamtausgabe*. Vol. 1: Schriften und Briefe 1522 bis März 1525. Edited by Gerhard Müller. Gütersloh: Gerd Mohn, 1975.

Paleotti, Gabriele. *De imaginis sacris et profanis*. . . . Ingolstadt: Sartorius, 1594.

Pedro de Gante. "Epistola alia eiusdem argumenti." In *Chronica compendiosissima ab exordio mundi*, 124–7. Antwerp: Simon Cock, 1534.

Peter Martyr of Anghiera. *De novo orbe*. Alcala de Henares: Eguia, 1530.

———. *De nuper sub d. Carolo repertis insulis,* . . . Basel, 1521.

———. *De orbe novo decades*. Alcala: Arnaldus Guillelmus, 1516.

———. *De rebus et insulis noviter repertisa sereniss. Carolo Imperatore,* . . . Nuremberg: Friedrich Peypus, 1524.

———. *Opera*. 1530. Facsimile, Graz: Akademische Drucke, 1966.

Petz, Hans. "Urkunden und Regesten aus dem königlichen Kreisarchiv zu Nürnberg." *JKSW* 10 (1889): xx–lxii.

Pius II, *Historia rerum ubique gestarum*. Venice: Colonia et Manthen, 1477.

Prouinciae sive regiones in India occidentali. . . . [1520].

Ptolemaeus. *Cosmographia*. Ulm, 1482. Facsimile, edited by R.A. Skelton. Amsterdam: Meridian, 1963.

Puga, Vasco de. *Provisiones, cedulas, instrucciones de su Magestad, ordenancas de difuntos y audiencia*. [Mexico: Pedro Ocharte, 1563].

Quiccheberg, Samuel. *Inscriptiones, vel tituli theatri amplissimi*. Munich: 1565.

Recueil de la diversité des habits qui sont de present en usaige tant es pays d'Europem Asie, Affrique et Illes Sauvages. Paris: Richard Breton, 1562.

Relacion muy verdadera del alto recibimiento, que la ciudad de Burgos hizo. . . [Valladolid: Bernardino de Santo Domingo, 1572].

Relacion verdadera, del recebimiento, que la muy noble y muy mas leal ciudad de Burgos . . . 1572.

Román y Zamora, Hieronymo. *Republicas del mundo divididas in XXVII. libros*. Medina del Campo: Francisco del Canto, 1575.

———. *Republicas del mundo. Divididas en tres partes*. Salamanca, 1595.

Römischer Keyserlicher Maiestat Christenlichste Kriegs Rüstung wider die vnglaubigen/ anzug in Hispanien vnd Sardinien/ Ankunfft in Africa/ vnd eroberung des Ports zu Thunisi im monat junio Anno 1535. Aus Teutschen/ Italianischen vnd Frantzosichen schrifften vnd abtrucken fleissig ausgezogen.

Römischer Küniglicher Maiestat Krönung zu Ach geschehen. Augsburg: Grimm und Wirsung, 1520.

Sachs, Hans. *Werke*. Edited by A. v. Keller and E. Goetze. Vols. 22–23. Hildesheim: Georg Olms: 1964.

Sahagún, Bernardino de. *Relacion de la conquista de esta Nueva España, como la contaron los soldados indios que se hallaron presentes* [1585]. Edited by S.L. Cline. Salt Lake City: University of Utah Press, 1989.

Salinas, Martin de. *El emperador Carlos V y su corte segun las cartas de Don Martin de Salinas, embajador del infante Don Fernando (1522–1539)*. Edited by Antonio Rodríguez Villa. Madrid: Fortanet, 1903.

Sánchez Cantón, F. J., ed. *Inventarios Reales: Bienes Muebles que Pertenecieron a Felipe II*, 2 vols. Real Academia de la Historia: Archivo Documental Español 10–11. Madrid: 1956–9.

Sandoval, Prudencio de. *Historia de la Vida y Hechos del Emperador Carlos V.* BAE 81. Madrid, 1955.

Santa Cruz, Alonso de. *Crónica del Emperador Carlos V.* 5 vols. Madrid: Patronato de Huérfanos de Intendencia é Intervención Militares, 1920–25.

Saville, Marshall H., "The Earliest Notices Concerning the Conquest of Mexico by Cortés in 1519," *Indian Notes and Monographs* IX. New York: Museum of the American Indian, 1919–1920.

Schaendlinger, Anton C. *Osmanisch-Türkische Dokumente aus dem Haus-, Hof- und Staatsarchiv zu Wien*, Teil 1. Wien: Österreichischen Akademie der Wissenschaften, 1983.

Schedel, Hartmann. *Liber chronicum*. Nuremberg: Koberger, 1493.

Schiltberger, Hans. *Hans Schiltbergers Reisebuch: nach der Nürnberger Handschrift*. Ed. Valentin Langmantel. Tübingen: Litterarischer Verein in Stuttgart, 1885.

Schramm, Albert. *Der Bilderschmuck der Frühdrucke*. Leipzig: K. W. Hiersemann, 1920–43.

Schroeder, H. J., ed. *Canons and Decrees of the Council of Trent*. B. Herder: St. Louis, 1941.

Schweigger, Salomon. *Ein Newe Reyssbeschreibung auss Teutschland nach Constantinopel und Jerusalem* (Nuremberg: Johann Lantzenberger, 1608). Facsimile, Graz: Akademische Druck u. Verlagsanstalt, 1964.

Schweyger, Franz. *Chronik der Stadt Hall 1303–1572*. Edited by David Schönherr. Tirolische Geschichtsquellen I. Innsbruck: Wagner, 1867.

Spandounes, Theodore. *Der Türcken heymligkeyt*. Bamberg: Erlinger, 1523.

———. *On the origin of the Ottoman Emperors* (1538). Edited and translated by Donald M. Nicol. Cambridge: Cambridge University Press, 1997.

Staden, Hans. *Warhaftig/ Historia und Beschreibung eyner Landt-/schafft der Wilden Nacketen Grimmigen Menschfressen*. Marburg, 1557.

Strauß, Jacob. *Ein kurtz Christenlich vnterricht des grossen irrthumbs/ so im heiligthüm zü eren gehalten/ das dan nach gemainem gebrauch der abgötterey gantz gleich ist*. Erfurt: Michael Büchführer, 1523.

Strauss, Walter L., ed. *The Book of Hours of Maximilian I*. New York: Abaris Books, 1974.

Tamara, Francisco. *El libro de las costumbres de todas las gentes del mundo, y de las Indias*. Antwerp: Martin Nucio, 1556.

Thevet, Andre. *La Cosmographie universelle*. Paris: Pierre Huillier, 1575.

Torre, Antonio de la, ed. *Testamentaría de Isabel la Católica*. Valladolid: 1968.

Translation uss hispanischer sprach zu Frantzösisch gemacht/ so durch den Vice Rey in Neapols/ Fraw Margareten Hertzoginn inn Burgundi zu geschriben. [Basel: Pamphilus Gengenbach, 1523].

Triumph und Frewdenfest, zu Ehren dem Heiligen Ertzengel Michael.... Munich, 1597.

Türckenbiechlin, Ain Nutzlich Gesprech oder Underrede etlicher personen [1522]. Facsimile in *Chronica unnd Beschreibung der Türckey,* ed. Carl Göllner, 121–164. Schriften zur Landeskunde Siebenbürgens, vol. 6. Vienna: Böhlau, 1983.

Uff dem Rychstag zu Worms gehalten sind in eygner personen gewesen. Speyer: Schmidt, 1521.

Ulloa, Alfonso. *Vita del potentissimo e christianiss. Imperatore Ferdinando Primo.* Venice: Camillo and Francesco Franceschini, 1565.

Unterkircher, Franz. ed. "Hieremias Gundlach: Nova Hispaniae Regnorum Descriptio." *JKSW* 56 (1960): 166–96.

Urban of Gurk. *Gaistliche Kriegsrüstung/ Das ist/ Christliche Buss vnnd Trostpredigen.* Vienna: Caspar Stainhofer, 1567.

Valdés, Alfonso de. *Diálogo de Mercurio y Carón* (1528). Reprint, Madrid: Cátedra, 1999.

―――. *Diálogo de las cosas ocurridas en Roma* [1528]. Reprint, Madrid, 1928.

Varthema, Lodovico. *Die ritterlich un[d] lobwirdig Rayss.* Augsburg: Hans Miller, 1515. Facsimile, edited by George Winius. New York: John Carter Brown Library, 1992.

Velenus, Ulrich. *In hoc libello gravissimis... probatur Apostolum Petrum non venisse... Romam.* [Basel: Cratander, 1520].

Vergil, Polydore. *De inventoribus rerum.* 1499.

Vergil, Polydore. *On Discovery.* Edited by Brian Copenhaver [1521 and 1525]. Cambridge, MA: Harvard University Press, 2002.

Vier warhafftige Missiven/ eine der frawen Isabella Königin vnd nachgelassene wittib in Ungern/ wie untrewlich der Türck vnd die iren mit ir vmbgangen. Die ander/ eines so in der belegerung bey der Konigin im Schloß gewest/ wie es mit Ofen/ vor und nach der belegerung ergangen. Die dritte/ eines Ungern von Gran/ wie es yetz zu Ofen zugehe. Die vierdte / des Türckischen Tyrannen an die Sibenbürter. [Nuremberg: Johann vom Berg and Ulrich Neüber, 1542].

Vincent of Beauvais, *Speculum historiale.* Strasbourg: 1473.

Vital, Laurent. "La relation du voyage de Charles-Quint en Espagne." In *Collection des Voyages des Souverains des Pays-Bas,* ed. Gachard and Piot, 1–303. Vol. 3. Brussels: Hayez, 1881.

Vitoria, Francisco de. *Relectio de Indis.* Ed. L. Pereña and J.M. Perez Prendes. Corpus Hispanorum De Pace, 5. Madrid: CSIC, 1967.

Voltelini, Hans von, ed. "Urkunden und Regesten aus dem k. u. k. Haus-Hof- und Staats-Archiv in Wien." *JKSW* 11 (1890): i-lxxxiii.

―――. "Urkunden und Regesten aus dem k. u. k. Haus-, Hof- und Staats-Archiv in Wien." *JKSW* 13 (1892): xxvi–clxxiv

―――. "Urkunden und Regesten aus dem k. u. k. Haus-, Hof- und Staats-Archiv in Wien." *JKSW* 15 (1894): xlix–clxxix.

―――. "Urkunden und Regesten aus dem k.u.k. Haus-, Hof- und Staats-Archiv in Wien." *JKSW* 20 (1899): i–cxxiv.

Vrsprung des Turkischen Reichs/ bis auff den itzigen Solyman/ durch D. Paulum Jouium/ Bischoff Nucerin an Keiserliche Maistat/ Carolum V. . . / Verdeutschet durch Justus Jonam. [1538].

Wagner, Hanns. *Kurtze doch gegründet beschreibung des Durchleuchtigen Hochgebornnen Fursten unnd Herren/ Herren Wilhalmen. . . Und derselben geliebten Gemahel/ der D. H. Furstin/ Frewlein Renata gebornne Hertzogin zu Lottringen. . . gehalten Hochzeitlichen Ehren Fests. . . in der Furstlichen Haubtstat Muenchen gehalten worden sein/ den zwenundzwaintzigsten und nachvolgende tag Februarii Im 1568. jar.* Munich: Adam Berg, 1568.

Wagner, Henry R. ed. and trans. "Documents: Three Accounts of the Expedition of Fernando Cortés, printed in Germany Between 1520 and 1522." *HAHR* 9 (1929): 176–212.

Warhafftig anzaygung wie Kaiser Carl der fünft ettlichen Fürsten auff dem Reychstag zü Augspurg im M.CCCC.XXX jar gehalten/ Regalia und Lehen under dem fan gelihen. . . . [1530].

Warhafftige Beschreibung/ welcher gestalt die königkliche wirde Maximilian/ vnd Frewlin Maria/ geborne Königin auß Hispanien/ dero Gemahel / zü Böhemischen König vnd Königin in Prag den 20. Septembris/ dieses 1562. jars gekrönet worden. . . Auch Ebrahim Strotschen/ deß Türckischen Keysers Bottschafft. . . . Frankfurt a. M.: Georg Raab, Sigmund Feyerabend, Weygand Hanen Erben, 1563.

Warhafftige newe zeitung von dem Tuercken/ welliche eyn gefangner Türck zü Wien/ auff die fragsstuck/ so hierinn begriffen gantwort. 1532.

Warhafftige vnnd kurtze bericht Inn der Summa/ wie es ietzo/ im Tausent Funff hundert vnd Siben vnd zayntzigsten jar Den vi. tag May/ durch Römischer Kayserlicher/ vnnd Hispanischer Küniglicher Mayestet kriegs volck/ In eroberunng der Stat Rom ergangen ist/ biß auff den xxi. tage Junii. [1527].

Warhafftigen Neuwe Zeytung / aus dem Vngerlandt vnd Türckey ins Deutsch Landt geschrieben/ aus dem Latein inn Deutsche sprach verdolmetscht. 1546.

Warhafftyge und aigentliche verzaichnüs der Allerdurchleichtigisten großmechtigisten unnserer aller gndedigsten herrn Kayser Karls des fünfften/ sambt seiner Kayser. Maiestat Brueders Künig Ferdinanden rc. Wegnemen. . . Election des Roe. Künigs. . . unnd die Croenung zü Aach. . . . [Vienna: Singriener, 1531].

Wegrayß / Keyserlicher Maiestat Legation / im.32.jar zü dem Türcken geschickt / wie und was gestalt / sie hinein / vnd widerumb herauß /komen ist / warhafftigklich / von denen die mit vnd bey gewest / in schrifft verfasset. 1532.

Weiditz, Christoph. *Das Trachtenbuch des Christoph Weiditz von seinen Reisen nach Spanien (1529) und den Niederlanden (1531/32).* Berlin: Walter de Gruyter, 1927.

Weinsberg, Hermann. *Das Buch Weinsberg. Kölner Denkwürdigkeiten aus dem 16. Jahrhundert.* Vols. 1–2. Leipzig: Alphons Dürr, 1886–7.

Wie das hochwirdigist Auch kaiserlich heiligthum/ Vnd die grossen Römischen gnad darzu gegeben. Alle Jaer außgeruefft vnd geweist wirdt/ In der löblichen statt Nüremberg. Nuremberg: P. Vischer, 1487.

Wie das hochwirdigist Auch keiserlich heiligthum/ Und die grossenn Romischen genad darzubegen ist und Alle Jare ausz gerufft vnd geweisst wirt/ In der loblichen stat Nüremberg. Nuremberg: Hans Mair, 1493.

Wie der Türkisch Tyrann Soleyman/ der itzung regiert/ seinen eltesten Son Mustapha.... Wittenberg, 1556.

Winzinger, Franz. ed. *Die Miniaturen zum Triumphzug kaiser Maximilians I.* Facsimile, Graz: Akademische, Druck 1972.

Wölcher gstalt Künigklicher Maiestet zu Hungern vnnd Behem bottschafftenn/ nemlich Herr Sigmund Weyxelberger/ vnd ein Hungerischer Herr/ zü dem Türckischen Kayser an vnd ankommen sind/ souil vngefärlich auß vergeben- licher sag erhalten worden ist. [Nuremberg: Kunigunde Hergot], 1529.

Wünsch, Josef, ed. *Der Einzug Kaiser Maximilians II in Wien 1563.* Vienna: Brzezowsky, 1914.

Wyngaert, Anastasius Van Den, ed. *Itinera et relationes Fratrum Minorum.* Sinica Franciscana, 1:3–130. Quaracchi, Florence: Collegium S. Bonaventura, 1929.

Xérez, Francisco de. *Verdadera relacion de la conquista del Peru.* Seville: B. Perez, 1534.

Zarco Cuevas, Julián, ed. *Inventario de las alhajas, pinturas y objetos... donados por Felipe II al Monasterio de El Escorial (1571–1598).* Madrid: 1930.

Zimerman, Heinrich, ed. "Urkunden, Acten und Regesten aus dem Archiv des k. k. Ministeriums des Innern." *JKSW* 7 (1888): i–lxxxiv.

_____. "Urkunden und Regesten aus dem k. u. k. Haus-, Hof- und Staats-Archiv in Wien," *JKSW* 3 (1885): xciii–cxxiii.

Zimmerman, Heinrich, ed. "Das Inventar der Prager Schatz- und Kunstkammer vom 6. Dezember 1621," *JKSW* 25 (1905): xiii–li.

(Z)weintzig Glauben oder Secten. Frankfurt: Christian Egenolff, 1532.

(Z)weintzig Glauben oder Secten. 2nd ed. Frankfurt: Christian Egenolff, 1534.

Zwingli, Huldrych, *De vera et falsa religione commentarius [1525], Sämtliche Werke* 3. Leipzig: Heinsius, 1916.

Secondary Sources

Abun-Nasr, Jamil M. *A History of the Maghrib in the Islamic Period.* Cambridge: Cambridge University Press, 1987.

Ackermann, Hans Christoph. "The Basle Cabinets of Art and Curiosities in the Sixteenth and Seventeenth Centuries." In *The Origins of Museums*, ed. O. Impey and A. MacGregor, 62–68.

Ács, Pál. "Tarjumans Mahmud and Murad: Austrian and Hungarian Renegades as Sultan's Interpreters." In *Europa und die Türken in der Renaissance*, ed. B. Guthmüller and W. Kühlmann, 307–16. Tübingen: Niemeyer, 2000.

Adams, Robert P. *The Better Part of Valor.* Seattle: University of Washington Press, 1962.

Adamson, John, ed. *The Princely Courts of Europe.* London: Weidenfeld and Nicolson, 1999.

Adorno, Rolena. "Censorship and Its Evasion: Jerónimo Román and Bartolomé de las Casas." *Hispania* 75 (1992): 814–827.

Ágoston, Gabor. "Information, Ideology, and Limits of Imperial Policy: Ottoman Grand Strategy in the Context of Ottoman-Habsburg Rivalry." In *The Early Modern Ottomans: Remapping the Empire*, 75–103. Cambridge: Cambridge University Press, 2007.

Allgemeine Deutsche Biographie. Edited by the Historische Kommission der Bayerischen Akademie der Wissenschaften. 56 vols. Leipzig: Duncker & Humblot, 1875–1912.

Altfahrt, Margit. "Die politische Propaganda für Maximilian II." *Mitteilungen des Instituts für Österreichische Geschichtsforschung* 88 (1980): 283–312; 89 (1981): 53–92.

Álvarez Nogal, Carlos. "El Conde de Moctezuma en el reino de Granada." In *El Reino de Granada y el Nuevo Mundo*, 106–116. Vol II. Granada: Diputación Provincial de Granada, 1994.

Anders, Ferdinand. "Der Federkasten der Ambraser Kunstkammer." *JKSW* 61 n.s. 25 (1965): 119–132.

Appadurai, Arjun. "Introduction: Commodities and the Politics of Value." In *The Social Life of Things*, ed. Arjun Appadurai, 3–63. Cambridge: Cambridge University Press, 1986.

Aram, Bethany. *Juana the Mad: Sovereignty and Dynasty in Renaissance Europe*. Baltimore: Johns Hopkins University Press, 2005.

Arbel, Benjamin. *Trading Nations: Jews and Venetians in the Early Modern Eastern Mediterranean*. Leiden: Brill, 1995.

Asad, Talal. "Pain and Truth in Medieval Christian Ritual." In *Genealogies of Religion*. Baltimore: Johns Hopkins University Press, 1993.

Asch, Ronald, ed. *Princes, Patronage, and the Nobility*. London: Oxford University Press for the Historical Institute, 1991.

Aulinger, Rosemarie. *Das Bild des Reichstages im 16. Jahrhundert*. Schriftenreihe der Historischen Kommission bei der Bayerischen Akademie der Wissenschaften 18. Göttingen: Vandenhoeck & Ruprecht, 1980.

Babinger, Franz. "'Bajezid Osman' (Calixtus Ottomanus), ein Vorläufer und Gegenspieler Dschem-Sultans." *La Nouvelle Clio* 3 (1951): 349–388.

———. *Mehmed the Conqueror and His Time*. Translated by Ralph Manheim. Princeton: Princeton University Press, 1978.

Bak, János. "The Late Medieval Period, 1382–1526." In *A History of Hungary*, ed. Peter F. Sugar, 54–82. Bloomington: Indiana University Press, 1990.

Bataillon, Marcel. *Erasmoo y España*. Translated by Antonio Alatorre. Mexico: Fondo de Cultura Económica, 1950.

———. "Hernán Cortés, Autor Prohibido." In *Libro Jubilar de Alfonso Reyes*, 77–82. Mexico City: Dirección General de Difusión Cultural, 1956.

Bate, Heidi Eberhardt. "Portrait and Pageantry: New Idioms in the Interaction Between City and Empire in Sixteenth-Century Nuremberg." In *Politics and Reformations: Communities, Polities, Nations, and Empires*, ed. Christopher Ocker et al., 121–41. Leiden: Brill, 2007.

Baudot, Georges. *Utopia and History in Mexico*. Niwot: University Press of Colorado, 1995.

Bauer, Rotraud. "The Coronation Mantle." In *The Secular and Ecclesiastical Treasures*. Guide to the Collections of the Kunsthistorische Museum, no. 35, 136–49. Vienna: Kunsthistorisches Museum, 1991.

Baxandall, Michael. *The Limewood Sculptors of Renaissance Germany*. New Haven: Yale University Press, 1980.

Bayerle, Gustav. "The Compromise at Zsitvatorok." *Archivum Ottomanorum* VI (1980): 5–29.

_____. *Ottoman Diplomacy in Hungary*. Uralic & Altaic Series, Vol. 101. Bloomington: Indiana University Press, 1972.

_____. "Turco-Hungarian Duels: Comments on a Letter of Ibrahim Agha from 1589." *Journal of Popular Culture* 16 (Summer 1982): 117–25.

Bayly, C.A. *Empire and Information*. Cambridge: Cambridge University Press, 1997.

Bedini, Silvio. "The Papal Pachyderms." *Proceedings of the American Philosophical Society* 125 (1981): 75–90.

Belting, Hans. *Likeness and Presence*. Chicago: University of Chicago Press, 1994.

Berggruen, J. Lennart and Alexander Jones, *Ptolemy's Geography*. Princeton: Princeton University Press, 2000.

Bennassar, Bartholomé and Lucile Bennassar. *Les Chrétiens d'Allah*. Paris: Perrin, 1989.

Bernhart, Max. *Die Bildnismedaillen Karls des Fünften*. Munich: Otto Helbing, 1919.

Bernheimer, Richard. *Wild Men in the Middle Ages: A Study in Art, Sentiment, and Demonology*. Cambridge: Harvard University Press, 1952.

Berschin, Walter. *Greek Letters and the Latin Middle Ages: From Jerome to Nicholas of Cusa*. Rev. ed. Translated by Jerold C. Frakes. Washington DC: Catholic University of America Press, 1988.

Bertelli, Sergio. *The King's Body: Sacred Rituals of Power in Medieval and Early Modern Europe*. Translated by R. B. Litchfield. University Park: Pennsylvania State University Press, 2001.

Bibl, Viktor. "Zur Frage der religiösen Haltung Kaiser Maximilians II." *AÖG* 106 (1918): 289–425.

Biechler, James. "A New Face toward Islam." In *Nicholas of Cusa in Search of God and Wisdom*, ed. G. Christianson and T. Izbicki, 185–202.

Biegman, N.H. "Ragusan Spying for the Ottoman Empire." *Belleten* 27 (1963): 237–239.

_____. *The Turco-Ragusan Relationship*. The Hague: Mouton, 1967.

Birnbaum, Marianna D. *Humanists in a Shattered World: Croatian and Hungarian Latinity in the Sixteenth Century*. UCLA Slavic Studies, Vol. 15. Columbus: Slavica, 1985.

Bisaha, Nancy. *Creating East and West: Renaissance Humanists and the Ottoman Turks*. Philadelphia: University of Pennsylvania Press, 2004.

Bobinger, Maximilian. *Kunstuhrmacher in Alt-Augsburg*. Abhandlungen zur Geschichte der Stadt Augsburg, Bd. 18. Augsburg: Hans Rösler, 1969.

Bobzin, Hartmut. *Der Koran im Zeitalter der Reformation*. Stuttgart: Steiner, 1995.

_____. "'A Treasury of Heresies': Christian Polemics against the Koran." In *The Qur'an as Text*, ed. Stefan Wild, 157–75. Leiden: Brill, 1996.

Bohnstedt, John W. *The Infidel Scourge of God: the Turkish Menace as Seen by German Pamphleteers of the Reformation Era*. Transactions of the American Philosophical Society n.s. 58/9. Philadelphia: American Philosophical Society, 1968.

Borah, Woodrow. "The Cortés Codex of Vienna and the Emperor Ferdinand I." *The Americas* 19 (1962): 79–92.

Bosbach, Franz. "The European Debate on Universal Monarchy." In *Theories of Empire, 1450–1850,* ed. David Armitage, 81–98. Aldershot: Ashgate, 1998.

———. *Monarchia Universalis: Ein Politischer Leitbegriff der Frühen Neuzeit.* Göttingen: Vandenhoeck & Ruprecht, 1988.

Bouwsma, William. *Venice and the Defense of Republican Liberty.* Berkeley: University of California Press, 1968.

Boxer, C.R. "Portuguese and Spanish Projects for the Conquest of Southeast Asia, 1580–1600." *Journal of Asian History* 3 (1968): 118–136.

Bracewell, Catherine W. *The Uskoks of Senj: Piracy, Banditry, and Holy War in the Sixteenth-Century Adriatic.* Ithaca: Cornell University Press, 1992.

Brading, D.A. *The First America: The Spanish Monarchy, Creole Patriots, and the Liberal State, 1492–1867.* Cambridge: Cambridge University Press, 1991.

Brady, Thomas A., Jr. *Turning Swiss: Cities and Empire, 1450–1550.* Cambridge: Cambridge University Press, 1985.

Brandi, Karl. *Kaiser Karl V.* Munich: F. Bruckmann, 1937.

Braudel, Fernand. *The Mediterranean and the Mediterranean World in the Age of Philip II.* Translated by Sian Reynolds. New York: Harper Torchbooks, 1976.

Braunfels, Wolfgang. "'Cuius Regio Eius Ars.'" In *Wittelsbach und Bayern,* ed. Hubert Gläser, II/1: 133–40.

Brodrick, James. *Robert Bellarmine.* Westminster: The Newman Press, 1961.

Brubaker, Leslie. "The Elephant and the Ark." *Dumbarton Oaks Papers* 58 (2004): 175–95.

Brummett, Palmira. "The Myth of Shah Ismail Safavi: Political Rhetoric and 'Divine' Kingship." In *Medieval Christian Perceptions of Islam,* ed. John V. Tolan, 331–59. New York: Garland, 1996.

Buchanan, Harvey. "Luther and the Turks 1519–1529." *ARG* 47 (1956): 145–60.

Bukovinska, Beket. "The Kunstkammer of Rudolf II." In *Rudolf II and Prague: The Court and the City,* ed. Eliška Fučíková, 199–208. London: Thames and Hudson, 1997.

Burmeister, Karl Heinz. *Sebastian Münster.* Basel: von Helbing & Lichenhahn, 1969.

Burns, Robert I. "The Significance of the Frontier in the Middle Ages." In *Medieval Frontier Societies,* ed. Robert Bartlett and Angus MacKay, 307–30. Oxford: Oxford University Press, 1989.

Cabello, Paz. "Los Inventarios de Objetos Incas Pertenecientes a Carlos V." *Anales del Museo de América* 2 (1994): 33–61.

Camille, Michael. *The Gothic Idol: Ideology and Image-Making in Medieval Art.* Cambridge: Cambridge University Press, 1989.

Campbell, Mary. *The Witness and the Other World: Exotic European Travel Writing, 400–1600.* Ithaca: Cornell University Press, 1988.

Cassirer, Ernst. "Giovanni Pico della Mirandola: A Study in the History of Renaissance Ideas." *JHI* 3 (1942): 123–44, 319–46.

———. *The Individual and the Cosmos in Renaissance Philosophy* [1927]. Translated by Mario Domandi. Philadelphia: University of Pennsylvania Press, 1963.

Cave, Terence. "Panurge, Pathelin and Other Polyglots." In *Lapidary Inscriptions: Renaissance Essays for Donald A. Stone, Jr.*, ed. Barbara C. Bowen and Jerry Nash, 171–82. Lexington: French Forum, 1991.

Cervantes, Fernando. *The Devil in the New World*. New Haven: Yale University Press, 1994.

Checa Cremades, Fernando. *Carlos V y la imagen del héroe en el Renacimiento*. Madrid: Taurus, 1987.

———. *Felipe II, Mecenas de las Artes*. Madrid: Nerea, 1992.

Chmelarz, Eduard. "Die Ehrenpforte des Kaisers Maximilian I." *JKSW* 4 (1886): 289–319 and Sonderband IV.

Chrisman, Miriam. *Lay Culture, Learned Culture: Books and Social Change in Strasbourg, 1480–1599*. New Haven: Yale University Press, 1982.

Christensen, Carl C. "Iconoclasm and the Preservation of Ecclesiastical Art in Reformation Nuernberg." *ARG* 61 (1970): 205–21.

Christian, William, A. Jr. *Apparitions in Late Medieval and Renaissance Spain*. Princeton: Princeton University Press, 1981.

———. *Local Religion in Sixteenth-Century Spain*. Princeton: Princeton University Press, 1981.

Christianson, Gerald and Thomas Izbicki. *Nicholas of Cusa in Search of God and Wisdom*. Leiden: Brill, 1991.

Classen, Albrecht. "The World of the Turks Described by an Eye-Witness." *Journal of Early Modern History* 7 (2003): 257–79.

Clemen, D. "Introduction to 'Vorwart zu dem Libellus de ritu et moribus Turcorum'." *WA* 30(2). Weimar: Böhlau, 1909.

Cline, Howard. "Hernando Cortes and the Aztec Indians in Spain." *The Quarterly Journal of the Library of Congress* 26 (1969): 70–90.

Cline, S.L. *Colonial Culhuacan*. Albuquerque: University of New Mexico Press, 1986.

Cohrs, F. and A. Goetze. "Introduction to 'Heerpredigt wider den Türken'." *WA* 30(2): 149–59.

———. "Introduction to 'Vom Kriege wider die Türken'." *WA* 30(2): 81–106.

Coleman, David. *Creating Christian Granada: Society and Religious Culture in an Old-World Frontier City, 1492–1600*. Ithaca: Cornell University Press, 2003.

Colin, Susi. *Das Bild des Indianers in 16. Jahrhundert*. Beiträge zur Kunstgeschichte, 102. Idstein: Schulz-Kirchner Verlag, 1988.

Comaroff, Jean and John L. Comaroff. *Of Revelation and Revolution: Christianity, Colonialism, and Consciousness in South Africa*. Vol. 1. Chicago: University of Chicago Press, 1991.

Craven, William G. *Giovanni Pico della Mirandolla: Symbol of His Age*. Geneva: Droz, 1981.

Cuneo, Pia. *Art and Politics in Early Modern Germany*. Leiden: Brill, 1998.

Daston, Lorraine and Katharine Park. *Wonders and the Order of Nature*. New York: Zone Books, 1998.

Davis, Natalie Z. "Beyond the Market: Books as Gifts in Sixteenth-Century France." *Transactions of the Royal Historical Society* 5th ser., 33 (1983): 69–88.

de Certeau, Michel. *The Writing of History*. Translated by Tom Conley. New York: Columbia University Press, 1988.

Dejeung, Christoph. "Sebastian Franck." *Bibliotheca Dissidentium*, VII: 39–117. Baden-Baden: Valentin Koerner, 1986.

Dettenthaler, Josef. "Hans Springinklee als Maler." *MVGN* 63 (1976): 145–77.

Devisse, Jean and Michel Mollat. *The Image of the Black in Western Art*. Vol. 2:2. Translated by William Granger Ryan. Lausanne: Office du Livre, 1979.

Diener, Hermann. "Die Kamera Papagalli im Palast del Papstes: Papagaeien als Hausgenossen der Päpste, Könige und Fürsten des Mittelalters und der Renaissance." *AKG* 49 (1967): 43–97.

Dilger, Konrad. *Untersuchungen zur Geschichte des Osmanischen Hofzeremoniells im 15. und 16. Jahrhundert*. Beiträge zur Kenntnis Südosteuropas und des Nahen Orients, IV. Munich: Trofenik, 1967.

Dilke, O.A.W. and editors. "Cartography in the Byzantine Empire." In *A History of Cartography*, ed. J.B. Harley and David Woodward, 1:267–70. Chicago: University of Chicago Press, 1987.

Dodgson, Campbell. "A Woodcut Illustrating the Relics of the Holy Roman Empire." *The Burlington Magazine* 30 (1917): 96–8.

Domínguez Ortiz, Antonio and Bernard Vincent. *Historia de los moriscos: Vida y tragedia de una minoría*. Madrid: Revista de Occidente, 1978.

Dotzauer, Winfried. "Die Ausformung der frühneuzeitlichen deutschen Thronerhebung." *AKG* 68 (1986): 25–80.

Ducchardt, Heinz. *Protestantisches Kaisertum und Altes Reich*. Wiesbaden: Franz Steiner, 1977.

Duindam, Jeroen. "The Court of the Austrian Habsburgs c. 1500–1750." In *The Princely Courts of Europe*, ed. J. Adamson, 165–85, 328–9.

Dunbabin, Jean. "The Reception and Interpretation of Aristotle's *Politics*." In *The Cambridge History of Later Medieval Philosophy*, ed. N. Kretzmann, A. Kenny, and J. Pinborg, 723–37. Cambridge: Cambridge University Press, 1982.

Dursteler, Eric. *Venetians in Constantinople: Nation, Identity, and Coexistence in the Early Modern Mediterranean*. Baltimore: Johns Hopkins University Press, 2006.

Earle, T.F. and K.J.P. Lowe, ed. *Black Africans in Renaissance Europe*. Cambridge: Cambridge University Press, 2005.

Ecker, Heather. "The Great Mosque of Córdoba in the Twelfth and Thirteenth Centuries." *Muqarnas* 20 (2003): 113–41.

Edelmayer, Friedrich. *Hispania-Austria II : Die Epoche Philipps II (1556–1598)*. Munich: Oldenburg, 1999.

———. "Die Neue Welt in den Berichten der kaiserlichen Gesandten." In *1492–1992: Spanien, Österreich und Iberoamerika*, ed. Wolfram Krömer, 131–47.

Edwards, Jr., Mark U. *Luther's Last Battles*. Ithaca: Cornell University Press, 1983.

Eichberger, Dagmar. *Leben mit Kunst: Wirken Durch Kunst*. Turnhout: Brepols, 2002.

———. "Margaret of Austria's Portrait Collection: Female Patronage in the Light of Dynastic Ambitions and Artistic Quality." *Renaissance Studies* 10 (1996): 259–79.

Eichberger, Dagmar and Lisa Beaven. "Family Members and Political Allies." *Art Bulletin* 77 (1995): 225–48.

Eire, Carlos. *From Madrid to Purgatory: The Art and Craft of Dying in Sixteenth-Century Spain.* Cambridge: Cambridge University Press, 1995.

_____. *War against the Idols.* Cambridge: Cambridge University Press, 1986.

Elbl, Ivana. "Prestige Considerations and the Changing Interest of the Portuguese Crown in Sub-Saharan Atlantic Africa, 1444–1580." *Portuguese Studies Review* 10/2 (2002): 15–36.

Elliott, J.H. "Final Reflections: The Old World and the New Revisited." In *America in European Consciousness, 1493–1750*, ed. Karen, Kupperman 391–408.

_____. "The Mental World of Hernán Cortés." In *Spain and Its World, 1500–1700*, 27–41. New Haven: Yale University Press, 1989.

_____. *The Old World and the New, 1492–1650.* 1970. Reprint with a new preface, Cambridge: Cambridge University Press, 1992.

European Americana. Edited by John Alden. Vol. 1. New York: Readex, 1980.

Evans, R.J.W. *The Making of the Habsburg Monarchy, 1550–1700.* Oxford: Clarendon Press, 1979.

_____. *Rudolf II and His World.* Oxford: Oxford University Press, 1973.

Falk, Tilman. *Hans Burgkmair. Studien zu Leben und Werk des Augsburger Malers.* Munich: Bruckmann, 1968.

Feest, Christian. "The Collecting of American Indian Artifacts in Europe, 1493–1750." In *America in European Consciousness, 1493–1750*, ed. Karen Kupperman, 324–60.

_____. "Vienna's Mexican Treasures: Aztec, Mixtec, and Tarascan Works from 16th Century Austrian Collections." *Archiv für Völkerkunde* 44 (1990): 1–64.

Feil, Ernst. *Religio*, 2 vols. Göttingen: Vandenhoeck & Ruprecht, 1986–1997.

Ferguson, John and Elizabeth H. Alexander. "Notes on the Work of Polydore Vergil 'De Inventoribus Rerum'," *Isis* 17 (1932): 71–93.

Fernández-Santamaria, J.A. *The State, War and Peace: Spanish Political Thought in the Renaissance 1516–1559.* Cambridge: Cambridge University Press, 1977.

Fichtner, Paula Sutter. "The Disobedience of the Obedient: Ferdinand I and the Papacy 1555–1564." *SCJ* 11 (1980): 25–34.

_____. *Emperor Maximilian II.* New Haven: Yale University Press, 2001.

_____. *Ferdinand I of Austria: the Politics of Dynasticism in the Age of the Reformation.* Boulder: East European Monographs, 1982.

Fillitz, Hermann. "Die Weltliche Schatzkammer – Wien." In *Schatzkammern Europas: Weltliche Schatzkammern*, ed. Erich Steingräber. Munich: Hirmer, 1968.

Findlen, Paula. "The Museum: Its Classical Etymology and Renaissance Geneaology." *The Journal of the History of Collections* 1 (1989): 59–78.

_____. *Possessing Nature: Museums, Collecting, and Scientific Culture in Early Modern Europe.* Berkeley: University of California Press, 1994.

Finlay, Robert. "Prophecy and Politics in Istanbul." *Journal of Early Modern History* 2 (1998): 1–31.

Fischer-Galati, Stephen. *Ottoman Imperialism and German Protestantism: 1521–1555.* Cambridge, MA: Harvard University Press, 1959.

————. "Ottoman Imperialism and the Religious Peace of Nürnberg." *ARG* 47 (1956): 160–79.

Fleischer, Cornell. "Shadow of Shadows: Prophecy in Politics in 1530s Istanbul." *International Journal of Turkish Studies* 13 (2007): 51–62.

Fleischhauer, Werner. "Die Kunstkammer des Grafen Ulrich von Montfort zu Tettnang, 1574." *Ulm und Oberschwaben: Zeitschrift für Geschichte und Kunst* 44 (1982): 9–28.

Forell, George. "Luther and the War against the Turks." *Church History XIV* (1945): 256–71.

Foulche-Doelbosch, R. "Un point conteste de la vie de don Diego Hurtado de Mendoza." *Revue Hispanique* 2 (1895): 290–303.

Frank, Ross. "The Codex Cortés: Inscribing the Conquest of Mexico." *Dispositio* 14 (1989): 187–212.

Frankl, Viktor. "Die Begriffe des mexikanischen Kaisertums und der Weltmonarchie in den "Cartas de Relación" des Hernán Cortés." *Saeculum* 13 (1962): 1–34.

Freedberg, David. "Johannes Molanus on Provocative Paintings." *JWCI* 34 (1971): 229–45.

————. *The Power of Images.* Chicago: University of Chicago Press, 1989.

Freys, E. and H. Barge. "Verzeichnis der gedruckten Schriften des Andreas Bodenstein von Karlstadt." *Zentralblatt für Bibliothekswesen* 21 (1904): 153–79, 209–43, 305–23.

Friede, Juan. "Las Casas and Indigenism." In *Bartolomé de Las Casas in History: Towards an Understanding of the Man and his Work*, ed. Juan Friede and Benjamin Keen, 127–234. De Kalb: Northern Illinois University, 1971.

Friedman, David. *Florentine New Towns: Urban Design in the Late Middle Ages.* Cambridge, MA: MIT Press, 1988.

Friedman, Ellen. *Spanish Captives in North Africa in the Early Modern Age.* Madison: University of Wisconsin Press, 1983.

Frübis, Hildegard. *Die Wirklichkeit des Fremden: die Darstellung de Neuen Welt im 16. Jahrhundert.* Berlin: Reimer, 1995.

Fučíková, Eliška. "The Collection of Rudolf II at Prague." In *The Origins of Museums*, ed. O. Impey and A. MacGregor, 47–53.

Fulton, Elaine. *Catholic Belief and Survival in Late Sixteenth-Century Vienna.* Aldershot: Ashgate, 2007.

Garber, Josef. "Das Haller Heiltumbuch mit den Unika-Holzschnitten Hans Burgkmairs des Älteren." *JKSW* 32 (1915): i–clxxvii.

García-Arenal, Mercedes. *A Man of Three Worlds.* Baltimore: Johns Hopkins University Press, 2003.

García Arenal, Mercedes and Miguel Ángel de Bunes. *Los Españoles y el Norte de África, siglos XV–XVIII.* Madrid: MAPFRE, 1992.

Geary, Patrick. *Furta Sacra: Thefts of Relics in the Central Middle Ages.* Princeton: Princeton University Press, 1978.

Gennep, Arnold van. *The Rites of Passage.* Translated by Monika B. Vizedom and Gabrielle L. Caffee. Chicago: University of Chicago Press, 1960.

Gibson, Charles. *The Aztecs under Spanish Rule.* Stanford: Stanford University Press, 1964.

_____. *Tlaxcala in the Sixteenth Century*. New Haven: Yale University Press, 1952.

Giesecke, Michael. "Die typographische Konstruktion der,Neuen Welt'." In *Gutenberg und die Neue Welt*, ed. Horst Wenzel, 15–32. Munich: Wilhelm Fink, 1994.

Gläser, Hubert, ed. *Wittelsbach und Bayern*. Vol. II/1–2. Um Glauben und Reich: Kurfürst Maximilian I. Munich: Hirmer, 1980.

Göllner, Carl. *Turcica*. 3 vols. Bucarest and Berlin: Academy, 1961–78.

Goodman, David C. *Power and Penury: Government, Technology and Science in Philip II's Spain*. Cambridge: Cambridge University Press, 1988.

Goodrich, Thomas. *The Ottoman Turks and the New World: A study of Tarih-i Hind-i garbi and Sixteenth Century Ottoman Americana*. Wiesbaden: Harrassowitz, 1990.

Gosman, Martin, Alasdair Macdonald, and Arjo Vanderjagt, ed., *Princes and Princely Culture 1450–1650*. Leiden: Brill, 2005.

Göttler, Christine. "'Nomen mirificum'. Rubens' *Beschneidung Jesu* für den Hochaltar der Jesuitenkirche in Genua." *Zeitsprünge* 1/2 (1997): 796–844.

Gow, Andrew. *The Red Jews: Anti-Semitism in an Apocalyptic Age, 1200–1600*. Leiden: Brill, 1995.

Grafton, Anthony. "The Ancient City Restored." In *Rome Reborn*. Washington DC: Library of Congress, 1993.

_____. "The Availability of Ancient Works." In *The Cambridge History of Renaissance Philosophy*, ed. Charles B. Schmitt, Quentin Skinner, Eckhard Kessler. Cambridge: Cambridge University Press, 1988.

_____. *Joseph Scaliger*. Oxford: Oxford University Press, 1993.

_____. *New Worlds, Ancient Texts*. Cambridge, MA: Belknap Press, 1992.

Grasshoff, R. *Die briefliche Zeitung des XVI Jahrhunderts*. Leipzig: C.W. Vollrath, 1877.

Greenblatt, Stephen. *Marvelous Possessions: The Wonder of the New World*. Chicago: University of Chicago Press, 1991.

Gregory, Brad. *Salvation at Stake*. Cambridge, MA: Harvard University Press, 1999.

Griffin, Clive. *The Crombergers of Seville*. Oxford: Clarendon Press, 1988.

Grimm, Harold J. *Lazarus Spengler: A Lay Leader of the Reformation*. Columbus: Ohio State University Press, 1978.

Gröblacher, Johann. "König Maximilians I. erste Gesandtschaft zum Sultan Baijezid II." In *Festschrift Hermann Wiesflecker zum sechzigsten Geburtstag*, ed. Alexander Novotny, 73–80. Graz: Historische Institut der Universität Graz, 1973.

_____. "König Maximilians I. zweite Gesandtschaft zum Sultan Baijezid II." In *Domus Austriae: Eine Festgabe Hermann Wiesflecker zum siebzigsten Geburtstag*, ed. Walter Höflechner, Helmut Mezler-Andelberg, Othmar Pickl, 159–69. Graz: Akademische Druck, 1983.

Groebner, Valentin. *Liquid Assets, Dangerous Gifts: Presents and Politics at the End of the Middle Ages*. Translated by Pamela E. Selwyn. Philadelphia, University of Pennsylvania Press, 2002.

Habich, Georg, ed. *Deutschen Schaumünzen des XVI Jahrhunderts*. Munich: Bruckmann, 1929.

Hagenbach, Karl. "Luther und der Koran vor dem Rathe zu Basel." *Beiträge zur vaterländischen Geschichte* 9 (1870).

Hale, J.R. *Artists and Warfare in the Renaissance*. New Haven: Yale University Press, 1990.

————. "The Soldier in German Graphic Art of the Renaissance." *Journal of Interdisciplinary History* XVII (1986): 85–114.

Halperin, Charles J. "The Ideology of Silence: Prejudice and Pragmatism on the Medieval Religious Frontier." *CSSH* 26 (1984): 442–466.

Hampe Martínez, Teodoro. *Don Pedro de la Gasca. Su Obra Política en España y América*. Lima: Fondo Editorial de la Pontificia Universidad Católica del Perú, 1989.

Hampton, Timothy. "'Turkish Dogs': Rabelais, Erasmus, and the Rhetoric of Alterity." *Representations* 41 (1993): 58–82.

Hankins, James. *Plato in the Italian Renaissance*, vol. 1. Leiden: Brill, 1990.

Hans Burgkmair. 1473–1973. Das Graphische Werk. Stuttgart: Graphische Sammlung Staatsgalerie [1973].

Hartog, François. *The Mirror of Herodotus: The Representation of the Other in the Writing of History*. Translated by Janet Lloyd. Berkeley: University of California Press, 1988.

Haskell, Francis and Nicholas Penny. *Taste and the Antique*. New Haven: Yale University Press, 1981.

Hay, Denys. *Polydore Vergil, Renaissance Historian and Man of Letters*. Oxford: Clarendon Press, 1952.

Hayden-Roy, Patrick. *The Inner Word and the Outer World: A Biography of Sebastian Franck*. Renaissance and Baroque Studies and Texts 7. New York: Peter Lang, 1994.

Headley, John M. "Gattinara, Erasmus, and the Imperial Configurations of Humanism." *ARG* 71 (1980): 64–98.

————. "Geography and Empire in the Late Renaissance." *RQ* 53 (2000): 1119–55.

————. "Germany, the Empire and *Monarchia* in the Thought and Policy of Gattinara." In *Das römisch-deutsche Reich im politischen System Karls V*, ed. Heinrich Lutz, 15–30. Munich: Oldenburg, 1982.

————. "The Habsburg World Empire and the Revival of Ghibellinism." *Medieval and Renaissance Studies* 7 (1978): 93–127.

————. "Rhetoric and Reality: Messianic, Humanist, and Civilian Themes in the Imperial Ethos of Gattinara." In *Prophetic Rome in the High Renaissance Period*, ed. Marjorie Reeves, 241–69. Oxford: Clarendon Press, 1992.

————. *Tommaso Campanella and the Transformation of the World*. Princeton: Princeton University Press, 1997.

Heath, Michael J. *Crusading Commonplaces: La Noue, Lucinge and Rhetoric against the Turks*. Geneva: Droz, 1986.

————. "Erasmus and War against the Turks." In *Acta Conventus Neo-Latini Turonensis*, ed. Jean-Claude Margolin, 991–9. Paris: Vrin, 1980.

Hecht, Christian. *Katholische Bildertheologie im Zeitalter von Gegenreformation und Barock*. Berlin: Gebr. Mann, 1997.

Heikamp, Detlef. "Mexikanische Altertümer aus süddeutschen Kunstkammern." *Pantheon* 28 (1970), 205–20.

Hernad, Béatrice. *Die Graphiksammlung des Humanisten Hartmann Schedel*. Munich: Prestel, 1990.

Hess, Andrew C. *The Forgotten Frontier: a History of the Sixteenth-Century Ibero-African Frontier*. Chicago: University of Chicago Press, 1978.

———. "The Moriscos: An Ottoman Fifth Column in Sixteenth-century Spain." *American Historical Review* 74 (1968): 1–25.

Heyd, Uriel. "Moses Hamon, Chief Jewish Physician to Sultan Süleyman the Magnificent." *Oriens* 16 (1963): 152–70.

Himmelein, Volker. "Uhren und wissenschaftliche Instrumente." *Welt im Umbruch: Augsburg zwischen Renaissance und Barock*. Vol. 2, 55–7. Augsburg: Augsburger Druck- und Verlagshaus, 1980.

Hirsch, Elisabeth Feist. *Damião de Gois: The Life and Thought of a Portuguese Humanist, 1502–1574*. The Hague: Martinus Nijhoff, 1967.

Hodgen, Margaret T. *Early Anthropology in the Sixteenth and Seventeenth Centuries*. Philadelphia: University of Pennsylvania Press, 1964.

———. "Ethnology in 1500: Polydore Vergil's Collection of Customs." *Isis* 57 (1966): 315–24.

Hoffmann, Detlef. *Altdeutsche Spielkarten, 1500–1650*. Nuremberg: Verlag des Germanischen Nationalmuseums, 1993.

Hofmann, Christina. *Das Spanische Hofzeremoniell von 1500–1700*. Erlanger Historische Studien, 8. Frankfurt a.M.: Peter Lang, 1985.

Hoogvliet, Margriet. "The Medieval Texts of the 1486 Ptolemy Edition by Johann Reger of Ulm." *Imago Mundi* 54 (2002): 7–18.

Housley, Norman. "Frontier Societies and Crusading in the Late Middle Ages." In *Intercultural Contacts in the Medieval Mediterranean*, ed. Benjamin Arbel, 104–19. London: Frank Cass, 1996.

Hsia, R. Po-Chia. *The Myth of Ritual Murder: Jews and Magic in Reformation Germany*. New Haven: Yale University Press, 1988.

———. *Trent 1475*. New Haven: Yale University Press, 1992.

Huschenbett, Dietrich and John Margetts, ed. *Reisen und Welterfahrung in der deutschen Literatur des Mittelalters*. Würzburger Beiträge zur deutschen Philologie 7. Würzburg: Königshausen & Neumann, 1991.

Impey, Oliver and Arthur MacGregor, ed. *The Origins of Museums: the Cabinet of Curiosities in Sixteenth- and Seventeenth-Century Europe*. Oxford: Clarendon Press, 1985.

Israel, Jonathan I. *European Jewry in the Age of Mercantilism 1550–1750*. Rev. ed., Oxford: Oxford University Press, 1989.

———. *Race, Class and Politics in Colonial Mexico, 1610–1670*. London: Oxford University Press, 1975.

Iversen, Eric. *The Myth of Egypt and Its Hieroglyphs*. Princeton: Princeton University Press, 1993.

———. *Obelisks in Exile*, vol. 1. Copenhagen: Gad, 1968.

Izbicki, Thomas. "The Possibility of Dialogue with Islam in the Fifteenth Century." In *Nicholas of Cusa in Search of God and Wisdom*, 175–83.

Jacquot, Jean, ed. *Fêtes de la Renaissance*, 3 vols. Paris: Centre national de la recherche scientifique, 1956–75.

Jahns, Sigrid. "Frankfurt am Main im Zeitalter der Reformation (1500–1555)." In *Frankfurt am Main: die Geschichte der Stadt in neun Beiträgen*, ed. Frankfurter Historischen Kommission, 198–203. Sigmaringen: Thorbecke, 1991.

Jansen, Dirk. "The Instruments of Patronage. Jacopo Strada at the Court of Maximilian II: A Case-Study." In *Kaiser Maximilian II. Kultur und Politik im 16. Jahrhundert*, ed. Friedrich Edelmayer and Alfred Kohler, 182–202. Wiener Beiträge zur Geschichte der Neuzeit 19. Vienna: Verlag für Geschichte und Politik, 1992.

Jardine, Lisa. *Worldly Goods: A New History of the Renaissance*. New York: Doubleday, 1996.

Jedin, Hubert. *Geschichte des Konzils von Trent*, IV/2. Freiburg: Verlag Herder, 1975.

Johnson, Carina L. "Negotiating the Exotic: Aztec and Ottoman Culture in Habsburg Europe, 1500–1590." Ph.D. dissertation, University of California at Berkeley, 2000.

Johnson, Christine R. *The German Discovery of the World: Renaissance Encounters with the Strange and Marvelous*. Charlottesville: University of Virginia Press, 2008.

Jones, Pamela M. "Art Theory as Ideology: Gabriele Paleotti's Hierarchical Notion of Paintings' Universality and Reception." In *Reframing the Renaissance: Visual Culture in Europe and Latin America, 1450–1650*, ed. Claire Farago, 127–39. New Haven: Yale University Press, 1995.

Jorzick, Regine. *Herrschaftssymbolik und Staat*. Vienna: Verl. für Geschichte und Politik, 1998.

Jütte, Robert. "Contacts at the Bedside: Jewish Physicians and Their Christian Patients." In *In and Out of the Ghetto*, ed. R. Po-Chia Hsia and Hartmut Lehman, 137–50. Cambridge: Cambridge University Press, 1995.

Kafadar, Çemal. "A Death in Venice (1575): Anatolian Muslim Merchants Trading in the Serenissima." *Journal of Turkish Studies* 10 (1986): 191–218.

Kantorowicz, Ernst. *The King's Two Bodies: A Study in Medieval Political Theology*. Princeton: Princeton University Press, 1957.

Katalog der Sammlung für Plastik und Kunstgewerbe. Part II. Vienna: Kunsthistorisches Museum, 1966.

Kaufmann, Thomas DaCosta. "From Treasury to Museum: The Collections of the Austrian Habsburgs." In *The Cultures of Collecting*, ed. John Elsner and Roger Cardinal, 137–54. Cambridge, MA: Harvard University Press, 1994.

———. *Mastery of Nature*. Princeton: Princeton University Press, 1993.

———. *The School of Prague*. Chicago: University of Chicago Press, 1988.

Kedar, Benjamin Z. *Crusade and Mission: European Approaches toward the Muslims*. Princeton: Princeton University Press, 1984.

Keen, Benjamin. "The Legacy of Bartolomé de Las Casas." In *Essays in the Intellectual History of Colonial Latin America*. Boulder: Westview Press, 1998.

Keen, Maurice H. *The Laws of War in the Late Middle Ages*. London: Routledge & Kegan Paul, 1965.

Kellenbenz, Hermann. *Die Fugger in Spanien und Portugal bis 1560*. Munich: E. Vogel, 1990.

_____. "Wirtschaftsleben der Blütezeit." *Geschichte der Stadt Augsburg*, ed. Gunter Gottlieb et al., 258–301. Stuttgart: Konrad Theiss, 1984.

Kelley, Donald R. "'Second Nature': The Idea of Custom in European Law, Society, and Culture." In *The Transmission of Culture in Early Modern Europe*, ed. Anthony Grafton and Ann Blair, 131–72. Philadelphia: University of Pennsylvania Press, 1990.

Kemp, Martin. "'Wrought by No Artist's Hand': The Natural, the Artificial, the Exotic, and the Scientific in Some Artifacts from the Renaissance." In *Reframing the Renaissance: Visual Culture in Europe and Latin America, 1450–1650*, ed. Claire Farago, 177–96. New Haven: Yale University Press, 1995.

Keunecke, Hans-Otto. "Friedrich Peypus (1485–1535). Zu Leben und Werk des Nürnberger Bruchdruckers und Buchhändlers." *MVGN* 72 (1985): 1–65.

Kircher, Albrecht. *Deutsche Kaiser in Nürnberg: Eine Studie zur Geschichte des öffentlichen Lebens der Reichsstadt Nürnberg von 1500–1612*. Nuremberg: Verlag die Egge, 1955.

Kissling, H.J. "Das Renegantentum in der Glanzzeit des Osmanischen Reiches." *Scientia* 96 (1961): 18–26.

Kleinlogel, Cornelia. *Exotik-Erotik: Zur Geschichte des Türkenbildes in der deutschen Literatur der frühen Neuzeit (1453–1800)*. Bochumer Schriften zur deutschen Literatur 8. Frankfurt a. M.: Peter Lang, 1989.

Klingensmith, Samuel. *The Utility of Splendor*. Chicago: University of Chicago Press, 1993.

Knappe, Emil. "Die Geschichte zur Kulturgeschichte einer Stadt während der Türkenzeit." Ph.D. dissertation, University of Vienna, 1949.

Koerner, Joseph. *The Reformation of the Image*. Chicago: University of Chicago Press, 2004.

Kohl, Karl-Heinz, ed. *Mythen der Neuen Welt: Zur Entdeckungsgeschichte Lateinamerikas*. Berlin: Frolich and Kaufmann, 1982.

Kohler, Alfred. *Antihabsburgische Politik in der Epoche Karls V*. Göttingen: Vandenhoeck and Ruprecht, 1982.

Kohler, Alfred and Friedrich Edelmayer, ed. *Hispania-Austria*. Vienna: Verlag für Geschichte und Politik, 1993.

Kramml, Peter Franz. "Der Erste Elefant in Österreich (1552) und die Geschichte des Salzburger 'Elefantenhauses' in der Sigmund-Haffnergasse." *Salzburg Archiv* 4 (1987): 49–70.

Kretschmayr, Heinrich. "Ludovico Gritti." *AÖG* 83 (1897): 1–106.

Kris, Ernst, ed. *Goldschmiedearbeiten des Mittelalters, der Renaissance und des Barock*. Vol. 1. Vienna: Schroll, 1932.

Kristeller, Paul Oskar. *Eight Philosophers of the Italian Renaissance*. Stanford: Stanford University Press, 1964.

_____. *The Philosophy of Marsilio Ficino*. Translated by Virginia Conant. New York: Columbia University Press, 1943.

Krömer, Wolfram, ed. *1492–1992: Spanien, Österreich und Iberoamerika.* Innsbruck: Institut für Sprachwissenschaft der Universität Innsbruck, 1993.

———, ed. *Spanien und Österreich in der Renaissance.* Innsbruck: Institut für Sprachwissenschaft der Universität Innsbruck, 1989.

Krstić, Tijana. "Illuminated by the Light of Islam and the Glory of the Ottoman Sultanate: Self-Narratives of Conversion to Islam in the Age of Confessionalization." *CSSH* 51 (2009): 35–63.

Kuntz, Marion Leathers. *Venice, Myth and Utopian Thought in the Sixteenth Century.* Aldershot: Ashgate, 1999.

Kupperman, Karen Ordahl, ed. *America in European Consciousness, 1493–1750.* Chapel Hill: University of North Carolina Press, 1995.

Kurz, Otto. *European Clocks and Watches in the Near East.* London: The Warburg Institute, 1975.

Lach, Donald F. *Asia in the Making of Europe.* I:1. Chicago: University of Chicago Press, 1965.

———. "Asian Elephants in Renaissance Europe." *Journal of Asian History* 1 (1967): 133–76.

Lafaye, Jacques. *Quetzalcóatl and Guadalupe.* Chicago: University of Chicago Press, 1976.

Laferl, Christopher. *Die Kultur der Spanier in Österreich unter Ferdinand I. 1522–1564.* Vienna: Böhlau, 1997.

Landes, David S. *Revolution in Time: Clocks and the Making of the Modern World.* Cambridge, MA: Harvard University Press, 1983.

Laschitzer, Simon. "Die Heiligen aus der ,Sipp-, Mag- und Schwägerschaft' des Kaisers Maximilian I." *JKSW* 4 (1886): 70–288.

Lawrance, Jeremy. "Europe and the Turks in Spanish Literature of the Renaissance and Early Modern Period." *Culture and Society in Habsburg Spain,* ed. Nigel Griffin et al., 17–33. London: Tamesis, 2001.

———. "The Middle Indies: Damião de Góis on Prester John and the Ethiopians." *Renaissance Studies* 6 (1992): 306–24.

Lazure, Guy. "Possessing the Sacred: Monarchy and Identity in Philip II's Relic Collection at the Escorial." *RQ* 60 (2007): 58–93.

Lazzaro, Claudia. "Animals as Cultural Signs: A Medici Menagerie in the Grotto at Castello." In *Reframing the Renaissance: Visual Culture in Europe and Latin America, 1450–1650,* ed. Claire Farago, 197–228. New Haven: Yale University Press, 1995.

Lestringant, Frank. *Mapping of the Renaissance World.* Translated by David Fausett. Berkeley: University of California Press, 1994.

Lewis, Bernard. "The Privilege Granted by Mehmed II to His Physician." *Bulletin of the School of Oriental and African Studies* XIV 3 (1952): 550–63.

Leyser, Karl. "Frederick Barbarossa, Henry II and the Hand of St. James." In *Medieval Germany and its Neighbors 900–1250.* London: Hambledon Press, 1982.

———. "The Tenth Century in Byzantine-Western Relationships." In *Medieval Germany and Its Neighbors 900–1250.* London: Hambledon Press, 1982.

Lieb, Norbert. *Die Fugger und die Kunst.* Studien zur Fuggergeschichte 10, 14. Munich: Schnell & Steiner, 1952–8.

Lietzmann, Hilda. *Das Neugebäude in Wien.* Munich: Deutscher Kunstverlag, 1987.

Lindemann, Margot. *Nachrichtenübermittlung durch Kaufmannsbriefe. Brief- "Zeitungen" in der Korrespondenz Hildebrand Veckinchusens (1398–1428).* Dortmunder Beiträge zur Zeitungsforschung, 26. Munich: Dokumentation, 1978.

Lockhart, James. *The Nahuas after the Conquest.* Stanford: Stanford University Press, 1992.

Lopes Don, Patricia. "Carnivals, Triumphs, and Rain Gods in the New World." *Colonial Latin American Review* 6 (1997): 17–40.

López de Coca Castañer, José Enrique. "Institutions on the Castilian-Granadan Frontier 1369–1482." In *Medieval Frontier Societies,* ed. Robert Bartlett and Angus MacKay. Oxford: Oxford University Press, 1989.

Loredo, Rafael. *Bocetos para la Nueva Historia del Peru: Los Repartos.* Lima: D. Miranda, 1958.

Lotz, Wolfgang. "Sixteenth-Century Italian Squares." *Studies in Italian Renaissance Architecture.* Cambridge, MA: MIT Press, 1977.

Louthan, Howard. *The Quest for Compromise: Peace-Makers in Counter-Reformation Vienna.* Cambridge: Cambridge University Press, 1997.

Low, Setha. "Indigenous Architecture and the Spanish American Plaza in Mesoamerica and the Caribbean." *American Anthropologist* 97 (1995): 748–62.

Lowe, Kate. "'Representing' Africans: Ambassadors and Princes from Christian Africa to Renaissance Italy and Portugal, 1402–1608." *Transactions of the Royal Historical Society,* 6th ser., 17 (2007): 101–28.

Luttenberg, Albrecht. "Pracht und Ehre: Gesellschaftliche Repräsentation und Zeremoniell auf dem Reichstag." *Alltag im 16. Jahrhundert,* 291–326. Wiener Beiträge zur Geschichte der Neuzeit, vol. 14. Vienna: Verlag für Geschichte und Politik, 1987.

Lutz, Heinrich. *Conrad Peutinger. Beiträge zu einer Politischen Biographie.* Augsburg: Die Brigg, 1958.

Lyell, James. *Early Book Illustration in Spain.* London: Grafton & Co., 1926.

MacCormack, Sabine. "Limits of Understanding: Perceptions of Greco-Roman and Amerindian Paganism in Early Modern Europe." In *America in European Consciousness, 1493–1750,* ed. Karen Kupperman, 79–129.

––––––. *Religion in the Andes.* Princeton: Princeton University Press, 1991.

MacDonald, Deanna. "Collecting a New World: The Ethnographic Collections of Margaret of Austria." *SCJ* 33 (2002): 649–63.

Maçzak, Antoni and Hans Jürgen Teuteberg, ed. *Reiseberichte als Quellen europäischer Kulturgeschichte.* Wolfenbüttler Forschungen 21. Wolfenbüttel: Herzog August Bibliothek, 1982.

Madrazo, Pedro de. "Über Krönungsinsignien und Staatsgewänder Maximilian I. und Karl V. und ihr Schicksal in Spanien." *JKSW* 9 (1889): 446–64.

Maravall, Jose Antonio. *Carlos V y el Pensamiento Politico del Renacimiento.* Madrid: Instituto de Estudios Políticos, 1960.

Martels, Zweder von. "On His Majesty's Service. Augerius Busbequius, Courtier and Diplomat of Maximilian II." In *Kaiser Maximilian II. Kultur und Politik im*

16. Jahrhundert, ed. Friedrich Edelmayer and Alfred Kohler, 169–81. Wiener Beiträge zur Geschichte der Neuzeit 19. Vienna: Verlag für Geschichte und Politik, 1992.

Martínez Millán, José. "Charles V. " In *Princes and Princely Culture, 1450–1650*, ed. M. Gosman, A. MacDonald, and A. Vanderjagt, 227–48.

Martz, Linda. "Converso Families in Fifteenth- and Sixteenth-Century Toledo." *Sefarad* XLVIII (1988): 117–67.

———. "Pure Blood Statues in Sixteenth-Century Toledo: Implementation as Opposed to Adoption." *Sefarad* LIV (1994): 83–107.

Mas, Albert. *Les turcs dans la littérature espagnole du siècle d'or.* 2 vols. Paris: Centre de Recherches Hispaniques, 1967.

Massing, Jean Michel. "Hans Burgkmair's depiction of native Africans." *Res* 27 (1995): 39–51.

Mattingly, Garrett. *Renaissance Diplomacy.* Baltimore: Penguin, 1955.

Matuz, Josef. "Die Pfortendolmetscher zur Herrschaftszeit Süleymans des Prächtigen." *Südost-Forschungen* 34 (1975): 26–60.

McGinness, Frederick. *Right Thinking and Sacred Oratory in Counter-Reformation Rome.* Princeton: Princeton University Press, 1995.

McLean, Matthew. *The Cosmographia of Sebastian Münster.* Aldershot: Ashgate, 2007.

McTighe, Thomas. "Nicholas of Cusa's Unity–Metaphysics and the Formula Religio una in Rituum Varietate." In *Nicholas of Cusa in Search of God and Wisdom*, ed. G. Christianson and T. Izbicki, 161–72.

Ménage, V.L. "The Mission of an Ottoman Secret Agent in France in 1486." *Journal of the Royal Asiatic Society of Great Britain and Ireland* 1965: 112–32.

Menéndez Pidal, Ramón. *Idea Imperial de Carlos V.* Buenos Aires: Espasa-Calpe, 1941.

Menzhausen, Joachim. "Elector Augustus's *Kunstkammer*: An Analysis of the Inventory of 1587." In *The Origins of Museums*, ed. O. Impey and A. Mac-Gregor, 69–75.

Meserve, Margaret. *Empires of Islam in Renaissance Historical Thought.* Cambridge, MA: Harvard University Press, 2008.

———. "News from Negroponte: Politics, Popular Opinion, and Information Exchange in the First Decade of the Italian Press." *RQ* 59 (2006): 440–80.

Michalski, Sergiusz. *The Reformation and the Visual Arts.* London: Routledge, 1993.

Mignolo, Walter D. *The Darker Side of the Renaissance: Literacy, Territoriality, & Colonization.* Ann Arbor: University of Michigan Press, 1995.

Minty, J.M. "Judengasse to Christian Quarter: the Phenomenon of the Converted Synagogue in the Late Medieval and Early Modern Holy Roman Empire." In *Popular Religion in Germany and Central Europe, 1400–1800*, ed. Bob Scribner and Trevor Johnson, 58–86. New York: St. Martin's Press, 1996.

Momigliano, Arnaldo. "Ancient History and the Antiquarian." *JWCI* 13 (1950): 285–315.

Monroe, James T. "A Curious Morisco Appeal to the Ottoman Empire." *Al-Andalus* 31 (1966): 281–303.

Morán, José Miguel and Fernando Checa. *El Coleccionismo en España. De la cámara de maravillas a la galería de pinturas*. Madrid: Cátedra, 1985.
Moraw, Peter, "The Court of the German Kings and of the Emperor at the End of the Middle Ages, 1440–1519." In *Princes, Patronage, and the Nobility*, ed. R. Asch, 103–37.
Moseley, C.W.R.D. Introduction to *The Travels of Sir John Mandeville*. New York: Penguin, 1983.
Moser, Stephanie. *Ancestral Images: The Iconography of Human Origins*. Ithaca: Cornell University Press, 1998.
Moxey, Keith. *Peasants, Warriors, and Wives: Popular Imagery in the Reformation*. Chicago: University of Chicago Press, 1989.
Mraz, Gottfried. "Die Rolle der Uhrwerke in der kaiserlichen Türkenverehrung im 16. Jahrhundert." *Die Welt als Uhr: Deutsche Uhren und Automaten, 1550–1650*, ed. Klaus Maurice and Otto Mayr, 39–54. Munich: Bayerisches Nationalmuseum, 1980.
Mukerji, Chandra. *From Graven Images: Patterns of Modern Materialism*. New York: Columbia University Press, 1983.
Mullaney, Steven. "Strange Things, Gross Terms, Curious Customs: The Rehearsal of Cultures in the Late Renaissance." *Representations* 3 (1983): 40–67.
Müller, Arnd. "Zensurpolitik der Reichstadt Nürnberg." *MVGN* 49 (1959): 66–169.
Müller, Uwe. "Herzog Wilhelm V. und das Reichsheiltum." *MVGN* 72 (1985): 117–35.
Mundy, Barbara. "Mapping the Aztec Capital." *Imago Mundi* 50 (1998): 1–22.
Nader, Helen. "Habsburg Ceremony in Spain: The Reality of the Myth." *Historical Reflections/ Réflecions Historiques* 15 (1988): 293–309.
Necipoglu, Gülru. "Süleyman the Magnificent and the Representation of Power in the Context of Ottoman-Habsburg-Papal Rivalry." *Art Bulletin* 71 (1989): 401–27.
Nirenberg, David. *Communities of Violence*. Princeton: Princeton University Press, 1996.
Nowotny, Karl. "Die Gastgeschenke des Motecuhçoma an Cortés." *Archiv für Völkerkunde* 2 (1947): 210–21.
_____. *Mexikanische Kostbarkeiten aus Kunstkammern der Renaissance im Museum für Völkerkunde Wien und in der Nationalbibliothek Wien*. Vienna: Museum für Völkerkunde, 1960.
Nutini, Hugo G. *The Wages of Conquest: The Mexican Aristocracy in the Context of Western Aristocracies*. Ann Arbor: University of Michigan Press, 1995.
Oberman, Heiko. *The Roots of Antisemitism in the Age of Renaissance and Reformation*. Philadelphia: Fortress Press, 1984.
_____. "The Stubborn Jews. Timing the Escalation of Antisemitism in Late Medieval Europe." *Leo Baeck Institute Year Book* XXXIV (1989): xi–xxv.
_____. "Teufelsdreck: Eschatology and Scatology in the 'Old' Luther." *SCJ* 19 (1988): 435–50.
Olaechea Labayen, Juan B. *El Indigenismo Desdeñado*. Madrid: MAFRE, 1992.

O'Malley, John W. *Giles of Viterbo on Church and Reform*. Leiden: Brill, 1968.
———. *Praise and Blame in Renaissance Rome*. Durham: Duke University Press, 1979.
Oohlau, Jürgen. "Neue Quellen zur Familiengeschichte der Spengler. Lazarus Spengler und seine Söhne." *MVGN* 52 (1963/64): 232–55.
Otte, Enrique. "Jacob und Hans Cromberger und Lazarus Nürnberger, die Begründer des Deutschen Amerikahandels." *MVGN* 52 (1963/4): 129–62.
Ozment, Steven. *Mysticism and Dissent*. New Haven: Yale University Press, 1973.
Özyurt, Şenol. *Die Türkenlieder und das Türkenbild in der deutschen Volksüberlieferung vom 16. bis zum 20. Jahrhundert*. Motive 4. Munich: Wilhelm Fink, 1972.
Pagden, Anthony. "Dispossessing the barbarian: the language of Spanish Thomism and the debate over the property rights of the American Indians." In *The Languages of Political Theory in Early-Modern Europe*, 79–98. Cambridge: Cambridge University Press, 1987.
———. *European Encounters with the New World*. New Haven: Yale University Press, 1993.
———. *The Fall of Natural Man*. Cambridge: Cambridge University Press, 1982.
———. *Lords of All the World: Ideologies of Empire in Spain, Britain, and France c. 1500–c. 1800*. New Haven: Yale University Press, 1995.
———. *Spanish Imperialism and the Political Imagination*. New Haven: Yale University Press, 1990.
Palencia-Roth, Michael. "The Cannibal Laws of 1503." In *Early Images of the Americas: Transfer and Invention*, ed. Jerry M. Williams and Robert E. Lewis, 21–64. Tucson: University of Arizona Press, 1993.
Pardo, Osvaldo F. *The Origins of Mexican Catholicism: Nahua Rituals and Christian Sacraments in Sixteenth-Century Mexico*. Ann Arbor: University of Michigan Press, 2004.
Pastor Bodmer, Beatriz. *The Armature of Conquest: Spanish Accounts of the Discovery of America 1492–1589*. Palo Alto: Stanford University Press, 1992.
Peirce, Leslie. *The Imperial Harem: Women and Sovereignty in the Ottoman Empire*. Oxford: Oxford University Press, 1993.
Pendergrass, Jan N. "Simon Grynaeus and the Mariners of *Novus Orbis* (1532)." *Medievalia et Humanistica*. n.s. 19 (1993): 27–45.
Pérez de Tudela, Almudena and Annemarie Jordan Gschwend. "Luxury Goods for Royal Collectors." *JKMW* 3 (2001): 1–127.
Perjés, Géza. *The Fall of the Medieval Kingdom of Hungary: Mohács 1526–Buda 1541*. Translated by Márió D. Fenyó. War and Society in East Central Europe, Vol. XXVI. Highland Lakes, NJ: Atlantic Research and Publications, 1989.
Perkins, Judith. *The Suffering Self*. London: Routledge, 1995.
Petkov, Kiril. *Infidels, Turks, and Women: The South Slavs in the German Mind, ca. 1400–1600*. Frankfurt a. M.: Peter Lang, 1997.
Petritsch, Ernst. "Der Habsburgisch-Osmanische Friedensvertrag des Jahres 1547." *Mitteilungen des Österreichischen Staatsarchiv* 38 (1985): 68–78.
———. "Tribute oder Ehrengeschenk?" *Archiv und Forschung*, ed. Elisabeth Springer and Leopold Kammerhofer, 49–58. Wiener Beiträge zur Geschichte der Neuzeit, 20. Vienna: Verlag für Geschichte und Politik, 1993.

———. "Die Wiener Turkologie vom 16. bis zum 18. Jahundert." In *Osmanistik–Turkologie–Diplomatik. Festgabe an Josef Matuz*, ed. Christa Fragner und Klaus Schwarz, 25–33. Islamkundliche Untersuchungen 150. Berlin: Klaus Schwarz Verlag, 1992.

Pettegree, Andrew. *Emden and the Dutch Revolt*. Oxford: Clarendon Press, 1992.

Pieper, Renate. "Die Berichterstattung aus der Neuen Welt im ausgehenden 16. Jahrhundert am Beispiel der Fuggerzeitungen." In *Die Neue Welt im Bewußtsein der Italiener und Deutschen des 16. Jahrhunderts*, ed. Adriano Prosperi and Wolfgang Reinhard, 157–74. Berlin: Duncker und Humblot, 1993.

———. "Informationszentren im Vergleich. Die Stellung Venedigs und Antwerpens im 16. Jahrhundert." In *Kommunikationsrevolutionen: die neuen Medien des 16. und 19. Jahrhunderts*, ed. Michael North, 45–60. Vienna, Cologne: Böhlau, 1995.

———. *Die Vermittlung einer Neuen Welt: Amerika im Nachrichtennetz des Habsburgischen Imperiums, 1493–1598*. Mainz: Philipp von Zabern, 2000.

Pölnitz, Götz Freiherr von. "Jakob Fuggers Zeitungen und Briefe an die Fürsten des Hauses Wettin in der Frühzeit Karls V, 1519–1525." *Nachrichten von der Akademie der Wissenschaften in Göttingen Phil.-Hist. Kl. 1941 N.F. 3* (1941): 122–6.

Poole, Stafford. "Church Law on the Ordination of Indians and *Castas* in New Spain." *HAHR* 61 (1981): 637–50.

———. "The Declining Image of the Indian among Churchmen in Sixteenth-Century New Spain." In *Indian-Religious Relations in Colonial Spanish America*, ed. Susan E. Ramírez, 11–19. Foreign and Comparative Studies, Latin America Series 9. Syracuse: Syracuse University, 1989.

Portillo Muñoz, José L. *La ilustracion grafica de los incunables sevillanos (1470–1500)*. Seville: Diputación Provincial de Sevilla, 1980.

Post, Chandler. *A History of Spanish Painting*. vol. 9. Cambridge, MA: Harvard University Press, 1947.

Pratt, Mary Louise. "Fieldwork in Common Places." In *Writing Culture: The Poetics and Politics of Ethnography*, ed. James Clifford and George Marcus, 27–50. Berkeley: University of California Press, 1986.

Press, Volker. "The Habsburg Court as Center of the Imperial Government." *Journal of Modern History* 58 (1986) suppl.: 23–45.

———. "The Imperial Court of the Habsburgs from Maximilian I to Ferdinand III, 1493–1657." In *Princes, Patronage, and the Nobility*, ed. R. Asch, 289–312.

Price, David H. *Albrecht Dürer's Renaissance*. Ann Arbor: University of Michigan Press, 2003.

Pulido Rubio, Jose. *El Piloto Mayor: Pilotos Mayores, Catedraticos de Cosmografia y Cosmografos de la Casa de la Contratación de Sevilla*. Seville: CSIC, 1950.

Rabe, Horst, ed. *Karl V. Politik und politisches System*. Constance: Universitätsverlag Konstanz, 1996.

Redworth, Glyn and Fernando Checa. "The Courts of the Spanish Habsburgs 1500–1700." In *The Princely Courts of Europe*, ed. J. Adamson, 43–65.

Reeves, Marjorie. *The Influence of Prophecy in the Later Middle Ages*. Oxford: Clarendon Press, 1969.

————. "A Note on Prophecy and the Sack of Rome (1527)." *Prophetic Rome in the High Renaissance Period*, ed. Marjorie Reeves. 271–8. Oxford: Clarendon Press, 1992.

Remensnyder, Amy G. "The Colonization of Sacred Architecture: The Virgin Mary, Mosques, and Temples in Medieval Spain and Early Sixteenth-Century Mexico." In *Monks & Nuns, Saints & Outcasts*, ed. Sharon Farmer and Barbara Rosenwein. 189–219. Ithaca: Cornell University Press, 2000.

Reynolds, L. D. ed. *Texts and Transmission*. Oxford: Clarendon Press, 1983.

Richgels, Robert W. "The Pattern of Controversy in a Counter-Reformation Classic." *SCJ* 11 (1980): 3–15.

Rill, Gerhard. *Fürst und Hof in Österreich von den habsburgischen Teilungsverträgen bis zur Schlacht von Mohács (1521/22 bis 1526)*. Vienna: Böhlau, 1993.

Rodríguez-Salgado, M.J. "The Court of Philip II of Spain." In *Princes, Patronage, and the Nobility*, ed. R. Asch, 205–44.

Rosenfeld, Jörg. "Reformatorischer Bildersturm – Export ins Nichts?" *ARG* 87 (1996): 74–89.

Rosenthal, Earl. "The Invention of the Columnar Device of Emperor Charles V at the Court of Burgundy in Flanders in 1516." *JWCI* 36 (1973): 198–230.

————. "*Plus ultra, Non plus ultra*, and the columnar device of Emperor Charles V." *JWCI* 34 (1971): 204–28.

Roth, Paul. *Die Neuen Zeitungen in Deutschland im 15. und 16. Jahrhundert*. Leipzig: B.G. Teubner, 1914.

Rothenberg, Gunther. *The Austrian Military Border in Croatia, 1552–1747*. Urbana: University of Illinois Press, 1960.

Rouillard, Clarence Dana. *The Turk in French History, Thought, and Literature (1520–1660)*. Paris: Boivin, 1940.

Rowe, John H. "Ethnography and Ethnology in the Sixteenth Century." *Kroeber Anthropological Society Papers* 30 (1964): 1–19.

Rowland, Ingrid. *The Culture of the High Renaissance*. Cambridge: Cambridge University Press, 1998.

Rowlands, John. *The Age of Dürer and Holbein: German Drawings 1400–1550*. London: British Museum, 1988.

Rubiés, Joan-Pau. *Travel and Ethnology in the Renaissance: South India through European Eyes, 1250–1625*. Cambridge: Cambridge University Press, 2000.

Rudolf, Harriet. "Türkische Gesandtschaften ins Reich am Beginn der Neuzeit – Herrschaftsinszenierung, Fremdheitserfahrung und Erinnerungskultur." In *Das Osmanische Reich und die Habsburgermonarchie*, ed. Marlene Kurz, Martin Scheutz, Karl Vocelka, Thomas Winkelbauer, 295-314. Vienna: Oldenbourg, 2005.

Rudolf, Karl. "Exotica bei Karl V., Philip II. und in der Kunstkammer Rudolfs II." *JKMW* 3 (2001): 173–203.

————. "Die Kunstbestrebungen Kaiser Maximilians II. im Spannungsfeld zwischen Madrid und Wien." *JKSW* 2nd ser. 55 (1995): 165–256.

Russell, Joycelyne G. *Diplomats at Work: Three Renaissance Studies*. Wolfeboro Falls: Alan Sutton, 1992.

———. *Peacemaking in the Renaissance*. Philadelphia: University of Pennsylvania Press, 1986.

Russell, P.E. "White Kings on Black Kings: Rui de Pina and the Problem of Black African Sovereignty." In *Medieval and Renaissance Studies in Honour of Robert Brian Tate*, ed. Ian Michael and Richard A. Cardwell, 151–63. Oxford: Dolphin, 1986.

Russell-Wood, A.J.R. "Settlement, Colonization, and Integration in the Portuguese-Influenced World, 1415–1570." *Portuguese Studies Review* 15 (2007): 1–35.

Russo, Alessandra. "Plumes of Sacrifice: Transformations in Sixteenth-Century Mexican Feather Art." *Res* 42 (2002): 227–49.

Ryan, Michael T. "Assimilating New Worlds in the Sixteenth and Seventeenth Centuries." *CSSH* 23 (1981): 519–38.

Sahlins, Marshall. *Islands of History*. Chicago: University of Chicago Press, 1985.

Sahlins, Peter. *Boundaries: The Making of France and Spain in the Pyrenees.* Berkeley: University of California Press, 1989.

Said, Edward. *Orientalism*. New York: Vintage, 1978.

Salles-Reese, Verónica. *From Viracocha to the Virgin of Copacabana*. Austin: University of Texas Press, 1997.

Sauer, Carl. *The Early Spanish Main*. Berkeley: University of California Press, 1969.

Saxl, Fritz. "Illustrated Medieval Encyclopaedias – 1. the Classical Heritage" [1939], *Lectures*, 228–41. London: The Warburg Institute, 1957.

Scarry, Elaine. *The Body in Pain*. Oxford: Oxford University Press, 1985.

Schadendorf, Wulf. "Peter Flötners Spielkarten für Francesco d'Este." *Anzeiger des Germanischen Nationalmuseums* 1954–1959: 143–169.

Schaendlinger, Anton C. "Der diplomatische Verkehr zwischen Österreich und der Hohen Pforte in der Regierungszeit Süleymans des Prächtigen." *Kultur des Islam*, ed. Otto Mazal. Biblos-Schriften 113. Vienna: Österreichische Nationalbibliothek, 1981.

Schäfer, Ernesto. *El Consejo Real y Supremo de las Indias*. Vol. 1. Seville: Carmona, 1935.

Schauerte, Thomas U. *Die Ehrenpforte für Kaiser Maximilian I*. Munich: Deutscher Kunstverlag, 2001.

Scheicher, Elisabeth. "The Collection of Archduke Ferdinand II at Schloss Ambras." In *The Origins of Museums*, ed. O. Impey and A. MacGregor, 29–38.

———. *Die Kunst- und Wunderkammern der Habsburger*. Vienna: Molden, 1979.

Schestag, Franz. "Kaiser Maximilians I. Triumph." *JKSW* 1 (1883): 154–81.

Schiller, Gertrud. *Iconography of Christian Art*. Vol. 2, The Passion of Jesus Christ. Translated by Janet Seligman. Greenwich, CT: New York Graphic Society, 1968.

Schlemmer, Karl. *Gottesdienst und Frömmigkeit in der Reichsstadt Nürnberg am Vorabend der Reformation*. Forschungen zur frankischen Kirchen- und Theologiegeschichte. Würzburg: Echter, 1980.

Schlosser, Julius von. *Die Kunst- und Wunderkammern der Spätrenaissance.* Leipzig: Klinkhardt & Biermann, 1908.

Schmitt, Charles. "Perennial Philosophy: From Agostino Steuco to Leibniz." *JHI* 27 (1966): 505–32.

Schmitt, Ludwig. *Der Kölner Theologe Nikolaus Stagefyr und der Franziskaner Nikolaus Herborn.* Freiburg im Breisgau: Herder'she Verlagshandlung, 1896.

Schnelbögl, Julia. "Die Reichskleinodien in Nürnberg, 1424–1523." *MVGN* 51 (1962): 78–159.

Schottenloher, Karl. *Flugblatt und Zeitung.* Bibliothek für Kunst-und Antiquitäten Sammler XXI. Berlin: Schmidt, 1922.

Schulz, Juergen. "Jacopo de' Barbari's View of Venice: Map Making, City Views, and Moralized Geography Before the Year 1500." *Art Bulletin* LX (1978): 425–74.

Schulze, Winfried. *Reich und Türkengefahr im späten 16. Jahrhundert: Studien zu den politischen und gesellschaftlichen Auswirkungen einer äußeren Bedrohung.* Munich: C.H. Beck, 1978.

Schwoebel, Robert. *The Shadow of the Crescent: The Renaissance Image of the Turk (1453–1517).* New York: St. Martin's Press, 1969.

Scribner, R. W. "Cosmic Order and Daily Life." In *Popular Culture and Popular Movements in Reformation Germany.* London: Hambledon Press, 1987.

———. "Why was there no Reformation in Cologne?" In *Popular Culture and Popular Movements in Reformation Germany.* London: Hambledon Press, 1987.

Seed, Patricia. "'Failing to Marvel': Atahualpa's Encounter with the Word." *Latin American Research Review* 26 (1991): 7–32.

Seelig, Lorenz. "The Munich *Kunstkammer,* 1565–1807." In *The Origins of Museums,* ed. O. Impey and A. MacGregor, 76–89.

Seling, Helmut W. "Silberhandel und Goldschmiedekunst in Augsburg im 16. Jahrhundert." *Welt im Umbruch: Augsburg zwischen Renaissance und Barock.* Vol. 3, 162–70. Augsburg: Augsburger Druck- und Verlagshaus, 1981.

Setton, Kenneth M. "Lutheranism and the Turkish Peril." *Balkan Studies* 3 (1962):133–68.

———. *Western Hostility to Islam and Prophecies of Turkish Doom.* Philadelphia: American Philosophical Society, 1992.

Shelton, Anthony Alan. "Cabinets of Transgression: Renaissance Collections and the Incorporation of the New World." In *The Cultures of Collecting,* ed. John Elsner and Roger Cardinal, 177–203. Cambridge: Harvard University Press, 1994.

Siegert, Bernhard. "Die Verortung Amerikas im Nachrichtendispositiv um 1500 oder: Die Neue Welt der Casa de la Contratación." In *Gutenberg und die Neue Welt,* ed. Horst Wenzel, 307–26. Munich: Wilhelm Fink, 1994.

Silverblatt, Irene. "Political Memories and Colonizing Symbols: Santiago and the Mountain Gods of Colonial Peru." In *Rethinking History and Myth,* ed. Jonathan D. Hill, 174–94. Urbana: University of Illinois Press, 1988.

Sitte, Alfred. "Tsausch Hedajets Aufenthalt in Wien (1565)." *AKG* 6 (1908): 192–201.

Skilliter, Susan. "Catherine de' Medici's Turkish Ladies-in-Waiting: A Dilemma in Franco-Ottoman Diplomatic Relations." *Turcica* VII (1975): 188–204.

Smith, Christine. *Architecture in the Culture of Early Humanism. Ethics, Aesthetics, and Eloquence 1400–1470.* Oxford: Oxford University Press, 1992.

Smith, Jeffrey Chipps. *Sensuous Worship: Jesuits and the Art of the Early Catholic Reformation in Germany.* Princeton: Princeton University Press, 2002.

————. "The Transformations of Patrician Tastes in Renaissance Nuremberg." In *New Perspectives on the Art of Renaissance Nuremberg,* ed. Jeffrey Chipps Smith, 83–100. Austin: University of Texas Press, 1985.

Smith, Pamela and Paula Findlen, ed. *Merchants and Marvels.* New York: Routledge, 2002.

Smoller, Laura. "Playing Cards and Popular Culture in Sixteenth-Century Nuremberg." *SCJ* 17 (1986): 183–214.

Sommer-Mathis, Andrea. "América en el teatro y en la fiesta." In *El teatro descubre América: fiestas y teatro en la casa de Austria.* Madrid: MAPFRE, 1992.

Soria Mesa, Enrique. "De la conquista a la asimilación." *Areas* 14 (1992): 49–64.

Spohn, Margret. *Alles getürkt: 500 Jahre (Vor) Urteile der Deutschen über die Türken.* Oldenburg: Universität Oldenburg, 1993.

Sporhan-Krempel, Lore. *Nürnberg als Nachrichtenzentrum zwischen 1400 und 1700.* Nürnberger Forschungen, 10. Nuremberg: Verein für Geschichte der Stadt Nürnberg, 1968.

Stagl, Justin. "The Methodising of Travel in the 16th Century." *History and Anthropology* 4 (1990): 303–38.

Starenko, Peter E. "In Luther's Wake: Duke John Frederick II of Saxony, Angelic Prophecy, and the Gotha Rebellion of 1576." Ph.D. dissertation, University of California at Berkeley, 2002.

Starn, Randolph and Loren Partridge. *Arts of Power: Three Halls of State in Italy, 1300–1600.* Berkeley: University of California Press, 1992.

Steinmetz, David C. "Calvin and Abraham." *Church History* 57 (1988): 443–55.

Steinruck, Josef. *Johann Baptist Fickler.* Münster: Aschendorff, 1965.

Stockbauer, J. *Die Kunstbestrebungen am Bayerische Hofe unter Herzog Albert V. und seinem Nachfolger Wilhelm V.* Quellenschriften für Kunstgeschichte und Kunsttechnik des Mittelalters und der Renaissance 8. Vienna: Braumüller, 1874.

Strauss, Gerald. *Nuremberg in the Sixteenth Century.* Rev. ed., Bloomington: Indiana University Press, 1976.

Strong, Roy. *Art and Power: Renaissance Festivals 1450–1650.* Berkeley: University of California Press, 1984.

Sturminger, Walter. *Bibliograhie und Ikonographie der Türkenbelagerungen Wiens 1529 und 1683.* Veröffentlichungen der Kommission für Neuere Geschichte Österreichs 41. Graz: Böhlau, 1955.

Subrahmanyam, Sanjay. *The Career and Legend of Vasco da Gama.* Cambridge: Cambridge University Press, 1997.

————. "Holding the World in Balance: The Connected Histories of the Iberian Overseas Empires, 1500–1640." *American Historical Review* 112 (2007): 1359–85.

Sugar, Peter F., ed. *A History of Hungary*. Bloomington: Indiana University Press, 1990.

Szakály, Ferenc. "The Early Ottoman Period, Including Royal Hungary, 1526–1606." In *A History of Hungary*, ed. Peter F. Sugar, 83–99. Bloomington: Indiana University Press, 1990.

———. *Lodovico Gritti in Hungary, 1529–1534*. Budapest: Akademiai Kiadó, 1995.

Szakály, Ferenc and Lajos Tardy. "Auf der Suche nach einem aus Ungarn stammenden Dolmetscher des Sultans." In *Osmanistik – Turkologie – Diplomatik. Festgabe an Josef Matuz*, ed. Christa Fragner and Klaus Schwarz. Islamkundliche Untersuchungen 150. Berlin: Klaus Schwarz Verlag, 1992.

Talbot, Cynthia. "Inscribing the Other, Inscribing the Self: Hindu-Muslim Identities in Pre-Colonial India." *CSSH* 37 (1995): 692–722.

Tanner, Marie. *The Last Descendant of Aeneas. The Hapsburgs and the Mythic Image of the Emperor*. New Haven: Yale University Press, 1993.

Tardy, Lajos. *Beyond the Ottoman Empire. 14th – 16th Century Hungarian Diplomacy in the East*. Translated by János Boris. Studia Uralo-Altaica 13. Szeged: Szeged. Universitas, 1978.

Tennant, Elaine C. "The Protection of Invention: Printing Privileges in Early Modern Germany." In *Knowledge, Science, and Literature in Early Modern Germany*, ed. Gerhild Scholz Williams and Stephan K. Schindler, 7–48. Chapel Hill: University of North Carolina Press, 1996.

Teply, Karl. "Türkische Gesandtschaften nach Wien (1488–1792)." *Österreich in Geschichte und Literatur* 20 (1976): 14–32.

Thomaz, Luis Filipe F.R. "Factions, Interests and Messianism: The Politics of Portuguese Expansion in the East, 1500–1521." *Indian Economic and Social History Review* 28 (1991): 97–109.

———. "L'idée impériale manuéline." In *Découverte, le Portugal et l'Europe*, ed. Jean Aubin, 35–103. Paris: Touzot, 1990.

Tietze, Hans and Erica Tietze-Conrat. *Kritisches Verzeichnis der Werke Albrecht Dürers* II:1. Basel and Leipzig: Holbein, 1937.

Tolan, John V. *Saracens: Islam in the Medieval European Imagination*. New York: Columbia University Press, 2002.

Trachtenberg, Marvin. *Dominion of the Eye: Urbanism, Art, and Power in Early Modern Florence*. Cambridge: Cambridge University Press, 1997.

Trexler, Richard. *The Journey of the Magi*. Princeton: Princeton University Press, 1997.

———. *Public Life in Renaissance Florence*. New York: Academic Press, 1980.

———. "We Think, They Act: Clerical Readings of Missionary Theatre in 16th Century Mexico." In *Church and Community, 1200–1600*. Rome: Edizioni di storia et letteratura, 1987.

Trinkaus, Charles. *In Our Image and Likeness*. 2nd ed. Notre Dame: University of Notre Dame Press, 1995.

Truman, Ronald W. *Spanish Treatises on Government, Society and Religion in the Time of Philip II*. Leiden: Brill, 1999.

Turan, Ebru. "Voices of Opposition in the Reign of Sultan Süleyman." In *Studies on Istanbul and Beyond*, ed. R. G. Ousterhout, 23–35. Philadelphia: University of Pennsylvania Museum of Archaeology and Anthropology, 2007.

VD 16 – Verzeichnis der im deutschen Sprachbereich erschienen Drucke des XVI. Jahrhunderts. Stuttgart: Hiersemann, 1989.

Valensi, Lucette. *The Birth of the Despot: Venice and the Sublime Porte*. Translated by Arthur Denner. Ithaca: Cornell University Press, 1993.

Vigneras, Louis-André. "Saint Thomas, Apostle of America." *HAHR* 57 (1977): 82–90.

Vilfan, Sergij. "Die wirtschaftlichen Auswirkungen der Türkenkriege aus der Sicht der Ranzionierungen, der Steuern und der Preisbewegung." In *Die Auswirkungen der Türkenkriege*, ed. Othmar Pickl, 71–130. Grazer Forschungen zur Wirtschafts- und Sozialgeschichte. Graz: Lehrkanzl. für Wirschafts- und Sozialgeschichte der Univ. Graz, 1971.

Vocelka, Karl. *Die Politische Propaganda Kaiser Rudolfs II. (1576–1612)*. Vienna: Österreichische Akademie der Wissenschaften, 1980.

———. "Eine türkische Botschaft in Wien 1565." *Beiträge zur neueren Geschichte Österreichs*, ed. Heinrich Fichtenau and Erich Zöllner, 102–14. Vienna: Böhlau, 1974.

Vogel, Klaus. "Cultural Variety in a Renaissance Perspective." In *Shifting Cultures*, ed. Henriette Bugge and Joan Pau Rubiés. Münster: Lit Verlag, 1995.

Vogler, Günter. *Nürnberg 1524/25. Studien zur Geschichte der reformatorischen und sozialen Bewegung in der Reichsstadt*. Berlin: Deutscher Verlag der Wissenschaften, 1982.

Walker, D.P. *The Ancient Theology*. Ithaca: Cornell University Press, 1972.

Wallraf-Richartz-Museum. *Die Gemälde der Altdeutschen Meister*. Cologne: Gutenberg, 1939.

Wandel, Lee. *Voracious Idols and Violent Hands: Iconoclasm in Reformation Zurich, Strasbourg, and Basel*. Cambridge: Cambridge University Press, 1995.

Watts, Pauline Moffitt. *Nicolaus Cusanus: A Fifteenth-Century Vision of Man*. Leiden: Brill, 1982.

———. "Talking to Spiritual Others." In *Nicholas of Cusa in Search of God and Wisdom*, ed. G. Christianson and T. Izbicki, 203–18.

Weiner, Annette B. "Cultural Difference and the Density of Objects." *American Ethnologist* 21 (1994): 391–403.

———. *Inalienable Possessions: The Paradox of Keeping-While-Giving*. Berkeley: University of California Press, 1992.

Weiss, Ullman. *Die frommen Bürger von Erfurt*. Weimar: Böhlau, 1988.

Weller, Emil. *Die ersten deutschen Zeitungen*. 1872. Reprint, Hildesheim: Olms, 1962.

Werner, Theodore Gustav. "Das kaufmännische Nachrichtenwesen im späten Mittelalter und in der frühen Neuzeit und sein Einfluß auf die Entstehung der handschriftlichen Zeitung." *Scripta Mercaturae* 9/2 (1975): 3–51.

Wertheimer, Eduard. "Der Geschichte des Türkenkrieges Maximilians II. 1565–1566." *AÖG* 53 (1875): 43–102.

Wiesflecker, Hermann. *Kaiser Maximilian I. Das Reich, Österreich und Europa an der Wende zur Neuzeit*. 5 vols. Munich: Oldenbourg, 1971–1986.

Wilckens, Leonie von. "Oriental Carpets in the German Speaking Countries and the Netherlands." *Oriental Carpets and Textile Studies* 2 (1986): 139–50.

Wilhelm, Raymond. *Italienische Flugschriften des Cinquecento (1500–1550)*. Tübingen: Max Niemeyer, 1996.

Winzinger, Franz. *Albrecht Altdorfer: Die Gemälde*. Munich: R. Piper, 1975.

———. *Albrecht Altdorfer: Graphik*. Munich: R. Piper, 1963.

Wisch, Barbara and Susan Scott Munschower, ed. *Art and Pageantry in the Renaissance and Baroque*. University Park: Pennsylvania State University, 1990.

Wolff, Larry. *Inventing Eastern Europe: The Map of Civilization on the Mind of the Enlightenment*. Stanford: Stanford University Press, 1994.

Wood, Christopher S. *Forgery, Replica, Fiction: Temporalities of German Renaissance Art*. Chicago: University of Chicago Press, 2008.

Yapp, M.E. "Europe in the Turkish Mirror." *Past and Present* 137 (1992): 134–55.

Yates, Frances. *Astraea*. London: Routledge, Kegan and Paul, 1975.

Zamora, Margarita. *Reading Columbus*. Berkeley: University of California Press, 1993.

Zeitlin, Judith Francis and Lillian Thomas. "Spanish Justice and the Indian Cacique: Disjunctive Political Systems in Sixteenth-Century Tehuantepec." *Ethnohistory* 39 (1992): 285–315.

Zika, Charles. "Host, Processions and Pilgrimages: Controlling the Sacred in Fifteenth-Century Germany." *Past and Present* 118 (1988): 25–64.

Žontar, Josef. "Michael Cernović, Geheimagent Ferdinands I. und Maximilians II. und seine Berichterstattung." *Mitteilungen des Österreichischen Staatsarchivs* 24 (1971): 169–222.

Zucker, Paul. *Town and Square*. New York: Columbia University Press, 1959.

Index

315

Made in the USA
Lexington, KY
01 December 2014